African-American Mayors

African-American Mayors

Race, Politics, and the American City

EDITED BY

DAVID R. COLBURN

AND JEFFREY S. ADLER

University of Illinois Press
URBANA AND CHICAGO

© 2001 by the Board of Trustees of the University of Illinois
All rights reserved
Manufactured in the United States of America
∞ This book is printed on acid-free paper.

Library of Congress Cataloging-in-Publication Data
African-American mayors : race, politics, and the American city /
edited by David R. Colburn and Jeffrey S. Adler.
p.   cm.
Includes index.
ISBN 0-252-02634-9 (alk. paper)
1. Afro-American mayors—History—20th century.
2. Afro-Americans—Politics and government—20th century. 3. United
States—Race relations—Political aspects. 4. Municipal government—
United States—History—20th century. 5. United States—Politics and
government—1945–1989. 6. United States—Politics and government—
1989–   . I. Colburn, David R. II. Adler, Jeffrey S.
E185.615.A5924   2001
324'.089'9607301732—dc21   00-010609

C 5 4 3 2 1

Contents

Acknowledgments

Although research and writing tend to be solitary enterprises, all historians know well how much they rely on the guidance and advice of friends and colleagues. In assembling a collection of essays, editors are particularly dependent on the goodwill and the professionalism of others.

We were unusually fortunate to have the support of and to work with many remarkably capable individuals. Daneen Denny kept the project afloat in numerous ways, including spearheading the correspondence relating to this collection and communicating with the contributors. Jason Parker and Mark Hove, two very talented doctoral candidates in the Department of History at the University of Florida, provided valuable research assistance. And a number of friends took time away from their research to help with particular portions of this book. We especially appreciate the help and advice of Tom Gallant, Bob McMahon, Jane Landers, Larry Rivers, George Wright, Maxine Jones, and Steve Lawson.

We were also fortunate to work with Richard L. Wentworth, who retired as director but still acquires manuscripts for the University of Illinois Press, and Theresa L. Sears, managing editor, who guided the project through the production process. We very much appreciate their good counsel and support of our efforts. Our copy editor, Polly Kummel, proved quite extraordinary and greatly aided the quality of the manuscript. We have also benefited enormously from the work of leading scholars in African-American and urban history, especially Richard Bernard, Taylor Branch, Clayborne Carson, William Chafe, Jim Cobb, David Garrow, David Goldfield, Darlene Clark Hine, Kenneth Kusmer, Steven Lawson, Earl Lewis, Aldon Morris, Robert J. Norrell, Jon Teaford, Mills Thornton, Joe Trotter, and Harvard Sitkoff.

Finally, we are indebted to our contributors, all of whom were thoroughly professional, remarkably prompt, and unfailingly considerate as we pieced this book together. We thank them for making this project particularly worthwhile.

Our deepest appreciation goes to our spouses: Marion Colburn and Donna Adler, who tolerated our work on this project during evenings and weekends. We dedicate this book to them in no small appreciation for their support and for giving our lives meaning.

African-American Mayors

Introduction

JEFFREY S. ADLER

ON NOVEMBER 7, 1967, voters in Cleveland, Ohio, and Gary, Indiana, elected new mayors to govern their cities. In the process they changed American urban and political history. Carl B. Stokes and Richard G. Hatcher became the first African Americans elected to urban executive positions in the history of the United States. After three and one-half centuries of complete or relative disfranchisement, African Americans rapidly assumed the mayor's office in nearly every major city in the nation. Within sixteen years of the great breakthrough three of the four largest urban centers in the United States had elected African-American mayors, and in 1990 the nation's biggest city, New York, followed suit. By 1993 African Americans had been elected mayor in sixty-seven cities with populations of more than fifty thousand residents, and most had majority-white populations.[1] Nor was the trend restricted to major urban centers or to the liberal bastions of the North. Only a decade after Stokes's and Hatcher's victories, more than two hundred African-American mayors headed U.S. cities, and by 1990 the figure exceeded three hundred, generating one of the most important shifts in twentieth-century American politics.[2]

This transformation—and the social and legal processes that undergirded it—produced a sea change in urban society. The scope of the transformation was particularly apparent at the local level. In 1962 Atlanta's city hall remained "strictly segregated with separate restrooms, drinking fountains, and employment listings" for African Americans and whites, the historian Jon C. Teaford has noted. Moreover, a local ordinance forbade African-American police officers from arresting whites.[3] Twelve years later Atlanta had an African-American mayor and an African-American police chief.[4]

The election of hundreds of African-American mayors during the decades after November 1967 was a complex phenomenon, one that defies simple explanation.[5] The civil rights leader Bayard Rustin predicted the change, arguing in a 1965 article that political power would flow from the civil rights movement.[6] To a considerable extent Rustin was right. Without the civil rights movement—and the ideological energy and political mobilization that it generated—Stokes, Hatcher, and others could not have achieved success at the ballot box.[7] But few of the first-generation mayors, as David R. Colburn notes here, moved directly from the civil rights movement to the political arena. To be sure, some early mayors, such as Hatcher, Kenneth Gibson of Newark, New Jersey, and Marion Barry of Washington, D.C., honed their skills as activists. Others, including Harold Washington and Eugene Sawyer of Chicago, Tom Bradley of Los Angeles, and David Dinkins of New York City, worked their way through local political organizations. In short, the notion that the first African-American mayors entered city hall after years of street activism obscures as much as it reveals about these political pioneers.

Nor was the rise of African-American mayors merely the latest chapter in a recurring process of group succession.[8] According to this view, for more than a century shifts in the character of the urban population have transformed municipal politics, with Irish Americans supplanting native-born residents, Italian Americans succeeding Irish Americans, and now African-American city dwellers gaining political power as the "ethnics" moved to the suburbs.[9] With each shift in the composition of the electorate, the balance of power within the ever-adapting big-city machine changed, remaking political alliances and producing new power brokers. Such a model accounts for a portion of the complex process that produced electoral victories for Stokes, Hatcher, and their counterparts. Without question, population changes prepared the ground for political ones. Moreover, political insiders such as Washington worked their way through the machine and seized greater influence as the demographic composition of the city changed. In addition, African-American mayors, like their Irish, Italian, and Jewish counterparts in earlier generations, mobilized their supporters but also relied on intergroup coalitions to gain office and to exercise power.[10] Just as Irish Americans rarely held a majority in the cities that they ran, African Americans, particularly in the first generation of African-American mayors, did not dominate the local electorate. Thus in both cases success depended on intergroup support and alliances.[11]

In crucial ways, however, group succession fails to explain fully the fortunes of African-American mayors. Because of the persistent influence of racism in American urban society, the experiences of African-American politicians stand apart from those of their ethnic predecessors, particularly with regard to governance itself. Established political institutions proved substantially less flexible for African Americans than for others. This is not to deny the effects of xenophobia, anti-Semitism, or other forms of prejudice or group conflict. Such discrimination, however, was not comparable to racial prejudice. If machine politicians, at least according to legend, learned new languages and dialects and embraced different customs to appeal to new voters, the process has been much more difficult when race was involved. Modern polling data and political science studies demonstrate the intractability of racial hostility.[12] A sizable segment of white voters have remained hostile to African-American candidates—and to their African-American neighbors. The chapters in this book are replete with examples of the race-based hostility of many white politicians, city employees, and voters. Harold Washington, for instance, faced a city council dedicated to opposing his efforts; as Arnold R. Hirsch explains, the battle became so fierce that the *Wall Street Journal* termed Chicago "Beirut on the Lake."[13] Similarly, Stokes, although a Democrat, received scant support and even some opposition from the county Democratic Party, according to Leonard N. Moore. Hatcher also faced considerable hostility from within his own party, James B. Lane finds. The chairman of Gary's Lake County Democratic Central Committee, John G. Krupa, supported the Republican candidate for mayor in 1967, explaining that "Mr. Hatcher was not the 'right kind' of Negro."[14] Some mayors struggled to deal with police officers—and even police administrators—who refused to support the initiatives of "nigger mayors."[15] Nor were intergroup political alliances, the traditional lubricant of the political machine, easily forged when race became an issue. In many instances hostile groups found a source of intergroup unity by championing "white" interests against African-American mayors; racial solidarity often trumped party affiliation in the emotionally charged world of late twentieth-century urban politics, prompting some long-time white Democrats to support Republican candidates rather than to vote for African-American Democratic candidates. Such political tactics, according to Heather R. Parker, helped Sam Yorty to defeat Tom Bradley in 1969. Similarly, in Cleveland's 1967 mayoral election Stokes's Republican opponent, Seth B. Taft, received 127,328 votes, although the city had only 39,000 registered Republicans.[16] A comparable shift occurred in Philadelphia in 1987, when an estimated 50,000 white Democrats changed their party affiliation to support the Republican candidate, Frank Rizzo.[17] In short, anti-Semitism, anti-Catholicism, and similar phenomena have long influenced municipal politics, but race-baiting has commanded unique power in American political history.[18] Thus the blossoming of African-American influence in urban politics has proved to be more complicated than simply the latest version of the familiar process of group succession.

* * *

Three profound and interrelated shifts in the late twentieth-century city set the stage for the election of African-American mayors, simultaneously shaping their political fortunes. The first shift was demographic. Migration patterns redefined the composition of urban society—and with it the urban electorate—during the twentieth century. The so-called Great Migration of the opening decades of the century represented the start of a massive population shift. Between 1890 and 1920 the net out-migration of African Americans from the South approached 900,000. By comparison, the total for the three-decade period after 1940 exceeded 4.3 million. During the twentieth century, African Americans went from being one of the least urbanized major groups in U.S. society to one of the most urbanized. Between 1910 and 1980 the proportion of African Americans living in cities rose from 27 percent to 85 percent, and since the 1950s African Americans have been more likely to live in cities than whites.[19] The African-American populations of the nation's central cities more than doubled between 1950 and 1970, rising by 3.6 million during the 1950s and by another 3.4 million during the 1960s.[20] African Americans became disproportionately concentrated in the largest U.S. cities. In 1990, 41 percent of the nation's African Americans lived in the central cities of metropolitan areas with more than one million residents, compared to 15 percent of whites.[21]

This population shift, in combination with two other factors, remade the urban electorate. First, the civil rights legislation of the 1960s lowered barriers to African-American political participation, though as a consequence of reapportionment, consolidation, and gerrymandering African Americans remained underrepresented among voters, particularly in many southern cities.[22] Hostility from well-entrenched political institutions also undercut the increasing political muscle of the African-American population. Nonetheless, African Americans in U.S. cities enjoyed growing influence as their numbers surged.

Another demographic shift reinforced their political clout. While African Americans flocked to central cities, whites migrated out of them. Government policies subsidized suburban development and urban sprawl in ways that fueled white flight. According to Roger Biles, two million whites left New York City alone during the 1970s. Chicago lost 700,000 (non-Latino) white residents, and Detroit lost nearly 400,000 residents, the majority of whom were white, during the decade. By 1980 one white resident in three had fled from Cleveland, desperate to escape urban problems, many of which whites associated with the influx of African Americans. In most central cities the out-migration of whites exceeded the in-migration of African Americans. During the 1960s the populations of Baltimore, Boston, Chicago, Cincinnati, Cleveland, Detroit, Minneapolis, New Orleans, Philadelphia, Pittsburgh, St. Louis, San Francisco, Washington, and other cities fell. Detroit's population, for example, dropped by more than 9 percent, Cleveland's and Pittsburgh's decreased by 14 percent, and St. Louis's shrank by 17 percent. By 1970 the populations of Chicago, Detroit, and Philadelphia had tumbled below their 1930 levels, whereas the populations of Pittsburgh, St. Louis, and Boston had plunged below their 1910 levels. For most of these cities the decline continued through the 1970s. At the end of the decade New York City recorded a larger population than forty-one states, yet it also had its smallest population since the Great Depression.[23] Cleveland's population drop attracted particular attention. According to Teaford, "If Cleveland's population continued to decline at the same absolute rate as it did during the 1970s, by the year 2013 there would be no one remaining in the Ohio metropolis."[24]

As the number of white urbanites plummeted and the number of African-American city dwellers soared, the latter comprised a growing proportion of the shrinking urban population. On the eve of World War II approximately one city dweller in twelve was African American. Three decades later more than one city dweller in five was African American. By 1970 one third of the residents of Chicago and Philadelphia were African American, as were approximately 40 percent of the residents of Detroit, St. Louis, Baltimore, Memphis, New Orleans, and Cleveland. African Americans comprised more than 50 percent of the residents of Gary, Atlanta, and Newark, New Jersey, in 1970 and more than 70 percent of the residents of Washington, D.C. In 1940 one Detroit resident in eleven was African American. Three decades later African Americans made up more than 40 percent of the city's population. During the 1970s migration patterns reinforced the concentration of whites in the suburbs and African Americans in Detroit, as 418,000 whites left the city and 102,000 African Americans entered the city. As a result, in 1980 African Americans comprised almost two thirds of the residents of Detroit.

The shifting and conflicting tides of migration concentrated African-American residents in the inner city, producing "hypersegregation" on the one hand and surging political power on the other. At least until the 1980s the cross-currents seldom produced African-American majorities, though the group often held a plurality, creating new political opportunities for African Americans. In a few cities that elected African-American mayors, whites continued to dominate the population; African Americans comprised less than 18 percent of the population when Los Angeles residents elected Tom Bradley and only 25 percent of the population when New Yorkers elected

David Dinkins, though more often cities chose their first African-American mayors when African Americans made up 35 percent to 45 percent of the local population. White city dwellers, in fact, remain in the majority in more than 70 percent of the large cities that elected African-American mayors. When Cleveland residents elected Stokes, African Americans comprised only 38 percent of the city's population. As the historian Kenneth L. Kusmer has noted, "racial solidarity alone" was not sufficient to get Stokes elected.[25] Furthermore, until barriers to voting were removed and unless activists mobilized the community and registered voters, an African-American popular majority did not necessarily translate into a voting majority. Many cities, such as Gary, Atlanta, and Newark, elected African-American mayors when African Americans constituted a majority of the population but a minority of voters. Put differently, the flow of migrants merely generated the potential for electoral success. African-American candidates, however, typically could not win without support from white voters. Latino voters assumed a crucial role in many cities, and particular subsets of the white electorate often emerged as key swing groups in municipal elections, a factor that significantly influenced the campaigns and platforms of African-American candidates.[26]

The second major change in the late twentieth-century city that shaped the experiences of African-American mayors involved jarring shifts in the structure of the urban economy. Deindustrialization, the rise of overseas and sun-belt competition, and the "New Federalism" contributed to the collapse of the urban economy in the rust belt, accelerating the flow of white and affluent residents from the crumbling central city. While African Americans were moving into the city and African-American mayors were entering city halls, jobs, particularly manufacturing jobs, were disappearing from urban America. In the fifteen years after the election of the nation's first African-American mayors—from 1967 to 1982—Philadelphia lost more than half its manufacturing jobs, Detroit and Chicago lost more than 49 percent of their manufacturing jobs, and New York, Baltimore, and Cleveland lost 41 percent to 46 percent of their manufacturing positions.[27]

Corporate headquarters abandoned older central cities as well, taking tax dollars and reinforcing the downward spiral. Between 1956 and 1974 the number of Fortune 500 companies headquartered in Chicago dropped by 30 percent, the number in Philadelphia fell by 43 percent, and the number in Detroit plunged by 67 percent. From 1965 to 1986 New York City suffered a 59 percent drop in the number of Fortune 500 corporate headquarters it housed.[28]

As jobs disappeared and central cities became poorer, downtown shopping districts withered and died. From 1960 to 1979, according to James B. Lane, the number of downtown businesses in Gary dropped by more than 90 percent. Similarly, during the decade after Stokes's victory (1967–77), retail sales in Cleveland's business district fell by 44 percent.[29] From 1977 to 1987 sales fell by an additional 16 percent. Nor were the Indiana and Ohio metropolises unique in this regard. Between 1977 and 1982 central business district sales dropped by 23 percent in Philadelphia and Baltimore, by 25 percent in Chicago, and by 43 percent in Detroit. To a considerable extent, sales receipts, like white consumers, left the city for the suburbs. During the 1970s, for example, Chicago lost 90,000 sales and clerical jobs, while its suburbs gained 115,000 such jobs.[30]

This economic transformation impoverished the central cities. During the 1970s the populations of the five largest cities dropped by 9 percent, though their poverty populations rose by 22 percent.[31] Unemployment rates for African Americans exploded, approaching 25 percent in Detroit in 1980.[32] Poverty rates spiked accordingly; among the residents of central cities, one African-American family in four lived below the poverty line in 1980, and the figure approached one in three by 1987.[33] As the sociologists Douglas S. Massey and Nancy A. Denton have argued, poverty became concentrated in the inner city and particularly in African-American neighborhoods.[34] The sociologist William Julius Wilson has identified a growing "mismatch" between the circumstances of inner-city residents and the economic structures and public institutions available to them. Working-class African Americans increasingly struggled to find jobs close to their neighborhoods or close to mass transit lines. Similarly, they lost access to adequate shopping facilities and health-care providers as businesses left the central city. The increasing poverty of ghetto residents in combination with the decreasing number of stable jobs in the central city, Wilson has explained, contributed to crime rates, teen pregnancy rates, and high school dropout rates, thus reinforcing the inclination of whites, middle-class residents, business owners, and investors to abandon the city.[35]

The downward spiral became self-perpetuating. As inner-city residents became poorer, downtown stores closed and employers fled, causing the local economy to deteriorate, property values to fall, and tax revenue to decrease. In turn, this process reduced the ability of municipal government to address the spate of growing problems. During the early 1970s Chicago's tax base contracted by $440 million, and Cleveland's assessed value of property dropped to levels not seen since the 1950s. Demand for city services (particularly health care and law enforcement) soared, but the narrowing tax base compelled city executives to slash municipal payrolls and to reduce services. Between 1977 and 1985, as crime rates exploded and public schools deteriorated, the number of city employees dropped by 15 percent in Philadelphia, by 16 percent in Cleveland and in Detroit, and by 17 percent in Baltimore.[36] During the mid-1970s New York City teetered on the edge of bankruptcy, and by the late 1970s Cleveland had plunged into default.

Changes in national politics contributed to the free fall. The so-called New Federalism of the late 1970s and the 1980s celebrated local responsibility for social problems and sharply constricted the flow of federal dollars to U.S. cities. In 1977–78, for example, the federal government provided 27 percent of Chicago's general revenue and 23 percent of Detroit's. By the mid-1980s the proportions had fallen to 12 percent and to 15 percent, respectively.[37] As Biles explains, "By 1991 federal aid accounted for just 9.3 percent of New York City's budget, down significantly from 17.9 percent ten years earlier." While poverty rates soared, tax revenues dwindled, municipal layoffs mounted, and jobs disappeared, federal aid to central cities contracted. Owing much of its popularity to an antiurban bias and to a racially charged feeling of besiegement among lower middle-class white ethnics, Reagan's New Federalism had a devastating effect on central cities and particularly on African-American residents. The historian Carl Abbott has estimated that cities "absorbed approximately two-thirds of the federal budget cuts" of the early 1980s.[38]

These structural changes affected African-American mayors in important ways. The economic crisis shaped their campaigns and commanded their attention as they moved into city hall. On the day that he assumed office, for example, the New York mayor David Dinkins faced a $1 billion deficit, a homeless population in excess of seventy-five thousand, and the immediate need for 250,000 new public housing units.[39] Detroit's Coleman Young, Heather Ann Thompson argues, "was never able to compensate for the economic evisceration of the Motor City occasioned by white flight." According to Teaford, "when blacks entered city hall to take the spoils of victory, they found that whites had carted away the wealth of the metropolis to suburban communities beyond central-city jurisdiction. The black-ruled fragments were little more than bankrupt relics of past greatness."[40]

The effects of this crisis shaped the experiences of African-American mayors. In view of the need for white support to secure election, to achieve policy goals, and to remain in office, African-American mayors faced particularly vexing difficulties.[41] Two sets of issues illustrate the problem. First, because these leaders usually assumed office during an economic downturn, they struggled both to staunch the flow of jobs from the central city and to meet the increasing needs of the poor residents who remained. Thus on the one hand African-American mayors—as well as white mayors during this period— tried to keep businesses in the central city or to lure them back into the city, offering tax breaks and various giveaways of land and services. Such policies contributed, at least in the short run, to the shrinking of tax bases. On the other hand mayors sought to provide badly needed services to poor city dwellers, most of whom were African American. The mayors tried to forge policies that simultaneously preserved the low tax rates sought by employers, appealed to liberal supporters hoping to address social problems, and enhanced social services badly needed by African-American and Latino residents while the federal government was reducing support to cities. "Institutional and financial restraints, as well as resistance from white politicians or business leaders," Kusmer has explained, "made it almost impossible for these mayors to bring about basic improvements in jobs and housing."[42]

Confronting crime proved to be equally problematic and even more politically charged for African-American mayors. Crime rates, particularly rates of violent crime, exploded between the late 1960s and the early 1990s, the period when African-American mayors assumed office. Moreover, the first African-American mayors were elected in the wake of the urban riots of the 1960s, and many white voters believed that such leaders could restore peace. Crime rates rose especially quickly in the largest cities, many of which had African-American mayors. For much of U.S. history, cities have had lower rates of violence than the nation as a whole, but this changed abruptly during the 1960s. New York's violent crime rate quadrupled during the late 1960s, and Baltimore's and Detroit's rates tripled. By the mid-1970s the thirty-two largest cities had 15 percent of the nation's total population but 38 percent of murders and 55 percent of robberies.[43] If Detroit's homicide rate of the 1970s had persisted, "a baby born in the city in 1974 and remaining there all of his life would have a one in thirty-five chance of being murdered. But if the murder rate continued to rise at the same pace as in the early 1970s, then the odds were one in fourteen."[44] The crime problem defied—and defies— simple solutions, though many residents held mayors, particularly African-American mayors, responsible for skyrocketing crime rates.

The concentration of violent crime in the central cities distorted public policy debates. For complex reasons relating to poverty, social dislocation, and demographics, African-American city dwellers suffered disproportionately.[45] By the mid-1980s homicide had emerged as the leading cause of death among young African-American men in U.S. cities. By the late 1980s young African-American men in Washington, D.C., were being murdered at nearly eighteen times the rate of their white counterparts.[46] Similarly, in the year that David Dinkins moved into Gracie Mansion, the homicide rate for young African-American men in New York City surged to twenty-four times the national rate. Even though crime rates have fallen in recent years, racially tinged images of inner-city gangs, "super-predators," and drive-by shootings have cemented popular assumptions about the relationship between race and violence.[47]

All mayors, but especially African-American mayors, faced conflicting pressures. Many residents, regardless of race, demanded additional police protection, more aggressive law-enforcement strategies, and tougher sentencing guidelines.[48] In some campaigns white candidates used a "law-and-order" platform to galvanize white support across party lines. According to one Philadelphia politico, "supercop" Frank Rizzo's slogan of "Rizzo Means Business" actually meant "Rizzo will keep blacks in their place."[49] In order to attract the white votes necessary for victory, African-American leaders had to appear hard-nosed regarding crime, even as they sought to address the underlying social problems that produced crime. Once in office the pressure became still more pronounced. Critics and potential opponents seized on the issue of urban crime; the former U.S. attorney Rudolph Giuliani, for example, used crime as the centerpiece in his successful challenge to Dinkins. Charges that African-American mayors were soft on crime damaged Stokes's reputation in Cleveland, undercut Dinkins's popularity with white ethnic voters in New York City, and contributed to Wilson Goode's catastrophic decision to use explosives on the Philadelphia house containing members of the MOVE commune, resulting in eleven deaths and the burning of two city blocks. In short, African-American mayors were buffeted by the incendiary rhetoric of entrenched foes and the unrealistic expectations of loyal supporters.

Third, political and institutional problems posed particular obstacles for African-American mayors. Municipal executives such as Stokes clashed with police officials reluctant to work with African-American executives. Moreover, when mayors attempted to address long-standing problems relating to the police harassment of minorities, white officers often balked, charging that the reforms amounted to political pandering and thus could be ignored. Hatcher appointed an African-American law-and-order police chief in order to resolve this dilemma, though the tension between "cracking down" on criminals and safeguarding the rights of minority city dwellers persisted in Gary and doomed the experiment to failure.[50]

But police officers were not the only officials to wage political war against African-American mayors. For some executives, such as Ernest Morial of New Orleans, Richard Hatcher, and Harold Washington, hostile state legislatures stymied efforts to stimulate economic recovery and to address issues of racial inequality. In many cities, such as Cleveland, New Orleans, and Chicago, city councils coalesced in opposition to African-American mayors and challenged nearly every legislative initiative.[51] The tattered remains of Richard J. Daley's machine possessed sufficient power within Chicago's city council to block many of Washington's reforms, while Stokes grew so frustrated with recalcitrant Cleveland city council members, Leonard N. Moore explains, that the mayor eventually instructed his cabinet members to stop attending council meetings.

In part, the intransigence of city councils reflected overt racism, but other—often related—factors contributed to the problem. In cities in which African Americans remained an electoral minority, pragmatic council members used race—or, more accurately, racial hostility—as the bond in creating political coalitions. Such a strategy often pitted new mayors against the remnants of political machines. Thus African-American mayors, as political outsiders, lacked the well-heeled system of alliances that had traditionally sustained political power in the city. In addition, these mayors struggled to maintain their fragile coalitions. Washington relied on Chicago's "lakefront liberals," and Dinkins and Bradley looked to Jewish voters and other liberal segments of the white electorate. In Washington, D.C., according to Howard Gillette Jr., Marion Barry "forged alliances with liberal and gay whites as well as low-income African Americans." Goode, Kurt Schmoke of Baltimore, and others looked to local business leaders for support, which reduced their ability to undertake social reform. Ronald H. Bayor finds that Maynard Jackson's efforts to establish such connections "limited long-term improvements for low-income blacks" in Atlanta. Nor did newcomers such as Stokes and Hatcher possess the political and administrative experience to vanquish their determined political and bureaucratic opponents. Likewise, in an era of economic decline and institutional retrenchment, African-American mayors lacked the range of patronage positions that, in other eras, had cemented political coalitions. In short, even after they secured office, African-American executives faced formidable political and institutional obstacles.

* * *

Scholarly assessments of the influence of the early African-American mayors vary enormously, as the essays in this collection demonstrate. Just as historians debate whether Reconstruction was a failure, a partial success, or a crucially important first step in a far-reaching process, commentators disagree about the achievements and the legacy of African-American municipal executives. To some extent the debate depends on the particular frame of analysis. The rise of African-American mayors may have represented a powerful symbolic change, but at the same time its influence on poverty and inequality might have been modest. Similarly, particular legislative and institutional reforms could be termed minor achievements or the first rumbles in a seismic shift in public policy and political power.

For many observers the groundswell initiated by Stokes and Hatcher graphically illustrated the racial polarization of modern America.[52] Whites often supported candidates such as Stokes in the hope that an African American could end the rioting that plagued central cities during the late 1960s; fear of African-American unrest, rather than faith in African-American leadership, thus motivated some whites to cross racial lines in municipal elections. Moreover, the rise of African-American mayors followed the concentration and isolation of African Americans in central cities, as white flight, redlining, and other processes contributed to racial segregation. In fact, African Americans secured office disproportionately in the most segregated cities. In 1980, for example, sixteen major cities suffered from hypersegregation.[53] Half of these cities elected African-American mayors during the 1980s, while only 38 percent of the sixteen largest urban centers elected African-American mayors.

Voting patterns provided little cause for optimism about a decline in racial polarization. To win at the ballot box African-American candidates needed virtually unanimous support from African-American voters; these mayors typically captured more than 90 percent of the votes cast by African Americans. During the first three decades of African-American political power, whites in large cities voted across racial lines in modest numbers. In Detroit's 1973 mayoral election, for example, the white candidate, police commissioner John F. Nichols, received 91 percent of the white vote, and Coleman Young received 92 percent of the African-American vote. Similarly, in 1987 Frank Rizzo received 98 percent of Philadelphia's white vote, while Wilson Goode captured 97 percent of the African-American vote. Such polarization extended into the 1990s as well.[54] In Memphis's 1991 mayoral election, for instance, 97 percent of white voters cast their ballots for the white candidate, while 99 percent of African-American voters supported the African-American candidate, W. W. Herenton. New Orleans voters in 1994 cast their ballots in comparable proportions.[55] More often, however, African-American candidates in the Northeast and the Midwest received between one fifth and one eighth of white votes. In 1967 Hatcher captured 95 percent of the African-American vote but only 12 percent of the white vote.[56] Even Tom Bradley and David Dinkins, both of whom triumphed in urban centers with relatively modest African-American populations, enjoyed only limited white support. Los Angeles and New York possessed unusually diverse populations—Latino and Asian-American voters redefined the political landscape. Dinkins won in 1990 with just one quarter of the white vote.

In the major urban centers electing African-American mayors, voting rarely crossed racial lines, and this pattern has not changed appreciably since Stokes and Hatcher triumphed in 1967. African-American incumbents and

African-American challengers have usually fared nearly as poorly with white voters, attracting the votes of only a small number of liberal whites. Atlanta's Maynard Jackson, for example, carried 17.5 percent of the white vote in 1973 and 19.5 percent of the white vote in 1977. In his study of race and voting the political scientist Keith Reeves has concluded that "whites, by and large, continue to harbor implacable hostility toward blacks."[57] If African-American mayors were commonplace in America's leading cities by the end of the twentieth century, the trend did not necessarily point to a decline in racial polarization. As the number (and proportion) of African-American city dwellers continues to rise, African-American candidates become less dependent on white support.

To be sure, the level of electoral polarization has been less pronounced in medium-sized cities, particularly in recent years, and in sun-belt cities. Voters in a number of cities in which African Americans comprised less than a third of the population, including Charlotte, North Carolina, and Seattle, Washington, elected African-American mayors during the 1980s, as did voters in Denver, Kansas City, and Dallas during the 1990s. Although African Americans made up only 2 percent of the population of Spokane, Washington, voters in that city chose an African-American mayoral candidate, James Chase, in 1981. Such cross-over voting may point to a softening of racial hostility. In the major urban centers of the nation's rust belt, however, racial polarization has proved to be persistent.

Many critics of African-American mayors also lament the policy failures of these executives. Some mayors, such as Stokes, were rarely able to translate their ideologies into policy because of local opposition, whereas others, such as Dinkins and Washington, did not remain in office long enough to tally significant legislative achievements. But many African-American mayors, according to critics, abandoned their reformist programs, opting to "sell out" to business interests.[58] Andrew Young, for example, forged enduring ties with Atlanta's Chamber of Commerce and attracted foreign investors to the Georgia city. In the process, according to the Reverend Hosea Williams and others, he sacrificed the interests of Atlanta's African-American community by supporting regressive taxes and other policies that yielded benefits principally to merchants and developers.[59] Such criticism, particularly of Young, may be justified, but it also reflects the enormous expectations that greeted early mayors and the limits of African-American political power.[60]

These charges notwithstanding, evidence abounds to support a more positive assessment of African-American leadership. To be sure, African-American executives could not instantly revive the flagging economies of rust-belt cities, and many changes that took place during their tenures can be credited to the on-going influence of the civil rights movement. Still, African-American mayors produced an impressive list of tangible improvements for their constituents and their cities. These mayors, for example, oversaw a revolution in minority hiring practices. Even while overall municipal employment contracted, employment of African Americans by municipalities spiked during the years of African-American leadership in cities such as Detroit and Atlanta. During Coleman Young's first four years in office, for instance, the proportion of administrative positions held by African Americans in Detroit increased by 94 percent. Similarly, four years before Maynard Jackson's election in Atlanta, African Americans held 7 percent of administrative jobs and 15 percent of municipal professional positions. Four years after Jackson assumed office, however, the figures had surged to 33 percent and 42 percent, respectively.[61] According to a study based on 1978 data, of the ten cities with the highest proportion of African-American administrators, eight had African-American mayors during the 1970s.[62] The political scientist Peter Eisinger has concluded that "city hiring represents one tangible benefit of black political power."[63]

Nowhere was the influence of African-American mayors felt more profoundly than in police departments. For much of the twentieth century, police action has been at the center of racial violence. Law-enforcement tactics triggered many riots of the 1960s and have sparked more recent turmoil as well, including riots in Miami in the 1980s and the spiral set off by the 1991 beating of Rodney King in Los Angeles. As many of the first African-American mayors quickly learned, police departments were often particularly resistant to change and unusually hostile to African-American executives. Yet between 1966–67 and 1978, a span in which African Americans became mayors in Atlanta and Detroit, African Americans on the Atlanta police force increased from 9 percent to 30 percent, and the proportion in Detroit rose from 5 percent to 30 percent.[64] Changes in police leadership were still more remarkable. Within five years of the election of the first African-American mayors, African-American police chiefs (or police commissioners) were appointed in Cleveland, Gary, Newark, Atlanta, Detroit, Washington, Chicago, and Philadelphia.[65]

African-American mayors enjoyed other significant policy achievements as well. Cities with African-American mayors devoted particular attention—and money—to social and welfare services.[66] The much-criticized Stokes, for example, more than doubled the number of public housing units in Cleveland during his first term.[67] The economic policies of African-American mayors also generated dividends, as many mayors used the private sector to improve the status of African-American city dwellers. When Jackson took office in Atlanta, less than 1 percent of city business went to African-American businesses. By the end of his second term, the figure exceeded 30 percent. While opponents lambasted Andrew Young's "trickle-down" approach, he trumpeted the effectiveness of the strategy, labeling it a "bubble-up" approach.[68]

Perhaps the most important aspect of African-American political ascendance is the most difficult to measure. Without question, the rise of these mayors marked a fundamental symbolic turning point for African Americans. The success of Stokes and Hatcher, and their counterparts in other cities, gave minority city dwellers greater access to city hall. The process also contributed to the political engagement of African Americans; according to political scientists, the success of African-American candidates changed the attitudes of African-American residents, encouraging greater interest in and knowledge of municipal affairs.[69] Similarly, as Colburn notes, race itself no longer infuses every mayoral campaign involving an African-American candidate. Although racially charged euphemisms, such as "crack head" and "welfare queen," continue to infect campaign rhetoric, overt racism has faded considerably since 1967.

Local events, rather than aggregate data, may best capture the symbolic significance of the rise of African-American mayors as well as the remarkable speed of social and political change. In 1963 Police Commissioner Bull Connor prowled the streets of Birmingham, Alabama, harassing African-American residents, and white extremists firebombed a local Baptist church, murdering four young girls in the process. Only sixteen years later Birmingham voters chose Richard Arrington, an African-American zoologist, to run their city. Nor was the change fleeting; Arrington held the office for sixteen years.[70] Although leaders such as Arrington proved unable to eliminate social and racial inequality or to garner significant white support, their political ascendance nonetheless signaled an important change in race relations in American urban society.

* * *

The essays that follow explore the experiences of African-Americans mayors between 1967 and 1995. Nine of the ten essays are original pieces of research, and the tenth, Arnold R. Hirsch's examination of Chicago's Harold Washington and New Orleans's Ernest Morial, is a revised version of a previously published essay. Eight essays focus on individual cities, and thus they highlight the role of local political and economic forces. Moreover, the essays underscore the variety and complexity of African-American political ascendance. The collection includes essays on African-American mayors in snow-belt cities, such as New York, Gary, and Detroit, and on African-American mayors in sun-belt cities, such as Atlanta, New Orleans, and Los Angeles. We have attempted to strike a balance in putting together this collection, blending essays that examine some of the most important pioneers with essays that explore the range of conditions and experiences that African-American mayors have confronted. Because more than three hundred African Americans had served as mayor by the mid-1990s, we could not include pieces on every important mayor or every important city. For sake of comparability and coherence, this collection concentrates on a cross-section of the first generation of African-American mayors of major urban centers.

Colburn opens the book with a far-ranging and provocative analysis of the campaigns and strategies that carried African-American mayoral candidates into office. While he notes the hostility and racism that these political leaders faced, he emphasizes the rapid pace of social change since Stokes and Hatcher ran in 1967. Colburn finds that levels of racial hostility have waned markedly, particularly in the smaller cities and sun-belt cities, and that race does not dominate political campaigns, as it did during the late 1960s and the 1970s. In short, Colburn argues that changes in campaigns and in campaigning reveal important shifts in race relations during the final third of the century.

As one of the first African-American mayors, Richard G. Hatcher confronted enormous obstacles, including intense racial hostility. James B. Lane examines Hatcher's extraordinary twenty-year tenure as the mayor of Gary, a rust-belt city ravaged by the effects of deindustrialization. With an unflinching commitment to civil rights and racial equality, Hatcher used the power of municipal government to help low-income Gary residents. But, as Lane explains, Hatcher battled hostile forces within his own party, entrenched opposition from the state legislature, and obstructionist campaigns by Gary's leading employer. In the end, Lane notes, Hatcher's experience as a five-term mayor represents "a case study into the limits of black political power."

Cleveland's Carl B. Stokes faced a similar combination of political and economic difficulties. Like Hatcher, Stokes struggled to overcome the opposition of local politicians from both parties and to shore up a sagging economy. Leonard N. Moore, however, identifies two additional problems that plagued Stokes. First, a series of scandals dogged him during his two terms in city hall, providing ammunition for his political enemies. Second, Stokes endured stinging criticism from middle-class African Americans. Like Lane, Moore concludes that pioneers such as Stokes pressed the "limits of black power."

Focusing on Ernest "Dutch" Morial of New Orleans and Harold Washington of Chicago, Arnold R. Hirsch also explores the influence of local political culture on the experiences of African-American mayors. Although Morial and Washington rose to political influence through very different channels, both championed social reform but confronted fierce opposition from local political institutions. Such formidable obstacles notwithstanding, Hirsch concludes that Morial and Washington tallied significant political achievements that had a "democratizing influence" on their cities.

Roger Biles's essay on David Dinkins focuses on the special political challenges that African-American mayors confronted in cities with small African-American populations. Because African Americans made up only 25 percent of New York City's population, Dinkins relied on a multiracial, multiethnic coalition. According to Biles, the necessity of maintaining such political alliances—in combination with the mayor's political shortcomings—limited Dinkins's ability to address issues of racial equality. Caught between the demands of conflicting constituencies in a era of economic decline, Dinkins proved to be politically vulnerable and was turned out of office after a single term. Biles explains that New York's political fragmentation facilitated the election of the city's first African-American mayor, but the city's financial woes and demographic composition also posed insurmountable challenges for Dinkins.

In examining the career of Los Angeles's Tom Bradley, Heather R. Parker also analyzes the experiences of a mayor of a major urban center with a small African-American population. She devotes particular attention to Bradley's relationship with the city's African-American community, which comprised less than one fifth of the population when he was first elected. Parker emphasizes Bradley's commitment to policies that were not race based. Although his efforts benefited African Americans, many members of the local African-American community accused him of being unresponsive to their needs. Thus Parker's essay underscores the challenges that African-American executives faced, as they struggled to meet the expectations of African-American voters while attempting to represent other constituencies and maintain fragile political coalitions.

Ronald H. Bayor's essay demonstrates that African-American mayors in southern cities frequently endured similar problems, though in Atlanta policy debates often revolved around efforts to sustain economic growth. When African-American municipal executives in Atlanta attempted to address issues relating to poverty and racial inequality, they clashed with powerful conservative white business leaders who insisted that public policy should, first and foremost, support downtown financial interests. Over time, according to Bayor, African-American mayors shifted their priorities, devoting greater attention to the demands from the business community and less attention to the needs of low-income Atlantans. Although Maynard Jackson, Andrew Young, and Bill Campbell worked to improve the lives of African-American residents, it was, ironically, the local business elite that benefited most from the policies of Atlanta's first African-American mayors.

Marion Barry's remarkable political career is the subject of Howard Gillette Jr.'s essay. While Barry's tenure as mayor of Washington, D.C., featured pitched battles with political adversaries, it was the mayor's flamboyant style that made his public life distinctive, according to Gillette. Barry's political career survived charges of mismanagement and marital infidelity, the public release of an FBI videotape involving extramarital sex and drug use, and his subsequent incarceration for cocaine possession. Moreover, Barry embraced political philosophies ranging from racial separatism to pragmatism, and at various points during his years as mayor his allies included Louis Farrakhan and Newt Gingrich. Gillette's essay, in short, explores the tumultuous public life of perhaps the most controversial mayor of the era.

In the final essay in this volume Heather Ann Thompson analyzes the political ideology that many African-American mayors embraced. Focusing on Detroit's Coleman Young, she argues that demographic shifts, deindustrialization, and the increasingly conservative leanings of white voters combined to transform the urban political landscape. Even as white urbanites disproportionately lost faith in activist government and moved to the right politically, African-American mayors maintained their commitment to government-sponsored solutions to poverty and racial inequality. Thus political leaders such as Young emerged as the most influential defenders of 1960s-style liberalism.

* * *

The essays here identify important themes relating to the rise of African-American mayors. They focus particular attention on the ways in which urban social and political conditions shaped the experiences of African-American executives. Much work, however, remains to be done on the topic. Historians need to learn more about the influence of Latino and Asian-American voters on the politics of race, especially in sun-belt cities. Moreover, a number of African-American women, including Sharon Pratt Kelly in Washington, D.C., Doris Ann Lewis Davis in Compton, California, and Sharon Sayles Belton in Minneapolis, have won mayoral elections, raising interesting questions about the relationship between race and gender in late twentieth-century municipal politics. Furthermore, studies of African-American mayors in medium-sized and smaller cities will contribute significantly to our understanding of race and politics in modern America. As Colburn's essay shows, in Raleigh, North Carolina; Roanoke, Virginia; Seattle, Washington; and other medium-sized cities, residents have voted across racial lines much more frequently than their counterparts in major urban centers. Although this book concentrates on the nation's largest cities, the success of African-American candidates in smaller communities raises intriguing questions about the influence that local political institutions exert on race relations. In short, we hope that these essays stimulate additional research and discussion on the topic.

Finally, we hope that this collection helps to connect the history of African-American mayors to the broader contours of twentieth-century political and urban history. As all the essays note, the experiences of African-American mayors cannot be understood apart from the history of the late twentieth-century city. Forces such as deindustrialization, white flight, and residential segregation both set the stage for the victories of African-American mayors and exaggerated the obstacles that these executives confronted. Recent trends in urban society, particularly the economic rebirth of many rust-belt cities and the sharp decrease in rates of violent crime, may signal the dawn of a new era in urban political history. Whether the trend begun by Stokes and Hatcher in 1967 continues in this century, however, will depend on the tenor of race relations in the American city.

Notes

1. Stephan Thernstrom and Abigail Thernstrom argue that eighty-seven cities with populations greater than fifty thousand elected African-American mayors between 1967 and 1993. It is not clear how the Thernstroms arrived at this figure. See Stephan Thernstrom and Abigail Thernstrom, *America in Black and White* (New York: Simon and Schuster, 1997), 286.

2. Richard M. Bernard suggests that the trend marked the "greatest change in twentieth-century urban politics." See Bernard's introduction to Richard M. Bernard, ed., *Snowbelt Cities: Metropolitan Politics in the Northeast and Midwest Since World War II* (Bloomington: Indiana University Press, 1990), 16.

3. Jon C. Teaford, *The Twentieth-Century American City: Problem, Promise, and Reality* (Baltimore, Md.: Johns Hopkins University Press, 1986), 149.

4. For an examination of African-American police officers, see W. Marvin Dulaney, *Black Police in America* (Bloomington: Indiana University Press, 1996), 121.

5. For important works on the topic see Roger Biles, "Black Mayors: A Historical Assessment," *Journal of Negro History* 77, no. 4 (Summer 1992): 109–25; William E. Nelson Jr. and Philip J. Meranto, *Electing Black Mayors: Political Action in the Black Community* (Columbus: Ohio State University Press, 1977); George C. Galster and Edward W. Hill, eds.,

The Metropolis in Black and White (New Brunswick, N.J.: Rutgers University Press, 1992); Rufus P. Browning, Dale Rogers Marshall, and David H. Tabb, *Protest Is Not Enough: The Struggle of Blacks and Hispanics for Equality in Urban Politics* (Berkeley: University of California Press, 1984).

6. Bayard Rustin, "From Protest to Politics: The Future of the Civil Rights Movement," *Commentary* 39 (February 1965): 25–31.

7. Many important pieces of civil rights legislation, such as the Voting Rights Act of 1965, however, most directly affected southern states—rather than the northern states with large cities. Thus, although such legislation mobilized African-American voters, its influence on the victories of early African-American mayors was indirect.

8. See William J. Grimshaw, *Bitter Fruit: Black Politics and the Chicago Machine, 1931–1991* (Chicago: University of Chicago Press, 1992); Peter Eisinger, *The Politics of Displacement: Racial and Ethnic Transition in Three American Cities* (New York: Academic Press, 1980). Also see Martin Kilson's important essay, "Political Change in the Negro Ghetto, 1900–1940s," in Nathan I. Huggins, Martin Kilson, and Daniel Fox, eds., *Key Issues in the Afro-American Experience,* vol. 2 (New York: Harcourt, Brace, Jovanovich, 1971), 167–85.

9. Robert C. Smith, "The Changing Shape of Urban Black Politics: 1960–1970," *Annals of the American Academy of Political and Social Science* 439 (September 1978): 28.

10. Bernard, introduction, 16.

11. Ibid.

12. For example, see Howard P. Chudacoff and Judith E. Smith, *The Evolution of American Urban Society,* 4th ed. (Englewood Cliffs, N.J.: Prentice Hall, 1994), 304, and Keith Reeves, *Voting Hopes or Fears? White Voters, Black Candidates, and Racial Politics in America* (New York: Oxford University Press, 1997), 62.

13. See Hirsch's essay (chap. 4) in this volume. Also see Hirsch, "The Cook County Democratic Organization and the Dilemma of Race, 1931–1987," in Bernard, *Snowbelt Cities,* 85–86; Paul Kleppner, *Chicago Divided: The Making of a Black Mayor* (DeKalb: Northern Illinois University Press, 1985), 217.

14. *New York Times,* November 8, 1967.

15. Quoted in Biles, "Black Mayors," 119.

16. *New York Times,* November 8, 1967.

17. Carolyn Teich Adams, "Philadelphia: The Private City in the Post-Industrial Age," in Bernard, *Snowbelt Cities,* 218.

18. For example, see Smith, "Changing Shape of Urban Black Politics," 28.

19. During the early 1970s, however, African Americans, particularly wealthier African Americans, began to leave central cities. For the social effects of this migration, see William Julius Wilson, *The Truly Disadvantaged* (Chicago: University of Chicago Press, 1987) and *When Work Disappears* (New York: Knopf, 1997).

20. U.S. Bureau of the Census, *Historical Statistics of the United States,* pt. 1 (Washington, D.C.: U.S. Government Printing Office, 1975), A73–A90; Reynolds Farley and Walter R. Allen, *The Color Line and the Quality of Life in America* (New York: Oxford University Press, 1989), 114.

21. Thernstrom and Thernstrom, *America in Black and White,* 290.

22. Biles, "Black Mayors," 114–15.

23. Daniel J. Walkowitz, "A Tale of Two Cities," in Bernard, *Snowbelt Cities,* 193.

24. Teaford, *Twentieth-Century American City,* 152.

25. Kenneth L. Kusmer, "African Americans in the City Since World War II," *Journal of Urban History* 21 (May 1995): 472.

26. Thernstrom and Thernstrom, *America in Black and White,* 295.

27. Jon C. Teaford, *The Road to Renaissance* (Baltimore, Md.: Johns Hopkins University Press, 1990), 213, 288.

28. Ibid., 211, 295.

29. Ibid., 208. To calculate the percentage drop in sales, Teaford adjusted the retail sales figures for inflation.

30. John D. Kasarda, "Urban Industrial Transition and the Underclass," *Annals of the American Academy of Political and Social Science* 501 (January 1989): 29.

31. Wilson, *The Truly Disadvantaged,* 46.

32. Thomas J. Sugrue, "The Structures of Urban Poverty: The Reorganization of Space and Work in Three Periods of American History," in Michael B. Katz, ed., *The "Underclass" Debate* (Princeton, N.J.: Princeton University Press, 1993), 110.

33. Paul Osterman, "Gains from Growth? The Impact of Full Employment on Poverty in Boston," in Christopher Jencks and Paul E. Peterson, eds., *The Urban Underclass* (Washington, D.C.: Brookings Institution, 1991), 126. Between 1969 and 1982 the number of African-American central-city residents living below the poverty line surged by 59 percent. See Wilson, *The Truly Disadvantaged,* 172.

34. Douglas S. Massey and Nancy A. Denton, *American Apartheid* (Cambridge, Mass.: Harvard University Press, 1993).

35. Wilson, *When Work Disappears,* 3–50.

36. Teaford, *Road to Renaissance,* 263.

37. Ibid., 262.

38. Carl Abbott, *Urban America in the Modern Age, 1920 to the Present* (Arlington Heights, Ill.: Harlan Davidson, 1987), 131.

39. Biles, "Black Mayors," 118.

40. Teaford, *Twentieth-Century American City,* 147.

41. For works dealing with related themes, see Mark H. Jones, "Black Political Empowerment in Atlanta: Myth and Reality," *Annals of the American Academy of Political and Social Science* 439 (September 1978): 90–117; Edmond J. Keller, "The Impact of Black Mayors on Urban Policy," *Annals of the American Academy of Political and Social Science* 439 (September 1978): 40–52.

42. Kusmer, "African Americans in the City," 472.

43. Wesley G. Skogan, "Crime in Contemporary America," in Hugh Graham Davis and Ted Robert Gurr, eds., *Violence in America* (Beverly Hills, Calif.: Sage, 1979), 381.

44. Teaford, *Twentieth-Century American City,* 135.

45. The scholarly literature on this topic is enormous. See, for example, Gary LaFree, "Race and Crime Trends in the United States," in Darnell F. Hawkins, ed., *Ethnicity, Race, and Crime* (Albany: State University of New York Press, 1995), 169–93.

46. Samuel Walker, *Sense and Nonsense About Crime and Drugs,* 3d ed. (Belmont, Calif.: Wadsworth, 1994), 7.

47. Randall Kennedy, *Race, Crime, and the Law* (New York: Vintage, 1997), 14–15, 366–80. Also see Thomas Byrne Edsall with Mary D. Edsall, *Chain Reaction: The Impact of Race,*

Rights, and Taxes on American Politics (New York: Norton, 1991). For recent changes in rates of violence, see Alfred Blumstein and Richard Rosenfeld, "Explaining Recent Trends in U.S. Homicide Rates," *Journal of Criminal Law and Criminology* 88 (Summer 1998): 1175–1216.

48. See Wilson, *When Work Disappears*, 23, 184, 188; Ken Auletta, *The Underclass* (New York: Vintage, 1982), 144–45; Franklin E. Zimring and Gordon Hawkins, *Crime Is Not the Problem: Lethal Violence in America* (New York: Oxford University Press, 1997), 8–15.

49. Teaford, *Road to Renaissance*, 195.

50. More recently, African-American mayors such as Kurt Schmoke of Baltimore struck a more successful balance between these often conflicting goals.

51. Biles, "Black Mayors," 119; Hirsch, "Cook County Democratic Organization," 85.

52. See Teaford, *Twentieth-Century American City*, 147.

53. Massey and Denton, *American Apartheid*, 76.

54. Adams, "Philadelphia," 218.

55. Thernstrom and Thernstrom, *America in Black and White*, 296.

56. Stanley Lieberson, *A Piece of the Pie: Blacks and Immigrants Since 1880* (Berkeley: University of California Press, 1980), 66.

57. Reeves, *Voting Hopes or Fears?* 62.

58. See Nelson and Meranto, *Electing Black Mayors*.

59. David R. Goldfield, "Black Political Power and Public Policy in the Urban South," in Arnold R. Hirsch and Raymond A. Mohl, eds., *Urban Policy in Twentieth-Century America* (New Brunswick, N.J.: Rutgers University Press, 1993), 174; David R. Goldfield, "Southern Politics: Showtime to Bigtime," in Paul D. Escott and David R. Goldfield, eds., *The South for New Southerners* (Chapel Hill: University of North Carolina Press, 1991), 130–32.

60. For a thoughtful discussion of the political and institutional obstacles that African-American mayors confronted, see Kusmer, "African Americans in the City," 472.

61. Peter K. Eisinger, "Black Employment in Municipal Jobs: The Impact of Black Political Power," *American Political Science Review* 76 (June 1982): 385.

62. Ibid., 384.

63. Ibid., 380. Eisinger argues that the effect was clear and measurable, although relatively modest in statistical terms.

64. Peter K. Eisinger, "Black Mayors and the Politics of Racial Advancement," in William C. McCready, ed., *Culture, Ethnicity, and Identity* (New York: Academic, 1983), 95–109.

65. For data on police chiefs see Dulaney, *Black Police in America*, 121.

66. Albert K. Karnig and Susan Welch, *Black Representation and Urban Policy* (Chicago: University of Chicago Press, 1980), 122–28.

67. Keller, "Impact of Black Mayors," 48.

68. Goldfield, "Black Political Power and Public Policy," 177; Richard M. Bernard, "Metropolitan Politics in the American Sunbelt," in Raymond A. Mohl, ed., *Searching for the Sunbelt* (Athens: University of Georgia Press, 1993), 76.

69. Smith, "Changing Shape of Urban Black Politics," 27; Karnig and Welch, *Black Representation and Urban Policy*, 109–11.

70. Bernard, "Metropolitan Politics," 75.

1. Running for Office: African-American Mayors from 1967 to 1996

DAVID R. COLBURN

WITH THE PASSAGE of the Voting Rights Act of 1965, the nation ended nearly a century of legalized segregation and hastened the integration of African Americans into the political mainstream. Aided by federal registrars, hundreds of thousands of southern blacks marched to the polls to reclaim the most basic right of citizens in a democratic society. Their determination, in turn, inspired northern blacks to recommit themselves to the electoral process.[1] Yet as this process unfolded, Bayard Rustin was one of a very few black leaders to recognize that a campaign for political power in the black community was about to supersede the activities of civil rights organizations.[2]

Black politics had long been commonplace in the urban North, especially after the mass migrations of black southerners in the early 1900s. Political involvement before the late 1960s, however, had resulted in only limited benefits for black communities and for select black leaders. A "plantation politics," or what the political scientist Martin Kilson has called "clientage politics," dominated the local scene in the North.[3] Although this political environment represented an improvement over the racial isolation of the late nineteenth and early twentieth centuries, it offered black residents a circumscribed voice in city life. Within this historical context the elections of African-American mayors beginning in 1967 portended a significant new chapter in the black experience and in urban politics.[4]

The swiftness of the evolution from social protest against de jure segregation to Carl Stokes's and Richard Hatcher's assuming elective office also caught most early writers off guard.[5] A widespread skepticism about white America's willingness to accept the civil rights reforms and to elect African-American political leaders prevailed among writers and activists. Three political scientists wrote in 1968, for example, that "Stokes and Hatcher won because black-voter power coalesced with a relatively small minority of liberal whites. It was not a victory of acceptance or even tolerance of Negroes, but a numerical failure of the powers of discrimination."[6] To dismiss the victory of Carl Stokes, a great-grandson of a former slave, over Seth Taft, the great-grandson of a former president, as simply "a numerical failure of the powers of discrimination" is not only bewildering but inaccurate. These and other authors of this era chose largely to ignore the significance for urban America of Stokes's and Hatcher's elections and for what they said about changes in race relations.

Many more recent scholars have been equally remiss in noting the significance of this development, despite black political achievements since the 1960s. Writing in the late 1980s, the historian David Chalmers noted the influence of the civil rights movement on a host of reform efforts in U.S. society in the 1960s but did not mention its influence on politics or the election of Stokes or Hatcher as one of its consequences. Equally glaring is the failure even to mention the election of African-American mayors or black politics in William Chafe's important 1986 survey of the era, *The Unfinished Journey,* which describes the social and political developments in the post–World War II era.[7] Both authors ignored the increase in the number of black mayors, from 2 in 1968 to 48 in 1973 and to 316 in 1990.[8] According to the Joint Center for Political and Economic Studies, in 1991 African Americans headed thirty cities with populations of fifty thousand or more, and sixteen led cities with white majorities.

The assassination of the Reverend Martin Luther King Jr. in 1968, a year after the elections of Stokes and Hatcher, was more than symbolic, however. King's death and the rise of these two men to the office of mayor represented the passing of one era and the emergence of another. The two developments placed in stark contrast what only Rustin had the prescience to observe: the transition of black activism from the streets to the halls of government.[9] This essay profiles sixty-seven black mayors who were elected to office between 1967 and 1996 in cities with populations greater than fifty thousand (see table 1.1). In doing so, I examine the mayors collectively and by cohort, based on whether they served in what has been called the first period of black leadership, from 1967 to 1976, or in the era that followed, to offer a better understanding of who they were, what they represented, and how they and their political agendas evolved over time.[10] I also analyze the evolution of the politics of race as it affected the campaigns of these mayors. Although African Americans were elected mayor in nearly every large city in the United States during this period, they encountered persistent opposition by whites, especially in the nation's oldest and largest cities. But these experiences do not provide a complete picture of the African-American experience. In a significant number of midsized cities, such as Berkeley, California; Roanoke, Virginia; Grand Rapids, Michigan; and Spokane, Washington, and in twenty-two sun-belt cities, including Raleigh and Charlotte, North Carolina; Dallas; and Los Angeles, African Americans captured the mayor's office with white voters paying surprisingly little attention to issues of race.[11]

Table 1.1. Black Mayors in Cities of 50,000 or More, 1968–96

City	Mayor	Years Served
Ann Arbor, Mich.	Albert Wheeler	1975–78
Atlanta, Ga.	Maynard Jackson	1974–82, 1990–94
	Andrew Young	1982–90
	Bill Campbell	1994–
Baltimore, Md.	Kurt Schmoke	1987–[a]
Berkeley, Calif.	Warren Widner	1971–79
	Gus Newport	1980–88
Birmingham, Ala.	Richard Arrington	1979–95
Camden, N.J.	Melvin Primas	1981–89
	Aaron Thompson	1990–
Charlotte, N.C.	Harvey Gantt	1983–87
Chicago, Ill.	Harold Washington	1983–90
Cleveland, Ohio	Carl Stokes	1967–72
	R. Michael White	1990–
Compton, Calif.	Doris Ann Lewis Davis	1973–77
	Walter Tucker	1987–93
Dallas, Tex.	Ron Kirk	1996–
Dayton, Ohio	James Howell McGee	1970–82
	Richard Dixon	1987–
Denver, Colo.	Wellington Webb	1991–
Detroit, Mich.	Coleman Young	1973–93
	Dennis Archer	1994–
Durham, N.C.	Chester Jenkins	1989–91
East Orange, N.J.	William Hart	1971–79
	Thomas Cooke Jr.	1979–83
	John Hatcher Jr.	1983–91
	Cardell Cooper	1991–95
East St. Louis, Ill.	James Estel Williams Sr.	1971–75
	William Edgar Mason Sr.	1975–79
	Carl Officer	1979–91
	Gordon Bush	1991–
Flint, Mich.	James Sharpe Jr.	1983–87
Gary, Ind.	Richard Hatcher	1966–87
	Thomas Barnes	1988–95
Grand Rapids, Mich.	Lyman Parks	1971–75
Hartford, Conn.	Thurman Milner	1981–87
	Carrie Saxon Perry	1987–93
Inglewood, Calif.	Edward Vincent	1983–95

Table 1.1. (cont.)

City	Mayor	Years Served
Kansas City, Mo.	Emanuel Cleaver	1991–
Los Angeles, Calif.	Thomas Bradley	1973–93
Memphis, Tenn.	W. W. Herenton	1991–
Minneapolis, Minn.	Sharon Sayles Belton	1994–
Mt. Vernon, N.Y.	Ronald Blackwood	1981–
Newark, N.J.	Kenneth Gibson	1970–86
	Sharpe James	1986–94
New Haven, Conn.	John Daniels	1990–
New Orleans, La.	Ernest Morial	1978–86
	Sidney Barthelemy	1986–94
	Marc Morial	1994–
New York, N.Y.	David Dinkins	1990–94
Oakland, Calif.	Lionel Wilson	1977–90
	Elihu Harris	1990–94
Philadelphia, Pa.	Wilson Goode	1984–92
Pontiac, Mich.	Wallace Holland	1974–86
	Walter Moore	1986–96
Portsmouth, Va.	James Holley III	1984–88
Raleigh, N.C.	Clarence Lightner	1973–75
Roanoke, Va.	Noel Taylor	1975–92
Rochester, N.Y.	William Johnson	1994–
Rockford, Ill.	Charles Box	1990–93
Seattle, Wash.	Norman Rice	1989–97
Spokane, Wash.	James Chase	1981–85
St. Louis, Mo.	Freeman Bosley	1993–97
Trenton, N.J.	Douglas Palmer	1990–
Washington, D.C.	Walter Washington	1974–79
	Marion Barry	1980–90, 1994–98
	Sharon Pratt Kelly	1990–94

Note: Total = 67 mayors. Those mayors whose final year in office is not identified were still serving as mayor at last examination in 1999.
  a. Elected to third term in 1995.

Virtually all the largest cities with a strong mayor system had elected a black mayor by 1996. Sixty-seven were elected mayor in citywide campaigns in forty-four cities, with several cities electing more than one African-American mayor. The largest number served in cities with a mayor-council form of government and a strong and independent mayor. The mayor-council governments tended to be concentrated in the older cities of the Northeast and the larger cities of the Midwest, whereas those elected mayor in cities where the mayor-commissioner government prevailed were disproportionately located in the South and West. Even in the latter cities, however, most mayors were elected in their own right (as opposed to being appointed by the board of commissioners), held substantive budgetary and personnel power, and exercised important symbolic leadership in setting the political agenda.[12]

Profiles of the First Black Candidates

In commenting in 1969 upon the emergence of black executive leadership in cities, the political scientist and U.S. senator Daniel Patrick Moynihan argued that the "current crop" of black leaders was nurtured in the Great Society programs of Lyndon Johnson's administration, which provided important training outlets for the development of black leadership. "Very possibly," he wrote, "the most important long-term impact of the community action programs of the 1960s will prove to have been the formulation of an urban Negro leadership echelon at just the time when the Negro masses . . . were verging toward extensive commitments to urban politics." At almost the precise moment that the civil rights movement was nearing its end, according to Moynihan, black leaders made the transition from the training ground of the Great Society to the political arena.[13]

An analysis of the backgrounds and campaigns of the sixty-seven black mayors elected to govern the nation's largest cities, however, offers little evidence to support Moynihan's claim about the political influence of the Great Society community action programs. It may well be that black political involvement in all its manifestations accorded with Moynihan's premise, but among black mayors in the nation's largest cities, the evidence suggests a different sort of paradigm.

The first major campaigns for mayor by black candidates followed directly on the heels of the Civil Rights Act of 1964 and the Voting Rights Act of 1965 and occurred in the midst of racial unrest and rioting in a number of the nation's major cities. It was not coincidental that these campaigns followed such political and social upheaval so closely, nor was it accidental that they overlapped the racial violence. The mayoral campaigns of Carl Stokes in Cleveland, Ohio, and Richard Hatcher in Gary, Indiana, simultaneously reflected black aspirations, the frustrations of black voters with a system that seemed to have little bearing on their physical and economic circumstances, their efforts to redefine and assert their racial identity, and recognition by a white minority of a new era in race relations.[14]

That such campaigns occurred first in the North resulted from certain political realities. African Americans in this region had the suffrage and were not dependent on special voting rights legislation or on the intervention of federal marshals dispatched by the Department of Justice to help them register. Although often subjected to an exploitative relationship with local white politicians, many northern blacks had nevertheless gained valuable political experience in the urban political machines. Such experience proved important in helping them mount local campaigns, raise money, mobilize support, and ultimately govern large complex cities.[15] Moreover, by the time Hatcher and Stokes ran for mayor, African Americans in cities throughout the Midwest and Northeast had gained experience at many levels of government, from city councils to state legislatures. This experience proved at least as significant and was more widespread for black candidates than the Great Society experience suggested by Moynihan.[16]

In a separate but related vein, black residents of these northern communities, many of whom had relatives in the South but who themselves were often little more than observers of the civil rights revolution in the South, were inspired by the struggle against segregation to pursue change in their cities. This desire for reform, together with the rise of cultural nationalism in black communities and its emphasis on black self-determination, spurred a major challenge to the notion of politics as usual.[17] A measure of northern black pride was a factor in the election of the first black mayors by voters who had watched the civil rights protests in the South from the sidelines. Moreover, many believed that their lives in the North would be significantly enhanced by electing one of their own as, they observed, it had been for other ethnic groups before them. Much like ethnic minorities, black voters wanted certain tangible benefits from government, such as influence over public policy, programs that would address their needs, and jobs. It had also become increasingly clear to black voters that white leaders were not willing to undertake the full range of reforms necessary to address the pervasive social and economic problems in black communities.[18]

The scholarly literature on the first black mayors generally suggests a two-pronged explanation of their political ascendancy. Richard Hatcher fit the so-called model of civil-rights-activist-turned-politician. He had been involved in NAACP activities during his student days at Indiana University and served as legal adviser for the Gary chapter of the NAACP after he settled in the community. He subsequently assumed a leadership role in assembling a black political organization in Gary to provide a training ground for black activists interested in political careers. Hatcher's involvement in civil rights activities would, in fact, significantly shape his mayoral agenda. But one could also argue that Hatcher was an example of the Horatio Alger model of the poor boy made good. Born to an impoverished family with thirteen children, he rose from humble origins to become a successful lawyer and prominent local and national political figure.[19]

Carl Stokes, who was elected mayor of Cleveland on the same day in 1967 as Hatcher, followed a path that conformed to a much more traditional model of political ascendancy. Like Hatcher, Stokes was born and raised in the slums. He dropped out of high school before enlisting in the army at eighteen. After his discharge, Stokes received a bachelor's degree from the University of Minnesota and a law degree from Cleveland-Marshall Law School while working days. In 1962 he won election to the Ohio legislature as a Democrat and became the state's first black legislator in the twentieth century. Stokes ran unsuccessfully for mayor in 1965, in a race that helped lay the basis for his successful campaign in 1967. Before he became mayor in 1968, Stokes had not been a member of the NAACP or any other civil rights organization. But, like virtually all black Americans, he had followed the civil rights demonstrations in the South and greatly admired King. Although Stokes identified with the movement, he was very much rooted in the political system, and he operated comfortably within it.[20]

These men illustrated two different paths to office. Most writers asserted that Hatcher's experience was typical of mayors during the early period of black governance from 1968 to 1976. An examination of the seventeen men and one woman (Doris Davis of Compton, California) who were directly elected mayor by voters during this era reveals, however, that Hatcher's route was not common at all. Although candidates took many paths to the office of mayor, the route that went through the civil rights movement was one of the least frequent for this first wave of successful mayoral candidates and for those who followed. Among the eighteen elected in this era, only Kenneth Gibson of Newark, New Jersey, shared with Hatcher a formal connection to the civil rights movement.

Personal and Political Profiles of Black Mayors

An analysis of the sixty-seven black mayors who were elected during the twenty-eight years from 1967 to 1996 reveals that they shared a variety of characteristics. The political scientist Lester Salamon has argued that the "expansion of black political participation and the opening of the political system to black office seeking . . . tapped new sources of talent outside the circle of the middle class professionals."[21] The backgrounds of the sixty-seven mayors reveal, however, that these black mayors represented the educational elite of the country and a rising group of middle-class professionals.[22]

Of those elected mayor between 1967 and 1996, nearly all were well educated, whether they served in the first cohort from 1967 to 1976 or the second cohort, from 1977 to 1996. Before 1976, 94.4 percent, or seventeen of eighteen mayors, had college degrees, compared to 92 percent of those elected after 1976. Among those in the first group, only Coleman Young of Detroit had not graduated from college. Nine mayors in this cohort had law degrees (50 percent), three (18 percent) had doctoral degrees, six (35 percent) had a master's degree (all three with doctoral degrees also had master's degrees), and Noel Taylor of Roanoke, Virginia, and Lyman Parks of Grand Rapids, Michigan, held the degree of doctor of divinity. In this first group all but one mayor with a bachelor's also had a postgraduate degree. Fifty percent of the first cohort of black mayors had law degrees, compared to 31 percent of the second cohort; 44.4 percent of the first group had graduate degrees, compared to 38 percent of the second cohort. The statistics in both cases represented a high degree of academic achievement compared to the general population and to that of other candidates running for mayor during this period. The educational background of the first cohort was particularly remarkable and underscored the observation of the political scientist Leonard Cole and others that the first black candidates often had to be supermen and superwomen to establish their viability as candidates and to secure support from voters.[23]

Backgrounds and credentials proved crucial in gaining the support of white voters, but they were also important in securing black votes in these early contests. Educational achievements eased concerns among some nonblack voters about the ability of these candidates to govern such large, complex communities. Many older blacks, accustomed to voting for whites throughout their adult years, preferred to vote for a black candidate who was well educated and articulate. Howard Lee, who served as the mayor of Chapel Hill, North Carolina, from 1969 to 1975, expressed concern about "those, both black and white, who constantly wonder whether a black man is really capable of handling the reins of municipal government."[24] Although education has always been an important factor in defining a candidate's qualifications for office, it had much greater meaning in this first decade of black political leadership than it would subsequently, when blacks and whites became more accustomed to black governance.

Historically, black colleges in the South were crucial in educating southern black leaders, whereas predominantly white colleges and universities frequently were the alma maters of those elected in the North and West.[25] Black colleges below the Mason-Dixon line enabled young black men and women to mature and develop leadership skills in a supportive environment, where the oppressiveness of racism intervened only occasionally. For northern blacks, their collegiate contacts with white students no doubt helped them understand the concerns and aspirations of whites, their racial prejudices, and, perhaps as important, how to communicate and interact with them.

Another prominent feature of these mayors was their maleness. The only African-American women elected mayor of a large city since 1980 have been Doris Davis of Compton, California; Carrie Saxon Perry of Hartford, Connecticut; Sharon Pratt Kelly of Washington, D.C.; and Sharon Belton of Minneapolis (or 6 percent of the sixty-seven mayors considered here).[26] The dominance of male candidates was not surprising in light of the prominence of black men in the civil rights movement, in local politics, and in the business community. Within the southern civil rights movement, for example, the ministers of the Southern Christian Leadership Conference were accustomed to running things and often expressed reservations about such activist women as Septima Clark and Ella Baker.[27] In the late sixties, the black power movement was exclusively male led. Although black women played a central role in the community as both wage earners and homemakers, they received little consideration when black candidates first ran for office. Gender relations in black America, indeed, had much in common with the gendered construction of white society.[28]

The work and political experiences of these black mayors varied over time, reflecting the changing racial environment in the United States and the middle-class aspirations of these men and women. Of the eighteen elected before 1976, the largest number, seven of eighteen, or 39 percent, had worked in the private sector as lawyers, another five (28 percent) served in the military, and four (22 percent) worked in education; only two worked in city government and another three worked in state government. Most of these mayors had multiple work experiences, with those who served in the military subsequently taking jobs in another sector of society. Only two men in this first group had been clergy previously, and only one, James Williams of East St. Louis, Illinois, had worked for the federal government—in the Veterans Administration. The fields of military service, education, and law dominated the work experiences of most of these men and one woman before they became mayor.

Of those elected after 1976, most worked in the private sector (57 percent), either as lawyers (35 percent) or as private businessmen and -women (35 percent). Only four in the first group worked in private business. As with the first group, many in the second group served in the military (20 percent) and in education (18 percent). But the diversity of work experiences was much broader in the second group, with three serving as judges, four as college professors, and three in the federal government.

The political experiences of the mayors in the two groups reveal similar differences over time. Of the sixty-seven mayors, all had some sort of experience at the federal, state, or local levels, and most had extensive political experience. More than 65 percent came out of local politics, where they had been members of a city council, city or county government, school board, or planning or development commission. When the two cohorts are combined, half had served on city councils. Members of the second cohort were more likely, however, to have experience as state legislators. Twenty-three percent of the second cohort of mayors served in the state senate or the state house of representatives. Another 14 percent served in federal elective and appointive positions. By contrast, only two mayors in the first cohort had held a state office, and none held a federal office.

The work and political experiences of the post-1976 group highlight the role of the civil rights movement, black voting, and the leadership of the pre-1976 group in opening up political opportunities. The experiences of these black mayors reveal that U.S. society had begun to accept, albeit gradually and with continuing white resistance, the participation of black citizens in a wide range of activities previously denied to them.

Throughout the era from 1967 to 1996, black voters and black candidates looked increasingly to the Democratic Party for political involvement. A black Republican candidate for mayor was about as rare as any endangered species, and none of the black mayors in large cities since 1967 has been a Republican. Black voters felt a special commitment to the Democratic Party for civil rights advances, affirmative action, and a host of Great Society programs that had helped the black poor. The election of black Democrats in cities across the country further cemented ties with the party. Moreover, black residents, who were left behind by the out-migration of manufacturing and the black middle class in the 1970s and 1980s, came to regard Democratic social programs as crucial to their personal and economic well-being. Because of this political commitment, black voters and black candidates were heavily dependent on the cities' remaining Democratic in order to achieve their political, social, and economic goals.[29]

These African-American mayors captured elections in a wide variety of cities across the country. Approximately 66 percent governed cities (a total of forty-four cities) in the older communities of the Northeast, Midwest, and South. Another 33 percent were elected to office in a range of midsized cities and sun-belt cities (twenty-two). Further analysis also reveals that African-American candidates were elected or reelected for twelve or more years in twenty of the sixty-six cities. Of these, eleven had a majority-black voter base, whereas nine had a white majority. (The discrepancy between the number of cities and the number of black mayors reflects the fact that some cities elected several black mayors.)

Campaign Platforms

Whether in cities like Newark, Charlotte, Baltimore, or Los Angeles, economic issues dominated the campaign platforms of these black mayors. In nearly every campaign they called for programs to enhance economic development, recruit new businesses, and develop enterprise zones. Sixty-three of the sixty-seven mayors (94 percent) proposed economic development, enterprise zones, and government-business partnerships. Combating crime stood a strong second, with forty-one of the sixty-seven mayors (61 percent) calling for larger police forces, drug prevention, and/or sterner measures to reduce crime. Education ranked third, with twenty-eight of sixty-seven mayors (42 percent) proposing programs to improve public schools. Urban renewal stood fourth, housing fifth, and transportation a more distant sixth. These issues resonated almost equally with urban white and black voters throughout the period from 1968 to 1996, although blacks more consistently favored new housing, whereas whites favored tax relief.[30]

Economic issues transcended region and individual candidates and highlighted the anxiety that touched the largest cities in this era. Successful candidates understood that programs to address these issues won supporters among blacks and whites. The stagflation of the 1970s, followed by mounting unemployment in the 1970s and 1980s, stagnating personal incomes, the out-migration of the white and black middle class in the 1970s and 1980s, and the transformation of the national economy from industry to service and high technology, nearly devastated the old industrial inner cities of the Northeast and Midwest. The recessions of the early 1980s and early 1990s added to the economic misery.[31] Black residents felt these pressures more than most, especially in the large cities of the industrial belt, where many resided in the 1970s and 1980s and where fundamental changes in the economy bypassed them and their communities.

The deteriorating economic conditions in many northeastern and midwestern cities and the general level of national economic uncertainty in the 1970s, 1980s, and early 1990s underscored why so many mayors called for programs to spur economic growth.[32] In the old industrial belt, Detroit was among the hardest hit, but conditions there were similar to developments throughout the region. The city lost nearly 400,000 people between 1970, when its population was 838,877, and 1980, when its residents numbered 444,730, as the economy drifted downward. The trend continued into the 1980s, with the black middle class accompanying the white middle class in fleeing the city, a pattern repeated elsewhere in the region. By 1988 more than 30 percent of Detroit's black community and more than 10 percent of white residents lived below the poverty level (for comparative population and unemployment statistics, see table 1.2).[33] The populations of most rust-belt cities fell below their 1930 levels, and the major corporations joined the exodus from these cities.[34]

The mayoral campaigns of black candidates in these and other cities emphasized redevelopment and job creation. They offered creative but essentially mainstream approaches to bringing the business and middle class back to the city and to creating employment opportunities for residents in an effort to turn their cities around. In 1978 Ernest Morial, for example, offered the business community in New Orleans "a partnership and a strong voice in my administration as long as we can agree that balanced growth is urban salvation."[35] The political scientist Peter Eisinger has pointed out that this decision meant Morial would consciously ignore black radicalism or separatism as counterproductive.[36] In fact, among black mayors, only Richard Hatcher offered a more radical economic approach to urban problems.

Crime also plagued these communities, and much of it arose from the depressed economic conditions. Drugs offered both escape and financial gain and preyed heavily upon the black community. The sociologist William Julius Wilson has noted that the departure of the black middle class not only hurt the city economically but added significantly to the breakdown of community in black neighborhoods. Black communities faced exceedingly difficult times, given the dramatic reduction in the number of middle-class residents, high rates of unemployment, and a decline in government assistance.[37] These conditions resulted in the social deterioration of many inner-city black neighborhoods.

Following the urban riots of the 1960s and amid the social and economic crises in many urban communities from 1970 to 1995, some white leaders began to support black mayoral leadership as a potential antidote to the decline of their cities. A number of scholars have argued that this economic degeneration was a primary incentive for many white and black residents to support black mayoral candidates, whether one was in the first or second cohort, throughout the period from 1967 to 1996.[38] In 1987, with the number of residents living at or below the poverty level at 23 percent in New York (up from 15 percent in 1975), and at 32 percent in New Orleans (up from 26 percent two decades earlier), and with 25 percent of Newark's residents and an equal percentage of Birmingham's residents on public assistance, most blacks determined that a black mayor had a better understanding of their economic plight and would be more likely to use local government to help them.[39] Richard Hatcher's success in attracting an estimated $150 million in federal funds during his first five years in office did not go unnoticed and suggested that black leadership could bring tangible benefits to black communities.[40]

Table 1.2. Cities Governed by Black Mayors

City	Population (1000s)			African Americans (%)			Unemployment (%)		
	1970	1980	1990	1970	1980	1990	1970	1980	1990
Ann Arbor, Mich.	100	108	110	7	9	9	3	11	4
Atlanta, Ga.	495	425	394	51	67	67	4	8	9
Baltimore, Md.	906	787	736	46	55	59	5	11	9
Berkeley, Calif.	114	103	103	24	20	19	8	7	6
Birmingham, Ala.	301	284	265	42	56	63	5	7	9
Camden, N.J.	103	85	87	40	53	56	6	18	16
Charlotte, N.C.	241	315	396	30	31	32	3	4	4
Chicago, Ill.	3400	3000	2700	33	40	39	4	10	11
Cleveland, Ohio	751	574	506	38	44	47	4	11	14
Compton, Calif.	79	81	90	74	75	55	10	12	14
Dallas, Tex.	844	905	1000	25	29	30	3	3	7
Dayton, Ohio	243	194	182	31	37	40	4	14	11
Denver, Colo.	515	493	468	9	12	13	4	5	7
Detroit, Mich.	1500	1200	1000	44	63	76	7	11	20
Durham, N.C.	95	101	137	39	47	46	3	5	5
East Orange, N.J.	75	78	74	54	83	90	4	9	12
East St. Louis, Ill.	70	55	41	69	96	98	10	10	25
Flint, Mich.	193	160	141	28	41	48	6	15	18
Gary, Ind.	175	152	117	53	71	81	6	15	17
Grand Rapids, Mich.	198	182	189	11	16	19	6	7	7
Hartford, Conn.	158	136	140	28	34	39	5	8	11
Inglewood, Calif.	90	94	110	14	57	52	6	7	10
Kansas City, Mo.	507	448	435	22	27	30	4	6	7
Los Angeles, Calif.	2800	2900	3500	18	17	14	7	6	8
Memphis, Tenn.	624	646	619	39	48	55	5	9	9
Minneapolis, Minn.	434	371	368	4	8	22	4	4	7
Mt. Vernon, N.Y.	73	67	67	36	49	55	3	5	7
Newark, N.J.	382	329	275	54	58	59	7	13	15
New Haven, Conn.	138	126	130	26	32	36	5	9	9
New Orleans, La.	593	558	497	45	55	62	6	6	13
New York, N.Y.	7900	7000	7300	21	25	29	4	7	9
Oakland, Calif.	362	339	372	35	47	44	8	9	10
Philadelphia, Pa.	1900	1700	1600	34	38	40	5	11	10
Pontiac, Mich.	85	77	71	28	37	42	12	15	14
Portsmouth, Va.	111	105	104	40	45	47	4	8	8
Raleigh, N.C.	123	150	212	23	28	28	3	4	4
Roanoke, Va.	92	100	96	19	22	24	3	6	6
Rochester, N.Y.	295	242	230	17	26	32	4	9	9
Rockford, Ill.	147	135	140	9	13	15	4	7	6
Seattle, Wash.	531	494	516	7	10	10	8	6	5
Spokane, Wash.	171	171	177	1	2	2	7	8	8
St. Louis, Mo.	622	453	397	41	46	51	6	8	11
Trenton, N.J.	105	92	89	38	45	49	5	10	11
Washington, D.C.	757	630	607	71	70	66	4	7	7

Two cities elected African-American mayors in 1997, just outside the period covered in this study:

City	Population (1000s)			African Americans (%)			Unemployment (%)		
Houston, Tex.	1230	1600	1630	19.3	18.1	28.1	3	3.4	8
San Francisco, Calif.	715	679	724	10.6	12	10.9	5.8	5.6	6

Note: Total = 44 cities.

Moreover, Carl Stokes's ability to walk into the inner-city areas of Cleveland and persuade militants not to riot in 1968 captured the attention of white leaders. Cleveland and Gary avoided much of the destruction that engulfed such white-governed cities as Newark and Detroit. Whites were eager to re-establish social stability in the chaotic environment of the 1960s, 1970s, and 1980s, and some white leaders viewed a black mayor as the community's last best hope.[41]

Although black mayors assumed office in many large cities in the Midwest and Northeast that were in crisis, this portrait of black political succession is not the whole picture. Black candidates were also elected to govern some of the more prosperous and successful cities in the nation—Seattle, Denver, Los Angeles, Raleigh, Charlotte, Spokane, Berkeley, Boulder, Santa Monica, and many other communities like them. These urban centers not only pros-pered in the era leading up to black governance but flourished throughout the era in which black mayors served (see table 1.1). Moreover, economic recession did not dominate the campaigns of black candidates in these cit-ies. In such communities black mayoral candidates emphasized programs to promote further economic growth and diversification, so that all residents would have opportunities. This part of the picture reveals that the selection of black mayors involved more than a simple racial appeal to black voters or an act of desperation by white supporters. This trend of black mayors' cap-turing elections in cities with strong economies continued in 1997 with the election of Willie Brown Jr. in San Francisco and Lee Brown in Houston.[42]

Black Versus White: Mayoral Campaigns from 1967 to 1994

In analyzing political developments in cities in the 1960s, the political scien-tists James Mathews and Donald Prothro observed that white hostility to-ward black political participation increased significantly as black residents approached 30 percent of the total population. Nearly twenty years later the political scientists Albert Karnig and Susan Welch incorporated Mathews and Prothro's argument in their analysis of black political involvement and as-serted that black candidates lost as the black population grew in proportion to the white community and won only when black residents reached a ma-jority. The political scientist Georgia Persons added later, "Most black may-ors have been elected in cities with a majority or near-majority black popu-lation."[43]

Table 1.2 shows that the sixty-seven black mayors won office in a broad range of communities—Cleveland, Chicago, New Haven, New Orleans, Phil-adelphia, and New York—where black voters were in the minority but where the black population had grown dramatically relative to the white community. Black candidates also did well in such cities as Atlanta, Gary, New Orleans, Newark, and Detroit, where the black community had attained a population majority but where whites still held a voting majority when the first black mayors were elected in the late 1960s and early 1970s. The table further reveals that thirty-four of the forty-six cities that elected black mayors have been predominantly white, although several were in transition and in the process of becoming much more racially and ethnically diverse.[44]

In most of the early campaigns from 1967 to 1976, race defined the voting results. Victorious African-American candidates captured more than 90 percent of the black vote and 10 percent to 20 percent of the white vote.[45] The racial split between voters was profound, and in many cases lifelong Democrats who were white chose to vote for the white candidate, even a Republican. But it also must be noted that the black candidates would have won few campaigns without support from a segment of white voters.[46] This was true even for Hatcher, who received 96 percent of the black vote but needed 12 percent of the white vote and 55 percent of the Latino vote win office.[47]

The literature of political science and American history has highlighted these voting patterns as evidence of persistent racial division in U.S. society, and race clearly did engulf the voting booth. In placing their emphasis on this racial divide, however, historians and political scientists have failed to note that African Americans were viable candidates in all sorts of cities barely fifteen years after the passage of the Voting Rights Act of 1965 and that they were elected in many sun-belt and midsized cities where blacks constituted a relatively small percentage of the electorate. This development was especially startling, given persistent racial divisions in U.S. society and white opposition to such issues as affirmative action and busing, which the black community strongly supported.[48]

In conducting their campaigns successful black mayoral candidates pursued essentially two strategies in which the racial makeup of voters was crucial. In the older large metropolises of the Northeast, Midwest, and the South, candidates sought to mobilize as much support among black constituents as possible and to increase their voter registration numbers while building coalitions with white supporters, mainly liberals and business people. The population shift to the suburbs between 1965 and 1980 left many of the oldest and largest cities with substantial black populations. Thus black candidates could garner sufficient votes to secure a runoff in the Democratic primary, but typically black voters alone could not determine the outcome of the primary or general election. The rhetoric of campaigns in black neighborhoods was rooted initially in the civil rights movement and in an emerging black consciousness.[49]

In the newer cities of the South and West, black candidates usually encountered much better economic and social conditions. As a consequence, their rhetoric and platforms tended to focus more on inclusive issues to address community-wide needs and to bridge potential racial opposition and less on targeted racial or ethnic appeals. Moreover, as black voters assumed a significant majority of the electorate in some older cities in the late 1980s and began to dictate not only the outcome of the primaries but the general election, issues other than race assumed greater significance.[50]

In plotting his strategy for the 1968 campaign, Carl Stokes began with the view that, first, "a Black Democratic candidate running in a Democratic city against a White Republican opponent could count on the solid support of every Black voter who turned out" and, second, that "seven in ten of the eligible Black voters would come out in this type of municipal contest with only a normal amount of organizational prodding."[51] Coleman Young's strategy in Detroit in 1973 and Harold Washington's in Chicago in 1983 built on Stokes's approach. They both sought to expand the black electorate through registration drives to ensure maximum support from the black community. In Detroit the Young campaign added about fifty-eight thousand black voters to the rolls, whereas in Chicago the number of black voters increased by nearly 20 percent.[52]

Black churches served as the organizational base for Stokes's and Washington's campaigns and virtually all the other campaigns, but mayoral candidates also called on a variety of black organizations, including fraternities, sororities, civil rights groups, newspapers, radio stations, and unions to sponsor meetings with the candidates and to help increase registration and turn out the vote.[53] What made this strategy so crucial in the early period, from 1968 to 1976, was that African Americans lacked connections with white civic organizations and the media that they could draw upon to publicize their candidacies. Moreover, in those communities where urban machines remained a political force, black candidates encountered such resistance that they were forced to turn elsewhere to mobilize supporters, as Washington did in Chicago. Throughout this period, and up to the 1990s, black candidates, such as Tom Bradley in Los Angeles, W. W. Herenton in Memphis, and Kurt Schmoke in Baltimore, found it essential to speak at black churches and public-housing projects to secure and enhance black support.[54]

The political strategies of black mayoral candidates in the nation's oldest cities often paralleled the campaign tactics of Irish-American politicians in the midnineteenth century. Irish candidates turned to the church, the pub, Irish neighborhoods, and the local political machine, and they appealed to Irish-American nationalism to mobilize the Irish community. With few ties to the larger community the Irish, like African-American candidates in the late twentieth century, remained heavily dependent on their own people and institutions for victory. They could count on little support from the larger community. Thus they focused heavily on Irish neighborhoods and on issues of concern to Irish voters to secure political office.[55]

A second key to victory for black candidates in the older cities of the Northeast and Midwest was a transitional period of black-white cooperation that made it possible for black candidates to capture at least 10 percent of the white vote. The election of a black mayor generally occurred after an election or series of elections in which a black-white coalition helped elect a white candidate and in which a white mayor eased the transition to black mayoral leadership by appointing a number of African Americans to leadership positions in city government. In Memphis, for example, Dick Hackett prepared the way for Herenton by appointing six African Americans as directors on his staff and by naming African Americans to 41 percent of the managerial positions in the city. William Donald Schaefer did much the same in Baltimore; the first majority-black school board was named during his first term as mayor.[56] The prominence of blacks in local leadership positions, and the cooperation between white and black managers, eased some white concerns about the ability of blacks to govern and about a black takeover. Such cooperation proved essential before white voters, white professionals, and white business leaders would consider supporting a black candidate.

In seeking white votes, whether in older mayor-council communities or in the newer mayor-commissioner cities, black candidates throughout this era looked principally to middle- and upper-class whites, and liberal elements within these two groups, for white votes. The political scientist Leonard Cole found that liberal whites have often comprised the margin of victory in the North.[57] Similarly, Thomas Pettegrew observed that white supporters of black candidates in Cleveland, Gary, Los Angeles, and Newark were disproportionately in the upper-income brackets and college educated.[58] Moreover, a study of the New York mayoral election of 1989 found a large proportion of the white New York City electorate that described itself as liberal shared many policy preferences with black and Latino New Yorkers.[59] Black voters and white liberals agreed on a number of issues but most especially on economic growth and crime control.[60] As part of his election strategy, Carl Stokes spoke to any white group that would receive him, from meetings in homes to public and private halls, to secure the requisite votes. His invitations came almost exclusively, however, from middle- and upper-class whites.[61] In 1990 Charles Box in Rockford, Illinois, tried to transcend the racial divisions in the community by having "Chats with Charles" in whites' homes on the east

side of town and in the homes of blacks and Latinos on the west and southwest sides. Box commented, "The key for us was to take the fear of the unknown out of the equation. I wanted to give people a reason to vote for me,
not against someone else."[62] In his 1990 campaign in Denver mayoral candidate Wellington Webb walked throughout the city, staying in black and white
homes to draw attention to the biracial nature of his campaign and trying
to persuade whites that they had no reason to fear his candidacy.[63] Despite
some claims that these black candidates were able to construct a biracial
coalition across class lines, the coalition that resulted in each case was almost
exclusively one of black candidates, white elites, and liberal members of the
white middle class.

In several cities small groups of whites began to recognize relatively early
that a black voting majority was not far off and that a political transition to
black leadership with white cooperation would be beneficial to them and to
community relations. Support came frequently from business people who
endorsed black candidates for pragmatic reasons. One Atlanta banker said
of Maynard Jackson, "I'd always been persuaded that Maynard was going to
be elected. So I thought somebody in the business community better get
behind this guy so that we'd have a line of communication." Thus he and
others concluded that black leadership was inevitable and that they could
continue to influence city government and secure their business interests by
being in on the ground floor of this political change. In Atlanta the business
community also had aspirations for the city to be the economic capital of
the South, and the business class did not want to jeopardize those ambitions
by maintaining a death grip on the past. The historians Steven Lawson and
Ronald Bayor have both noted that black candidates often embraced such
white support with an understanding that they would have to redefine their
political goals to enhance their chances of election.[64]

Another factor attracting white support in these cities concerned the number of blacks holding office and the frequency with which they did so. The
more often blacks served in prominent political positions and as mayor, the
more acceptable they were to white and other minority groups. This trend
was especially evident in reelection campaigns and in elections in the 1980s
and 1990s as black candidates became more commonplace and as black mayors demonstrated they could govern these complex cities no less fairly and
wisely than whites.[65] The fears of whites diminished gradually, and the focus
of campaigning began to shift away from race and toward the black candidate's record and political agenda for the city.[66]

Not surprisingly, black candidates had to walk a political tightrope in their
simultaneous appeal to black and white voters. In New York David Dinkins

conducted a campaign at two levels. One was citywide and directed to liberal whites and Latinos; the other was localized in the black community. His message differed, and he and his aides were careful to prevent his message to black residents from becoming publicized citywide and perhaps alienating supporters in the liberal white and Latino communities.[67]

As the ethnic and racial mix changed in large metropolises, a number of black candidates began reaching out to other minority groups. Jesse Jackson's success in bringing Latino and black voters together on various policy issues during his presidential campaign in 1984 was instructive to black mayoral candidates.[68] Before Jackson formed his Rainbow Coalition, Tom Bradley had demonstrated that black candidates could win support in the Latino community in his 1982 campaign in Los Angeles. During a television debate that year he highlighted a letter from an Latino boy who sent Bradley $4 that he had earned mowing yards because he hoped to be governor one day and saw Bradley as his role model. Despite the simplicity of this approach, it was not insignificant to an ethnic group whose voters had been largely ignored by previous candidates and mayors. Harold Washington and his advisers, among them Jesse Jackson, sought Latino support in Chicago through neighborhood and community action groups and through economic development initiatives. Washington's endorsement of bilingual education and opposition to the Simpson-Mazoli bill, which would have tightened legal immigration, garnered him significant support in the Latino community.[69] In his 1989 campaign John Daniels of New Haven, Connecticut, quite consciously mimicked Jackson's attempt to build a coalition of minority groups. The multiracial politics of the Daniels campaign was also evident in the Dinkins campaign in New York City and the Washington campaign in Chicago. Such a strategy developed in response to the increasing number and diversity of minorities in these cities, especially in communities where blacks constituted a minority of the voters. It also did not alienate liberal white voters, many of whom embraced the politics of diversity.[70]

In the newer mayor-commissioner cities in the sun belt and in the West, in particular, black candidates also began by securing their support in the black community and then reached out to certain key constituencies in the white community. Those constituencies most frequently included civic and business groups and liberal organizations in the city. Personality, issues, and political competency typically dominated these campaigns in cities such as Dallas, Raleigh, Charlotte, Denver, Seattle, and Los Angeles. Because black candidates for mayor were initially quite novel, they commanded a great deal of attention. The free publicity cut two ways. It gave these candidates free advertising and thus an early boost, but it also generated fear and hostility

among some whites. The skill with which these candidates used this to political advantage and the receptivity of whites to a black candidate ultimately determined the electoral outcome. Successful black candidates generally
sought to debate their white opponents in order to persuade white voters of
their moderation and ability to govern the city. They also followed Webb's
example in Denver, visiting whites at home and at work to ease racial concerns. Moreover, the absence of both rigid segregation patterns and an urban political machine to mobilize whites against a black candidate, together
with a prosperous economy, enhanced the prospects of African-American
candidates. White support for successful black candidates in these newer sun-
belt cities and midsized cities was often substantial, beginning at 30 percent
and rising to 40 percent in the successful campaigns.[71]

Race and Political Campaigning from 1967 to 1994

Paradoxically, despite sharp racial divisions in voting, race seldom became
an overt issue in campaigns from 1967 to 1994, even though it was often part
of the strategy used by both white and black candidates. Public condemna-
tion of the rhetoric of extremists like Orval Faubus of Arkansas and George
Wallace of Alabama combined with the passage of the civil rights laws of the
1960s to discourage blatant racist appeals, especially in big-city campaigns.
The absence of such appeals did not mean, however, that race was absent from
these campaigns. The percentage of white and black voters casting ballots for
someone of their own race, especially in the older cities, makes clear that race
was an important factor. A. L. "Sonny" DeMaiorbus, chairman of the Cuyahoga County (Cleveland) Republican Party, commented bluntly in 1967:
"Whether we like it or not, . . . the inclination of Negroes is to vote for a
Negro, and it's going to be vice-versa in white areas. There's no use kidding
ourselves. We don't want to inject race, but it's there."[72]

Black mayoral candidates were such a novelty in the first part of this era,
from 1967 to 1976, that most white voters were quite conscious of their presence on the ballot without their white opponents' making an issue of it. White
candidates often appealed to white anxieties, or what the political scientist
Asher Avian refers to as "race-based anxiety," to make sure white voters were
aware of the implications of black governance. Many whites feared a black
takeover and were uneasy about black candidates in this first period. Mayoral candidate Sam Massell, for example, warned Atlanta voters in 1973 that
Maynard Jackson was unqualified to lead a dynamic city like Atlanta and used
the slogan "Atlanta's Too Young to Die" to discourage white support for Jackson.[73] Massell's slogan was more pointed than that used by most white can-

didates, but it was not uncommon for whites to attack black opponents as inexperienced and unfit to govern or to label them as political hacks. Significantly, the educational backgrounds of these early black candidates helped serve as a counterbalance to derisive comments about their qualifications. White candidates also played on white fears of a racially polarized city by promising that they "would represent all residents," suggesting that their black opponents would represent only the interests of black residents.[74]

While white candidates generally avoided overt racist appeals, their aides did not, especially when talking to neighborhood groups. Such was the case in Philadelphia in 1983. Although the campaign appeared almost totally free of racism on the surface, Wilson Goode complained that Frank Rizzo and his aides were "running an 'underground campaign' that included racist slanders."[75] In Chicago, Ed Vrdolyak, council member and party leader, called on whites in neighborhood meetings to vote for Jane Byrne against Harold Washington in 1983, noting, "It's a racial thing. Don't kid yourself. I'm calling on you to save your city, to save your precinct. We're fighting to keep the city the way it is."[76]

As black governance became more commonplace, white candidates turned increasingly to certain key issues to undermine the candidacy of their black opponents. Avian calls them "race-correlated agenda items," and they included crime, drugs, homelessness, and urban violence. Most black candidates throughout the country found it necessary to defend themselves on these issues as their opponents questioned their ability to address them satisfactorily.[77] The implication was that these issues were endemic to the black community and that a black mayor was not equipped to resolve them.

While white candidates manipulated race to their political advantage, black candidates were not immune to using their own racial strategies. Linda Williams, associate director of research at the Joint Center for Political Studies in Washington, D.C., argued that the post-1980 group of "black mayors . . . consciously shaped their images so as not to be threatening to middle-class blacks or to white America."[78] There is every indication, however, that all successful black candidates from 1968 on sought to deracialize their campaigns and their political images to some degree, especially when communicating with white audiences or when campaigning in predominantly white cities. Carl Stokes's case was typical. At one point he reassured a white Cleveland audience that his victory "would not mean a Negro takeover. It would not mean the establishment of a Negro cabinet." Nearly every black mayoral candidate has repeated the comments of Stokes in one form or another to ease white anxieties.[79] Black voters seemed to understand the compromises black candidates had to make and were will-

ing to accept such statements so long as candidates did not turn their backs
on the black community.

Throughout this era black candidates also used race to build solidarity
among black voters, much like the Irish used an ethnic appeal more than a
century earlier. In 1983, for example, Harold Washington campaigned heavily
in churches, "a practice that he had used extensively while in Congress." The
political scientist William Grimshaw wrote that Washington's supporters
blocked his white opponents from gaining entry to black churches, contend-
ing that such access would constitute "a desecration." The end result was that
only Washington was able to move freely among all potential black voters.
This development had particular significance for the mayoral campaign,
because, as Grimshaw observed, the churches became ward organizations for
the elections—"voter registration drives were held along with get-out-the-
voter rallies, and on Sunday the ministers whipped their congregations into
line like old-time ward bosses."[80]

Many of the rust-belt campaigns in the economically bleak 1970s and 1980s
also included a call for black renewal and a heightened black consciousness.
Harold Washington's campaigns in 1983 and 1987, for example, "were steeped
in religious symbolism," and they more often resembled civil rights gather-
ings and "Baptist revival" meetings than political events, the historian Paul
Kleppner has observed.[81] The first stages of the David Dinkins campaign in
New York in 1989 also resembled a crusade, with such activists as Jesse Jackson, Louis Farrakhan, and Al Sharpton each bringing his own supporters and
racial agenda to Dinkins's election effort. Marches and rallies on behalf of
Dinkins reminded onlookers of civil rights rallies and were often rich in
African-American symbolism, as Dinkins and his advisers looked for creative
ways to keep the black community mobilized throughout a very difficult
primary and general election.[82]

In examining the 1989 mayoral campaign in New York, the writer Scott
McConnell contended that the race card became a key part of the political
strategy of Dinkins and his supporters to mobilize black voters. During the
Dinkins-Koch campaign, McConnell noted, Dinkins used the alleged rape
of Tawana Brawley by whites to highlight "racial brutality" in New York and
the need for new, more progressive leadership. McConnell argued that because this line of attack proved to be an asset in mobilizing black interest in
his campaign, Dinkins continued to pursue it for weeks after it became clear
that Brawley and her advisers were not reliable.[83] After Yusef Hawkins, a black
teenager, was murdered as he walked through the predominantly Italian section of Bensonhurst, Jesse Jackson noted not so subtly at the funeral that "that
boy . . . could make David Dinkins the next mayor."[84] Although Jackson was

heavily criticized for his statement, his comment came nearer to the truth than most were ready to acknowledge.

By the 1990s some black candidates in tight races attempted to use race overtly to mobilize black voters against their opponents. In Cleveland, George Forbes, who had almost no support among whites in the city, sought to use race to undermine the campaign of his black opponent, Michael White, who had considerable support in the white community, by referring to him derisively as "White Mike" and a slumlord. Elihu Harris, the African-American mayor who faced a stiff challenge from a Chinese-American opponent in his 1994 reelection campaign in Oakland, California, told an audience of black voters, "When I see black folks tell me they're going to vote for a Chinese man, it makes me angry." Blacks must vote for their own people, he insisted.[85]

Although appeals to racial solidarity served as a key component in the campaigns of black candidates, they were not sufficient by themselves to maintain black support. Black voters did not automatically cast their ballots for a black candidate, nor did middle-class blacks and lower-class black voters always vote the same. A failed mayor, for example, could not overcome such political problems by simply calling for black solidarity. Neglecting the community once elected or failing to solve economic problems proved politically devastating. By 1993, for example, Carrie Perry of Hartford, Connecticut, had so alienated many black and white voters with her failed economic policies that even the assistance of Jesse Jackson and Sen. Carol Moseley Braun of Illinois proved insufficient to persuade the black middle class to support her reelection. In 1987 the community of Norfolk, Virginia, voted to recall Mayor James Holley, with black voters strongly supporting the initiative. Holley's economic development program had largely ignored the concerns of black residents for low-income housing, neighborhood improvements, and participation in downtown redevelopment. Moreover, long-serving mayors Richard Hatcher and Kenneth Gibson went down to defeat at the hands of black opponents within a year of one another because of these mayors' inability to offset the corrosive effects of persistent economic and social problems in their cities. And in 1996 the predominantly black community of Gary selected a white man, Scott King, to govern the city because of concerns about the community's economic future.[86]

In many campaigns in the older big cities of the Northeast and Midwest, race played a crucial factor in the strategies of candidates and in influencing the outcome of the campaigns. Well into the 1980s and even into the 1990s, black candidates in these cities faced a huge hurdle in trying to attract white voters. Race was also a factor in campaigns in the newer cities of the South and West, but it was much less a barrier to the campaign efforts of black mayors, especially in more recent years. In these newer sun-belt and midsized cities successful black candidates had to offer an agenda that resonated with voters and to engage in racial bridge building to dispel initial white fears.[87] But personality and issues, rather than race, more often decided these campaigns.

Conclusion

As this essay reveals, race has never been a constant in the political campaigns of these mayors. They and their white opponents shifted the language of race, their campaign platforms, and appeals to voters according to the composition of the community, the strength and the race of their opponents, the issues that mobilized constituents, and the time period in which they were campaigning. The race card remained a viable political weapon, especially in large cities, although it has diminished over time and was used in a much more subtle fashion by white and black candidates in the 1980s and 1990s. As the political scientist Zoltan Hajnal has argued, "The impact of race is highly variable across time and context" and race "need not be a permanent, central fixture in American politics."[88] The political scientist John Mollenkopf also asserted in the 1990s that "urban politics is no longer a simple matter of black and white, where black political leaders can consolidate minority empowerment primarily on appeals to black solidarity," or through appeals to all "people of color" alone. In the future "the course of urban politics will depend on who can construct broader and more complex coalitions."[89]

Had black and white voters grown weary of the racial overtones in urban campaigns by the mid-1990s, and did they seek out candidates who offered concrete solutions to local problems, as David Bositis, a senior political analyst with the Joint Center for Political and Economic Studies, and others have contended?[90] Several campaigns of the 1990s suggest that voters were tired of the same old rhetoric by the same old candidates, but nothing, of course, was new about that.

To dismiss race as an issue, however, would be naive at best. The election patterns in the larger cities of the Northeast and Midwest, for example, continue to point to race as a persistent problem in these regions. The defeat of black mayors seeking reelection in New York and Philadelphia in 1991 suggests that race is alive and well in the voting booth.[91] Moreover, the absence of new black mayoral candidates, which may be the more telling development in these older, predominantly white cities, seems to underscore the persistence of race.

At the same time, election results in the sun belt and midsized cities from

Raleigh to Charlotte, Dallas, Denver, Spokane, Seattle, and, more recently, San Francisco and Houston, offer a different picture. Race too has been a factor in the elections in these cities, but the sizable white vote for these black mayors shows that it is not insurmountable. Clearly, the absence of deeply entrenched political machines, combined with economies that were generally thriving and a more fluid racial environment, was conducive to a more progressive response to racial change and to the candidacies of African-American mayors. In these cities race appears to have been replaced by what the journalist Jim Sleeper has called "a can-do pragmatism and a common civic identity that is more than the sum of skin tones, genders, sexual orientations, and resentments."[92]

The process of racial advancement in urban politics thus remains a mixed one. The electoral process in cities with African-American mayors points to some positive developments, but it also denotes the persistence of race and the nation's continuing struggle with its great dilemma. Not all is as it was when Stokes and Hatcher were elected in 1967, however. As Eisinger has stated, most whites have come to recognize that black representation is a legitimate "product of the democratic processes."[93] Moreover, these mayors have breathed new life into communities in economic and social turmoil, offering hope and opportunity to groups of residents who had not been privy to such possibilities under previous local governments. And they did this, for the most part, with remarkably traditional campaign platforms and a pattern of political alliances that crossed racial boundaries at several levels. As well-educated men and women, most of whom had gained middle-class status through education, hard work, and employment, their political activities unfolded within a well-established framework that emphasized educational and economic opportunity and interracial public-private partnerships.[94] At the same time, their campaigns also offered inclusion and political opportunity to people who had been previously ignored, and their leadership gave these cities a political future, even under extraordinarily difficult social and economic circumstances. Thus, despite the considerable problems that remain, the political scientist Richard Bernard is certainly correct when he writes, "The greatest change in twentieth-century urban politics in the Snowbelt as well as the Sunbelt has been the coming to power of blacks."[95]

Notes

1. Black voter registration increased from 1,472,000 in April 1962 to 3,112,000 in the spring of 1968 as a result of the civil rights movement and the Voting Rights Act of 1965. See James C. Harvey, *Black Civil Rights During the Johnson Administration* (Jackson: University Press of Mississippi, 1973), 27, 168; Steven Lawson, "From Boycotts to Ballots: The

Reshaping of National Politics," in Armstead L. Robinson and Patricia Sullivan, eds., *New Directions in Civil Rights Studies* (Charlottesville: University Press of Virginia, 1991), 188.

2. Bayard Rustin, "From Protest to Politics: The Future of the Civil Rights Movement," *Commentary,* 39 (February 1965): 25–31.

3. Martin Kilson, "Political Change in the Negro Ghetto, 1900–1940s," in Nathan I. Huggins, Martin Kilson, and Daniel Fox, eds., *Key Issues in the Afro-American Experience,* vol. 2 (New York: Harcourt Brace Jovanovich, 1971). Also see James Q. Wilson, who made a similar argument about machine politics and black voters eleven years earlier in *Negro Politics: The Search for Leadership* (New York: Free Press, 1960), 21–47.

4. Some scholars have questioned the connection between the civil rights movement and black politics, arguing that only candidates in the South had ties to the movement. In commenting on the significance of the link with the civil rights movement, however, the historian Steven Lawson has observed, "Voter registration campaigns connected electoral and protest politics" (Lawson, *Running for Freedom: Civil Rights and Black Politics in America Since 1941* [Philadelphia: Temple University Press, 1991], 146–47). The early registration and campaign efforts often seemed indistinguishable from the religious and emotional intensity of the movement, whether in the South or the North. Black candidates sought to tie their campaigns to the major civil rights campaigns of the early 1960s for a practical reason: it helped mobilize black voters, who provided the cornerstone of their support. The connection between black nationalism and the civil rights movement in the emergence of black politics is potentially an extremely interesting and complex one. It merits further study by historians who are examining issues of race and politics in urban America. The political scientist William Keech, writing in 1968, contended that the ballot was a limited political resource for the black community. But Keech was writing at a time when black politics was in its infancy. See William Keech, *The Impact of Negro Voting: The Role of the Vote in the Quest for Equality* (Chicago: Rand McNally, 1968).

5. These scholars assumed it would be quite some time before blacks assumed political leadership at any level. See, for example, Benjamin Muse's *Ten Years of Prelude* (New York: Viking, 1964). Peter Eisinger was one of the few early writers to identify the significance of this transition. See Peter K. Eisinger, "Black Mayors and the Politics of Racial Economic Advancement," in Harlan Hahn and Charles H. Levine, eds., *Readings in Urban Politics: Past, Present, and Future* (New York: Longman, 1980), 249.

6. Jeffrey K. Hadden, Louis H. Masotti, and Victor Thiessen, "The Making of the Negro Mayors," *Trans-Action* 5 (January–February 1968): 30.

7. David Chalmers, *And Crooked Places Made Straight: The Struggle for Social Change in the 1960s* (Baltimore, Md.: Johns Hopkins University Press, 1991); William Chafe, *The Unfinished Journey* (New York: Oxford University Press, 1986). David Farber, *The Age of Great Dreams: America in the 1960s* (New York: Hill and Wang, 1994), is equally remiss. By contrast, the editors Rufus Browning, Dale Rogers Marshall, and David Tabb conclude in *Racial Politics in American Cities,* 2d ed. (New York: Longman, 1997), "There is no denying the enormous gain from the virtual exclusion of blacks in 1950 to their achievement of governmental position and leadership in 1968" (287).

8. Frank McCoy, "Black Power in City Hall," *Black Enterprise,* August 1990, pp. 148–52.

9. *Black Elected Officials: A National Roster and Profiles of Black Mayors in America* (Washington, D.C.: Joint Center for Political Studies and Johnson Publishing, 1991). Ver-

non Jordan observed later that black political success "is the ultimate realization of what the march from Selma to Montgomery was all about" (W. John Moore, "From Dreamers to Doers," *National Journal,* February 13, 1988, p. 373).

10. I chose the years 1967 to 1976 to represent one cohort, based on the early literature that identified this as a distinct period of black governance. As readers will note, I do not find this argument persuasive, but it is a useful construct at times in making comparisons of these mayors to those who followed them, to the general population, and to their white opponents.

11. Also see Zoltan Hajnal, "Solving the Puzzle of Black Incumbent Success: White Learning Under Black Mayors" (Ph.D. diss., University of Chicago, 1997), available at *<http://polisci.spc.uchicago.edu/research/american/zoli.htm>* (August 23, 2000). Hajnal argues, "When white voters recognize how little actually changes, they learn that they have little to fear from black political leadership."

12. A number of African Americans also served as mayors in cities where the mayor was chosen by the other members of the city commission, but this study considers only mayors elected in citywide races. The most recent big cities to elect an African-American mayor are Houston, which elected Lee P. Brown, and San Francisco, which elected Willie Brown, in November 1997. Profiles of the sixty-seven candidates were taken from many different sources, including local and national newspapers. Also see *Black Elected Officials.* In addition, see Thomas E. Cavanagh and Denise Stockton, *Black Elected Officials and Their Constituencies* (Washington, D.C.: Joint Center for Political Studies, 1981); and James E. Conyers and Walter L. Wallace, *Black Elected Officials* (New York: Russell Sage Foundation, 1976). By the end of 1990, 185 municipalities had black mayors; 153 of these jurisdictions had fewer than twenty thousand residents. The 185 mayors represented an increase from 43 in 1973. In 1993 black mayors governed 38 cities with populations greater than fifty thousand, and 8,015 black elected officials held office throughout the nation (Roger Witherspoon, "Black Mayors on the Fiscal Tightrope," *Black Enterprise,* January 1991, pp. 31–32; *Black Elected Officials, 1993,* 24). Also see Alex Poinsett, "The Changing Color of U.S. Politics," *Ebony,* August 1991, pp. 30, 32–35.

13. Quoted in Roger Biles, "Black Mayors: A Historical Assessment," *Journal of Negro History* 77, no. 4 (Summer 1992): 114; also see Lawson, *Running for Freedom,* 149. See as well Bette Woody, *Managing Crisis Cities: The New Black Leadership and the Politics of Resource Allocation* (Westport, Conn.: Greenwood, 1982), 83; Woody credits the Great Society programs with providing blacks with managerial experience in private and public institutions that became key to their success in city halls around the country.

14. David R. Colburn and George E. Pozzetta, "Race, Ethnicity, and the Evolution of Political Legitimacy," in David Farber ed., *The Sixties: From Memory to History* (Chapel Hill: University of North Carolina Press, 1994), 121.

15. Doug Gills, "Chicago Politics and Community Development: A Social Movement Perspective," in Pierre Clavel and Wim Wiewel, eds., *Harold Washington and the Neighborhoods: Progressive City Government in Chicago, 1983–1987* (New Brunswick, N.J.: Rutgers University Press, 1991), 37.

16. Kilson, "Political Change in the Negro Ghetto," 167–92. Also see Lawson, *Running for Freedom,* 171.

17. Paul Kleppner, *Chicago Divided: The Making of a Black Mayor* (DeKalb: Northern

Illinois University Press, 1985), 253. Kleppner notes that blacks in the North, in particular, felt great impatience with the slow pace of civil rights reform. Wilbur C. Rich, in *Coleman Young and Detroit Politics: From Social Activist to Power Broker* (Detroit: Wayne State University Press, 1989), notes that many Detroiters had relatives in the South and responded to their call for black mobilization nationally (77). Also see Allen J. Matusow, *The Unraveling of America: A History of Liberalism in the 1960s* (New York: Harper and Row, 1984), 359, and Richard M. Bernard, ed., *Snowbelt Cities: Metropolitan Politics in the Northeast and Midwest Since World War II*, 2d ed. (Bloomington: Indiana University Press, 1990), 15–16. Bernard observes that only in the campaign for voting rights did northern blacks "find civil rights tactics that were directly applicable" to their own situation (16).

18. See Browning, Marshall, and Tabb, *Racial Politics in American Cities*, 9.

19. Jon C. Teaford, "King Richard Hatcher: Mayor of Gary," *Journal of Negro History* 77, no. 3 (Spring 1992): 126–40. Also see Hadden, Masotti, and Thiessen, "Making of the Negro Mayors," 21–30; Wilbur C. Rich, *Black Mayors and School Politics: The Failure of Reform in Detroit, Gary, and Newark* (New York: Garland, 1996), 65; and Charles H. Levine, *Racial Conflict and the American Mayor* (Lexington, Mass.: Lexington Books, 1974). Hatcher's organization was named Muigwithania after Jomo Kenyatta's organization and newspaper in Kenya. Much like Kenyatta's campaign in Kenya, the Muigwithania movement in Gary sought to facilitate the election of black candidates.

20. Hadden, Masotti, and Thiessen, "Making of the Negro Mayors," 21–30; Thomas Campbell, "The Struggle for Stability," in Bernard, *Snowbelt Cities*, 118–23.

21. Lester Salamon, "Leadership and Modernization: The Emerging Black Political Elite in the American South," *Journal of Politics* 35 (1973): 624.

22. Among many other scholars, the historians William Julius Wilson, Stephan Thernstrom, and Abigail Thernstrom note the rise of the substantial black middle class during this era. The Thernstroms identify eighty-seven African-American mayors during this period, a figure they calculate "from a list of all blacks elected mayor of cities with populations of 50,000 or more, compiled from the Joint Center for Political and Economic Studies' invaluable series of volumes, 'Black Elected Officials: A National Roster,' and supplemented with cases gleaned from newspapers and other periodicals" (287). I have been able to identify only sixty-seven elected mayors in cities with a population greater than fifty thousand. Because we used the same sources, I suspect the difference results from their having counted mayors elected as city council or city commission members and chosen by the other members to serve as mayor. I counted only black mayors who were elected by voters to the position of mayor. A second possibility is that a number of cities had nearly fifty thousand residents when a black mayor was elected. Those that had fewer than fifty thousand residents and declined in population in the late twentieth century did not make my list. Those that had slightly fewer than fifty thousand residents at the time of the election of an African-American mayor and grew to more than fifty thousand shortly thereafter do appear on my list. Perhaps these two factors account for the differences between our lists. See Wilson, *The Truly Disadvantaged: The Inner City, the Underclass, and Public Policy* (Chicago: University of Chicago Press, 1987), esp. pp. 55–57, and Stephan Thernstrom and Abigail Thernstrom, *America in Black and White: One Nation Indivisible* (New York: Simon and Schuster, 1997), 183–202.

23. Leonard A. Cole, *Blacks in Power: A Comparative Study of Black and White Elected Officials* (Princeton, N.J.: Princeton University Press, 1976), esp. pp. 37–55.

24. Ibid., 5.

25. Some notable exceptions among northern blacks were W. W. Herenton, who attended LeMoyne College but received his doctoral degree at Southern Illinois University.

26. The number of black women elected to political office was significantly larger than the number elected as mayors of large cities. From 1976 to 1986 black women comprised 27 percent of the 5,384 elected black officials. See Sheila F. Harmon-Martin, "Black Women in Politics: A Research Note," in Hanes Walton Jr., ed., *Black Politics and Black Political Behavior* (Westport, Conn.: Praeger, 1994), 210. Also see "Carrie Saxon Perry: More Than a Pretty Hat," *Ebony,* April 1988, pp. 45, 62, 64.

27. See, for example, Lawson, *Running for Freedom,* 71. The NAACP was also led by men, and few women chaired state chapters from 1954 to 1970.

28. Black women were more reluctant to condemn male chauvinism in their community, because most felt that racism was a greater concern and that it accounted for the sharply defined roles for men and women in the black community. Albert Karnig and Susan Welch, *Black Representation and Urban Policy* (Chicago: University of Chicago Press, 1980), also noted this pattern among black elected officials before 1980.

29. The political scientists Elsie Barnes and Ronald Proctor found that most Republicans did not receive more than 6 or 7 percent of the black vote in Virginia. See Barnes and Proctor, "Black Politics in Tidewater, Virginia," in Walton, ed., *Black Politics,* 87. Kilson roots the black political commitment to the Democratic Party in the 1920s and 1930s when local political machines reached out to black leaders and provided them with greater political opportunities than the Republicans did. This development, in concert with federal relief programs provided by the New Deal in the 1930s, was crucial to the shift of black voters to the Democratic Party (Kilson, "Political Change in the Negro Ghetto," 191). Some black Republicans were elected as mayor. James Usry in Atlantic City, for example, took office as a Republican, but I do not include him in this study because the city had fewer than fifty thousand residents at the time of his election and the city's population has continued to decline since. Others were elected by members of the city council or city commission and, again, are not part of this study.

30. By the mid-1990s education began to replace crime as the second agenda item for black mayors.

31. Witherspoon, "Black Mayors on the Fiscal Tightrope," 32. For a fuller assessment of the effects of the structural transformation and the out-migration of the black middle class, see Wilson, *The Truly Disadvantaged,* 55–57, and Douglas S. Massey and Nancy A. Denton, *American Apartheid: Segregation and the Making of the Underclass* (Cambridge, Mass.: Harvard University Press, 1993).

32. Lester Salamon takes a different point of view, arguing that "blacks with traditional backgrounds . . . evidence a change-oriented set of values that distinguishes them" from white mayors ("Leadership and Modernization," 624). The evidence suggests, however, that the social and economic decline of these cities required black mayors to respond differently than their white counterparts, who governed in healthier times.

33. Wilbur C. Rich, "The Politics of Casino Gambling, Detroit Style," *Urban Affairs*

Quarterly 26 (December 1990): 275. Also see Rich, *Coleman Young and Detroit Politics*. Other cities of the Midwest, like Cleveland, suffered almost as much. Cleveland saw more than 370,000 people depart between 1960 and 1990, leaving the community with a population just over 500,000 residents. See Saundra C. Ardey and William E. Nelson, "The Maturation of Black Political Power: The Case of Cleveland," *PS: Political Sciences and Politics* (June 1990): 149.

34. Jon C. Teaford, *The Road to Renaissance* (Baltimore, Md.: Johns Hopkins University Press, 1990), 208–13, 262–63.

35. Arnold R. Hirsch, "Race and Politics in Modern New Orleans: The Mayoralty of Dutch Morial," *Amerikastudien/American Studies* 35, no. 4 (December 1991): 470.

36. Eisinger, "Black Mayors and the Politics of Racial Economic Advancement," 257.

37. Rich, *Coleman Young and Detroit Politics*, 100–120; Wilson, *The Truly Disadvantaged*, and Wilson, *The Declining Significance of Race: Blacks and Changing American Institutions* (Chicago: University of Chicago Press, 1978), 139–41.

38. See Wilson, *Declining Significance of Race*, 139. Also see Peter H. Rossi and Richard A. Berk, "Generalized Performance Measures for Urban Political Systems," paper prepared for the 69th Annual Meeting of the American Political Science Association, New Orleans, September 4–8, 1973, p. 31, cited in Levine, *Racial Conflict and the American Mayor*, 119.

39. By comparison, Detroit's population living at or below the poverty level reached 32.5 percent, up from 14.6 percent two decades earlier (Cole, *Blacks in Power*, 161). Also see Asher Arian, Arthur S. Goldberg, John H. Mollenkopf, and Edward T. Rogowsky, *Changing New York City Politics* (New York: Routledge, 1991), 4.

40. Levine, *Racial Conflict and the American Mayor*, 77.

41. Ibid., 60.

42. In other communities economic conditions were not even the dominant factor. In Norfolk, for example, the issue of quality education for black students was the prominent issue among black voters for much of the 1970s and 1980s (Barnes and Proctor, "Black Politics in Tidewater, Virginia," 89).

43. See Donald R. Mathews and James W. Prothro, "Social and Economic Factors and Negro Voter Registration in the South," *American Political Science Review* 57 (1963): 29; Karnig and Welch, *Black Representation and Urban Policy*, 64; Georgia Persons, "Racial Politics and Black Power in the Cities," in George C. Galster and Edward W. Hill, eds., *The Metropolis in Black and White: Race, Power, and Polarization* (New Brunswick, N.J.: Center for Urban Policy Research, 1992), 174.

44. Hadden, Masotti, and Thiessen, "Making of the Negro Mayors," 462, 468–69. Blacks constituted a 54 percent majority of the population in Newark but were a minority of voters in 1969. Gibson got 56 percent of the vote. In Cleveland, Stokes won an estimated 16,000 white votes in the Democratic primary and 30,000 in the general election. Hatcher received only about 5,000 white votes in Gary in his first election but could not have won without them. Michael Preston has pointed out that the election of black mayors in cities where blacks are a distinct minority dispels the argument that black candidates can win only where blacks are a majority. See Preston, "Limitations of Black Urban Power: The Case of Black Mayors," in Louis H. Masotti and Robert L. Lineberry, eds., *The New Urban Politics* (Cambridge, Mass.: Ballinger, 1976), 112.

45. Bruce Ransom, "Black Independent Electoral Politics in Philadelphia: The Election

of Mayor W. Wilson Goode," in Michael Preston, Lenneal J. Henderson Jr., Paul L. Puryear, eds., *The New Black Politics: The Search for Political Power* (New York: Longman, 1987), 257. Ransom contends that until 1987 black candidates needed at least 20 percent of the white vote to win the mayoralty in cities where the black community constituted less than 50 percent of the population.

46. Marcus D. Pohlmann and Michael P. Kirby, *Racial Politics at the Crossroads: Memphis Elects Dr. W. W. Herenton* (Knoxville: University of Tennessee Press, 1996), xix.

47. Levine, *Racial Conflict and the American Mayor*, 72.

48. Harry S. Ashmore, *Civil Rights and Wrongs: A Memoir of Race and Politics, 1944–1996* (Columbia: University of South Carolina Press, 1997), 242–43, 309–11. Also see Thomas Byrne Edsall with Mary D. Edsall, *Chain Reaction: The Impact of Race, Rights, and Taxes on American Politics* (New York: Norton, 1992), 123–28.

49. See Bernard, *Snowbelt Cities,* esp. p. 15 in the introduction, and the subsequent chapters on cities of the Northeast and Midwest. Also see Arian et al., *Changing New York City Politics,* 198.

50. John Mollenkopf, "New York: The Great Anomaly," in Browning, Marshall, and Tabb, *Racial Politics in American Cities,* 110–11, and *Memphis Commercial Appeal,* September 24, 1995, p. 1.

51. Penn Kimball, *The Disconnected* (New York: Columbia University Press, 1972), 153–54; also see Levine, *Racial Conflict and the American Mayor,* 56–57.

52. Rich, *Coleman Young and Detroit Politics,* 105; Clavel and Wiewel, *Harold Washington and the Neighborhoods,* 27.

53. Washington's forces mobilized local black activist organizations, including Jesse Jackson's Operation PUSH, the Urban League, and the Chicago Black United Communities. See Gills, "Chicago Politics and Community Development," 42, 43. Also see Chuck Stone, *Black Political Power in America* (Indianapolis, Ind.: Bobbs-Merrill, 1968), 223–24, and Edward C. Banfield and James Q. Wilson, *City Politics* (Cambridge, Mass.: Harvard University Press, 1963), 158.

54. Pohlmann and Kirby, *Racial Politics at the Crossroads,* 155; *Houston Chronicle,* January 2, 1998, p. 1.

55. Kerby A. Miller, *Emigrants and Exiles: Ireland and the Irish Exodus to North America* (New York: Oxford University Press, 1985), esp. pp. 320–44; also see Peter Eisinger, *The Politics of Displacement: Racial and Ethnic Transition in Three American Cities* (New York: Academic Press, 1980). Eisinger compares the rise of the Irish in Boston politics and the Yankee response to it with the response of white elites to the rise of black politics in Atlanta and Detroit.

56. Pohlmann and Kirby, *Racial Politics at the Crossroads,* 135. Wilson Goode was named managing director (city manager) in Philadelphia by William Green, a Kennedy-style liberal Democratic mayor (Carolyn Teich Adams, "Philadelphia: The Private City in the Postindustrial Era," in Bernard, ed., *Snowbelt Cities,* 217). Also see Browning, Marshall, and Tabb, *Racial Politics in American Cities,* who find that some form of urban reform and racial inclusion was necessary before blacks were elected mayor. See especially the chapter by Huey L. Perry, "The Evolution and Impact of Biracial Coalitions and Black Mayors in Birmingham and New Orleans," 182–83. Browning, Marshall, and Tabb and their contributors, especially Marion Orr in "The Struggle for Black Empowerment in

Baltimore: Electoral Control and Governing Coalitions," 209, found this to be the case in Los Angeles, Philadelphia, New York, Chicago, Atlanta, New Orleans, Birmingham, Baltimore, and Denver. In Philadelphia a highly competitive political environment meant that the regular Democratic organization was "forced to court black voters" (Richard A. Keiser, "After the First Black Mayor: Fault Lines in Philadelphia's Biracial Coalition," 69). In Chicago Jane Byrne mobilized black voters in the 1979 city election and received nearly 84 percent of the black vote, preparing the way for Washington in 1983 (Dianne M. Pinderhughes, "An Examination of Chicago Politics for Evidence of Political Incorporation and Representation," 125).

57. Cole, *Blacks in Power,* 35; also see Kleppner, *Chicago Divided,* 152, 219.

58. Thomas F. Pettegrew, "When a Black Candidate Runs for Mayor: Race and Voting Behavior," in Harlan Hahn, ed., *People and Politics in Urban Society* (Beverly Hills, Calif.: Sage, 1972), 99–105. Pettegrew too noted that such white supporters were Democratic and Jewish.

59. Arian et al., *Changing New York City Politics,* xi.

60. Peter Ross Range, "Capital of Black Is Bountiful," *New York Times Magazine,* April 7, 1974, pp. 28–29, 68–78, and Steven V. Ross, "He's One of Us," *New York Times Magazine,* February 24, 1974, pp. 16–20, 24, 28–30, 35. Also see Keiser, "After the First Black Mayor," 77.

61. Huey L. Perry and Alfred Stokes, "Politics and Power in the Sunbelt: Mayor Morial of New Orleans," in Preston, Henderson, and Puryear, *The New Black Politics,* 236; Hadden, Masotti, and Thiessen, "Making of the Negro Mayors," 23.

62. Cole, *Blacks in Power,* 118. White elites were generally willing to accept a black consciousness and sensitivity among mayoral candidates as long as it did not come at the expense of the overall needs of their cities.

63. "The Mile High City Is Standing a Little Taller," *Business Weekly,* July 1, 1991, p. 36.

64. The banker is quoted in Clarence N. Stone, *Regime Politics: Governing Atlanta, 1946–1988* (Lawrence: University Press of Kansas, 1989), 136. Also see Lawson, *Running for Freedom,* 150–51, and Ronald H. Bayor, "Race, Ethnicity, and Political Change in the Urban Sunbelt South," in Randall H. Miller and George E. Pozzetta, eds., *Shades of the Sunbelt: Essays on Ethnicity, Race, and the Urban South* (New York: Greenwood, 1988), 127–42.

65. Cole, *Blacks in Power,* 223.

66. S. M. Watson, "The Second Time Around: A Profile of Black Mayoral Election Campaigns," *Phylon* 45 (1984): 165–75, esp. 172.

67. Arian et al., *Changing New York City Politics,* 199.

68. Ibid., 41. Arian et al. find that Jackson's 1988 campaign was particularly successful in bringing black and Latino political leaders together and laying the basis for Dinkins's mayoral victory in 1989 (67).

69. Gills, "Chicago Politics and Community Development," 35. Also see Maria de los Angeles Torres, "The Commission on Latino Affairs: A Case Study of Community Empowerment," in Clavel and Wiewel, *Harold Washington and the Neighborhoods,* 171, and Kleppner, *Chicago Divided,* 152–53.

70. Mary Summers and Philip A. Klinker, "The Election and Governance of John Daniels as Mayor of New Haven," in Huey L. Perry, ed., *Race, Politics, and Governance in the United States* (Gainesville: University Press of Florida, 1996), 129–33.

71. See Browning, Marshall, and Tabb, *Racial Politics in American Cities;* Mylon Winn, "The Election of Norm Rice as Mayor of Seattle," *PS: Political Science & Politics* 23 (June 1990): 158–59; Richard M. Bernard and Bradley R. Rice, eds., *Sunbelt Cities: Politics and Growth Since World War II* (Austin: University of Texas Press, 1983).

72. Kenneth G. Weinberg, *Black Victory: Carl Stokes and the Winning of Cleveland* (Chicago: Quadrangle, 1968), 182.

73. Arian et al., *Changing New York City Politics,* xi; the slogan comes from Stone, *Regime Politics,* 80.

74. Arian et al., *Changing New York City Politics,* xi.

75. Thomas B. Edsall, "Poles Apart in Philadelphia: The Rizzo-Goode Battle in Dividing the Races," *Washington Post Weekly,* September 21, 1987, pp. 17–18. Also see Keiser, "After the First Black Mayor," 76.

76. Kleppner, *Chicago Divided,* 177. Writing in 1985, Kleppner argued, "Since at least the mid-1960s, race has been the dominant fact of Chicago's electoral politics" (90); also see Arnold R. Hirsch, "Chicago: The Cook County Democratic Organization and the Dilemma of Race, 1931–1987," in Bernard, ed., *Snowbelt Cities,* 85, and Dempsey J. Travis, *An Autobiography of Black Politics* (Chicago: Urban Research Institute, 1987), 593.

77. Winn, "Election of Norm Rice," 159.

78. Moore, "From Dreamers to Doers," 373.

79. Ardey and Nelson, "Maturation of Black Political Power," 148–51. Stokes is quoted in Weinberg, *Black Victory,* 88. Coleman Young denied his election would represent a black takeover: "I am trying to field a team that has balance—racially, ethnically and politically" (Rich, *Coleman Young and Detroit Politics,* 104). The one exception in this regard was Harold Washington, who announced after his victory in 1983: "Now it's our turn." He quickly backed away from this statement, however, when whites protested the implications (Kleppner, *Chicago Divided,* 154–55).

80. William J. Grimshaw, "Unraveling the Enigma: Mayor Harold Washington and the Black Political Tradition," *Urban Affairs Quarterly* 23, no. 2 (December 1987): 204. Also see Grimshaw's *Bitter Fruit: Black Politics and the Chicago Machine, 1931–1991* (Chicago: University of Chicago Press, 1992), 173–74. Kleppner noted that, in an effort to get out the vote, the Reverend George Clements, a black priest, told his parishioners that failure to register was a sin (Kleppner, *Chicago Divided,* 146).

81. Kleppner, *Chicago Divided,* 154–55.

82. Scott McConnell, "The Making of the Mayor, 1989," *Commentary* 89 (February 1990): 29–38. Many black mayoral candidates, like Willie Herenton in Memphis, turned to Jesse Jackson and Martin Luther King III in the 1990s for help in turning out the black vote. See Pohlmann and Kirby, *Racial Politics at the Crossroads,* 161.

83. McConnell, "Making of the Mayor," 31–33.

84. Arian et al., *Changing New York City Politics,* 75, 76, 82, 201.

85. Ardrey and Nelson, "Maturation of Black Political Power," 149; Harris is quoted in the *Sacramento Bee,* October 16, 1994, and the *Los Angeles Times,* October 31, 1994.

86. Barnes and Proctor, "Black Politics in Tidewater, Virginia," 92; Rich, *Black Mayors and School Politics,* 141.

87. The mayoral race in which two black candidates squared off occurred in Detroit in 1977 when Ernest Brown ran against Coleman Young. See Rush, *Coleman Young and De-*

troit Politics, 109–10. I have mentioned a few key mayoral elections after 1996, so that readers can see the ways that race unfolded after the period of this study.

88. Hajnal, "Solving the Puzzle."

89. Mollenkopf, "New York," 110–11. Thomas Barnes, an African American who defeated Richard Hatcher in Gary, echoed Mollenkopf and added, "We were allowed a very long honeymoon, an extremely long honeymoon, and that won't happen anymore." From now on, he added, "We will be judged on performance, not hype" (Moore, "Dreamers and Doers," 375).

90. *Memphis Commercial Appeal,* September 24, 1995, p. 1.

91. Mollenkopf, "New York," 109, and Persons, "Racial Politics and Black Power," 174.

92. Jim Sleeper, "The End of the Rainbow? America's Changing Urban Politics," *New Republic,* November 1993, pp. 20–25.

93. Eisinger, "Black Mayors and the Politics of Racial Economic Advancement," 249.

94. Abdul Alkalimat notes that Harold Washington was rooted in the black middle class and in the Democratic mainstream. See Alkalimat, "Chicago: Black Power, Politics, and the Crisis of the Black Middle Class," *Black Scholar* (April 1988): 45. Washington was not alone. Nearly all his peers shared a similar background.

95. Bernard, *Snowbelt Cities,* 16. Also see Joseph Arnold, "Baltimore: Southern Culture and a Northern Economy," in Bernard, *Snowbelt Cities,* 31.

2. Black Political Power and Its Limits: Gary Mayor Richard G. Hatcher's Administration, 1968–87

JAMES B. LANE

> The role of leaders changes. The nature of the advocates changes. In the early years there is a campaign to essentially dismantle apartheid. What happens then?
>
> —Henry Hampton, executive producer of *Eyes on the Prize*[1]

RARELY HAS THE advent of a mayoral administration taken on the symbolic importance of the inauguration of Richard Gordon Hatcher on January 1, 1968, in Gary, Indiana, the self-proclaimed "City of the Century" of approximately 170,000 people. To the chagrin of the local political establishment and economic elite, and to the delight of African Americans and liberal well-wishers across the country, Hatcher, a thirty-four-year-old community activist, had captured city hall after a bitter grassroots struggle. He and Cleveland's Carl Stokes became the first African-American mayors of large American cities. But unlike Stokes, Hatcher opposed the city's regular Democratic organization. At his inauguration Hatcher referred to the special problems and opportunities he faced and vowed to bring about "a healthy, vital black nationalism." Sympathetic federal bureaucrats were eager to embrace the new mayor by turning on the faucet of Great Society funds, so that Gary would prosper as a truly multiracial city and as a model of black empowerment. Major changes in the racial and political climate of the United States and in its antiurban biases would have to take place, however, before this could occur.[2]

The time, setting, and circumstances of Hatcher's ascension made his mayoralty unique. In 1967 the civil rights movement had entered an "angry" phase perceived by many as menacing to the established order. The slogan "black power" crystallized a plethora of conflicting impulses. Underlying Hatcher's political insurgency was the implied threat that Gary was on the verge of going up in flames, as had recently happened in Harlem, Watts, Newark, Detroit, and a host of other inner cities. But despite his militant rhetoric, Hatcher was not interested in tearing down "the system." Rather, he simply wanted African Americans included as full political, social, and economic partners. He may have agreed intellectually with Malcolm X's slogan of "by any means necessary," but Hatcher realized he could most effectively serve the cause in the political arena. At successive stages during his twenty-year tenure, Hatcher tried to nourish black entrepreneurship in three important ways, first through insisting that black-owned businesses get a lion's share of city contracts and that the city be tapped into federal programs such as Model Cities, revenue sharing, and the Comprehensive Employment and Training Act (CETA); second, through "Gary Genesis" activities, which were intended to instill black pride, attract outside black capital, and keep residents' money in the city; and third, by calling for new federal urban initiatives comparable to the momentous Marshall Plan of economic stimulus for Western Europe in the late 1940s.[3]

Born on July 10, 1933, Hatcher was the youngest of thirteen children, six of whom died before reaching maturity. He grew up in a small waterfront area known as the Patch in Michigan City, Indiana (a mostly white city of twenty-six thousand located twenty-five miles east of Gary). His father, Carlton, a semiskilled laborer at Pullman Standard, was barely literate but wise in the ways of the world. He also was a Baptist deacon. Richard's mother, Katherine, worked at a foul-smelling "hair" factory, plucking pigs' tails for cushion stuffing. During the Depression the family lived on a diet of powdered milk, powdered eggs, margarine, dried prunes, and potatoes, supplemented occasionally by handouts of small fish from the trawler captains of Lake Michigan. Richard Hatcher was an introverted child who stuttered badly, and he found acceptance on the football field and the track team, where he set a school record. With an athletic scholarship and help from two older sisters and two black churches, Hatcher attended Indiana University in 1951. After graduation he went to Valparaiso (Indiana) University Law School while working full-time as a psychiatric aide at Beatty Memorial Hospital. In 1958 he and several friends organized a sit-in at Brownie's Griddle in Michigan City, where he had once worked as a teenager.[4] Following law school, he was hired as a deputy prosecutor in Lake County and from there he entered local politics, rising to become president of the city council and then mayor of Gary in 1967.

Hatcher served five terms as mayor, becoming the most visible and prominent black urban leader in the nation. His administration is important for a host of reasons, not the least of which is as a case study of the limits of black political power. The history of his administration exemplified the travail of U.S. industrial cities during the late twentieth century. He held office when elective politics became, in the words of the social scientist Monte Piliawsky, the "dominant strategy in the search by blacks for equality in the United States." Both demographics and changing attitudes fueled the evolution from protest to governance. Furthermore, the alternatives of ignoring or over-throwing the U.S. political system were self-defeating and unrealistic. Was Hatcher a liberator, destroyer, scapegoat, or cipher of history, trapped in a public office inherently irrelevant to the cause of black liberation and forced to contend with myriad structural and economic restraints beyond his con-trol? The constraints on black mayors were less obvious in 1968 than three decades later, but Hatcher realized that black political power was but one of several prerequisites to the full liberation of African Americans. He would need political, administrative, and inspirational skills aplenty to overcome the roadblocks. As was the case for his parents' Georgia ancestors during the first era of Reconstruction a century earlier, federal support would be fleet-ing and come with strings attached. Hatcher was the only African-American mayor to be the full beneficiary of Great Society largesse, but he would also have to deal with Republican presidents during fifteen of his twenty years in office. His legacy has been the subject of much debate, but when he left office in 1987, no one could deny that, to quote the historian Lance Trusty, "the great Gary experiment, through which Washington tried to transform a black northern community into a model city, was over."[5]

The 1967 Election

The struggle for black urban political empowerment was a by-product of ethnic succession, antimachine insurgency, and the crusading spirit of the civil rights movement. Before 1967 black residents had been the most loyal but least rewarded component of Gary's corrupt Democratic machine. That organi-zation was weakened in 1962 when the popular Greek-American boss, May-or George Chacharis, pleaded guilty to charges of tax evasion. Hatcher, who had moved to Gary just two years earlier to start a law practice, quickly be-came prominent in local struggles involving discrimination in education, law enforcement, hiring practices, parks, hospitals, and housing. Though African Americans constituted half the city's population, they found most residen-tial neighborhoods and public facilities off-limits to them. At a time when Martin Luther King Jr. was the most admired role model among the city's African-American electorate, Hatcher developed impeccable civil rights cre-dentials by participating in police brutality cases and a school desegregation suit. He also volunteered in Mississippi during the Freedom Summer. He was a leader of Gary's NAACP Youth Council and a founder of Muigwithania, a politically minded group of young black professionals whose name in Swahili meant "Unity" or "We are together." Hatcher had been involved in protests since his days at Indiana University and Valparaiso University Law School and was inspired to enter public life, he said later, by King, John F. Kennedy, and Kenya's Jomo Kenyatta, who had also come to power under the banner of Muigwithania. In 1963 Hatcher won an at-large seat on the Gary Common Council and promptly allied himself with a white good-government faction, which elected him to chair the council. His support within the black community included union activists at U.S. Steel, women community leaders, high school teachers, and veterans of local civil rights battles. In 1966 one of the civil rights activists, John Grigsby, presented Hatcher with a petition signed by five thousand people urging him to run for mayor. Grigsby had collected most of the signatures at beauty parlors and barbershops.[6]

Winning the 1967 election was a two-step process. The incumbent mayor, Democrat A. Martin Katz, was seeking reelection. When a second white candidate, Bernard Konrady, entered the Democratic primary, Hatcher had an unexpected opportunity to win it if he could wean most black voters away from what he called the "plantation politics" of the Democratic machine. Konrady was popular among Gary residents who had voted for the segregationist George Wallace in Indiana's 1964 Democratic presidential primary (the Alabama governor had carried nearly every white precinct in Gary). To the chagrin of these voters, Mayor Katz had supported the common council's decision to establish a human relations commission and give it the power to subpoena companies accused of discriminating against minorities in employment, public accommodations, or housing. Konrady, on the other hand, was a maverick who believed that illegal machine activities had cheated his late brother Emery in the 1963 mayoral race. In the 1967 Democratic primary Katz received more than 30 percent of the black vote, while Hatcher won just 4.5 percent of the white vote. Nonetheless, Hatcher received a plurality of more 3,000 votes, garnering 20,272 votes to 17,190 for Katz and 13,133 for Konrady. The results set off a jubilant block party along Broadway, Gary's main thoroughfare, halting traffic for four hours. Although he was disappointed at the results, Konrady was nevertheless heard to say, "We did it, Emery."[7]

Because Gary was virtually a one-party fiefdom, Hatcher's nomination would have assured his election had he not earned the wrath of John Krupa, the chair of the county Democratic central committee who disliked the nominee's antimachine rhetoric. Krupa privately offered his support if he could select Hatcher's controller and chief of police, terms Hatcher refused. Publicly, Krupa demanded that Hatcher disassociate himself from the views of the actor Marlon Brando (a Vietnam critic) and Stokely Carmichael and H. Rap Brown, leaders of the Student Non-Violent Coordinating Committee, all three of whom were dangerous extremists, in Krupa's view—conditions Hatcher could never accept, given his commitment to a black united front. His campaign theme, in fact, was, "Let's Get Ourselves Together." Because most white Democratic precinct captains were supporting Republican Joseph Radigan, a furniture dealer with no previous political experience, Hatcher needed not only near-unanimous support from black voters but also help from white liberals, both locally and nationally, as well as federal court action to prevent vote fraud. On the eve of the election a federal appellate court forced the county Board of Registrars to add to the list of eligible voters 5,286 residents from the Central District, where most blacks lived, and to remove more than a thousand "ghost" names—of people who had either moved out of Gary or who had died. Predictions of rioting if Hatcher lost led Gov. Roger D. Branigan to put five thousand national guardsmen on alert. In a close but honest election by local standards, Hatcher won by 1,865 votes out of 77,759 cast, receiving 96 percent of the black vote and a mere 12 percent of the white vote (he got crucial support, however, from a group of mostly Jewish lakefront liberals known as the Miller Mafia). As one jubilant onlooker put it, Gary's black people had "gotten it together." The political columnist Joseph Alsop opined, "Hatcher represents black power in the best American tradition—and thank God for it!—just as President Kennedy represented the culmination of Irish power."[8]

In Office

During Hatcher's first days in office his staff was preoccupied with, among other things, constituent requests for jobs, interviews, guided tours of city hall, and answers to homework questions. One woman, for example, wanted to know whether the mayor could marry couples, another whether he could get an errant husband out of the house. With a bankrupt treasury, eroding local tax base, state-imposed limitations to home rule, and a wary business community, Hatcher moved cautiously in personnel matters, retaining many holdovers from the Katz regime, in part because so few African Americans were qualified for department-level jobs. One adviser compared the situation to a former African colony, where a national liberation regime needed the old bureaucracy to run public services.[9]

Centrifugal forces bedeviled the mayor as well. He acted decisively to dismantle Gary's "red-light" district, but the antivice crusade contributed to an alarming rise in street crime. His efforts to reach out to youth gangs, such as the Sin City Disciples, produced a white backlash. While Hatcher proved adept at crisis management, especially in situations where ghetto anger threatened to explode, he could do little to counter the impression—conveyed by the local media and fueled by a number of muggings, including an assault on a Serbian Orthodox priest—that Gary was undergoing a public safety crisis. In fact, although he worked tirelessly to defuse several potentially violent incidents, including near riots following the assassination of Martin Luther King on April 4, 1968, critics unfairly blamed the mayor for a school boycott, several sit-ins, and even a 1969 "eat-in" at the Gary Armory that disrupted a Republican reception for Gov. Edgar D. Whitcomb, who succeeded Branigan and had recently vetoed a welfare measure and who had refused to meet with a delegation representing the Aid for Dependent Children Mothers Club. Hatcher talked the protesters into vacating the armory—but not until some youngsters had helped themselves to pie.[10]

Strategy 1: Urban Laboratory

Hatcher achieved much greater rapport with federal officials and East Coast foundations that were eager to steer racial protest into constructive channels than he did with local or state agencies. With the support of Great Society programs funded by Lyndon B. Johnson's Office of Economic Opportunity, Hatcher focused on making Gary an urban laboratory. His administration put together one of the most constructive community-based Model Cities experiments in the country, one that provided a path to leadership and entry into the middle class for talented ghetto residents. Hatcher considered Model Cities "the most important work taking place in the nation." The influx of money and consultants was a mixed blessing, however, because it fostered a dependence on distant bureaucrats, aroused unrealistic expectations, and created opportunities for waste and graft. The motivation for some programs was more to quiet ghetto unrest than to elevate poor people. Summer youth programs were well and good, for instance, and the Hatcher administration would have been negligent not to pursue such funds diligently, but the mayor had little concrete to point to when critics wondered where all the money had gone. More than most mayors, Hatcher really believed in "maximum feasible participation" and encouraged citizen boards to design and implement antipoverty programs. The tragedy was that the experiment, launched at the tail end of the Johnson administration, was never given a decent interval to measure its progress. Gary faced a significant decline in federal revenues for social programs after the Nixon administration doubled the number of cities qualified to receive Model Cities money.[11]

In addition to perhaps escalating white flight and disinvestment (phenomena also occurring in nearby Hammond and East Chicago), Hatcher's leadership style stunted Gary's geographical expansion. Had he not espoused civil rights goals so forcefully, Gary's boundaries probably would have expanded south to include Merrillville, where more than $1 billion was subsequently invested by banks and retail stores formerly located in downtown Gary. Impetus might have grown for a regional "unigov" plan similar to the one adopted by Indianapolis; it would have diluted black political power in Gary but fostered regional planning in such matters as transportation, tourism, and redevelopment. But Hatcher's election and perceptions of his administration as an experiment in black power prompted suburban white Merrillville to incorporate, although not until Indiana's state legislators granted a controversial exemption from a "buffer zone" law that prohibited suburban incorporation in areas adjacent to cities. Hatcher's election also sparked an unsuccessful de-annexation movement among whites in Gary's Glen Park district and a ten-year court battle by residents in unincorporated Black Oak who objected to being annexed. These events reinforced Gary's negative image as a city immobilized by racial tensions. During his first term Hatcher used the phrase "City on the Move." Critics quipped, "Yes, Gary's on the move; everyone's moving out!" For Hatcher's detractors "City on the Move" denoted "the boarding up of Gary" or "Plywood City" (a reference to covering over the windows of vacant buildings). Some former residents sarcastically asked, "Will the last one out please turn off the lights?"[12]

Clearly, Gary was undergoing a fundamental metamorphosis. Except for a few lakefront enclaves, most white homeowners and merchants who could afford to relocate were leaving. Neither "Community Watch" programs, new recreation centers, nor the banning of "For Sale" signs could arrest the trend or keep arsonists from turning the downtown commercial district into a disaster area. Nixon's freeze on grants by the U.S. Department of Housing and Urban Development (HUD) brought in-progress housing projects to a standstill. While a murderous drug war accelerated disinvestment, critics harped on the mayor's tendency to always "cry race," as one put it. Gary's darkening complexion was evidence of the cynical definition of "neighborhood integration" as that brief period between the arrival of the first African Americans and the departure of the last whites.[13]

Despite predictions that disillusionment and apathy would curtail his political career, Hatcher secured a second term in 1971, handily defeating

African-American Alexander S. Williams, a machine-supported county coroner. But 1960s "seed money" from East Coast foundations and Great Society programs had dried up. Hatcher's administration experienced a diminution of community initiatives and a brain drain. City salaries were so low that the mayor's press secretary was literally living below the poverty line. Not the most efficient administrator, Hatcher could be maddeningly slow at decision making, yet he became impatient at delays when he was finally ready to act. One thing that energized him was a speech to a national organization or a university audience. Hatcher relished such opportunities to hold forth on leading issues of the day, as when he hosted the 1972 National Black Political Convention at Gary West Side High School. The historic conference, co-chaired by the playwright Imamu Baraka, attracted more than four thousand delegates and sought to forge a liberationist agenda palatable to the broadest spectrum possible.[14]

Although redevelopment and neighborhood preservation became top administration priorities, the city's economic problems worsened. To revive civic pride Hatcher promoted an annual Founder's Day celebration and lured the Miss Black America pageant to the city. Former heavyweight champ Muhammad Ali promised to build a top-quality restaurant. But Ali's plans never materialized, and two years later the Miss Black America pageant was moved elsewhere. With the construction of Southlake Mall and other suburban shopping centers, the number of downtown businesses decreased dramatically, from more than five hundred in 1960 to fewer than forty by 1979 (a similar phenomenon plagued nearby Hammond, whose mayor was white). Even a threatened boycott (supported by Jesse Jackson's Operation PUSH) did not deter Sears from abandoning its retail outlet, which was still doing a brisk business but supposedly was plagued by shoplifters. The decision was part of a national strategy by Sears to relocate to the suburbs (one such store anchored Southlake Mall) and was predicated on the belief that two stores within a ten-mile area were counterproductive and that black customers could be lured to Merrillville more easily than whites could be lured to downtown Gary. The financially troubled Holiday Inn closed in January 1975. "Gary's real problem," Hatcher declared, "has been the lack of private capital investment." As the 1975 election approached, Hatcher's pet project—a civic center—was stalled in the state legislature, partly the result of opposition from U.S. Steel, the Chamber of Commerce, and the *Post-Tribune* (which had dropped "Gary" from its masthead).[15]

During the 1970s, before most black leaders articulated the connection between pollution and corporate racism, Hatcher was in the forefront of two important environmental battles. The first involved enforcing an antipollution ordinance against U.S. Steel's coke plants, despite threats from the city's largest employer to close the mills down. The second arose when Gary became an intervenor in a suit to prevent the Northern Indiana Public Service Co. (NIPSCO) from building a nuclear power plant on the lakefront in neighboring Porter County. The delaying actions against NIPSCO proved successful; the utility eventually scuttled its nuclear power plant after cost estimates skyrocketed, and the Three-Mile Island accident in Pennsylvania heightened public concerns about atomic energy. According to Charles Ruckman, who served as city attorney, Hatcher seemed almost to relish these fights, even if they earned him the enmity of local corporate leaders. These were issues dear to some of his most loyal white supporters, including several who held key advisory positions in his administration. Hatcher's doggedness had U.S. Steel on the run until the state took enforcement powers against polluters away from the city. The lack of home rule also frustrated the mayor. The City of Gary had been the creation of the U.S. Steel Corp., which was its principal source of tax revenue, and the company's vast facilities still were grossly underassessed. City officials were virtually powerless to correct the situation, however, because tax assessment was in the hands of a township official, whose actions U.S. Steel could appeal to a state board.[16]

Strategy 2: Gary Genesis

Hatcher launched his third term with a new strategy, which he called "Genesis of a New Gary." Using references to death and rebirth, he sought to transform the city into a sort of mecca for African Americans. Redevelopment plans called for a civic center, a medical facility, development of the Gary airport, a marina on Lake Michigan, a downtown minimall, and reopening the old Holiday Inn. Hatcher quickly encountered obstacles, however. Save for the hotel project, which proved to be quite costly, the administration's efforts bogged down. Despite gestures of friendship, President Jimmy Carter proved to have tighter purse strings than Richard Nixon had had. Moreover, the common council opposed Hatcher's budget requests for spending the shrinking supply of revenue-sharing funds. Hatcher termed the council's position a politically inspired vendetta, a "reign of legislative terror" that imperiled "the normal operations of city functions." Meanwhile, the U.S. Attorney's Office launched grand jury investigations of numerous operations, including various youth jobs programs (Neighborhood Youth Corps, MANPOWER, Metro Corps), the Bishop Freeman Housing Project, the police department, and even the city dump. Convinced that Nixon holdovers were out to get him, Hatcher declared that "the person who pushes down the doors pays a great price; he bears the scars and hostilities." Other black mayors faced similar federal harassment. In Gary, despite the periodic leaking of rumors to the contrary, the probe results were inconsequential. The most incriminating revelation about the mayor, apparently, was the effort to encourage department heads to sell tickets to campaign fund-raisers, such as his annual "Evening to Remember," which featured black celebrities, including Harry Belafonte, Nancy Wilson, and Dick Gregory. In 1978 Hatcher turned down a White House position when it evidently did not come with a staff or specific responsibilities and turned instead to various "Genesis" projects, including an abortive "Buy-in-Gary" campaign ("there's no place in town to buy a quality suit," complained a local member of the clergy) and a successful upgrading of intracity bus services. Housing projects for the elderly were completed, but U.S. Steel's refusal to honor a commitment to build an office building downtown jeopardized a crucial grant from HUD under the Urban Development Action Grant program.[17]

Shelving his confrontational leadership style, at least temporarily, Hatcher announced that "reunion and reconciliation" would be the goals of his fourth term, which began in 1980. That Hatcher meant it was symbolized by the attendance at his swearing-in of his political rival Dozier T. Allen, cofounder of Muigwithania, one-time common council president, and the township trustee in charge of dispensing welfare. He praised the mayor's devotion to great dreams and to the pursuit of great goals. Other signs of reconciliation included a Chamber of Commerce luncheon at the Sheraton (the old Holiday Inn) and Hatcher's attendance at an Urban League banquet in Merrillville, which ended the mayor's boycott of such events in white suburbs. Hatcher also established a working relationship with U.S. Rep. Adam Benjamin, a Democrat who proved remarkably effective at obtaining funds for a transportation center and highway construction to link downtown Gary with I-65 and the Indiana Toll Road (Benjamin died in 1982). Hatcher reorganized his administration into four superdivisions (city operations, community services, physical and economic development, and protective services) and finally found an able police chief in New Yorker Frederick Kowsky. Most important, Gary became one of three cities (along with St. Paul, Minnesota, and Dayton, Ohio) included in a massive redevelopment experiment called negotiated investment strategy (NIS), developed by the Kettering Foundation to coordinate grants and planning by federal, state, and local agencies involved in urban redevelopment. The process led ultimately to the completion of the civic center (christened the Genesis Center) and the transformation of the defunct Hotel Gary into Genesis Towers, a beautiful high-rise for senior citizens. Ronald Reagan's election was a sour note, however, so far as other federal aid was concerned; plans for a minimall foundered when no developer put up matching funds.[18]

In the early 1980s the motto of "Reunion and Reconciliation" gave way to public feuds with Dozier T. Allen (regarding patronage) and Robert Pastrick, who chaired the Lake County Democratic Central Committee and refused to support any of Hatcher's candidates on the official Democratic slate. The mayor also hectored the area banking establishment for its redlining practices and remained a frequent critic of the state legislature (calling one of its "vindictive" actions "another midnight raid by the downstate KKK"). Gary's last two downtown department stores (Hudson's and Goldblatt's) closed, and U.S. Steel, the *Post-Tribune*, and the Chamber of Commerce opposed a bond issue to build a sports complex, drawing Hatcher's ire. No local newspaper was less a booster to its home city than the *Post-Tribune*, Hatcher charged. Mill officials were cooperative only when they needed a favor. Like the Chamber of Commerce, U.S. Steel Corp. generally opposed bond issues on the ground that they were indirect forms of taxation, even though Hatcher had enabled the company to float Indiana development bonds that enabled the company to borrow $100 million at low interest for pollution abatement. Much to the chagrin of his city planner, Hatcher had asked for nothing in return. "The mayor didn't do what you might call tit for tat," Robert Farag recalled.[19]

Despite Hatcher's hope that Gary could be the economic center of black America, the city's economic woes continued. Muslim leader Louis Farrakhan's promise of a fish-processing plant went unfulfilled, and a state commission blocked plans for a black-controlled bank. By 1983 the city tax base had so eroded that drastic cuts in services and personnel were unavoidable. The budget crisis was so severe that Gary could not pay its utility bills, slashed its departmental budgets by 10 percent, and laid off 384 employees. In the spring of 1984 came a ray of hope. City departments were under instructions to spruce up the Genesis Center and the Sheraton Hotel (where some welfare recipients had been moved) in preparation for about thirty-five thousand delegates to the National Baptist Convention who were coming to town. But wider use of the Genesis Center during Hatcher's fifth term had no noticeable effect on economic revitalization. In fact, the Sheraton closed, which left the city with only a single motel: the Interlude, which showed XXX-rated videos and rented rooms by the hour. When Thomas V. Barnes, the township assessor, foiled a plan to float bonds to pay for new police and fire equipment by registering his objections with the state tax board, the mayor's political fortunes began to slide. First, he lost his chairmanship of the First District Democratic Committee.

Then in 1985 he was replaced as a vice chair of the Democratic National Committee. Hatcher-backed candidates for Congress and for township and county offices fared poorly. Automation, suburbanization, and racial polarization continued to cast a wide shadow. In May 1985, after much effort to upgrade the Gary Municipal Airport, Britt Airlines began daily flights to Detroit and Indianapolis but closed down within three months because of lack of customers. Suburban detractors killed the experiment, Hatcher charged, by writing "poison pen" letters to Britt and taking the attitude that "I will be dead before I'll go to the Gary Airport." While Hatcher could take pride in numerous accomplishments during his fifth term—among them, completion of a transportation terminal and a city-run sports and fitness center, a declining crime rate, and the attraction of dozens of small steel-processing firms—they were overshadowed by a six-month steel strike in 1986 that crippled the local economy and dramatized the decline of the steel industry as a source of decent-paying jobs.[20]

Strategy 3: Changing National Priorities

During the mid-1980s Hatcher concentrated much of his energies on national and international issues. In 1984 he was campaign director for Jesse Jackson's bid for the Democratic presidential nomination and served in that role again in 1988. Jackson endorsed many agenda items formulated at the 1982 Black Economic Summit (which Hatcher had convened), including an economic aid program for U.S. cities comparable to the effort spent to save Western Europe from communism during the postwar period. The idea was to place large amounts of investment capital in the hands of minority entrepreneurs. As the chairman of TransAfrica, an organization that pressured Congress to slap trade sanctions on South Africa, Hatcher spent the night of November 29, 1984, in jail in Washington, D.C., charged with picketing within a prohibited zone in front of the South African embassy. Hatcher, noted one Gary reporter, should have been running a civil rights organization, "where there's no politics involved, just image and charisma and leadership."[21]

Some admirers wished Hatcher had moved on to Congress or perhaps to an ambassadorship in an African nation. Unlike Sen. Richard Lugar, who while mayor of Indianapolis had benefited from close ties to Indiana's political and economic elite, Hatcher had no realistic chance of political advancement so long as the Republican Party controlled state politics and the presidency. Hatcher admired the acumen of Lugar and his mayoral successor, Republican William Hudnut, and envied their clout with Indiana legislators, who usually looked askance at Gary as a "Hoosier stepchild." "Lugar was bright," recalled Hatcher, "but I felt I was as bright as he was. His real advantage was being a Republican at a time when the state senate, the assembly, and the governor's office were all controlled by Republicans. To top it all off, President Nixon was a Republican. That's a winning combination." Whereas Lugar (whom admirers had called "Nixon's favorite mayor") once seemed the anachronism, by the 1980s Hatcher seemed a throwback to a vanishing era of confrontation. Meanwhile, the new breed of pragmatic black mayors was emphasizing managerial skill rather than race consciousness.[22]

Structural problems also contributed to Gary's downward spiral. Nationally, disinvestment was least pronounced in cities such as Atlanta and Detroit that were blessed with Fortune 500 companies whose assets were so wedded to their home offices as to make relocation economically impractical. In Gary the central business district along Broadway had changed little since the Roaring Twenties and was destined to become, like hundreds of other downtowns, a casualty of suburbanization. Except for U.S. Steel, whose facilities had been drastically streamlined, the private sector collapsed, or, more accurately, cut and ran. Taking a narrow view of what was in their economic self-interest, northwest Indiana's business elite opted to relocate to the suburbs after accusing Hatcher of being inaccessible and a poor administrator, charges commonly leveled at black mayors elsewhere.[23]

How much this had to do with the mayor's leadership style and administrative ability became a matter of much debate. Downtown became a ghost town, not only in Gary but in neighboring Hammond and East Chicago, where white mayors could not stem the tide any better than Hatcher. Elsewhere, even when enterprise zone and redevelopment policies gave old commercial districts a face-lift, the trickle-down effect on black residents was disappointingly small. Critics often compared the satellite cities of Gary and Newark, New Jersey (which was twice as large with more than 300,000 residents) and the obstacles that had bedeviled five-term mayor Hatcher and four-term mayor Kenneth Gibson, who was unseated in 1986 by Sharpe James, a member of the city council. Gibson had been the more successful of the two in refurbishing downtown Newark but less successful in combating neighborhood decay. Like Tom Bradley of Los Angeles, Gibson was more conciliatory toward his city's white power structure than Hatcher, who found himself passed over for leadership positions within national organizations in favor of Bradley and Gibson. By the time Hatcher's fifth term in office began in 1984, about 250 U.S. cities had African-American mayors, twenty of whom presided over cities of more than 100,000 people. Even so, the more than five thousand blacks holding office represented only 1 percent of the total number of U.S. elected officials. Cities with black mayors were often those most beset by economic blight, debilitating racial polarization, middle-class flight, and shrinking revenue. Thus city hall turned out to be a hollow prize, signifying to some critics that the system was not responsive to the black masses. Put in office as much to maintain order as to resolve problems, they became care-takers of dying cities. But as events would later demonstrate in Chicago, New York, and even Gary, African Americans did not have a lock on city hall, as once presumed.[24]

Declension

In addition to being dubbed "America's Murder Capital" because of its record homicide rate, Gary in the mid-1980s was shaken by several events that seemed to symbolize a breakdown in community cohesion. One was the fatal stab-bing of an elderly women by a group of teenaged girls, including fifteen-year-old Paula Cooper, whose death sentence received worldwide publicity. In another case several children died while trapped in a slimy, untended, sup-posedly empty public swimming pool. Whereas legions of youngsters once held federally subsidized summer jobs, now the city could not even maintain its recreational facilities.[25]

After twenty years the electorate seemed ready for a new approach, for a less abrasive second-generation black mayor. In 1987 Hatcher's political enemies formed the so-called no-name group, and he faced his most formidable black mayoral opponent, Thomas Barnes, the township assessor, whose "Clean Up Gary" campaign emphasized competence in providing general services, such as garbage collection and snow removal, and cooperation with neighboring communities in matters of regional planning. Barnes reminded voters that Hatcher had been vainly promising marinas and minimalls for twenty years and that programs originally funded by the federal government had become a drain on the city budget once the flow of money from Washington dried up. In his previous campaigns for reelection Hatcher had charged that outsiders were plotting to grab control of Gary. This time the tactic failed. In 1983 Hatcher had amassed almost 28,000 votes to defeat Council President Thomas Crump. By 1987, however, age and apathy had depleted the ranks of his followers. Al-though Barnes won, he received only 2,000 more votes than Crump had gar-nered in 1983, but Hatcher's total dropped to fewer than 20,000.[26]

Hatcher's loss signaled that his confrontational leadership style had become a political liability. Before the election *Post-Tribune* reporter Chris Isadore had written that Hatcher "says he wants to cooperate with the city's predominantly white neighbors. But he says he first demands respect for Gary's political power, its resources and its residents." That much was true. So too was the conclu-

sion of a sociological study that found northwest Indiana to be the most segregated area in the nation. "When I have mentioned these problems," said
Hatcher, "I have been termed a racist." Jean Thurman, a community activist,
had learned what voters were thinking as she tried to solicit votes for Hatcher.
Former supporters, for example, told her, "He's been there long enough. It's
time for a change. Let somebody else try." She mentioned that Hatcher's enemies wanted his cooperation on projects that were not good for Gary, such as
bus service to suburban malls and allowing non-Garyites to control the airport board. Thurman added: "I'm glad he didn't cooperate. I never felt he was
antibusiness and antiwhite. He was just pro-poor and pro-black, and militantly
so, and that's why I admired him." Hatcher himself summed up his political
philosophy in this way: "All other considerations are secondary to this moral
requirement: that there must be opportunity for all Americans, regardless of
race, regardless of status." Hatcher loyalist Charlotte Johnson put a positive spin
on the small voter turnout that doomed Hatcher's efforts for a sixth term: "You
hear a lot of people say, 'I think he's tired. He needs a rest. Let somebody else
have the headaches.' These are the people who didn't bother about voting at
all. They just simply didn't go to the polls."[27]

Assessment

Whenever he was asked how his being mayor had made a difference, Hatcher liked to talk about individuals whose lives were enriched by the "human
services" his administration provided: the senior citizen able to move from
a basement hovel to a safe, attractive apartment; the black contractor who
gained a piece of the action and went on to sit on corporate boards; the Olympic sprinter who won a full college scholarship after she competed in city
youth programs; the welfare mother who became a respected state legislator after participating in Model Cities planning projects; the high school
dropout who became a successful caterer after attending classes held by Career Services. For hundreds, perhaps thousands, the Hatcher administration
was an opportunity provider on the path to self-respect. The mayor's top
priorities, as one critic succinctly put it, were civil rights, civil rights, and civil
rights. Atop his agenda were (1) efforts to provide quality care for dependent
groups (children, senior citizens, the disabled); (2) initiatives to eradicate the
last vestiges of institutional racism for minority workers and homeowners;
and, (3) affirmative action programs to redress past discrimination, especially
against aspiring black entrepreneurs. Hatcher's biggest disappointment was
that black political power did not lead to economic empowerment for more
African Americans. On those occasions when he attempted to mobilize black

business people for investment purposes, white-controlled area banks, skeptical state agencies, a hostile press, and/or local apathy doomed Hatcher's plans. That is why, once he was out of office, he concluded that only a fundamental reordering of national priorities could secure meaningful economic opportunities for African-American entrepreneurs.[28]

In assessing Hatcher's record as mayor, it is necessary not only to look at the successes or failures of his economic redevelopment effort and at the improvement or deterioration of general services under his watch but also to factor in his leadership. He considered himself a freedom fighter and wounded the pride of many opponents even as he engendered feelings of intense loyalty among faithful followers. His style may have been a barrier to regional harmony, but it also was a by-product of his life and times. Hatcher's friends and foes generally agreed that although he was outspoken, he was sincere and not a demagogue. He demanded respect and in matters of principle would not compromise (some called this stubbornness). He was not uncomfortable with whites, with whom he had worked throughout his schooling and public life, and he brought people of all races into his administration, expressing hope that Gary could remain a multiracial city. But, like most first-generation black mayors, he feuded frequently with local and state officials whom he perceived as racist and was slow to forgive old enemies or forget past slights. He obtained large amounts of federal funding for Gary and was an honest public servant, but opponents thought much was wasted on projects of debatable merit or slipped through the fingers of incompetent underlings.[29]

The Hatcher years were tumultuous but not riot torn, in part because the mayor steered black protest into constructive channels. Few of his critics suggested viable alternatives that would have lifted Gary from its morass. Some claim he paid too little attention to downtown urban renewal projects until it was too late, but his constituents had not elected him to build edifices inaccessible to ghetto residents, so it was hardly surprising that his antipoverty programs mainly targeted impoverished black neighborhoods. At any rate, when he did turn to downtown projects, the white power structure reacted apathetically and even negatively. Even so, during his tenure Gary's black residents came to have the highest proportion of homeownership in the nation. That this did not produce a healthy climate for black enterprise reflects the elusiveness of investment capital for black power, especially in a rundown mill town like Gary.[30]

First-generation black mayors were pioneers. According to Roger Wilkins, they tended to be haughty activists rather than mere housekeepers, facilitators, or accommodationists (the worst insult for African-American leaders of Hatcher's generation was to be called an Uncle Tom). They had taken a leap of faith that their elevation would have a ripple effect on the lives of their black constituents. They felt a particular obligation to tackle racial injustice. First-generation black mayors tended to assume the role of surrogate parent, promoting a bootstrap ethic of self-help and racial solidarity. "Even if Great Society programs were working perfectly," Hatcher said in 1967, "it wouldn't be enough. We must draw upon our basic spirit to survive and rely upon our innate abilities to grow because the rightness of our cause doesn't mean automatically that we'll succeed." First-generation black mayors also tended to take on the image of warrior or prophet (admirers frequently called Hatcher a black Moses). Although the mayors' jeremiads were often valid, and hectoring the white establishment was politically necessary, both approaches made it more difficult for these mayors to be coalition builders. The less beholden they were to the white power structure, the more threatening they seemed to the status quo. In Hatcher's view their situation was analogous to the dilemma of performing a heart transplant: necessary for the long-term health of the body politic but likely to trigger defense mechanisms designed to reject the foreign element.[31]

Some first-generation black mayors often were effective in combating police brutality and other vestiges of institutional racism but experienced less success in implementing their social welfare agenda. Although Hatcher was somewhat of an exception in this regard, the prime beneficiaries of black urban empowerment seem to have been middle-class African Americans, such as Richard Hatcher's colleagues in Muigwithania. Furthermore, according to Peter K. Eisinger, black mayors were more successful in improving capital-intensive services like street and park maintenance and delivering and water and sewerage than in improving services such as employment, housing, and public safety. Most felt compelled by economic circumstances to seek business alliances and public funding that curtailed their ability to effect meaningful change and threatened to make them, in the words of the political scientist Adolph Reed Jr., "virtual handmaidens to private development interests." For example, perhaps because of his background as a labor organizer, Coleman Young saw nothing wrong with Detroit that a few large factories could not cure. Former civil rights activist Andrew Young made his peace with capitalism and worked to create a vagrant-free zone in downtown Atlanta, a city that one critic compared to Calcutta at the height of the British Empire.

Again, Hatcher was the exception. Unable to forge a meaningful alliance with Gary's business leaders, Hatcher instead tapped into a plethora of federal programs that treated the symptoms of Gary's ills without curing the disease. Had Sen. Robert F. Kennedy not been assassinated during the spring of 1968, and instead gone on to the White House, Gary would have been the beneficiary of continued federal generosity, both in the funding for Great Society programs already underway and in new initiatives fostering black entrepreneurship such as had been pioneered in the Bedford-Stuyvesant ghetto of New York City. As the commitment from Washington, D.C., ebbed and then slowed to a trickle, Hatcher realized, perhaps too late, that the most important variable in successful urban development was the attitude and commitment of local business leaders and whether they were looking to invest in the city. When area business leaders talked about regional cooperation, the discussion usually involved matters that Hatcher believed would dilute his city's influence, such as expanding the board of the Gary Municipal Airport, or would be a detriment to Gary businesses, such as extending to suburban malls Gary's excellent bus services, which were a consequence of Hatcher's skill in securing federal funds.[32]

In a sense Hatcher transcended the limits of black political power by using the mayor's office as a forum for articulating the needs of black people in Gary and in the nation. Despite some similarities between Hatcher and Chicago's Harold Washington, there is virtually no American elected official to whom the Gary mayor can be compared in terms of doggedly working within the murky system of municipal government in pursuit of full freedom for African Americans. Nothing was artificial or guileful about his image of rectitude tinged with militancy. Eager to be a role model, opportunity provider, and spokesman for blacks, he wanted his constituents to know his priorities and to judge him on those terms. He had little concern for amassing personal wealth or seeking higher office, although he saw the mayor's office as an appropriate forum for articulating the needs of black people in the United States and throughout the world. Had he become executive director of the NAACP during the late 1970s, as had been rumored, he might have been spared the frustrations of office during the Reagan years. He was a better politician than most critics gave him credit for, however, surviving five terms despite unrelenting opposition. He might, in a different time or place, have become as important a city resource, as, say Baltimore's Kurt Schmoke or Birmingham's Richard Arrington. Instead, Hatcher was demonized by those who, in all likelihood, would have relocated to suburban environs no matter who controlled city hall. He left office as he entered it, unbossed, unbought, and with head unbowed.[33]

Notes

1. Hampton (who was not speaking specifically of Hatcher here) is quoted in Bill Barol, "A Struggle for the Prize," *Newsweek*, August 22, 1988, p. 63. The sequel to the acclaimed

television series *Eyes on the Prize* devoted a lengthy segment to the 1972 National Black Political Convention hosted by Hatcher at Gary West Side High School.

2. Gary, the "City of the Century," has existed in the shadow of Chicago culturally and economically since its founding in 1906 by the U.S. Steel Corp. See Powell A. Moore, *The Calumet Region: Indiana's Last Frontier* (Indianapolis: Indiana Historical Bureau, 1959), 257–303; Graham R. Taylor, *Satellite Cities: A Study of Industrial Suburbs* (1915; reprint, New York: Arno, 1970); Raymond A. Mohl and Neil Betten, *Steel City: Urban and Ethnic Patterns in Gary, Indiana, 1906–1950* (New York: Holmes and Meier, 1986); Alex Poinsett, *Black Power, Gary-Style: The Making of Richard Gordon Hatcher* (Chicago: Johnson, 1970); James B. Lane, *City of the Century: A History of Gary, Indiana* (Bloomington: Indiana University Press, 1978), 282–91; John Grigsby to James B. Lane, December 29, 1987, copy in the Calumet Regional Archives [hereafter CRA], Gary; William E. Nelson Jr., *Black Politics in Gary: Problems and Prospects* (Washington, D.C.: Joint Center for Political Studies, 1972); Richard G. Hatcher, interview by author, July 17, 1992 (CRA). Interviews cited subsequently were conducted by the author and are housed in the CRA unless otherwise noted. Among the nationally prominent Democrats who helped raise money for Hatcher were Vice President Hubert H. Humphrey and New York senator Robert F. Kennedy, both of whom had presidential ambitions. What Hatcher meant by "vital black nationalism" can be summarized by the slogan "black pride." Among the things Hatcher and his supporters later did to heighten black pride were to sing the "Negro national anthem," "Lift Every Voice," at public events and to dedicate a branch library in honor of W. E. B. DuBois.

3. William L. O'Neill, *Coming Apart: An Informal History of America in the 1960s* (Chicago: Quadrangle, 1971), 173–75; Allen J. Matusow, *The Unraveling of America: A History of Liberalism in the 1960s* (New York: Harper and Row, 1984), 345–75; Edward Greer, *Big Steel: Black Politics and Corporate Power in Gary, Indiana* (New York: Monthly Review Press, 1969); Eugene Carrabine, former Gary city council member, interview, October 5, 1988. On the effect of urban riots on federal policy, see James W. Button, *Black Violence* (Princeton, N.J.: Princeton University Press, 1978). When he was out of office during the late 1980s, Hatcher began suggesting that black investors deserved federal help equal to the aid packages developed for former communist countries such as Poland and the Soviet Union.

4. Lane, *City of the Century,* 282–84.

5. Monte Piliawsky, "The Impact of Black Mayors on the Black Community: The Case of New Orleans' Ernest Morial," *Review of Black Political Economy* 12 (Fall 1982): 18; Albert K. Karnig and Susan Welch, *Black Representation and Urban Policy* (Chicago: University of Chicago Press, 1980), 8–12; Chuck Stone, "Politics: Participate or Perish," *Black Collegian* (March–April 1974): 39; Zane L. Miller, *The Urbanization of Modern America: A Brief History* (New York: Harcourt Brace Jovanovich, 1973), 199–229; James B. Lane, "The Rise of Richard G. Hatcher," *Steel Shavings* 25 (1996): 82–94; Lance Trusty, "End of an Era: The 1980s in the Calumet," *Steel Shavings* 12 (1992): 5; Paul R. Eberts and Janet M. Kelly, "How Mayors Get Things Done: Community Politics and Mayors' Initiatives," *Research in Urban Policy* 1 (1985): 42. Of the four types of mayors that Eberts and Kelly describe (ceremonial-manager, caretaker–support seeker, entrepreneur-innovator, activist-executive), the last is most applicable to Hatcher.

6. Thulani Davis, "Black Mayors: Can They Make the Cities Work?" *Mother Jones,* July

1984, pp. 35–36; interviews of Hatcher (March 11, 1995), Nathaniel Coleman, a Hatcher political adviser (September 8, 1988), and Dolly Millender, a Gary city council member (January 10, 1989); James B. Lane and Ronald D. Cohen, *Gary: A Pictorial History* (Norfolk, Va.: Donning, 1983), 169. The Democratic Party in Gary had been dominated by the so-called Irish Mafia in the 1930s and 1940s and Eastern European ethnic leaders in the 1950s and early 1960s. The latter belonged to an organization called Club SAR that was similar to Muigwithania.

7. Interviews of Katie Hall, former member of Congress from Indiana's First District (September 12, 1988), and Charlotte Johnson, Hatcher's former administrative assistant (February 4, 1988); Katie Freeman, "Dancing in the Street," *Steel Shavings* 6 (1980): 29; Nelson, *Black Politics in Gary.* 384—96. Many of Konrady's supporters were concerned about the busing of black students to their neighborhood schools and believed that busing would lead to a decline in property values.

8. *Post-Tribune,* January 2, 1968; interviews of Hatcher (August 10, 1995), Charlie Brown (May 6, 1992), and Jesse Bell, Hatcher's opponent in 1979 (November 10, 1988); James Haskins, *A Piece of the Power: Four Black Mayors* (New York: Dial, 1972); Charles H. King, *Fire in My Bones* (Grand Rapids, Mich.: Eerdmans, 1983); Chuck Stone, *Black Political Power in America* (New York: Dell, 1970), 22; Joseph Alsop, *New York Times,* November 9, 1967, and various issues of the *Post-Tribune.* Charlie Brown, a teacher who became Hatcher's youth coordinator and later a state representative, recalled meeting black people from other cities who would say, "You folks in Gary really have got it together." He told me that he'd sometimes say to himself, after African-American members of the common council began feuding with Hatcher, "If they only knew."

9. Interviews of Eugene Kirkland, a Republican city council member during the 1960s (November 29, 1988); Calvin Fossett, a city planner in the Hatcher administration (December 11, 1987); Bell (November 10, 1988); and Jean Thurman, a community activist (November 27, 1988).

10. Lane, *City of the Century,* 291–300; "The Battle of the Pie," *Calumet Voice,* June 1969, p. 1; and Gloria Feignbaum, Hatcher's secretary, interview by Alex Poinsett, transcript in CRA; William E. Nelson Jr. and Philip Meranto, *Electing Black Mayors: Political Action in the Black Community* (Columbus: Ohio State University Press, 1977), 339–40; Harlan Hahn and Charles Levine, *Urban Politics: Past, Present, and Future* (New York: Longman, 1980); Edward Greer, "The Liberation of Gary, Indiana," *Trans-Action* 8 (January 1971): 30–39. Greer worked for Hatcher as a consultant during the mayor's first term. He and others were critical of Hatcher for not keeping his grassroots coalition together as a sort of pressure group, whereas others were critical of the new mayor for appointing too many supporters to city positions.

11. Marshall Frady, "Gary, Indiana: 'For God's Sake, Let's Get Ourselves Together,'" *Harper's,* August 1969, pp. 35–45; Terry N. Clark and Lorna C. Ferguson, *City Money: Political Processes, Fiscal Strain, and Retrenchment* (New York: Columbia University Press, 1983); interviews of Hatcher (June 3, 1994) and William Staehle, a city planner for mayors Katz and Hatcher (May 26, 1988).

12. Interviews of Charles Allen, city planner during the early 1970s (February 17, 1988), Charles Ruckman, city attorney in the Hatcher administration (February 5, 1988), Ray Wild, Hatcher's first press secretary (February 24, 1988), A. Martin Katz (March 12, 1991),

and Thomas Crump, a Gary politician who later ran for mayor (June 19, 1992); Gary Runner, "Will the Last One out Please Turn out the Lights?" (unpublished paper, ca. 1982), CRA. Indiana legislators discriminated against Gary in other ways, curbing the mayor's control over the police department and making the selection of area judges appointive rather than elective, as in the rest of the state.

13. Robert A. Catlin, "The Decline and Fall of Gary, Indiana," *Planning* (June 1988): 10–15.

14. Charles H. Levine and Clifford Kaufman, "Urban Conflict as a Constraint on Mayoral Leadership: Lessons from Gary and Cleveland," *American Politics Quarterly* 2 (January 1974): 78–106; "Elections: Assessing the Contests," *Time,* November 15, 1971, p. 16; interviews of Ray Wild (February 24, 1988), Charles Allen (February 17, 1988), Charlie Brown (January 28, 1989), Hatcher (June 30, 1992), Barbara Farrar, head of Emergency Referral, a disaster relief agency, during the 1970s (November 15, 1988), and Jesse Bell (November 11, 1988). Copies of many of Hatcher's national addresses, including "The Age of a New Humanity" (marking the end the DuBois Centennial Year, given at Town Hall, New York City, February 22, 1969) and "On the Shoulders of Giants" (African-American Summit Conference, New Orleans, April 21, 1989), are in the CRA.

15. Catlin, "Decline and Fall of Gary," 10–15; Edmond J. Keller, "Electoral Politics in Gary: Mayoral Performance, Organization, and the Political Economy of the Black Vote," *Urban Affairs Quarterly* 15 (September 1979): 43–63; interviews of Robert Gasser, former president of Gary National Bank (June 1, 1988), Charles Allen (February 17, 1988), and Hatcher (June 30, 1992). Some business leaders wanted the proposed civic center built by Indiana University Northwest, which was located near two expressways (the east-west Tri-state [I-80] and the north-south I-65), rather than downtown, as Hatcher wanted.

16. James E. Newman, "The Bailly Fight," *Steel Shavings* 16 (1988): 1–4; Andrew Hurley, *Environmental Inequalities: Class, Race, and Industrial Pollution in Gary, Indiana, 1945–1980* (Chapel Hill: University of North Carolina Press, 1995), 111–53; interviews of Art Daronatsy, a Hatcher political adviser (November 15, 1988) and Charles Ruckman (February 5, 1988); George Crile, "A Tax Assessor Has Many Friends," *Harper's,* November 1972, pp. 102–11.

17. Davis, "Black Mayors," 35–36; *Post-Tribune,* March 3, 1977, October 28, 1976, and April 5, 1992; interviews of Hatcher (August 9, 1995); Robert Farag, city planner (February 29, 1988); Carolyn McCready, Hatcher's press secretary during the 1980s (June 17, 1992); and Calvin Fossett (December 11, 1987).

18. *Post-Tribune,* January 2, 1980; interviews of Dozier T. Allen (June 2, 1988) and Hatcher (March 2, 1995). For more on NIS, see Lawrence E. Susskind and Sarah McKearnan, "The Evolution of Public Dispute Resolution in the United States" at <http://www.martin.uidaho.edu/SATP/neg EPDR article.htm> (June 13, 2000).

19. Interviews of Dozier T. Allen (June 2, 1988), Robert Farag (February 29, 1988), and Hatcher (March 2 and 11, 1995); *Post-Tribune,* May 6, 1981.

20. "Gary, Indiana: A City Federal Millions Haven't Helped," *U.S. News and World Report,* November 22, 1982, pp. 79–80; Catlin, "Decline and Fall of Gary"; interviews of Thomas Crump (June 19, 1992); Earline Rogers, former Gary city council member (November 17, 1988), and Jackie Shropshire, Hatcher's former law partner (January 20, 1988); Robbin Brodner, "Lockout," *Steel Shavings* 21 (1992): 65; Trusty, "End of an Era," pp. 6–7.

According to Trusty, in the 1980s the most dramatic development in the Calumet region, the industrial area southeast of and adjacent to Chicago that includes Gary, was the decline in influence of organized labor because of the precipitous loss of mill jobs from automation and "contracting-out" practices. Hatcher had staunch support from steelworker locals but supported a union for city workers only during his last months in office.

21. *Post-Tribune,* November, 30, 1984; Hatcher interview (March 11, 1995).

22. "Brash Mayor Stirs Indianapolis," *Business Week,* October 3, 1970, pp. 84–85; interviews of Richard G. Hatcher (March 11, 1995) and William Staehle (May 26, 1988). First Lady Nancy Reagan was evidently so angry at comments Hatcher made after a White House session with black leaders that she ordered that he be banned from future meetings.

23. Robert A. Catlin, *Racial Politics and Urban Planning: Gary, Indiana, 1980–1989* (Lexington: University of Kentucky Press, 1992); Trusty, "End of an Era," 6–7; interviews of Hatcher (esp. August 2, 1995); D. R. Judd, "Electoral Coalitions, Minority Mayors, and the Contradictions in the Municipal Policy Agenda," in Mark Gottdiener, ed., *Cities in Stress* (Beverly Hills, Calif.: Sage, 1986), 165; Gregory D. Squires, "Investment Policy for Economic Revitalization," *Focus* 11 (August 1983): 4–5.

24. Peter K. Eisinger, *The Politics of Displacement: Racial and Ethnic Transition in Three American Cities* (New York: Academic Press, 1980), 83; interviews of Ray Wild (February 24, 1988) and Hatcher (May 11, 1995); Alex Poinsett, "A 'Sharp' Change in Newark," *Ebony,* September 1986, pp. 128–32; Eisinger, *Politics of Displacement,* 3; Bruno Cortosio, "U.S. Black Mayors: What Next? A European Perspective," *Monthly Review* 37 (June 1985): 27; Jeffrey K. Hadden, Louis H. Masotti, and Victor Thiessen, "The Making of the Negro Mayors," *Trans-Action* 5 (January–February 1968): 21–30; Michael Preston, "Limitations of Black Urban Power: The Case of Black Mayors," in Louis H. Masotti and Robert L. Lineberry, eds., *The New Urban Politics* (Cambridge, Mass: Ballinger, 1976), 128; Davis, "Black Mayors," 30–37; W. John Moore, "From Dreamers to Doers," *National Journal,* February 13, 1988, p. 372; David R. Goldfield and Blaine A. Brownell, *Urban America: From Downtown to No Town* (Boston: Houghton Mifflin, 1979), 382–405; Pete Daniel, *Standing at the Crossroads: Southern Life in the Twentieth Century* (New York: Hill and Wang, 1986), 206. The percentage of black officeholders was higher in the South than the national average. In the North, who could have imagined in 1968, when anything seemed possible and committed politicians like Hatcher appeared to be the country's best hope for the future, how far to the right U.S. politics would move in little more than a decade?

25. Interviews of Charles Ruckman (July 6, 1988) and Thomas Barnes (May 9, 1988). See also *Post-Tribune* coverage.

26. Interviews of Earline Rogers (November 17, 1988); Alexander S. Williams, Hatcher's opponent in 1971 (May 11, 1988); Thomas Barnes (May 9, 1988); and Hatcher (March 11, 1995). See also *Post-Tribune* coverage. Several key Hatcher political operatives died during his fifth term, including former campaign manager Henry Coleman, who had played a major role in getting out the vote.

27. *Post-Tribune,* October 29, 1987, and September 24, 1989; Jean Thurman interview (October 27, 1988). Johnson is quoted in James B. Lane, "An Oral History of Richard G. Hatcher's Administration," *Steel Shavings* 21 (1992): 101.

28. David G. Nelson, research notes for "Black Reform and Federal Resources (University of Chicago thesis, 1972), CRA; various interviews of Hatcher. Hatcher was especially proud of appointing Katie Hall to succeed Adam Benjamin after the productive member of the House of Representatives died.

29. Robert A. Catlin, "Decline and Fall of Gary," 10–15.

30. Ray Wild interview (February 24, 1988).

31. Moore, "From Dreamers to Doers," 372; Hatcher interview (June 30, 1992); *Wall Street Journal,* November 8, 1976; Manning Marable, *From the Grassroots: Social and Political Essays Toward Afro-American Liberation* (Boston: South End Press, 1980), 224; James W. Button, "Southern Black Elected Officials: Impact on Socioeconomic Change," *Review of Black Political Economy* 12 (Fall 1982): 29–45; Matthew Holden Jr., "Black Politicians in the Time of 'New Urban Politics,'" *Review of Black Political Economy* 11 (Fall 1971): 68; Hatcher interview (June 30, 1992).

32. Peter K. Eisinger, "Black Employment in Municipal Jobs: The Impact of Black Political Power," *American Political Science Review* 76 (June 1982): 380–92; Phil W. Petrie, "Do Black Mayors Make a Difference?" *Black Enterprise,* July 1979, pp. 25–33; Adolph Reed Jr., "The Black Urban Regime: Structural Origins and Restraints," in Michael Peter Smith, ed., *Power, Community, and the City* (New Brunswick, N.J.: Rutgers University Press, 1988), 156, 159–60; Eberts and Kelly, "How Mayors Get Things Done," 42; Georgia A. Persons, "Reflections on Mayoral Leadership: The Impact of Changing Issues and Changing Times," *Phylon* 46 (September 1985): 205–18; Waldo Katz Fishman, Jerome Scott, Ralph C. Gomes, and Robert Newby, "The Politics of Race and Class in City Hall," *Research in Urban Sociology* 1 (1989): 135–77; interviews of Hatcher.

Hatcher groused at the "reach-out-to-the-suburbs" policies of his successor, Thomas Barnes, and made an ill-advised, unsuccessful effort to unseat him in 1991. While Barnes thought Gary's future lay in developing the lakeshore for tourism and bringing in lakefront casinos, Hatcher continued to insist that the only real boost in decent-paying jobs would come from expanding the city's municipal airport and transforming it into the Chicago area's third major facility. Even then, Hatcher believed, African Americans would not share fully in the benefits that an airport would bring unless they remained vigilant in guarding their civil rights.

33. Dempsey J. Travis, *An Autobiography of Black Politics* (Chicago: Urban Research Institute, 1987); interviews of Tom Knightley, a former *Post-Tribune* reporter (February 15, 1990) and Hatcher (esp. June 30, 1992); L. H. Whittemore, *Together: A Reporter's Journey into the New Black Politics* (New York: Morrow, 1971). Hatcher used the words *unbought* and *unbossed* in his 1971 reelection campaign. They stemmed from an autobiography by U.S. Rep. Shirley Chisholm of New York entitled *The Good Fight* (New York: Harper and Row, 1973).

3.   Carl Stokes: Mayor of Cleveland

LEONARD N. MOORE

ON NOVEMBER 7, 1967, Carl B. Stokes was elected mayor of Cleveland, Ohio, becoming, with Richard Hatcher of Gary, the first black mayors of major U.S. cities in the twentieth century. While Stokes's election symbolized the emergence of black power in U.S. politics, his four-year tenure was beset with racial and political problems. In particular, conservative whites and middle-class blacks made it difficult for him to achieve his political goals of aiding the city's black poor, who had suffered from years of poor housing, employment discrimination, inadequate educational opportunities, and unfair police protection. As one of the nation's first big-city black mayors, he was also the first to experience the limits of black power.

* * *

Born in Cleveland on June 21, 1927, Carl Burton Stokes was the second son of Charles and Louise Stokes. Tragedy soon struck the Stokes family when Charles died unexpectedly in 1929, leaving Louise to care for her two sons, Carl and Louis. To support her family Louise Stokes found work as a domestic. As with the majority of the city's black residents, the Stokeses were poor. "We lived in a rickety ol' two family house," Carl Stokes remembered. "We covered rat holes with the tops of tin cans. The front steps always needed fixing, one of them always seemed to be missing. The coal stove kept the living room warm, we used heated bricks and an old flatiron wrapped in flannel to keep warm in the back room, the three of us shared one bedroom." Their housing conditions improved in 1938 when they were one of the fortunate families to secure an apartment in Outhwaite Estates, the nation's first federally funded housing project. For the Stokes boys Outhwaite was a joy because it contained "a sink with hot and cold running water and an actual refrigerator."[1]

Stokes got his first look at politics while working with the Young Progressives, a youth organization affiliated with Henry Wallace's Progressive Party. Stokes's political indoctrination came in the summer of 1949 when he worked for the long-time civil rights activist John O. Holly, who had gained popularity in the 1930s when he led the Future Outlook League "in launching several 'don't buy where you can't work' campaigns." As Holly's chauffeur, Stokes often heard him speak of the need for a black political base. Aided by Holly's influence, Stokes subsequently found work as a state liquor agent, a job in which he witnessed first hand the dual standard of law enforcement. His experience with this agency led him to acquire a bachelor of law degree from the University of Minnesota, and shortly thereafter he enrolled in Cleveland-Marshall Law School in downtown Cleveland.

While pursuing his law degree, he worked full time as a probation officer and realized that he had an obligation to help the less fortunate. "The job as a probation officer enlarged my sense of social commitment and enraged me. . . . That job brought me again and again into contact with people who were not making it, people whose spirits were broken by oppression, filth, and squalor," Stokes later recalled. "I was supposed to be their advocate and guide, but I began to see that they needed advocates at the highest level of government." After graduating from law school, he took a position as an assistant prosecutor as he set his sights on a political career.[2]

* * *

By 1950 Cleveland's black population stood at approximately 147,000, or 20 percent of the city's population. Black migrants continued to flood in from the South in search of better living conditions, stretching the geographical boundaries of the black community. With their numbers steadily increasing, black voters began to elect African Americans to seats on the city council. In 1950 four African Americans sat on Cleveland's twenty-two-person city council, and by 1957 seven held seats, more than any other city in the country. But despite holding a third of the seats on the council, black representatives rarely, if ever, acted as a unified body. Instead, many eschewed race-based politics in favor of patronage.[3]

Stokes began in politics as a campaign manager. In the 1957 Cleveland City Council elections he successfully chaired Lowell Henry's campaign to defeat the long-time Jewish incumbent, Joseph Horowitz. After that election Stokes increased his civic and political involvement by becoming active in the Cleveland Urban League, the local NAACP, the County Federated Democrats of

Ohio, and the Young Democrats. In these settings he became acquainted with the city's political and business elite. In 1958 he sought a seat in the Ohio Senate, but with virtually no money and little name recognition he was soundly defeated in his bid to become the first black Democrat of the modern era to sit in the Ohio state legislature. Stokes, in fact, had not planned to win this race. Rather, the campaign was part of the political groundwork he believed he needed to lay. Two years later he ran for state representative, only to lose again after a lengthy and controversial recount.[4]

As conditions continued to worsen for black Clevelanders in the 1960s, Stokes resigned his position with the prosecutor's office to concentrate full time on building a black power base. By 1960 the majority of Cleveland's 250,000 black residents lived in the Central/Hough area, where 21 percent of all black-occupied housing was either dilapidated or substandard and where the median income of African Americans was roughly 65 percent that of local whites. Unemployment in Central/Hough stood at 17.6 percent largely as a result of deindustrialization. Between 1953 and 1963 approximately eighty thousand blue-collar jobs disappeared from the central city, only to be replaced with twenty thousand white-collar positions. As a staunch Democrat, Stokes believed that government had an obligation to assist the less fortunate. When he again ran for the statehouse in 1962, Stokes stressed the need for increased educational opportunities and for a state minimum wage. The voters responded by making him the first black Democrat to sit in the Ohio legislature.[5]

During the years 1963 and 1964 black residents protested the worsening housing and employment conditions in the city and conducted a nine-month protest against labor union discrimination and segregated schooling. Marches, rallies, sit-ins, and riots characterized the campaign. Mayor Ralph Locher exacerbated tensions by refusing to listen to the demands from the black community. Because of Locher's neglect, Stokes decided to enter the mayor's race in 1965.

Despite criticism of his administration, Locher announced that he would seek another term as the city's Democratic mayor. Republicans meanwhile had nominated Ralph Perk Jr. as their mayoral candidate. Because black Cleveland represented only 37 percent of the city's population, Stokes knew that to win he needed a three-way race, so he filed as an independent. Moreover, by running as an independent, Stokes became more visible in the black community. Most African Americans were ready for a change, having tired of the patron-client relationship that had governed black politics for decades.

Operating on a shoestring budget of $44,000, Stokes waged primarily a grassroots campaign. He spent more than 90 percent of his time on the black

East Side, stressing urban renewal, housing, improved city services, and fair employment. Although the major newspapers ignored Stokes during the primary campaign, his efforts received a tremendous boost when Martin Luther King Jr. made Cleveland the focal point of a 1965 voter registration drive. The effort by King to get out the black vote was critical, because eight of the city's ten black city council members refused to support Stokes. Many black council members figured that Stokes did not have a chance to win.[6]

In soliciting white votes Stokes faced two obstacles: the traditional racism of white ethnics and backlash from civil rights activity. Stokes placated the fears of white ethnics by adopting a race-neutral posture: "I want to get the Negro question out of the way, then we can talk about issues. My election would not mean a Negro takeover, it would not mean the establishment of a Negro cabinet. My election would mean that the mayor just happened to come from the Negro group." Stokes's use of separate campaign strategies in the black and white communities became a model for subsequent black candidates. He placated white fears by downplaying race while drawing upon black support by campaigning as a brother.[7]

Although black voters turned out in record numbers and Stokes received 85.4 percent of their vote, he polled badly in white areas, receiving only 5 percent of the white vote. Locher edged out Stokes by 2,548 votes. Stokes nonetheless considered his campaign to have been a moral victory.

Local developments soon propelled Stokes into the national spotlight. The U.S. Commission on Civil Rights visited Cleveland in April 1966 to review the city's racial problems. Throughout four days of hearings black residents told harrowing tales of police brutality, school segregation, employment discrimination, and poor housing. In July racial tensions in Hough erupted in four days of riots, millions of dollars in property damage, numerous casualties, and four fatalities. Officials of the Cleveland chapter of the Congress of Racial Equality (CORE) blamed city officials who failed to "meaningfully address themselves to the basic problems that confront the black community." Locher came under fire from the black community for failing to address its needs, and his credibility took a further blow in the white community when Robert Weaver, secretary of the U.S. Department of Housing and Urban Development (HUD) cut off Cleveland's urban renewal dollars because of the city's incompetence in completing projects. Weaver also withdrew a previously committed grant of $10 million, and he rejected an application for Model Cities money because it was incomplete.[8]

As the 1967 mayoral primary grew closer, Locher, despite his party's wishes, announced that he would seek another term. Seth Taft emerged as the GOP candidate. Stokes considered running as an independent again but decided instead to run as a Democrat. He chose this course for two reasons: Taft had told him that he would withdraw from the race rather than be used as a tool to split the white vote, and Stokes received a commitment for support from the national Democratic Party, which lacked faith in Locher yet wanted Cleveland to remain in Democratic hands.[9]

In the early days of the campaign Stokes was denied local party support, so he was once again forced to wage a grassroots effort. He also won the business community's support by stressing that he was the only candidate who could prevent another outbreak of racial violence. Many members of the business community were horrified by the damage from the Hough riot and wanted a mayor who could keep the black community from rioting again. Stokes also received assistance from local civil rights organizations. In July the NAACP, Cleveland Urban League, CORE, and the Southern Christian Leadership Conference launched voter registration drives on the East Side, registering in all more than fifty thousand black voters, many of whom who had been dropped from voting registers as a result of confusing election laws. These efforts also energized the black community to get behind Stokes's campaign.[10]

In contrast to his 1965 effort, Stokes spent much of his time in white areas, because he recognized that he needed a larger portion of the white vote if he hoped to win. In meetings with business leaders he emphasized that Cleveland's racial problems created an unhealthy business environment. The Cleveland business community liked Stokes's moderate views and agreed to support him, but the rest of the city's white population did not. Indeed, on several occasions during the campaign Stokes's workers were assaulted while canvassing in white neighborhoods, his West Side headquarters were vandalized, and one of his security men was shot at while guarding the same West Side office.[11]

Despite efforts of party leaders to derail his candidacy by alleging that Stokes's election would result in Martin Luther King Jr.'s running the city, Stokes defeated Locher by an 18,000-vote margin in the Democratic primary. The key to Stokes's victory was support from 15 percent of the white voters and his virtual sweep of the black vote. Locher had been a major hurdle, but Stokes's road had not become easy, for he now faced Taft in the general election.[12]

Taft was a wealthy suburbanite whose only previous political experience had come when he served as mayor of the wealthy suburb of Pepper Pike. He had little knowledge of inner-city conditions, and the Republican Party had been relegated to second-party standing in Cleveland. Stokes's defeat of Locher, however, changed the election dynamics. Working-class whites, for example, immediately threw their support to Taft, solely because he was white. Stokes quickly realized that he was in for a tough fight and that he had to attract some white support to defeat Taft. To prevent the desertion of more white Democrats, Stokes stressed several themes: as the Democratic nominee, he was entitled to their support; he would be a mayor of all the people; and his inner-city background and political experience made him the most qualified candidate. Although Stokes received little support from the county Democratic Party, he obtained a substantial boost when Vice President Hubert H. Humphrey and John Bailey, chair of the Democratic National Committee, openly endorsed him.[13]

As the campaign entered the final weeks, Stokes and Taft held three televised debates in which Stokes sought to allay concerns of white voters by laying out his plans for a responsive city hall, reorganization of the police department, new recreation centers, and a revived urban renewal program. Stokes also used the debates to stress Taft's unfamiliarity with the plight of the poor and working class. Taft had no idea, Stokes insisted, what it meant to be "hungry, without shoes, without clothes," or for his children to go hungry. Although Stokes respected Taft's "intellect and integrity," he wondered whether voters were willing to "entrust the problem of finding a job to a person who never knew the shock of the unemployment line in his own life or in his family."[14]

On November 7, 1967, Carl Stokes narrowly defeated Taft, 129,396 to 127,717. Stokes captured virtually all the black vote, but he also won critical support from middle-class whites and business people that ensured his victory. For Cleveland's black poor Stokes's victory had symbolic meaning. These residents felt they now had one of their own in Cleveland City Hall. As twenty-year-old Hough resident Billy Henson remarked: "Stokes understands our problems. He lived with us. He knows what the black man thinks. Maybe he'll open up opportunities for us." Fifteen-year-old Debbie Smith saw a personal message in Stokes's victory: "Stokes makes Negroes proud, makes us want to work harder." Norris Bunch, a ninth grader, was personally inspired: "I know he was a high school dropout . . . but he finished and went on to college. If he can make good, why can't I?"[15]

* * *

After campaigning so hard to get elected, Stokes acknowledged that he had no idea what to do once he took office. "We went into those sessions [after the election] with wild-eyed dreams of the reforms we would wreak on this corrupt machine, only to discover that we didn't even know where some of the buttons were!" Stokes later confessed that his team did not even know where some of the city departments were housed.[16]

In the weeks after the election Stokes appointed his cabinet with careful thought to the concerns of his supporters and to racial divisions in Cleveland. Joseph McManamon and Michael Blackwell, both white, became safety director and police chief, respectively, to allay white concerns about black governance. But Stokes also named three African Americans to important posts. Municipal Judge Paul White was named law director (city attorney); Ralph Tyler was picked to head city services; and Richard Green of Boston was appointed to lead the city's Department of Community Development. By appointing an interracial cabinet, Stokes sought to establish a broad biracial coalition, and he also wanted to reinforce his election promise that a Stokes victory would not mean a black takeover.[17]

Stokes recognized from the beginning that his administration would be under intense public scrutiny. "We had so much to learn, we had to find people to take the key jobs, and we had to do it right. Everything had to be right because everything we did was in the limelight. Celebrity is a two-edged sword." Stokes also felt enormous pressure to be a "credit to my race. That meant I had to be more witty, more thorough, than any other mayor in the country. Every move had to be exciting and a confirmation of everyone's confidence in me. I was their boy."[18]

Local journalists looked for any hint of mismanagement or scandal, and early on they found one. While Stokes was vacationing in the Caribbean during the early part of January 1968, the *Cleveland Press* revealed that Geraldine Williams, one of Stokes's executive assistants and a long-time supporter, was active in the business affairs of an illegal after-hours nightclub. Although Williams denied her involvement, her affiliation was confirmed when her signature was found on the state liquor permit, club minutes, and canceled checks. Stokes was incensed, particularly because he had questioned her about her relationship with the club before appointing her. Because Stokes was out of the city when the story broke, he and his aides did not provide an immediate response. When Stokes was informed, he dismissed Williams immediately. "The imperatives of this administration require maximum integrity and the public must be able to maintain confidence at all times in those administering their efforts," Stokes remarked. A number of black supporters felt Stokes had overreacted, however, and criticized the mayor for not allowing Williams a hearing.[19]

Stokes faced more serious problems with the Cleveland Police Department. Stokes told McManamon and Blackwell that he wanted them to reorganize the department with the goal of integrating select units, placing black officers in white areas, and placing more patrol officers on the streets. McManamon and Blackwell delegated the responsibility to their subordinates, who deliberately made the transfers as "awkward, embarrassing, and infuriating to the police as possible," with the obvious intent of embarrassing Stokes. Despite the transfer fiasco, the reorganization was well received in the black community. White officers responded to the reorganization with the blue flu. Black Clevelanders, however, were especially pleased that patrol officers were ordered to stop wearing their white helmets, which created a Gestapo-like atmosphere.[20]

In late February 1968 Stokes got some good news when Weaver, the HUD secretary, lifted the freeze on Cleveland's urban renewal funds. Stokes had appealed to Weaver to restore the city's funding after appointing the nationally known Green to chair the community development department. The local media, area residents, and city council applauded Stokes's ability to get the money released. The *Plain Dealer* characterized HUD's reversal as a triumph for Stokes and a victory for the City of Cleveland. Equally laudatory was the black weekly, the *Call and Post,* which echoed many of the same sentiments under the headline, "Stokes Makes Good on Campaign Promise." The mayor announced that the money would go toward building three hundred housing units for low-income Hough residents, and he was confident that a new era in Hough was underway. "Urban renewal, under my administration, is going to be what the people want," Stokes proclaimed, "it's going to make this and other neighborhoods better places to live." Stokes's success in getting the HUD money released earned him the influential support of the business community, which had been hit hard by former mayor Locher's political ineptness. Although some members of the business community were still unsure of Stokes's ability to lead, they all gave him credit for restoring millions of dollars to Cleveland's economic development efforts.[21]

Just as Stokes's popularity was increasing, he was faced with his first potential crisis that April when Martin Luther King was assassinated. Violence erupted throughout the country following the announcement of King's death. In all, 110 cities experienced rioting that left thirty-nine dead and millions of dollars in property damage. Cleveland was spared the violence, however, because of Stokes. He was attending a program at Baldwin-Wallace College on the city's far West Side when he learned of King's death. He immediately left the campus and headed for local TV stations to urge that the public remain calm. "I appeal to all Clevelanders to do honor to the memory of MLK by reacting to this tragic loss in the peaceful manner in which he lived." Although Stokes assured black youth that he understood the bitterness they were expressing, he told them that a violent reaction would be an injustice to King.

Instead of sending the predominantly white police department into the black community to keep the peace, he assembled an all-black patrol made up of ministers, black nationalists, community leaders, and members of his cabinet to patrol the tense areas. Riding in city vehicles, members of the patrol consistently told black youths to "keep it cool." Most responded by telling patrol members, "We will." Stokes's decision to keep the police out was a controversial one. He knew the historic relationship between the department and the black community, and he realized that on many occasions Cleveland's police often exacerbated tensions rather than quelling them.[22]

The local media, civic leaders, and citizens all cheered Stokes's success in keeping Cleveland calm. The *Plain Dealer*'s editorial typified the white perspective. Under the headline, "Good Work by City Leaders," the editors attributed Stokes's success to his ability to "communicate" to the black poor. Although Stokes was able to prevent rioting, the black community still felt much frustration over King's death. In response, Stokes gave all nonessential employees a half-day off in observance of "black Tuesday."[23]

Days after King's assassination business leaders flooded Stokes with calls. They wanted to know how they could help maintain racial peace. Stokes told them that, because of the conditions in the inner city, the slightest incident could trigger a riot. They told him to come up with a plan, and they would support it. At an April 12 meeting with business leaders Stokes called for new program entitled "Cleveland Now!" and asked them for $10 million to create eleven thousand jobs for the hard-core unemployed.[24]

Cleveland Now! subsequently became a $1.5 billion package that focused on housing and job creation over a ten-year period. The short-range goals called for spending $177 million in the first year to attack the major problems in six areas—employment, youth resources, health and welfare, neighborhood rehabilitation, economic revitalization, and city planning. The funds were to be a mixture of city, state, federal, and private contributions. Cleveland Now! would undertake to train and employ at least eleven thousand full- and part-time workers. The employment aspect was perhaps the most critical, followed by housing. Despite a countywide unemployment rate of 2.45 percent, one of the lowest in the country, the inner-city jobless rate was 15.5 percent. The new jobs were to be in both the private and public sectors; some would be part time and seasonal positions. The Aim-Jobs program of the Council for Economic Opportunities in Greater Cleveland was scheduled to create four thousand jobs, and the National Alliance of Businessmen signed up to supply another four thousand. Additionally, the job-training program of the city, in conjunction with the Cleveland Urban League, promised eighteen hundred jobs, and the U.S. Department of Labor's Development and Training Administration pledged twenty-five hundred positions. For the city's youth, Cleveland Now! would oversee a $750,000 program that would provide a wide array of programs, such as neighborhood clean-ups, work training, cultural enrichment, education, and recreation. Stokes also planned to establish ten multiservice health centers and ten day-care centers.[25]

Under Cleveland Now! the City Planning Commission would receive $1.75 million in city and federal funds to create a policy planning and program evaluation center to be used to avoid duplicating and/or overlapping projects. The program earmarked $61 million for economic revitalization to accelerate the existing urban renewal projects, with particular emphasis on downtown development. The greatest expenditure, $86 million, was geared for neighborhood rehabilitation, largely to make available forty-six hundred new and rehabilitated housing units throughout the city for low-income families. Of that amount, $20 million was to be used for housing inspection, while $10 million was to be set aside for homeownership programs. Money was also set aside for expanding small business opportunities.[26]

To market the program Stokes used radio and television ads, billboards, bumper stickers, pennants, and other gimmicks to grab people's attention. The reaction to Cleveland Now! was extremely positive—people had a sense that the city was at last moving forward. James Terrell, a part-time construction worker, felt that Cleveland Now! was "a wonderful program . . . we should of had someone like Mayor Stokes here years ago." Hough resident Arthur Danley was equally excited, saying Stokes was "the best damn mayor Cleveland ever had." Even suburban whites were excited about the program. In the days after the announcement private donations poured in from all corners of the city. Businesses, corporations, civic leaders, and even students contributed to the Cleveland Now! fund. By May 15, less than two weeks after the program was announced, Stokes had raised more than $11 million, which immediately triggered the release of $74.8 million in federal funds.[27]

The private money raised by Cleveland Now! allowed Stokes to use his discretion in its distribution. Because it was not tax money, the city council had little say in how the money would be used. Stokes was in complete charge of all disbursements. With his success in getting HUD funding restored, his ability to keep the peace after King's assassination, and the establishment of Cleveland Now! Stokes had emerged as one of the most popular politicians in the country. He was making this experiment in black urban governance look easy.

Stokes's popularity, however, came to an end on July 23, 1968, with the crazed actions of Fred "Ahmed" Evans.

* * *

Fred Evans, who was born in Greenville, South Carolina, moved to Cleveland with his family in the mid-1930s. After serving in the Korean War, he became concerned about the endless cycle of poverty and deprivation in the black community. "In 1964 I visited the headquarters of the Black Nationalists in Harlem and became a member," he later recalled. "Upon my return to Cleveland I became a full-time member of an organization known as the Black Nationalists of New Libya. By this time I had become Ahmed. I wasn't Fred anymore." By 1966 Evans was the leader of this small clique and gave numerous lectures on African culture and history. His lectures were often laced with a critique of the traditional black leadership class and the need for black self-determination. Evans also gained headlines for his predictions—some claimed his advocating—of racial violence. "I predicted that there would be trouble in Cleveland. I said it would happen in the months of June or July, and the Hough riots happened in July. I could do this through the studies I had taken in astrology," he said.[28]

By expounding the tenets of black nationalism and predicting race wars, Evans came under close police surveillance. In Evans's eyes Cleveland police began to harass him as soon as he gained a foothold with local youth. "This was when the police began to raid my apartment. They came to ask questions at first, then they came with a sledgehammer and wrecked the joint. They came in numbers, sometimes forty or fifty. They had various weapons, submachine guns and sometimes grenades. I heard once they brought a bazooka, but I didn't see it. We were always under surveillance."[29]

On Monday, July 22, police officials received an anonymous tip that Evans and his followers had gone to Detroit and Pittsburgh to pick up a cache of weapons in preparation for a July 23 showdown with police. Stokes was out of town that Tuesday and not due back until later that night, leaving the newly appointed law director, Clarence James, an African American, in charge (Paul White had resigned). James and police officials, including McManamon and Blackwell, met and decided the department would set up roving surveillance in front of Evans's apartment and that George Forbes, a city council member, and Walter Beach, a member of Stokes's cabinet, would go to Evans's place to monitor the situation. Both were African American.

When Forbes and Beach arrived at Evans's apartment, they noticed that the police were parked and had not set up the roving surveillance. Evans summoned Forbes and Beach to his backyard, where he expressed his displeasure with the police presence. Forbes and Beach then tried to assure him that everything would be fine. As Forbes and Beach were leaving, Evans told them, "Tell the big brother (Stokes) downtown everything will be alright." Forbes and Beach left Evans's around 8:05 P.M. under the impression that there would be no trouble, and they relayed their thoughts to Mayor Stokes, who had just returned to the city. They were wrong.[30]

At 8:30 P.M. Evans and his followers came out of the apartment complex firing weapons at two tow-truck operators whom they misidentified as police officers. As police rushed to the scene, they were fired upon as well. By 8:40 P.M. three white police officers and two New Libya members were dead. Sam Levy, a sergeant who was one of the first officers to arrive, recalled the shootings. "As I started up the driveway . . . I was hit . . . they kept shooting and I was hit again. They shot at anybody who moved." By 9:30 P.M. the shooting had stopped but not before two more had died, another white officer and another member of New Libya. Evans was captured at 12:24 A.M. As he was being placed in the patrol car, he was informed that three of his followers had been killed. His response: "They died for a worthy cause."[31]

Near Evans's apartment was the popular Lakeview Tavern, and as the shootings occurred, several patrons were trapped inside. Louise Brown, twenty-one, was one of several women in the tavern when police came in and sexually assaulted her. "The policeman ripped my clothes off me, he felt me in between my privacy, in between my legs," she said. Her friend, Jean Grisby, suffered a similar fate as two officers "searched" her by putting their hands up her skirt. John Pegues was shot at point-blank range as the police fired shots and tear gas into the tavern, and Arthur Radan was beaten with a shotgun while the police yelled, "We're going to kill this black motherfucker." Also brutally beaten was Trenton Irwin, who suffered several cracked ribs before he was knocked unconscious.[32] Despite the widespread brutality by police, not a single officer was ever indicted.

The police carnage continued in the vicinity of the shootings as the night progressed. The police shot at Andrew Wright as he drove through the area, and Albert Forrest had to dodge police bullets as he attempted to aid a wounded civilian. "One of them jammed a shotgun in my ribs and told me he was going to blow my guts out and the police behind him came across his shoulder with his rifle butt and jammed me in my face and knocked me down," he told an interviewer from the American Civil Liberties Union.[33]

Black youth sought revenge against police. Throughout the night they attacked white property, white motorists, and white police officers. Twenty-one-year-old Officer Herbert Reed was pulled from his patrol car and severely beaten as he attempted to observe the rioting. Blocks away, a new police cruiser went up in flames. By morning the casualty and arrest list was heavy. With black youths and white police officers reacting violently, all eyes turned to Mayor Stokes, who had assured the public that he could maintain racial peace.[34]

After conferring with Safety Director McManamon and Police Chief Blackwell, Stokes decided to bring in the national guard temporarily to gain control of the situation. The next morning Stokes met with more than one hundred leaders from the black community and solicited their advice. "What shall we do?" he asked. Although no consensus was reached, Stokes decided to pull the police and national guard out and let black community leaders patrol the area, just as he had done after King's assassination. Stokes instructed the national guard to cordon off the riot-torn area, and he stationed white officers along the perimeter. They were not allowed to enter the area: only black police officers and community leaders could do so. "The problem is in the black community and the black community will handle it," Stokes told reporters.[35] When Stokes announced his plans, the police rank-and-file expressed outrage by hurling racial slurs at the mayor over the police radio.

The five-hundred-person peace patrol gradually eased tensions, but significant looting and property damage continued. While Stokes expressed disappointment at the looting, he nonetheless considered the decision to pull out a success because there were no additional fatalities. The black community applauded Stokes's actions, but the police and large segments of the white community did not approve of his decision to remove white officers from the area. As a result of continued criticisms by the police department, Stokes disbanded the black peace patrol and allowed white officers back in to the area. With the help of the national guard, things returned to normal on Saturday, July 27.[36]

Days after the tragedy Stokes's credibility suffered a severe blow when it was revealed that Ahmed Evans had received a $10,000 grant from Cleveland Now! to open a community center and that he had used the money to buy the weapons that were used in the shoot-out. Stokes defended his decision to approve the grant to Evans: "What is the alternative to such a grant? Do you leave a man like Evans free to float in the community, to justify his resentments and nourish hatreds? Do you leave him in isolation, or do you try by any means at your disposal to reach him? It seems to me that you have no alternative but to embrace the socially dispossessed person, especially when he is a leader."[37]

While Stokes attempted to justify his actions, donations to Cleveland Now! dried up. "Many businessmen who had made pledges to the Cleveland Now! program quietly turned their backs, and we could see there would be no support for its continuance," wrote Stokes in his memoir.[38]

As Stokes's troubles mounted locally, he nevertheless remained popular nationally. He delivered the keynote address at the annual meeting of the American Federation of Teachers, where he was warmly received, and he gave the nominating speech for Hubert H. Humphrey at the 1968 Democratic National Convention. As his first year in office came to a close, Stokes could look back with both pride and disappointment, but he realized that, in the aftermath of the Ahmed Evans tragedy, he was in for the political fight of his life.

* * *

As Stokes began his second year in office, he undertook a plan for scattered-site public housing. To alleviate the plight of the black poor, who were largely confined to the slum areas of Hough, Stokes planned to build a public housing development of 274 single-family homes in the black middle-class community of Lee-Seville. The plans called for single-family homes on large lots in a variety of designs. The homes were to be similar to those found throughout the Lee-Seville community and that often sold for $20,000 (about $100,000 today). Scattered-site housing was the brainchild of the new Cuyahoga Metropolitan Housing Authority (CMHA) director, Irving Kriegsfeld. Although the subdivision was to be built on CMHA land, Stokes and the housing authority needed the approval of the city council to make the necessary street improvements. Plans for the subdivision were moving along until Clarence Thompson and George White, the African-American council members who represented the Lee-Seville area, began voicing opposition. Thompson and White objected to the project for two reasons: first, that city services could not handle the increased population, and second, that lower-income blacks should not rely on government to improve their situation. At an emotional city council meeting White argued, "We don't have adequate schools now; we don't have adequate recreation now; we don't have adequate police now; we don't have adequate police protection now." Stokes informed the council that the city would improve schools, recreation, and police protection, but Thompson and White remained unconvinced.[39]

Stokes resorted to heavy-handed politics to win support for his project, stating publicly that two blacks on Cleveland City Council were unconcerned about the welfare of the black poor. The controversy became ugly when Stokes labeled opponents of the project "black bigots." He explained: "If you permit bigoted black middle-class persons with a bigoted black public official representing them to stop the utilization of unused land for housing . . . you have failed to support everything we want to do with housing in this city and you will have struck a blow against expanding opportunities for all persons to live anywhere in the city and in the greater community." Thompson was incensed: "We are concerned about the poor in our city! How many of us have been poor? Many have come from farms. I never lived in metro housing. My

dad was a farmer. We have struggled hard for what we have attained." A segment of Thompson's constituents agreed. "I had to work fourteen hours a
day and seven days a week to earn a down payment on my house, why should
I say 'come on Charlie you can have it all for free,'" one voter told the *New
York Times*.[40]

Stokes became discouraged when he considered the long-term effects of
the opposition to Lee-Seville. While speaking about the controversy at Yale
University, Stokes warned that "if trouble comes to Cleveland this summer
it could well be over city council's failure to approve housing for the Lee-
Seville area." The mayor was also concerned about the future of scattered-
site public housing in general. "If we can't get council's approval for the Lee-
Seville project . . . then . . . we can't go to the suburbs with such a plan if we
can't demonstrate we can do the same thing in Cleveland."[41]

At a council meeting on June 2 supporters of the development greeted city
council members outside city hall and demanded hearings on the legislation.
But the Thompson-White forces stood firm. The next council session was
preceded by a "Citizens' Rally for Lee-Seville Housing" on the grounds of
city hall. During this session Stokes's supporters on council took dead aim
at Thompson and James Stanton, the city council president. "The legislation
is not unreasonable. If the people of Lee-Seville don't want it, we do in our
neighborhood," said James Bell, another member of the council. He went on
to say that he was "concerned and sorry that such an important service to
the people of Cleveland has been dropped into a struggle for power."[42]

At the last city council meeting before the summer recess, the city council
voted 20-13 not to bring the legislation out of committee. Stokes voiced his
displeasure: "Ladies and Gentlemen of council, the issue of public housing
in Lee-Seville is entirely up to you. My responsibility as mayor has been
fulfilled and while I am open to suggestions about what can be done, I must
state candidly that I am at a loss to know what it could be." Stokes could
readily understand white opposition to his housing agenda, but he was surprised at the fighting among his supporters. The class dimensions of this
conflict spoke directly to the limits of black political power.[43]

The rejection of Stokes's housing reform proposal paralleled his struggles
to reform the police department. After reorganizing the department and
securing the resignation of Chief Blackwell in October 1968 for insubordi-
nation, the mayor sought to increase promotions for black officers and place
more African Americans on the force. Historically, blacks had been grossly
underrepresented. Although black Clevelanders accounted for approximately
37 percent of the city's population, they held only 5 percent of the positions
on the police force. Likewise, black officers filled less than 1 percent of the

administrative positions. Shortly after taking office Stokes changed the make-up of the five-person Civil Service Commission, the city agency in charge of all testing of city personnel. The first order of business for the Stokes-dominated commission was to change the nature of police examinations. For the promotional exam applicants were now required to read twenty-five books dealing with police-community relations. Titles included Ralph Ellison's *Invisible Man* and *Dark Ghetto* by Kenneth Clark. In addition, the commission added an interview phase. These new testing procedures were drastically different; previously, exams simply measured a candidate's knowledge of particular details of departmental rules and regulations. When white officers received word of the new procedures, they responded angrily. "Our men are virtually in a state of shock due to city hall intervention with the civil service examinations," a representative of the Fraternal Order of Police told the *Plain Dealer*. "We understand there will be oral interviews given too, we are going to stop this by law." Continued complaints forced the commission to postpone the test twice, and when it was finally administered, Police Chief Patrick Gerity (who replaced Blackwell after Stokes asked Blackwell to resign) nullified it on the ground that proper security measures were not maintained. In fact, Gerity nullified the results because many white officers had done poorly.[44]

Stokes also took measures to add more blacks to the department. He approved a Cleveland Now! grant of $15,600 to help the local NAACP conduct a police recruitment campaign and to help black applicants prepare for the exam. The white-dominated Fraternal Order of Police (FOP) was outraged by Stokes's actions, and many white officers accused Stokes of lowering the standards in order to get more blacks on the force.[45]

As a result of continued complaints by the white rank-and-file of the police department, Visiting Judge Thomas Mitchell ordered the grand jury to look into alleged cheating on the promotional exam and testing irregularities in the first patrol officers' exam given on October 19. The grand jury report found that there were "security leaks" with the promotional test and that a copy of the exam had been found "folded and coffee-stained on the exam room floor." It labeled this test "the greatest tragedy and misuse of manpower and public funds . . . that any Grand Jury could ever expect to find." The grand jury was equally critical of the administration of the patrol officers' exam. The report stated that the NAACP recruits were given "unfair advantages" by being allowed to register after the deadline and by being granted fee waivers. It also stated that the practice test given at the NAACP training site was the exact exam given on October 19 and that the psychologists who drafted the actual test were also instructors at the NAACP training site. In closing, the report stated that the responsibility for correcting the damage was the mayor's.[46]

The county grand jury also issued interim indictments against Civil Service Commission members Jay White and Charles Butts, both Stokes appointees, on felony charges of perjury. They were also charged with destroying commission records. The report further implied that the two commission members had sold copies of the two exams. They resigned immediately and later pleaded guilty to misdemeanor charges of destroying records in exchange for dismissal of the perjury charges. Despite the indictments, Stokes defended his recruitment efforts and the role of the NAACP and the role of the NAACP in coaching black candidates for the exam. He pointed out that there was no "direct evidence presented of any wrongdoing" by the recruiters. He also criticized the grand jury for failing to investigate the role of white police officers in acquiring the promotional tests. But Stokes was particularly upset with his appointees, noting that when the blacks "I had brought into city hall let themselves get mixed up in things like this I would sit and think . . . here I am trying to put something together for all of us and they go and get involved in something like this. I would feel so helpless." Although Stokes was never implicated in the scandal, he had made the appointments and launched the initiative to get more black police officers and police administrators. In the eyes of white Clevelanders, Stokes was a man who would go to any lengths to place blacks on the police force. To make matters worse, Stokes now had to gear up for a reelection bid.[47]

* * *

After a rocky first term, Stokes found himself struggling in his reelection bid in the fall of 1969. In the Democratic primary he soundly defeated the local George Wallace imitator, Robert Kelly, who failed to attract voters to his law-and-order campaign. The general election promised to be more difficult, because Stokes faced the more experienced county auditor, Ralph Perk, the Republican candidate. Throughout the campaign Stokes stressed the accomplishments of his first term: the establishment of a city health department; the revitalization of the community development department; new city equipment; new housing for the poor; and a new department of human resources and economic development. Perk developed his campaign around the themes of law and order and fiscal mismanagement. "Here in the city of Cleveland our streets are so unsafe that residents . . . are afraid to come out at night . . . the streets are so unsafe that people are even afraid when they come out in the daytime," Perk declared. Perk also hit hard at Stokes's expenditures for social programs. On several occasions he implied that city hall was "doubling as a welfare office." He said nothing about housing, employment, or health and welfare.[48]

Although Stokes was certain that he had the black vote, he sought to retain as much support among white moderates as possible. During the campaign he spent much of his time on the white West Side, where he was able to convince white voters of three things: that despite the Evans tragedy, his administration could control black unrest; that his administration had created a positive environment for local business; and that he needed two more years to implement his programs. One businessman noted, "He should be allowed to pursue his programs . . . now that he has more knowledge of the job, of the city, and of his mistakes." The support of white moderates and the business community was instrumental in Stokes's victory. He defeated Perk by nearly 4,000 votes, a margin larger than in his 1967 election.[49]

What made Stokes's reelection so notable was that he had to contend with the election-day intimidation tactics of the Cleveland Police Department. When black voters went to the polls, they were confronted by white police officers. One of Stokes's security men observed the intimidation. "I talked to the polling officials, the presiding judge, and the other ladies who were there, and they were frightened, just totally intimidated. They said that these policemen had been interrogating the citizens who came to vote and just browbeat them. And they [the police] were handling the polling books, which is against the law." Moreover, the officers made no attempt to disguise the purpose of their visit: to ensure that Stokes was defeated.[50]

As Stokes began his second term, he remained committed to reforming the police department. The black community pressed Stokes to remove Gerity as police chief. When Safety Director Joseph McManamon resigned for health reasons in December 1969, Stokes decided to dismiss Gerity and find replacements for both positions. He needed someone whose credentials would be unquestioned and who would reestablish Stokes's credibility with the entire city. Stokes chose Benjamin O. Davis Jr., the first black general in the U.S. Air Force, as safety director. "A military man! A general! Black or not the people would have to respect him. And, being black, he would have to be the kind of man who would agree with what I wanted to do," Stokes wrote in his memoir. What impressed Stokes the most about Davis was his military background. Stokes believed that white officers would respect Davis. In making the appointment, Stokes stated that he expected Davis to restore discipline to the police department: "He is a doer, not a talker; he honestly wants to do something to curb the crime rate in Cleveland, not sit around and discuss it, as many people do."[51]

With Davis's approval, Stokes then appointed William Ellenburg, police chief of Grosse Point, Michigan, to head the police department. Within hours of Ellenburg's appointment, the Detroit media ran a story concerning Ellenburg's alleged involvement in an illegal abortion clinic while he was a member of the Detroit Police Department. Stokes came under fire for not examining Ellenburg's background more closely. In the midst of the controversy Ellenburg voluntarily resigned, realizing "that these charges . . . until cleared . . . would seriously impair my effectiveness." Stokes then appointed Inspector Lewis Coffey, who had come up through the ranks in Cleveland, to head the city police force. Although the charges against Ellenburg were never verified, many of Stokes's critics and supporters were growing tired of his administrative blunders. Thomas Vail, editor and publisher of the *Cleveland Plain Dealer,* summed up the opinion of many: "Time is running out, the people of Cleveland will not stand for another fiasco in public safety."[52]

Within months Stokes faced another crisis in law enforcement when General Davis came under intense criticism from the black community for his conservative approach to law enforcement. Several incidents throughout the spring convinced the black poor and working class that Davis was more interested in maintaining the status quo than reform. In March, Davis praised the SWAT team for breaking up a demonstration by black students at Cuyahoga Community College; one month later he failed to investigate the near beating death of an African exchange student in Little Italy. Later that month he went against the mayor's wishes and ordered thirty thousand high-powered bullets, and he gave officers permission to carry private weapons while on duty. Davis drew further criticism from the black community in June 1970 when he authorized a raid on the local headquarters of the Black Panther Party, then rejected a request for an investigation into the raid. The actions by Davis convinced Stokes and his supporters that the chief had no intention of reforming the department.[53]

Davis and Stokes also clashed over the mayor's rapport with local black nationalist organizations such as the Afro-Set and the Black Panthers. On several occasions Davis asked Stokes to sever administrative ties with them. When Stokes failed to act on Davis's request, the general abruptly resigned. "I find it necessary and desirable to resign as director of public safety," he said. "The reasons are simple, I am not receiving from you and your administration the support my programs require, and the enemies of law enforcement continue to receive support and comfort from you and your administration." In response Stokes stated that he had "no problems with his charge that I give them support and comfort." However, he disagreed with Davis's allegations that they were racists and anti–law enforcement. Rather, they were just groups and individuals "who work within the system but disagree with it."[54]

The local media trumpeted Davis's charges and added to Stokes's reputation as an opponent of strong law enforcement. Because of the Evans tragedy, these allegations crippled Stokes's leadership in the white community and among law-enforcement officers.

* * *

Midway through his second term Stokes decided to institutionalize his political power by spearheading the formation of the all-black 21st District Caucus. The caucus was formed in an attempt to unify the city's black politicians, to institutionalize the Stokes power base, and to make the Cuyahoga County Democratic Party, which had long taken the black vote for granted, responsive to black interests and concerns. Despite considerable black support, the county Democrats had failed to give blacks leadership positions in the party and most recently had given Stokes only tacit support. The caucus launched its first challenge to the county Democrats in May 1970 when it made three demands: 20 percent membership on the county executive committee; a black appointee as deputy director of the election board; another black appointee to the position of chair, vice chair, secretary, or treasurer. Unless these demands were met, Stokes and his followers would leave the party. "If we cannot have a voice in the Democratic Party, maybe it is time that black people determined they do not belong to either party," said Arnold Pinkney, one of Stokes's closest aides. County Democrats responded by agreeing to let the caucus name a county party secretary but then blocked the nomination when they discovered that the secretary was second in command under the party's constitution. Instead, the Democrats created three special vice chairmanships and told the caucus that it could "pick the black person" to fill one of the positions. After negotiations failed to produce a candidate the Democrats and the caucus could agree on, Stokes and the caucus withdrew from the party. Stokes was particularly upset that county Democrats often failed to consult him on party issues. "They can't exclude the mayor of the largest city from their talks in the development of the party, and then expect him to ratify their talks and actions," Stokes said.[55]

In the fall elections the caucus supported three Republican candidates, and it helped defeat Democrat Frank Gorman's bid for reelection to the county board of commissioners. Although this was the only race in which the caucus defeated a fellow Democrat, it was committed to charting a new path for black politics.[56]

As Stokes began his fourth year in office, his relationship with the city council grew increasingly antagonistic. By November 1970 the city was in the midst of a financial crisis, and Stokes launched a campaign to increase the city income tax. The proposal meant that suburbanites and big business would pay 72 percent of the income taxes the city collected. Because of the constant decline of the city's tax base, imbalanced tax reciprocity with the suburbs, and wage increases for an expanded municipal workforce, the city needed to generate an additional $133.1 million in revenue to operate for the next fiscal year. The anti-Stokes faction on the city council immediately came out against the income tax hike but as a compromise agreed to let voters make the final decision. In the weeks leading up to the special election, Stokes staked his political reputation on the proposal, mounting a massive public relations effort that included town hall meetings, door-to-door canvassing, and a thirty-minute television special. Conservative opponents labeled the tax plan a "Stokes Tax," and conjured up images of fiscal mismanagement, slush money to black nationalists, and increased social welfare programs for the black poor. The plan failed miserably, 106,410 to 76,277, and so did Stokes's political leadership.[57]

In the wake of the defeat of the tax increase, Stokes announced that the city would lay off thirty-two hundred workers and that "there will be no new programs of any kind." By announcing the cuts, Stokes sought to embarrass those on the city council who had asserted the city did not need a tax increase. Months later Council President Anthony Garofoli announced his tax plan, which called for a 0.6 percent increase in the income tax because the city was on the verge of financial ruin. Although Garofoli was instrumental in defeating the earlier tax proposal, Stokes asked city voters to approve the tax hike. "This is not a matter of Carl Stokes versus any other individual or faction, it is a question of whether or not Cleveland will survive as a city," the mayor said. Despite pleas by Garofoli and Stokes, the question failed. As in the earlier tax campaign, the black wards voted for its passage, while the predominantly white wards voted against it. Many observers argued that the defeated tax levy was a "plebiscite on the mayor's popularity . . . the people lacked confidence in his administration."[58]

As the relationship between Stokes and city council grew worse, the weekly council meetings became a virtual battleground. Throughout Stokes's tenure the Monday night meetings served as an opportunity for city council members to blame the administration for the city's problems. In early 1971 the attacks became personal. At the weekly council session on February 22, council member Francis Gaul accused Thomas Stallworth, commissioner of markets, weights, and measures, of "malfeasance, misfeasance, and nonfeasance." Gaul stated that his charges were based on personal investigations of local grocery stores, where he found a number of short-weighted meat packages. Gaul ended his comments by calling for an official council investigation into Stallworth's department. Stokes responded to Gaul's comments by declaring, "That kind of language is uncalled for." When Stokes tried to assert that the personal attacks violated the council's courtesy rule, Garofoli rebuffed him, arguing that the courtesy rule applied only to members of the city council. Stokes was angry: "What you have said is that the same standard will not be afforded to the administration. I must insist that the privileges and protections be equal. You have made it quite clear, and I am going to instruct my cabinet members to remove themselves from council chambers and we will not return until the same standards are extended to both branches of government." As he and his cabinet left the floor, Stokes shouted, "I don't want to get caught up on rules. I'm just asking for respect." For the remainder of his tenure Stokes and his cabinet did not attend council meetings.[59]

At a dinner party on April 16, 1971, Stokes told close friends and family that he would not seek reelection. He subsequently appeared on a local TV news broadcast and announced his decision to the public: "I have decided not to seek a third term as mayor of the city of Cleveland." One resident blamed Stokes's decision on "the racist councilmen and the envious blacks who knew they couldn't do as well as the Mayor." By contrast, many white residents were quite pleased at Stokes's announcement. "This is the best news we've heard in the last four years, I hope the city comes back again. It couldn't get much worse," said Francis Gavin, while another white resident remarked that he was glad to see Stokes leave because "the city has been going downhill under his leadership."[60]

In the fall election the 21st District Caucus supported Arnold Pinkney, a long-time Stokes lieutenant, who entered the race as an independent. However, Pinkney and the Stokes machine lost to GOP candidate Ralph Perk by 16,000 votes. This defeat signaled the end of the experiment in black political power in Cleveland.

* * *

As the first black mayor of a major city, Stokes was driven by two goals: to improve the lives of the black poor and to give black people a voice in municipal government. Although he had some successes, he was unable to achieve his goals. A declining tax base, an increasingly conservative federal and state government, and the continual influx of poor people into the city undermined his efforts to elevate the living conditions of the city's black poor.

While structural obstacles presented one set of challenges, Stokes's primary constraint was race. Bitter disputes occurred with the Cleveland Police Department and city council and were frequently laced with racial overtones.

Once the threat of a black revolt in Cleveland evaporated, whites no longer regarded Stokes as essential to the preservation of racial peace. Consequently, much of the white moderate and business support that had been so helpful during his early months in office vanished.

Last, Stokes's own confrontational and careless style of governance worked to his detriment. Throughout his tenure Stokes spent a considerable amount of political capital on issues he had little chance of winning. His repeated administrative blunders also gave his enemies the impression that he was incapable of governing.

Despite his political shortcomings, Stokes managed to capture the heart of black America. He heartened those who considered political power and black leadership as the next stage of the black freedom struggle. In fact, he considered his tenure a logical extension of the civil rights movement. Years after he left office, blacks in other cities would use the Stokes model to elect mayors of their own.

But subsequent black mayors held one notable advantage over Stokes: they were cognizant of the limits of black power. When he took office, Stokes did not want to be merely a symbolic black mayor. As a 1960s idealist, Mayor Stokes was confident that the city's structural problems could be solved by city hall and that structural changes could improve the lives of the black poor and working class. Stokes's basic mistake proved to be his unrealistic optimism.

Notes

1. Carl B. Stokes, *Promises of Power: A Political Autobiography* (New York: Simon and Schuster, 1973), 23–25. For a more in-depth discussion of Stokes's childhood and political career, consult early drafts of his autobiography: Container 64, Folders 1209–1210, Carl B. Stokes Papers (hereafter, CBS Papers), Western Reserve Historical Society (note that many documents in the CBS Papers are undated). Also consult several Stokes interviews at the Schomburg Center for Research in Black Culture, Harlem, New York.

2. Stokes, *Promises of Power*, 32–34, 39–40. For a worthwhile study of Holly and the Future Outlook League see Kimberley Phillips, *AlabamaNorth* (Urbana: University of Illinois Press, 1999).

3. *Call and Post*, November, 2, 9, and 16, 1957, January 28, 1958.

4. *Cleveland Press*, September 10, 1957; Stokes, *Promises of Power*, 48–49.

5. Ernest C. Cooper, *The Negro in Cleveland: An Analysis of the Social and Economic Characteristics of the Negro Population, 1950–1963* (Cleveland, Ohio: Urban League, 1964); U.S. Commission on Civil Rights, *Hearing Before the United States Commission on Civil Rights Held in Cleveland, Ohio* (Washington, D.C.: U.S. Government Printing Office, 1966).

6. *Cleveland Plain Dealer*, May 14, 1965; Carl B. Stokes, "Speech Announcing Candidacy," Container 2, Folder 2, CBS Papers; *Call and Post*, July 17, October 9, and October 30, 1965; *Cuyahoga County Democratic Executive Newsletter*, October 21 and 27, 1965, Container 5, Folder 75, CBS Papers.

7. Stokes is quoted in William E. Nelson Jr. and Philip Meranto, *Electing Black Mayors: Political Action in the Black Community* (Columbus: Ohio State University Press, 1977), 100. See also *Cleveland Press*, October 23, 1965; *Cleveland Plain Dealer*, October 23, 1965.

8. U.S. Commission on Civil Rights, *Hearing*, 514–15, 607; Ohio Advisory Committee, Cleveland Subcommittee, U.S. Commission on Civil Rights, *Cleveland's Unfinished Business in Its Inner-City: A Report* (Cleveland, Ohio: Cleveland Subcommittee, 1968); *Hough Grand Jury Report on the Superior and Hough Disturbances*, issued after a series of community meetings at Liberty Hill Baptist Church to determine the extent of police brutality during the riots (pp. 93–95), report on file at the Cleveland Public Library; *Call and Post*, July 2, 1966. CORE officials are quoted in Marc Lackritz, "The Hough Riots," unpublished paper on file at the Cleveland Public Library. See also *New York Times*, May 21, 1967; Nelson and Meranto, *Electing Black Mayors*, 110–11.

9. Nelson and Meranto, *Electing Black Mayors*, 114–15.

10. Adam Fairclough, *To Redeem the Soul of America* (Athens: University of Georgia Press, 1987), 352–53; David J. Garrow, *Bearing the Cross* (New York: Morrow, 1986), 563, 566.

11. Nelson and Meranto, *Electing Black Mayors*, 185.

12. Ibid., 140.

13. Ibid., 144.

14. Ibid., 150–51; *Cleveland Plain Dealer*, October 11, 1967. Stokes is quoted in "Transcript of First Debate Between Carl Stokes and Seth Taft," Container 2, Folder 40, CBS Papers.

15. *Cleveland Press*, November 10, 1967.

16. Stokes, *Promises of Power*, 108.

17. *Call and Post*, November 9, 1967, February 24, 1968; *Cleveland Press*, November 14, 1967, February 20, 1968; *Cleveland Plain Dealer*, February 20, 1968.

18. Stokes, *Promises of Power*, 111.

19. *Cleveland Press*, January 15–17, 1968; *Cleveland Plain Dealer*, January 18, 1968; *Call and Post*, January 20, 1968; Walter Burks, city personnel director, interview in July 1971 by Richard Murway, Stokes's press secretary, for the mayor's 1971 "Accomplishment Report," Container 6, Folder 97, CBS Papers; Murway, mayor's 1971 "Accomplishment Report," Container 7, Folder 104, CBS Papers. Stokes is quoted in "Statements by Carl Stokes," January 1, 1968, Container 51, Folder 956, CBS Papers.

20. Joseph McManamon, interview by Murway, July 1971, Container 7, Folder 103, CBS Papers.

21. *Cleveland Press*, March 1, 9, 1968; *Cleveland Plain Dealer*, March 2, 5, and 10, 1968. Stokes is quoted in the *Call and Post*, March 9, 1968.

22. Minutes of the Community Relations Board, Executive Board Meeting, April 11, 1968, Container 88, Folder 1745, CBS Papers; *Cleveland Plain Dealer*, April 9, 1968; *New York Times*, April 5, 7, and 9, 1968.

23. Neil J. Carruthers to Carl B. Stokes, April 8, 1968; Richard Seelback to Carl B. Stokes, April 6, 1968, both in the CBS Papers; *Cleveland Plain Dealer*, April 7, 1968.

24. *Cleveland Plain Dealer*, May 5, 1968.

25. Cleveland Now! Brochure, Container 1, Folder 5, Cleveland Now! Papers, Western Reserve Historical Society, Cleveland, Ohio.

26. Ibid.

27. *Cleveland Plain Dealer*, May 10, 11, 16, and 21, 1968; *Cleveland Press*, May 15, 1968;

Greater Cleveland Growth Association, memo, "Employees Campaign," Container 1, Folder 5, Cleveland Now! Papers. Stokes is quoted in the *Cleveland Press,* May 2, 1968.

28. Frank Keegan, *Blacktown, U.S.A.* (Boston: Little, Brown, 1971), 323.

29. Ibid., 325

30. Sgt. Bosie Mack, Safety Director Joseph McManamon, Law Director Clarence James, interviews by Louis H. Masotti and Jerry Corsi, September 1968 (in preparation for their subsequent book), all in Container 84, Folder 1655, CBS Papers; Police Chief Michael Blackwell, interview by Masotti and Corsi, September 1968, Container 84, Folder 1654, CBS Papers; press conference, "Glenville Disturbances," Container 84, Folder 1663, CBS Papers; "Chronological Report of Events: Glenville Area Disturbance," Container 84, Folder 1666, CBS Papers. The Evans quote appears in Louis H. Masotti and Jerome R. Corsi, *Shoot-out in Cleveland: Black Militants and the Police, July 23, 1968* (New York: Bantam, 1969). See also Keegan, *Blacktown,* 317–32, 396–414.

31. Masotti and Corsi, *Shoot-out in Cleveland,* 56–59.

32. Sworn testimony of Louise Brown, "Showing of Probable Cause: Documentary Evidence Tending to Show Criminal Activity by Cleveland Police During the Glenville Incident, July 23, 1968," report issued by the ACLU of Greater Cleveland, Container 9, Folder 41, CBS Papers; testimony of Jean Grisby, John Pegues, Arthur Radan, Trenton Irwin, all in ACLU report.

33. Andrew Wright and Albert Forrest, interviews in ACLU report, CBS Papers; *Call and Post,* August 3, 1968.

34. Masotti and Corsi, *Shoot-out in Cleveland,* 61–62; Cleveland Police Department, memo, "Looting Reports," Container 82, Folder 1582, CBS Papers; Cleveland Police Department, memo, "Arrest Record List," Container 84, Folder 1663, CBS Papers.

35. Masotti and Corsi, *Shoot-out in Cleveland,* 67–69; McManamon interview; Walter Beach, interview by Masotti and Corsi, September 1968, Container 84, Folder 1564, CBS Papers; William Silverman, interview by Masotti and Corsi, September 1968, Container 83, Folder 1636, CBS Papers; Walter Burks, interview by Masotti and Corsi, September 1968, Container 83, Folder 1636, CBS Papers; *Call and Post,* August 3, 1968. Stokes is quoted in *Cleveland Press,* July 24–25, 1968.

36. Masotti and Corsi, *Shoot-out in Cleveland,* 76–77; McManamon interview; Beach interview; ACLU of Greater Cleveland, "Showing of Probable Cause," Container 9, Folder 41, CBS Papers.

37. "Proposal for an African Culture Shop," Container 84, Folder 1665, CBS Papers; *Cleveland Press,* July 25–26, 1968; *Cleveland Plain Dealer,* July 27–28, August 10, 1968. Stokes is quoted in *Presbyterian Life,* date and author unknown, Container 90, Folder 1778, CBS Papers.

38. Stokes, *Promises of Power,* 224.

39. "Cleveland's New Look in Public Housing," brochure on Lee-Seville housing, Container 88, Folder 1735, CBS Papers; "Housing in Lee-Seville: Facts You Should Know," Container 88, Folder 1735, CBS Papers; "The Lee-Seville Story," Container 88, Folder 1734, CBS Papers; *New York Times,* September 5, 1968. White is quoted in *Cleveland Press,* July 16, 1968. See also *Cleveland Plain Dealer,* July 19, 1968; "Chronology of Events Concerning Lee-Seville," Container 32, Folder 578, CBS Papers; Sidney Spector, administrative assistant to the mayor, to Ralph Tyler, director of Utilities Dept., September 30, 1968,

Container 88, Folder 1734, CBS Papers; Sidney Spector to McManamon, safety director, Container 88, Folder 1734, CBS Papers; Sidney Spector to Edward Baugh, director of public properties, Container 88, Folder 1734, CBS Papers; Sidney Spector to Richard Green, community development director, Container 88, Folder 1734, CBS Papers; Linwood Smith, administrative assistant, community dev., to Carl B. Stokes, September 30, 1968, Container 88, Folder 1734, CBS Papers.

40. "Quotes on Lee-Seville Housing Proposal," Container 84, Folder 1735, CBS Papers. Stokes, Thompson, and the constituent are quoted in the *New York Times,* September 5, 1968.

41. *Cleveland Press,* March 12, April 3, 1969; *Cleveland Plain Dealer,* April 5, 1969.

42. *Cleveland Press,* June 3, 13, 1969; *Call and Post,* June 7, 13, 1969.

43. *Call and Post,* June 21, 1969.

44. Joseph Nook, foreman, "Cuyahoga Grand Jury Report," April 1969 term, to the Honorable George J. McMonagle, presiding judge, April 1969 term, Container 87, Folder 1721, CBS Papers; Estelle Zannes, *Checkmate in Cleveland* (Cleveland, Ohio: Case Western Reserve Press, 1972), 148–57; *Cleveland Plain Dealer,* October 3, 1968; Stokes, *Promises of Power,* 232.

45. *Call and Post,* September 14 and 17, 1968; "Police Recruitment Program," Container 3, Folder 45, CBS Papers; *Cleveland Plain Dealer,* October 6, 1968.

46. Nook, "Cuyahoga Grand Jury Report," Container 87, Folder 1721, CBS Papers; *Call and Post,* September 20, 1969; *Cleveland Press,* September 13, 1969.

47. Stokes, *Promises of Power,* 233–34; *Point of View,* March 19, 1970; *Call and Post,* July 5, 1969.

48. Perk is quoted in *Cleveland Press,* June 15, 1969. See also "The Stokes Record," Container 5, Folder 72, Container 5, Folder 73, CBS Papers; Bilinski campaign materials, Container 5, Folder 68, CBS Papers; Dick Murway to Carl B. Stokes, "Taft's City Club Remarks," October 23, 1969, Container 5, Folder 68, CBS Papers.

49. The businessman is quoted in *Plain Dealer,* October 22, 1969. See also *Plain Dealer,* March 27, 1969; *Cleveland Press,* November 5–6, 1969.

50. *Call and Post,* October 25, 1969; Arnold Pinkney, interview by Dick Murway, Container 7, Folder 105, pp. 1–25, CBS Papers; Carl B. Stokes to Police Chief Gerity, November 4, 1969, Container 81, Folder 1577, CBS Papers; "Memo from the Mayor's Office Concerning Illegal Activity by the Police," November 5, 1969, Container 81, Folder 1577, CBS Papers; Sidney Spector, interview by Dick Murway, Container 7, Folder 105, pp. 1–12, CBS Papers; Officer Barrett (the security man quoted), interview by Dick Murway, Container 6, Folder 97, pp. 25–29, CBS Papers; Clarence James, interview by author, February 26, 1998.

51. Stokes, *Promises of Power,* 182; *Cleveland Press,* January 9, 1970.

52. *Cleveland Press,* February 2–3, 1970; *Plain Dealer,* February 3, 1970; WJBK-TV, editorial, February 4, 1970, Container 81, Folder 1578, CBS Papers; Stokes press release regarding William Ellenburg, Container 82, Folder 1612, CBS Papers; *Cleveland Press,* February 2–3, 1970; *Plain Dealer,* February 3, 1970. See also Stokes, *Promises of Power,* 187–88; *Plain Dealer* March 3, 1970; *Cleveland Press,* March 3, 1970; Carl Stokes, "Statement on Ellenburg's Resignation," Container 81, Folder 1578, CBS Papers.

53. Thomas Monahan, interview by Dick Murway, Container 7, Folder 104, pp. 10–11, CBS Papers; *Call and Post,* August 1, April 4, June 20, August 8, 1970; Stokes, *Promises of Power,* 191–92, 195–96.

54. Davis is quoted in "Transcript of Press Conference on the Resignation of Benjamin Davis," July 27, 1970, Container 9, Folder 170, CBS Papers, and Stoke is quoted in Statement by Stokes, July 29, 1970, Container 81, Folder 1574, CBS Papers. See also *Call and Post,* July 11, 1970; *Cleveland Press,* July 2, 20, 27–29, 1970; Stokes, *Promises of Power,* 200; *Plain Dealer,* July 27, 1970.

55. Pinkney is quoted in Statement by Arnold Pinkney, May 20, 1970, Container 10, Folder 162, CBS Papers, and Pinkney interview; and Stokes is quoted in *Call and Post,* May 23, 1970. See also *Cleveland Press,* February 12, May 16, 18, 20, 26, 1970; *Plain Dealer,* May 12, 17, 23, 1970; Stokes, *Promises of Power,* 242.

56. *Plain Dealer,* November 4, 1970; *Cleveland Press,* November 7, 18, 1970.

57. Clarence James to Philip Dearborn, "Municipal Tax Increase, Reciprocity Credit," July 10, 1970, Container 74, Folder 1411, CBS Papers; "Task Force Membership," Container 57, Folder 1111, CBS Papers; Task Force to Carl B. Stokes, "Tax Reform," July 21, 1970, Container 74, Folder 1411; Carl B. Stokes to A. A. Sommer, task force chair, July 24, 1970, Container 74, Folder 1411, CBS Papers; "Payroll Information: Comparison of Municipal Employees," Container 23, Folder 402, CBS Papers; file on "Police Costs, 1968–1970," Container 55, Folder 1031, CBS Papers; flyer on "Safety Budget: 1960 and 1970," Container 55, Folder 1031, CBS Papers; "Effect of Reciprocity on Municipal Income Tax Receipts, 1969," Container 74, Folder 1411, CBS Papers; *Plain Dealer,* June 30, July 25, 1970; *Cleveland Press,* July 23 and 24, August 11, September 10 and 13, 1970; editorial reply by Dennis Kucinich, August 11, 1970, WJW-TV (Cleveland), Container 74, Folder 1411, CBS Papers; John Liebtag, personnel department employee, interview by Richard Murway, July 1971, Container 7, Folder 102, CBS Papers; Joseph Harris, executive secretary to the director of city services, interview by Richard Murway, July 1971, Container 6, Folder 100, CBS Papers; flyer on Issue #7, Container 55, Folder 1031, CBS Papers; Task Force on City Finances to Task Force members, memo, "Door-to-Door Canvassing," October 27, 1970, Container 55, Folder 1031, CBS Papers; "Fact Sheet for Issue #7," Container 74, Folder 1418, CBS Papers; "Exemptions Under Proposed City Income Tax," Container 23, Folder 402, CBS Papers; *Plain Dealer,* October 30, 1970; Greater Cleveland Growth Association memo, October 2, 1970, Container 59, Folder 111, CBS Papers; *Call and Post,* October 24, 31, 1970; *Plain Dealer,* November 3, 1970.

58. Stokes in quoted in *Plain Dealer,* November 3, 1970, and *Call and Post,* January 30, 1971; the criticism of the tax levy appeared in *Cleveland Press,* February 2, 1971. See also *Plain Dealer,* November 5, 1970, and February 1–2, 1971; *Call and Post,* February 6, 1971.

59. Stokes is quoted in *Call and Post,* February 27, 1971; *Cleveland Press,* February 23, 1971; *Plain Dealer,* February 23, 1971.

60. *Cleveland Plain Dealer,* April 17–18, 1971.

4. Harold and Dutch Revisited: A Comparative Look at the First Black Mayors of Chicago and New Orleans

ARNOLD R. HIRSCH

SINCE THE 1967 elections of Richard Hatcher in Gary, Indiana, and Carl Stokes in Cleveland, Ohio, the emergence of black mayors in major U.S. cities has been a distinguishing characteristic of local politics in the United States. Coming in the midst of the long, hot summers that plagued the mid-1960s, such political victories appeared initially as a potential alternative to violent street protest. Following hard on the heels of the Watts riot in Los Angeles (and nearly coinciding with explosions in Detroit and Newark), the successful resort to the electoral process by African Americans meant that an opened door now beckoned those previously denied access to the political and economic mainstream. And, given the passage of the Voting Rights Act of 1965, the promise of the open door could not be regionally contained. The end of disfranchisement in the South complemented black insurgencies and declarations of independence from machines and patrons in the North. The system, it appeared, could be revolutionized peacefully from the inside. Such staggering change would seem to herald the ultimate success of the civil rights revolution. Was this not, after all, what it was all about?

It is clear, however, that if the pattern of municipal officeholding has undergone a dramatic shift, the conditions that initially sparked black protest and political mobilization remain stubbornly persistent. Certainly rates of unemployment for African Americans living in the urban core have not dropped below those of the Vietnam era. And in charting the so-called pathologies of inner-city life—rates of crime, illegitimacy, illiteracy, single parent households, and the like—the violent 1960s look almost like a golden age whose problems seem manageable in comparison to those of the 1980s and 1990s. While the black middle class has indeed mushroomed, a seemingly chronically dependent urban black "underclass" (as it came to be called in the 1980s) also has emerged.

The black community, in short, is more complex and diverse today than it was a generation earlier. If the ghetto has been gilded for some and escaped by others, it now presents the dual problems of race and poverty in a new and concentrated form. The implicit political and ideological content of the concept of the "underclass" sparks legitimate concern, but the term's popularity stemmed, at least in part, from its apparent descriptive utility. The elevation of a new class of African-American officeholders has not, in short, substantially altered the social structure of urban America.

This essay offers a brief examination of two black mayors—Ernest Nathan "Dutch" Morial of New Orleans and Harold Washington of Chicago—in an effort to shed some light on the problems and forces they confronted. Certainly it is helpful to scrutinize African-American administrations in a northern city and a southern one to see whether any regional differences are significant, but no one should assume that Washington and Morial are representative of black mayors as a class. If anything, Dutch Morial and Harold Washington were among the toughest and smartest of those municipal executives dedicated to attacking the status quo; each was concerned more with pursuing and exercising power than accumulating mere honors. In sum, if any local officeholders could shape their immediate environments as individuals, these two would be likely candidates for producing visible results.

It is useful to examine the careers of Washington and Morial at three points. First is the acquisition of power. In looking at Morial's rise to the mayor's office in 1978 and Washington's in 1983 it is immediately clear that each reached that pinnacle when blacks represented both population and voting minorities in New Orleans and Chicago. That simple fact, ultimately, had serious implications for the ability of these mayors to govern. Second is the actual exercise of power. How did each function as chief executive? What obstacles did he confront and how successful was he in overcoming them? The final point involves the succession of power. Morial left city hall in 1986, turned out of office after two consecutive terms by a city charter term limitation that he tried and failed to repeal. Washington, in contrast, had been reelected to a second term in a city that honored a tradition of extended, multiple terms for its mayors but simply died in his office in 1987. How permanent were the advances made during their administrations? Did their legacies include an irresistible momentum for change? Had either, in other words, set his city on a new course?

* * *

The rise of Dutch Morial and Harold Washington makes clear, first, that they must be understood within their local political contexts. The study of American race relations has a tendency to homogenize everything into simple matters of black and white. A study of African-American mayors, however, reveals that within the framework provided by the U.S. racial dichotomy, an understanding of local culture is critical to an understanding of the individual.

If Atlanta's Andrew Young, for example, entered city hall through the ministry, and Coleman Young became industrial Detroit's chief executive officer after an extended stint as a labor radical and organizer for the United Auto Workers, it was similarly true that the first black mayors of New Orleans and Chicago launched their early careers in the most powerful local black institutions available. Local variables conditioned, if they did not dictate, the channels through which talented and ambitious African-American leaders developed their skills and became prominent figures.

In New Orleans and Chicago those institutions were neither the black church (though it was not without influence) nor the labor movement. For Dutch Morial that central institution was the National Association for the Advancement of Colored People (NAACP). It was not only the most important vehicle for protest and the civil rights movement in New Orleans but the institutional home for the remnants of a radical black Creole community that provided much of the city's leadership during the era of Reconstruction and kept alive a tradition of resistance to the color line since the dawning of the Jim Crow era. That Creole radicalism, personified by Homer Plessy's moral and legal challenge at the end of the nineteenth century, survived in New Orleans to tie the first and second eras of Reconstruction together.[1]

Morial was born and raised in New Orleans's Seventh Ward, the very epicenter of the downtown Creole community. He was an integral part of it and assumed the presidency of the local branch of the NAACP during the height of the civil rights agitation of the early 1960s. The New Orleans chapter of the NAACP, created in 1915, was one of the first branches established in the Deep South and displayed roots similar to Morial's. Its chief legal counsel, through the middle of the twentieth century, was A. P. Tureaud, another Seventh Ward Creole and Dutch Morial's senior partner and mentor.

Tureaud and Morial, more than any other individuals in the Crescent City, became identified with the dismantling of the legalized system of segregation. It was a fitting role for Morial, who was himself a walking civil rights revolution. The first black to graduate from the Louisiana State University Law School in 1954, he went on to accumulate an impressive array of other "firsts":

the first black assistant U.S. Attorney in New Orleans (1965), the first elected
to the state legislature in the modern era (1967), the first named to the Juve-
nile Court bench (1970), the first elected to the state's Fourth Circuit Court
of Appeal (1972), and, ultimately, the first elected mayor. In short, Dutch
Morial made his career by opposing, as Rodolphe Desdunes, another black
Creole, put it, the "fanaticism" of caste. The local branch of the NAACP also
became more than a vehicle for the legal assault on Jim Crow under Morial's
direction as it directed voter registration campaigns that proved instrumental in the successful launching of his political career. Initially locked out of the
system, Morial mounted an onslaught from outside, demolishing racial barriers while building an institutional base within the black community.[2]

In Chicago the NAACP was incapable of performing similar services. When,
early in the civil rights era, it had threatened to become an activist protest
organization, the black political boss William Levi Dawson simply had his
precinct captains infiltrate the organization as new voting members. A moderating change in leadership followed. That episode, however, provided a clue
to where the path to political power lay in Chicago—in the Cook County
Democratic Organization, the famed Chicago "machine" itself.

Indeed, Harold Washington had been raised in the very bosom of the organization he would later defeat. The Democratic political machine in Chicago, and its subordinate black branch, provided a wealth of opportunity for
those who could gather concentrated black votes in Chicago's highly segregated neighborhoods. Demography, geography, and the peculiar features of
Chicago's political landscape made that arena an attractive one for skilled and
ambitious players. Indeed, Chicago's South Side black belt proved a verita-
ble political hothouse, developing a sophisticated cadre of movers and shakers
by the turn of the twentieth century. Indeed, it was that scarred battleground
on the South Side, not the far larger New York, that by 1928 produced the first
black representative to the U.S. Congress elected from a northern district.[3]

Harold Washington's father, Roy Washington, was an attorney, an African
Methodist Episcopal preacher, a dabbler in real estate, and a precinct captain in the Democratic organization. Indeed, he was active at the beginning
of the 1930s, which made him one of the earliest black Democratic stalwarts.
Politics formed the core of the dinner table discussions Harold Washington
recalled from his childhood. And Harold did more than absorb stories about
the machine. He watched it operate at close hand as when—in 1947—his
father strapped a gun on his hip and went looking for the Democratic ward
committeeman who had covertly undermined Roy Washington's campaign
for a seat as an alderman on the city council.[4]

If Harold Washington was never quite an unthinking machine loyalist (he characterized himself at one point as an "independent machine politician"), he gave it enough obeisance early in his career to emerge as one of its most promising stars. He had taken over the South Side Third Ward precinct worked by his father and filled the elder Washington's slot in the corporation counsel's office following his death in 1953 (Harold Washington earned his law degree at Northwestern University in 1952). Though he was considerably younger than the Third Ward's Democratic committeeman (committeemen were the key political officers in each ward), the former Olympic star and rising machine politician Ralph Metcalfe, Washington had more finely honed political skills. Who, exactly, was mentoring whom is not entirely clear.

Finally rewarded with a seat in the state legislature, Washington became something of a renegade after his posting to Springfield (first in the state House of Representatives and, later, in the state Senate) in 1964. He confronted Mayor Richard J. Daley directly on the issue of police brutality and strayed from the party line on a host of lesser concerns. Washington soon found himself beyond Metcalfe's protective mantle and on his own. He made a longshot's futile run for city hall in 1977 after Daley died, and Washington fought off the organization's retaliatory attempt to purge him from the Illinois senate. In the party primary for the state senate race the following year, Washington had to survive an election in which the organization ran three opponents—two of them named Washington—against him. The attempt to confuse Washington's electoral base into submission fell barely 200 votes short of success. Washington then confirmed his independence by successfully challenging the machine's nominee and winning a seat in the U.S. House of Representatives in 1980. Having shown he could outdraw the machine in his home district, he became a vocal critic of the Reagan administration, which further ingratiated Washington with his South Side constituency.

Thus both Dutch Morial and Harold Washington built solid black political bases. Morial's was rooted in the downtown Creole community but extended uptown to the old "American" sector of the city. As an activist and as a candidate for the legislature, he mined those neighborhoods for supporters for both the NAACP's civil rights crusades and for his campaign. For Harold Washington home was Chicago's massive South Side, particularly those growing middle-class black wards that were proving less than reliable for the machine. That provided the base from which he could reach out to whites (he ultimately settled in the integrated Hyde Park community that surrounds the University of Chicago) and the newer, growing ghetto on the West Side. It is important to note also that neither Morial nor Washington

emerged overnight. In both cases long years of service and an extended political apprenticeship forged an organic unity between the community and
the candidate. The extraordinarily high levels of black voter turnout and
solidarity that they enjoyed in their surprising initial victories were testimo-
nies, ultimately, to their long-established credibility as well as the magic of
their respective moments.

In each case the assertiveness of the black candidates and their ability to
forge solid African-American electoral bases allowed them to surprise divided
white communities that did not take them seriously as political threats. In
dissecting their winning coalitions, however, analysts have split regarding the
relative significance of the solid black base as opposed to the essential white
fragment that provided, in theory, their margins of victory. Often rooted in
political or racial interests, at least some of this attention is misplaced. The
key factor, it seems, is the black base in combination with the ignorance and
arrogance that led to the underestimation of the African-American candidates in the white community and the internal white divisions that opened
the door for seemingly quixotic challenges.

In 1977 Dutch Morial faced three major white opponents that sharply divided New Orleans's white vote in an open (nonpartisan) primary that would
pit the top two finishers against one another if no one earned a majority of
the ballots cast. Morial was seen as nothing more than a spoiler at the outset, and his relative lack of financial resources and his grassroots campaign
in the black community led mainstream analysts to dismiss his prospects in
a city in which black registrants amounted to no more than 43 percent of the
vote. His influence on the campaign was discussed primarily in terms of how
he would affect the tallies of Nat Kiefer and Toni Morrison, the "serious"
white candidates who were actively courting black supporters. The fourth
candidate, Joseph DiRosa, ran a white populist campaign that made no pretense of seeking black votes.[5]

In the end, the traditional paternalistic ties that linked white political elites
to some African-American leaders and voters were no match for the communal ties forged by Morial during his long career. Morial's base returned a sizable majority of the black vote in the primary, eviscerating the campaigns of
both Kiefer and Morrison. They split the white vote with DiRosa and then
divvied up a small slice of the minority pie. Morial thus squeezed into the
runoff with DiRosa, a candidate who had thoroughly alienated the business
community and carried his own ethnic baggage. In the final showdown Morial swept 97 percent of an exceptionally high black turnout and just enough
whites, about 20 percent, to enable him to win a close contest.[6]

Similarly, Harold Washington was given no chance to win when he announced his candidacy for the mayoralty in 1983. He had, after all, won only 11 percent of the vote in his 1977 warm-up, and blacks still represented less than 40 percent of Chicago's electorate. The "real" race would be in Chicago's Democratic primary between the incumbent, Jane Byrne, and her major white challenger, Richard M. Daley, the son of Chicago's legendary Richard J. Daley. Until the final days of the primary campaign, Washington enjoyed nearly a free ride. The mainstream white press virtually ignored his prospects while concentrating on Byrne and Daley. For their part the mayor and her challenger refrained from attacking Washington. Because they were seeking some portion of the black vote for themselves in the primary, they certainly did not wish to alienate that constituency and hoped to pick it back up in the general election. Only in the closing days of the campaign did it become clear that, indeed, Washington, not Daley, was Byrne's most threatening opponent. That turn of events prompted Democratic Party chairman Ed Vrdolyak's now-famous dictum that the election had become a "racial thing." He called on whites to desert Daley in defense of racial interests. The raw appeal backfired. With Byrne and Daley neatly dividing the white ballots almost in half, Washington won the Democratic nomination for mayor with but 36 percent of the total primary vote. His showing in the black community—he had won 85 percent of a 70 percent turnout there following a massive increase in voter registration—carried the day. Part political campaign, part religious crusade, the Washington movement capitalized on a long series of racial provocations by Mayor Jane Byrne and Ronald Reagan that had energized black Chicagoans.[7]

Historically, winning the Democratic nomination for mayor in Chicago was tantamount to winning the election. No Republican had been elected mayor since 1927, and the GOP's numbers were so few that Democrats were often pressed into service as nominally "Republican" election judges so that the precincts might be properly staffed. Washington's seizure of the Democratic nomination, however, suddenly reinvigorated Chicago Republicanism. The national Republican Party raised hundreds of thousands of dollars for the campaign, provided media expertise, and furnished advice on how to run a racially divisive campaign without mentioning race—all this to secure the election of a man who won his party's nomination with but 11,000 votes (in contrast, Washington's 424,131 outpolled Byrne's 387,986 and Daley's 344,590). More important, of the fifty Democratic ward committeemen, more endorsed Washington's opponent in the general election, Bernard Epton, than supported the nominee of their own party; and even those nominally in Washington's corner often provided Epton with covert assistance in the attempt to undermine Washington. Still, in a bitter, racially charged campaign, Washington took just under 52 percent of the vote, winning by fewer than 50,000 of the nearly 1.3 million ballots cast. He managed to eke out about 12 percent of the white vote and 62 percent of the city's growing Latino vote (if Latinos are counted as "whites," Washington's white vote increased to 16 to 18 percent). That support supplemented the 97 to 99 percent of the black voters who backed Washington with an astounding 85 percent turnout. He won every black vote in the city, as one Epton supporter put it, "except for the accidents."[8] If Morial's victory seemed characteristic of an outsider's ferocious storming of dearly protected battlements, Washington's rise seemed more like an insider's palace coup.

Whites in New Orleans and Chicago, who had initially taken neither the Morial nor the Washington campaign seriously, and were hardly prepared even to share power, now found they had actually lost control of city hall to aggressive black challengers. A great deal of fear, uncertainty, and resentment were, consequently, primary political realities facing the victors. Because they had mobilized little more than one in ten, or, at best, less than one in five, white voters on their behalf, Washington and Morial faced white communities seemingly unprepared to deal with powerful black political figures. More, those whites who supported their campaigns often viewed themselves as king makers and were not prepared for the independence displayed by the new mayors or their determination to address the needs of their core constituency.

Once in office both Morial and Washington also had to deal with certain structural political realities that prevented them from having a free hand to retool their city. Morial had to deal not only with the atavistic racial attitudes still characteristic of a majority of the white population in his southern city but a fragmented governmental structure designed precisely to keep mayors weak and the public sector under the control of a conservative economic and social elite.

Nearly a century before, in the late nineteenth century, the pillars of the New Orleans commercial community had begun to pull key powers out of city hall as the ethnic Irish were coming to control the electoral arena. The Crescent City's economic and social elite, no longer in control of the ballot box, sought alternatives to the Regular Democratic Organization, one of the few big-city machines to appear in the South. The power brokers made a series of end runs to the governor and state legislature and, largely through the use of influence in Baton Rouge, succeeded in creating a network of appointed boards and commissions from which they could effectively protect their interests. Because they controlled key city functions such as tax rates, riverfront development, and drainage, they could still dictate the pace and nature of urban development from perches on the Board of Liquidation, City Debt (created in 1880), the Sewerage and Water Board (created in 1900), and the Board of Commissioners of the Port of New Orleans (created in 1896 and known simply as the "Dock Board"), among others. When coupled with a later city charter provision that limited the mayor to two terms, such structures placed the city's elected chief executive at a considerable disadvantage. The attempt to defuse one ethnic challenge from below at the end of the nineteenth century produced a government structure that impeded another one a hundred years later.[9]

In Chicago, Harold Washington's chief obstacle was not the formal structures of government but the informal political structure of the city. The Democratic machine, the Cook County Democratic organization, controlled the city council and virtually every other city agency that confronted the new black mayor. Harold Washington's entire first term, therefore, was taken up with political battles and the struggle for control of the city's government and its budget. This was the era of Chicago's stalemated "council wars," which pitted white city council opposition (29 of the council's 50 votes, enough to frustrate mayoral initiatives but not sufficient to overcome executive vetoes) led by "Darth" Vrdolyak against Harold "Skytalker," his largely black supporters, and a handful of "reform" representatives. The white majority controlled the powerful and patronage-rich council committees and refused to approve hundreds of Washington appointments that would have threatened the status quo in other city agencies. The factionalism and infighting became so intense that the *Wall Street Journal* branded Chicago "Beirut on the Lake."[10]

It is crucial to understand that these political difficulties meant that both Morial and Washington confronted deep structural problems that transcended narrow or immediate issues of race and that their attempts at reform, even absent the race issue, would have provoked tenacious resistance. The race issue greatly added to their burdens, of course, and provided cynical political manipulators with a powerful club they did not hesitate to use. It also meant that both mayors had to work hard at democratizing their cities and that each necessarily referred frequently to the need to "open" his town's political and economic structures.

In Dutch Morial's case the concept of an open New Orleans included a redefinition of the mayor's role that was sharply at odds with tradition. Morial asserted a primary role in urban governance for the city's democratically elected chief executive. His race—or at least the public's fascination with it—obscured the fundamental political challenge to the social and economic oligarchy that dominated public affairs from seats of social privilege on those primarily nonelected boards and commissions. Indeed, in a speech before the Metropolitan Area Committee, a civic leadership group, Morial let the city know what was coming. He made pointed reference to the 1971 study by the Tulane University political scientist Charles Chai, "Who Rules New Orleans?" and informed his audience that he was "astounded" that Chai had not included the mayor on his list of "influentials," compiled after discussions with community leaders. It was inconceivable to Morial that "a majority of the people [consulted] failed to even mention the mayor as a man essential to the communal equation." He added diplomatically that he "would like to think that that perception has changed." What he meant, of course, was that he would change it. The mayor's office was no longer the province of the ruling class, nor could Morial or any other democratically responsive, independent chief executive be willing to serve only its narrow ends. Such independence represented a real threat to the traditional elite's interests. Thus Morial's speech was a challenge that would have set off a political firestorm for any mayor—black or white—who dared to stake out such a position.[11]

Indeed, Morial's long-standing efforts to democratize New Orleans's government—his support for a 1975 discrimination lawsuit challenging the exclusive composition of the Board of Liquidation, City Debt, antedated his election as mayor—continued once he attained office. He believed a revitalized system of public education held the key to economic growth, and he attacked the city's Board of Education and the "anachronism" that "separate[d] the schools from the public consensus as expressed in the powers and person of the office of mayor." Similarly, the deteriorating position of the Port of New Orleans led him to go after the Dock Board as well, and he raised "the serious question as to whether this management, set so distinctly apart from the public consensus, will not eventually bear the same bitter fruit as the antiquity of our school board policy." Though the lawsuit against the Board of Liquidation ultimately proved successful, efforts to extend mayoral influence over the Board of Education (Morial sought to add two mayoral appointees to an otherwise elected board) and Dock Board were distinctly less so. Combined with a long acrimonious public dispute with the Sewerage and Water Board regarding access to its jobs and contracts by minorities and women (a bitter struggle in which Morial eventually prevailed), the mayor's efforts produced mixed results.[12]

The tenor of the times, however, is perhaps best revealed in Morial's also finding himself forced to play defense. Using the powers of the state to attack the office of the mayor and the City of New Orleans was a well-worn strategy in Louisiana that constituted the primary thrust of earlier Progressive era "reforms" as well as both Huey and Earl Long's bids to dominate the state. Whether legislative initiatives advanced by ostensible good-government forces or brutal frontal assaults launched by ambitious governors, they were all self-serving power grabs that threatened the city's independence. In the early 1980s Morial had to fight off attempts to remove the mayor as president of the Sewerage and Water Board and an effort to strip the city's authority over the metropolitan airport and Aviation Board. Morial was successful in these defensive battles, and he similarly fought off multiple attempts by the uptown social elite to wrest Audubon Park from the city's hands. Morial's city attorney, Sal Anzelmo, bluntly linked this last dispute to changing demographic realities and a broader pattern of conduct when he stated that "the State takeover is an effort by those in the Uptown establishment to keep blacks from getting control of the Zoo Commission. . . . They want to keep it under white control. They don't want blacks to sit on the Zoo Commission, the Aviation Board, . . . the Sewerage and Water Board or anything. They say they want to 'regionalize' everything. Well, that just means they want a controlling majority of whites who aren't even from Orleans Parish."[13] Unable to extend his authority to areas he deemed vital, Morial had to expend considerable time and energy fighting to retain what powers he had.

In Chicago, Harold Washington defeated the Cook County Democratic organization by energizing an unprecedentedly large black base and by plugging into a long-standing stream of antimachine reform politics that brought a significant number of white voters to his coalition. Byrne had done much the same four years before but returned to the machine fold as she pondered the difficulty of transforming an electoral majority into a governing one. Indeed, the organization's success in recapturing Byrne led several ward leaders to hope that the same could be done with Washington. It was Washington's resistance to this scenario—"I'm not going to pull a Byrne," he declared at one point—that precipitated the showdown with the machine's leadership. His continued attacks on patronage led one organization stalwart, Alderman Roman Pucinski of the Northwest Side, to claim that he could support a machine-oriented African American for mayor but that Washington's desire to dismantle the organization asked too much. "Why should I give him the guillotine with which to cut off my head?" Pucinski retorted. Finally, when Washington moved against party chairman Ed Vrdolyak by attempting to remove him from his powerful leadership post on the zoning committee, Vrdolyak solidified the twenty-nine-vote bloc that opposed Washington. There is no doubt that Vrdolyak and his retinue would have done the same to Jane Byrne had she had the courage of her stated convictions—or that they would have been able to do business with a more compliant and subservient Washington.[14]

Stalemated legislatively, Washington took a number of executive actions that placed him firmly in the reform camp. He cut his own salary by 20 percent and mothballed the limousine traditionally placed at the mayor's disposal. He also issued a "freedom of information" executive order that opened the city's records to public scrutiny, held budget hearings in the neighborhoods, and signed the Shakman decree, which prohibited the hiring or firing of city employees for political reasons. He also announced a self-imposed cap of $1,500 on campaign contributions by companies doing business with the city and cut the city payroll by seven hundred employees in the attempt to resolve the city's fiscal crisis.[15]

In the end, Washington's antimachine crusade received an incomparable boost from the federal courts. Finding that the city council's ward reapportionment plan under Jane Byrne was an outrageous racial gerrymandering that discriminated against blacks and Latinos, the courts ordered the drawing of new district boundaries and special elections in seven wards in 1986. The machine threw everything it had into these contests but could not prevent Washington from garnering four new supporters on the council. The city council was now divided 25-25, with Mayor Washington casting all tie-breaking votes; he had pieced together his governing majority on his own terms.[16]

Changes followed rapidly. The mayor either stripped the machine's ward barons of their leadership posts on the council or diluted their authority and then watched as the council passed a new ethics ordinance and a Tenant's Bill of Rights, amended taxi regulations to break up an existing near monopoly, and approved his executive appointments that had, literally, been held hostage for years. This last development was of the utmost importance, for it finally gave Washington control of such agencies as the Chicago Park District, a quasi-independent power base and source of patronage for machine opponent Edmund Kelly. Soon stripped of his powers, Kelly resigned.[17]

As was the case in New Orleans, Chicago's black mayor also had to play defense. Like Dutch Morial, Harold Washington proved largely successful in this endeavor. Hostile interests introduced measures in the state legislature that would strip the city of its control over the park district, the McCormick Place convention centers, Navy Pier, and the Port Authority. Another proposal called for the creation of a regional airport authority (taking O'Hare and Midway airports away from the city), and the opposition-controlled Finance Committee of the city council tried to arrogate unto itself the right to approve all city contracts. There was even a sudden, expressed desire for an elected school board.[18] Even as Dutch Morial struggled unsuccessfully to get a couple of mayoral appointees on New Orleans's elected school board, Harold

Washington's presence led some Chicagoans to question the merit of their mayor-appointed body.

The most telling episode, however, involved the effort, inspired by mayoral hopeful Richard M. Daley, to institute an open nonpartisan primary that would be followed by a runoff, given the likelihood that no candidate would win an outright majority in the next election. Stung by the charge that he had been the white spoiler that paved the way for Washington's victory, Daley wanted to make certain that the strongest white candidate in 1987 would be able to face Washington one on one. Petitions circulated throughout the city as sponsors of the measure hoped to get enough signatures to place it quickly before the people in a referendum. Washington forces on the city council countered by placing three other innocuous referenda on the ballot before the nonpartisan primary petitions could be collected and validated. Under an obscure Illinois law no more than three such propositions could be considered by a city at one time; Washington's council majority had preempted the ballot and blocked the attempt to change the rules in the middle of the game. Even his enemies grudgingly admired his deft political touch and the act of parliamentary legerdemain that left them standing in the dust. He had learned his lessons well.[19]

Washington's coup set the stage for his reelection in 1987 and a second term that promised, finally, substantive accomplishment. Washington had watched his first term be consumed by endless political wrangling before he ultimately consolidated his position and prepared to move forward. It was at this point that the trajectories of the Washington and Morial administrations sharply diverged.

Morial's most notable achievements were primarily confined to his first term. The short-lived oil boom of the early 1980s and the Morial administration's management skills kept the city afloat despite underlying weaknesses and the beginning of federal retrenchment; a burst of new downtown construction and the steady growth of tourism contributed to the early sense of well-being. The mayor clearly recognized that the city's long-term health demanded greater economic diversification and fiscal reform, and he tried to nudge the city in that direction. The optimism of the moment, however, and the political ethos of the city and the state proved impossible to overcome, and the city's fortunes declined radically in mid-1980s. Still, Morial's successful handling of a police strike, the streamlining of government, and a record of scandal-free, sound administration all graced his first four years.

During his second term Morial found himself constrained. The two-term limit placed on mayors by the city charter made him a lame duck as soon as he was reelected. More, the incoming city council included what Morial later called the "Gang of Five." In New Orleans's seven-member city council (five elected by districts, two at large), the five representatives who rose in opposition could not only blunt his initiatives but override his vetoes. Consisting of three whites elected from districts and two blacks (one of whom was elected at large), Morial's antagonists harassed him at every turn. When the city's fiscal problems combined with the full weight of Ronald Reagan's budget cuts, Morial's second term was characterized more by stagnation than progress. Unseemly controversies regarding a pay raise for the mayor, a shopping mall near the Superdome, and—particularly—Morial's unsuccessful efforts to remove the two-term limitation from the city charter provided less than edifying public theater.[20]

The course taken by Harold Washington's reign was exactly the opposite. Beset by difficulties in the beginning, he enjoyed more freedom toward the end of his administration. He had gained control of the city council and then had made particular strides in retiring the city's debt through a combination of payroll reductions and new taxes and had succeeded in restoring Chicago's favorable credit rating. Equally significant, because he was feeling politically secure, the mayor extended an olive branch to his adversaries, endorsing candidates Richard M. Daley and Aurelia Pucinski (Roman Pucinski's daughter) for high county offices and retaining eight former Vrdolyak supporters as council committee chairs. Former adversaries, who believed Washington's claim he would occupy city hall longer than Richard J. Daley had, began to move into his orbit after his reelection early in 1987; the most recalcitrant, such as Ed Vrdolyak, simply left the Democratic Party altogether. Just as he was preparing to move forward in building a genuine biracial coalition, Washington died. It was the day before Thanksgiving, little more than a half-year after his second victorious campaign.[21]

Politically unassailable within their respective communities, Dutch Morial and Harold Washington nonetheless endured significant undercurrents of black opposition that proved of great importance for their successions. Some opposition was the result, at least in part, of the impossibility of meeting inflated expectations and the enormous difficulty in dealing with deep-seated urban problems and institutions. Few areas were of greater concern to New Orleans's and Chicago's African Americans, for example, than housing, particularly public housing, and education. Yet it was precisely in these areas that Morial and Washington proved unable or unwilling to stimulate progressive change. The political resistance that manifested itself when Morial tried to tinker with the Crescent City's school board apparently convinced him that the risks were not worth a bitter battle with uncertain outcomes; he quickly backed off and did not pick up the issue again. Similarly, in dealing with the Chicago Housing Authority, Harold Washington inherited a political wasteland that, for the previous generation, had served as little more than a dumping ground for the black poor and a patronage trough for the machine. It clearly demanded more attention and resources than he was willing to commit.[22] Less than forceful leadership thus combined with the inertia of these large bureaucracies and a deteriorating economic climate beyond mayoral control—long-standing trends toward deindustrialization in Chicago and the oil bust in New Orleans (not to mention federal cutbacks that affected both)—to increase poverty and the demands placed on already inadequate and dysfunctional systems of public service.[23] If anything, problems in these areas got worse rather than better. Still, the overwhelming popularity of both Morial and Washington with the poor and with residents of public housing meant that their opposition was rooted in more than their inability to successfully address long-standing urban ills.

Machine or machine-style patronage politicians within the black community in each city existed in an uncomfortable relationship with Morial and Washington, as did those who might be considered racial nationalists or ethnic chauvinists. In New Orleans, Dutch Morial's predecessor, Moon Landrieu, had cultivated his own coterie of black officials, and Morial found them in place, already on the public payroll and with strong ties to city government. They certainly expected to be treated no less well by the city's first black mayor and were, in fact, stunned and embittered when Morial staffed his administration with blacks and whites from private business, academia, and the professions. Morial conducted a minipurge and even discharged large numbers of those who had entered public employment under the aegis of their former white patron. They were confused by the radical Creole who stressed merit and tried to transcend traditional racial divisions, and they accused the mayor of hiring only "superblacks" who had been held to unrealistically high standards.[24]

Harold Washington similarly had to deal with a number of black ward committeemen and aldermen who found themselves tied to his cause by an aroused constituency but who felt distinctly ill at ease with the mayor's reform posture. Creatures of the Democratic machine for most of their careers, they saw no reason to eschew spoils politics just as one of their own earned the keys to the city vault. Unable to oppose Washington openly—to do so would have been racial treason as defined by the nationalists and political suicide—they bided their time as nominal converts to a crusade in which they had no faith.[25]

The New Orleans and Chicago experiences diverge at this point to the extent that a segment of the black spoils politicians in the southern metrop-

olis embraced the rhetoric and goals of racial nationalism in their thirst for
the emoluments of office—the novelty of the black presence in New Orleans's
political life meant that the patronage seeker's racial "militancy" could have
a ring of plausibility. In Chicago, however, the African-American machine
politicians had so long been affiliated with Richard J. Daley's organization
that they could not credibly rattle the racial saber. Instead, Chicago had a
larger, more institutionalized, more vocal nationalist community that had
played its own distinct role in Washington's initial campaign and placed its
own demands on his administration. The nationalist community was no less
distressed than the machine politicians (albeit for quite different reasons) by
Washington's transition team, cabinet of advisers, patronage policies, political priorities, and campaign endorsements, and they increasingly found
themselves distanced from his administration.[26] That the mayor's "Dream
Slate" for county elections in 1988 included names such as Daley and Pucinski bespoke the grave differences in their agendas.

Indeed, the democratization of Chicago and New Orleans, pursued ardently by both Washington and Morial, offered something less to insiders (whether political or racial) seeking favor than either the machine loyalists or the
nationalists wanted. As far as conventional, and more narrowly defined, racial interests were concerned, however, both mayors apparently had an influence in moderating the behavior of their respective police departments
(long a primary irritant in the relations between black communities and
successive municipal administrations and an achievement not to be underestimated) and in the vigor with which their cities pursued affirmative action initiatives in the granting of public jobs and contracts. If their efforts in
the latter instance were denounced by their white opponents as mere patronage in disguise, and by black dissenters as meager and insufficient, their attempt to open up the municipal polity and bring African Americans into the
mainstream apparently had the approval of the vast majority of black voters, who swept both to a second term. Finally, the sheer strength of their
personalities and their combative, aggressive, "tell it like it is" styles of governance and politics undoubtedly provided an enormous psychological boost
to communities that identified closely with their travails and, apparently,
values. In Chicago those pursuing a chauvinistic black agenda found themselves further hemmed in by their own success in making support for Washington a litmus test for "blackness" during his first campaign—they could
hardly oppose him later without appearing to undermine their community's champion.

The chaos surrounding Harold Washington's succession, and the more
deliberate, systematic procedures that orchestrated Dutch Morial's, illustrate

one last dimension of the racial struggle for political power in urban America. In each case, white opponents of the first black mayors demonstrated the resourcefulness and resolve to catapult themselves back into control by dominating the processes through which Chicago and New Orleans selected their second black mayors. And the African-American communities of the two cities, fearful and fragmented after the deaths of their most historic political figures (Morial died in December 1989, in the middle of his successor's re-election campaign), retreated to a narrower brand of racial politics that left them more isolated from power than before.

In Chicago the white ethnic bloc on the city council won over a handful of former black allies who had been tied to the machine but could not openly oppose Harold Washington while he lived. After this unseemly alliance failed to negotiate the recapture of city hall for the old white leadership, it threw its support to a compliant black machine operative, Eugene Sawyer, who accepted the backing in a raucous city council meeting that ran past 4:00 A.M. With blacks and whites gathered outside city hall in the predawn hours chanting "No deals," waving dollar bills, and throwing coins at Sawyer, a majority vote of the city council anointed him Chicago's second black mayor.[27] What remained of the machine had shamelessly donned blackface to salvage its fortunes and selected a candidate who became immediately and irredeemably tainted in the eyes of the black community. His Conveniency's administration inevitably shattered Washington's coalition, separating nationalists from machine loyalists, and both from Washington's reform-minded heirs.

The special mayoral election of 1989, and every subsequent contest for city hall, provided the ultimate measure of Harold Washington's strength, skill, and vision. Where he had harnessed the city's disparate black factions in his service, they now flew apart, each asserting its exclusive right to speak for the community. Most revealingly, Sawyer's hold on his black electoral base proved so tenuous that he lacked the freedom and will to immediately fire a lieutenant whose anti-Semitic rants had been exposed by the *Chicago Tribune*. A marginal figure in both the Sawyer administration and nationalist circles, Steve Cokely lingered on the city payroll for a week before public pressure overwhelmed the mayor's fear of breaking racial ranks. In the end, the hesitant and timid reaction of the city's black leadership in this matter—including that of Sawyer's chief African-American rival, Timothy Evans (whose ostensible "reform" candidacy had been hijacked by the nationalists)—made the resurrection of Washington's electoral coalition a virtual impossibility. Instead, the black contenders engaged in a mutually destructive political standoff, bitterly refusing either to bow out or endorse the other; Sawyer subsequently fell in the Democratic primary, and Evans, representing the freshly minted Harold

Washington Party, went down in the general election. Neither challenger was able to unify the black community or to look beyond it in conceiving, let alone executing, a successful campaign strategy.

The primary beneficiary of this black political disarray was none other than Richard M. Daley, known locally as the "Son of Boss" (SOB) or R2D2. Without a serious white ethnic competitor, Daley secured his base and proceeded to emulate Harold Washington. His popular appointment of African-American reporter Avis LaVelle as his press secretary aimed not only at winning a fragment of the black vote but, more important, at reassuring white liberals of his "progressive" leanings. Crucial here were the "East 40s" (wards 42, 43, 44, 46, 48, and 49) and the lakefront high-rises that delivered decisive (and many Jewish) votes for Washington. Additionally, Daley actively wooed the rapidly growing Latino community and won the calculated endorsement of Alderman Luis Gutierrez, formerly a key Washington ally; it was no accident that Daley wrapped up his campaign with a rally in Gutierrez's Twenty-sixth Ward. In the primary Daley defeated Sawyer by more than 100,000 votes, winning thirty-one of the city's fifty wards and 56 percent of the total vote. In each of the East 40s and the Latino wards his margin topped 60 percent. In the general election he dispatched Evans by 150,000 votes, earning 55 percent of the ballots cast. Tellingly, an exit poll revealed that 30 percent of his voters had formerly pulled the lever for Harold Washington.[28]

Successive campaigns produced similar results. All told, in seven different contests (primary and general elections in 1989, 1991, and 1995 and a nonpartisan primary in 1999) Daley the Younger defeated seven different black candidates. Activist or "movement" elements within the black community have practiced an insular brand of what one commentator has called "tribal politics" and have consistently failed to unify and mobilize African Americans around their racial standard, even as they refused to contemplate supporting serious white or Latino challengers to the new Daley regime. The result has been not merely that black candidates have been defeated but that, politically, the community remains divided and dispirited. In Harold Washington's 1987 campaign, 58.5 percent of all voting-age blacks (not just registered voters) turned out on election day; in 1991 that figure dropped to 26.9 percent. At one point it seemed as though Washington could indeed occupy city hall longer than the legendary Richard J. Daley. Death prevented that, and now his achievements seem more personal than institutional. It must be remembered, however, that Richie Daley's administration is not, and in fact could not be, built in his father's image; if he succeeds in shattering the family record for longevity in office, he will owe as much to the model provided by Harold Washington as that furnished by his own flesh and blood. Indeed, his 1999 victory over U.S. representative and former Black Panther Bobby Rush followed a ten-year courtship of black and Latino voters, which had been necessitated by the loss of nearly two million white Chicagoans between his father's first term and his own (whites represented less than a third of the city's population by the end of the century). The younger Daley had seized the political high ground and left his most embittered racial opposition appearing reactionary and chauvinistic. Whether such noteworthy results constitute a repudiation of his father's brand of racial politics or merely a clever adaptation remains arguable and to be seen.[29]

In New Orleans regular election procedures made Sidney Barthelemy, another Creole of color, the mayor after Dutch Morial failed in his attempts to change the city charter. Barthelemy, a leading opponent of Morial's campaign for unlimited terms as well as his second effort, to permit "Just 3," represented the strong assimilationist tendency among some New Orleans Creoles and was the antithesis of the fading Creole radicalism personified by Morial. A Moon Landrieu protégé, Barthelemy had strong ties to the local Urban League and enjoyed close contact with the white civic and economic leadership. Running against another black candidate in what had become, during the Morial era, a majority-black city, Barthelemy turned Dutch Morial's winning electoral coalition inside out. Where Morial had been elected with solid and massive black support, combined with a liberal fragment of white backing, Barthelemy went into office with 85 percent of the white vote and the support of barely one in four black voters. Morial's progressive biracial coalition had been transformed into a conservative one that knit together whites and a patronage-oriented black leadership that had no agenda beyond its own enrichment and perpetuation. White New Orleans had found itself a black mayor it could live with—one that would protect, rather than challenge, the status quo.[30]

Ironically, when Barthelemy ran for reelection in 1990, he campaigned as the hope of the black community. In facing Donald Mintz, a white candidate with a good civil rights record, Barthelemy ran (in the weeks immediately after Morial's unexpected death) as a racial champion. As was the case with Eugene Sawyer, another emergent black politician who had left no tracks in the snow of the civil rights revolution, Barthelemy exploited symbolic racial issues and fears. But unlike Sawyer, he ran in what was now a majority-black city and won. His second winning coalition appeared, then, as an unlikely combination that mixed conservative whites at the top of his campaign structure with a mass of black voters at the bottom. It was a shotgun marriage of the rankest sort.

New Orleans's second black mayor, who held office for two terms, as opposed to Sawyer's two years, walked a policy tightrope. Some blacks—at least those tied directly to Barthelemy's political entourage—received the traditional rewards that have flowed to urban minorities that have become electoral majorities. The doling out of the patronage associated with the Housing Authority of New Orleans, Regional Transit Authority, New Orleans Exhibition Hall Authority, Aviation Board, and other agencies proved a consuming endeavor at city hall. For the rest of the African-American community, Barthelemy made the occasional symbolic gesture (such as dismantling offensive street barricades put up by neighboring suburban Jefferson Parish) and the promise of economic development. By the end of his administration, however, two of his heralded "achievements" stood as mute testimony to his lack of success. A major Pic 'N' Save distribution warehouse lay in ashes in eastern New Orleans, not to be rebuilt, and an unfinished land-based casino stood as an empty shell on valuable downtown property, a ghostly and ghastly reminder of the pitfalls of doing business in Louisiana.[31]

Barthelemy proved more adept at serving as a cheerleader for those corporate and social interests that needed public support for their initiatives. Most significantly, members of the Audubon Park Commission—who had been embroiled in so many bitter struggles with Dutch Morial—fought alongside Barthelemy to retain term limits and later supported him in his own mayoral run. The mayor now returned the favor, leading the charge for a referendum that secured public funds for the construction and operation of a new aquarium, and he offered no opposition to the creation of a new private nonprofit entity, the Audubon Institute, which would run it all on a "business" basis. If this did not represent the "regionalization" of the old commission, it accomplished what Morial's earlier adversaries desired: insulation from the pressures of a democratic polity in a majority-black city without sacrificing public financial support.[32]

Dutch Morial's legacy, however, would not be so easily or completely undone. The term limits that brought Barthelemy into office in 1986 took him out in 1994. Dutch's son, Marc H. Morial, won a hard-fought campaign against the same white challenger earlier dispatched by Barthelemy and then coasted to reelection, virtually unopposed, in 1998. The younger Morial's popularity stemmed, in large part, from a significant drop in crime and his earnest efforts to professionalize a notoriously brutal and corrupt police department that seemed to sink to new depths during the Barthelemy years. Most notably, the mayor went to Washington, D.C., to recruit outsider Richard Pennington as police superintendent, a move that has been widely credited for the city's turnaround. Willing to attack difficult issues of broad social concern, such as the revamping of public housing and education, the second Morial administration holds forth at least the promise of change. Marc Morial has even traveled to Chicago to confer with Richard M. Daley on educational reform, experiments in privatization, and mayoral responsibility. The sons, if they do not always occupy common ground, at least share common problems.

Clearly, Sawyer and Barthelemy resembled each other more than their assertive predecessors. The second black mayors of Chicago and New Orleans each fronted a white countercoup that tried to turn back the clock. Still, the long shadows cast by Harold Washington and Dutch Morial cloak their respective cities and the current dynastic occupants of their city halls. If the Morial legacy is direct and obvious in New Orleans, Richard M. Daley, at least, has wrapped himself in the mantle of reform and stolen a page from Harold Washington's political playbook. Given the reconfigured political landscape in Chicago, it is also evident that Daley II cannot afford to address racial issues as cavalierly or arrogantly as did his father. While the promise and rhetoric of reform and racial egalitarianism may outstrip the substance, the current administration cannot ignore the Washington legacy. In any event, fundamental structural change may well prove elusive in both cases. Changes in the global economy as well as the federal government's retreat from urban affairs have rendered purely local responses to municipal problems partial answers at best. To the extent that such solutions might be ameliorative, however, Chicago and New Orleans are perhaps better situated now than they were a short generation ago. If they are, it is due in no small measure to the lasting, democratizing influence of Harold Washington and Dutch Morial.

Notes

An earlier version of this chapter appeared in Raymond A. Mohl, ed., *The Making of Urban America* (Wilmington, Dela.: Scholarly Resources, 1997), 265–82. The author wishes to acknowledge the generous support of the American Council of Learned Societies (ACLS) in the preparation of this chapter.

1. For an introduction to the concept of Creole radicalism, see Arnold R. Hirsch and Joseph Logsdon, eds., *Creole New Orleans: Race and Americanization* (Baton Rouge: Louisiana State University Press, 1992), esp. pp. 189–319.

2. Rodolphe Lucien Desdunes, *Our People and Our History,* trans. and ed. Olga Dorothea McCants (Baton Rouge: Louisiana State University Press, 1973), 141. A somewhat more detailed look at Dutch Morial's political career is offered in Arnold R. Hirsch, "Race and Politics in Modern New Orleans: The Mayoralty of Dutch Morial," *Amerikastudien/ American Studies* 35, no. 4 (December 1991): 461–84.

3. For early black politics in Chicago see Charles Branham, "Black Chicago: Accommodationist Politics Before the Great Migration," in Melvin G. Holli and Peter d'A. Jones, eds., *The Ethnic Frontier: Essays in the History of Group Survival in Chicago and the Midwest* (Grand Rapids, Mich.: Eerdmans, 1977), 211–62; see also Branham's dissertation, "A

Transformation of Black Political Leadership in Chicago, 1864–1942" (Ph.D. diss., University of Chicago, 1981). Other important works are St. Clair Drake and Horace Cayton, *Black Metropolis: A Study of Negro Life in the Northern City* (New York: Harper and Row, 1970); Harold F. Gosnell, *Negro Politicians: The Rise of Negro Politics in Chicago* (Chicago: University of Chicago Press, 1967); Allan H. Spear, *Black Chicago: The Making of a Negro Ghetto, 1890–1920* (Chicago: University of Chicago Press, 1967); William M. Tuttle Jr., *Race Riot: Chicago in the Red Summer of 1919* (New York: Atheneum, 1970); John W. Allswang, *A House for All Peoples: Ethnic Politics in Chicago, 1890–1936* (Lexington: University Press of Kentucky, 1971).

4. For Harold Washington's early life and career see Florence Hamlish Levinsohn, *Harold Washington: A Political Biography* (Chicago: Chicago Review Press, 1983); Gary Rivlin, *Fire on the Prairie: Chicago's Harold Washington and the Politics of Race* (New York: Holt, 1992); Robert McClory, "Up from Obscurity: Harold Washington," in Melvin G. Holli and Paul M. Green, eds., *The Making of the Mayor: Chicago, 1983* (Grand Rapids, Mich.: Eerdmans, 1984), 3–16; William J. Grimshaw, *Bitter Fruit: Black Politics and the Chicago Machine, 1931–1991* (Chicago: University of Chicago Press, 1992); Dempsey J. Travis, *An Autobiography of Black Politics* (Chicago: Urban Research Institute, 1987).

5. For the primary election see Hirsch, "Race and Politics in Modern New Orleans," 465–68; for a broader context and essential background see also Hirsch, "Simply a Matter of Black and White: The Transformation of Race and Politics in Twentieth-Century New Orleans," in Hirsch and Logsdon, *Creole New Orleans,* 262–319, and Hirsch, "New Orleans: Sunbelt in the Swamp," in Richard M. Bernard and Bradley R. Rice, eds., *Sunbelt Cities: Politics and Growth Since World War II* (Austin: University of Texas Press, 1983), 100–137; see also Edward M. Haas, *DeLesseps S. Morrison and the Image of Reform: New Orleans Politics, 1946–1961* (Baton Rouge: Louisiana State University Press, 1974).

6. *Times-Picayune,* October 3, November 13, 14, 1977; *(New Orleans) Figaro,* May 4, August 3, October 5, 12, 19, November 16, 1977; *Louisiana Weekly,* November 12, 1977.

7. For Harold Washington's first mayoral triumph, see Grimshaw, *Bitter Fruit,* 167–96; Holli and Green, *Making of the Mayor;* Levinsohn, *Harold Washington,* 189–300; Travis, *Autobiography of Black Politics,* 528–610; and Paul Kleppner, *Chicago Divided: The Making of a Black Mayor* (DeKalb: Northern Illinois University Press, 1985).

8. Rivlin, *Fire on the Prairie,* 196.

9. Joy J. Jackson, *New Orleans in the Gilded Age: Politics and Urban Progress, 1880–1896* (Baton Rouge: Louisiana State University Press, 1969); Peirce F. Lewis, *New Orleans: The Making of an Urban Landscape* (Cambridge, Mass.: Ballinger, 1976).

10. For Chicago's "council wars," see Grimshaw, *Bitter Fruit,* 184–86, 189, 191, 213; Rivlin, *Fire on the Prairie,* 205–344; Melvin G. Holli and Paul M. Green, *Bashing Chicago Traditions: Harold Washington's Last Campaign* (Grand Rapids, Mich.: Eerdmans, 1989), 166. The headline is cited in Rivlin, *Fire on the Prairie,* 233.

11. Morial's speech is reprinted in its entirety in *(New Orleans) Figaro,* January 25, 1978; Charles Y. W. Chai, "Who Rules New Orleans?" *Louisiana Business Survey* 2 (October 1971): 2–7.

12. Hirsch, "Race and Politics in Modern New Orleans," 469–70, 472, 473, and passim.

13. *Louisiana Weekly,* September 18, 1982; July 23, 1983.

14. Rivlin, *Fire on the Prairie,* 187, 222.

15. Ibid., 235–36.

16. Grimshaw, *Bitter Fruit*, 189–90; Kleppner, *Chicago Divided*, 140; Rivlin, *Fire on the Prairie*, 348–58.

17. Rivlin, *Fire on the Prairie*, 357–61; Holli and Green, *Bashing Chicago Traditions*, 35–36.

18. Rivlin, *Fire on the Prairie*, 400–401.

19. Alderman Ed Burke, a bitter Washington foe, denounced the derailment of the nonpartisan primary proposition as a political ploy. With knowing appreciation, however, he added that he had to "compliment whoever thought of it." See Holli and Green, *Bashing Chicago Traditions*, 36–43.

20. A more detailed summary of Morial's two terms can be found in Hirsch, "Race and Politics in Modern New Orleans," 461–84.

21. Holli and Green, *Bashing Chicago Traditions*, 170, 187–88; Rivlin, *Fire on the Prairie*, 400.

22. Hirsch, "Race and Politics in Modern New Orleans," 473; Rivlin, *Fire on the Prairie*, 384–90.

23. The social and economic trends for Chicago are closely examined in Gregory D. Squires, Larry Bennett, Kathleen McCourt, and Philip Nyden, *Chicago: Race, Class, and the Response to Urban Decline* (Philadelphia: Temple University Press, 1987).

24. Hirsch, "Simply a Matter of Black and White," 310–16.

25. Grimshaw, *Bitter Fruit*, 133–36; Rivlin, *Fire on the Prairie*, 403–20.

26. The black nationalist role in Harold Washington's campaigns and his administration, and its growing sense of estrangement, are handled in depth and throughout Rivlin, *Fire on the Prairie*. See also Abdul Alkalimat and Doug Gills, *Harold Washington and the Crisis of Black Power in Chicago* (Chicago: Twenty-First Century Books, 1989).

27. For some background and context see Arnold R. Hirsch, "Chicago: The Cook County Democratic Organization and the Dilemma of Race, 1931–1987" in Richard M. Bernard, ed., *Snowbelt Cities: Metropolitan Politics in the Northeast and Midwest Since World War II* (Bloomington: Indiana University Press, 1987), 63–90. For Sawyer's rise (and fall), see Grimshaw, *Bitter Fruit*, 197–224, and Rivlin, *Fire on the Prairie*, 403–20.

28. See the essays collected in Paul M. Green and Melvin G. Holli, eds., *Restoration: Chicago Elects a New Daley* (Chicago: Lyceum, 1991).

29. Salim Muwakkil, "Daley Won't be Dethroned by Rush's Stale Strategy," *Chicago Tribune*, August 17, 1998; Neal Pollack, "Searching for the Great Black Hope," *Reader*, December 2, 1994. For contrasting assessments of Richard M. Daley, see Grimshaw, *Bitter Fruit*, 197–224, and Melvin G. Holli, "Daley to Daley," in Green and Holli, *Restoration*, 193–207.

30. Hirsch, "Simply a Matter of Black and White," 317–18.

31. The casino has since opened but failed to generate its predicted (*promised* might be more accurate) level of business. As this book went to press, profit shortfalls were provoking speculation that the casino would soon seek financial relief in the form of tax concessions from the state legislature.

32. Robert K. Whelan, Alma H. Young, and Mickey Lauria, "Urban Regimes and Racial Politics in New Orleans," *Journal of Urban Affairs* 16 (1994): 1–21.

5. Mayor David Dinkins and the Politics of Race in New York City

ROGER BILES

NEW YORK CITY has frequently been the pacesetter among urban places in the United States, but not until 1989, more than twenty years after the breakthrough by Carl Stokes in Cleveland, Ohio, and Richard Hatcher in Gary, Indiana, did the voters in the largest U.S. city choose a black politician as mayor. The comparative lateness of David Dinkins's election, along with the decision of the electorate to replace him after just one term in office, can be understood only with an appreciation of New York City's demographic and political history. Paramount in Dinkins's election in 1989 were issues regarding race and ethnicity, and they resurfaced repeatedly during his mayoralty and figured prominently in his unsuccessful reelection campaign in 1993. The city's first black mayor constructed a fragile multiracial coalition that failed to survive his troubled four years in office.[1]

By the late twentieth century, New York City was home to an extraordinarily diverse mixture of races and ethnic groups. In 1990 whites remained the single largest racial group in the city, but they were no longer a majority (see table 5.1). With the liberalization of U.S. immigration policy since 1970, the number of immigrants soared; Kennedy Airport became the Ellis Island of the modern era. The 1990 census recorded two million immigrants—approximately one fourth of the city's population—living within the five boroughs.

The largest single group of newcomers, blacks from such Caribbean nations as the Dominican Republic, Haiti, and Guyana, constituted a third of the immigrants to the city. Asian immigrants, though relatively small in number by comparison, accounted for more than 20 percent of New York City's foreign-born residents by 1990. As a consequence of such intense immigration

Table 5.1. Population Changes in New York City, 1980–90

	1980		1990		Change
Total population	7,071,639		7,322,564		3.55%
Whites	3,668,738	(51.9%)	3,163,125	(43.2%)	−13.79
Blacks	1,694,127	(23.9%)	1,847,049	(25.2%)	9.03
Latinos	1,406,024	(19.8%)	1,783,511	(24.3%)	26.85
Asians	300,406	(4.2%)	489,851	(6.7%)	63.06
Other	2,344	(0.2%)	39,028	(0.6%)	1,565.02

Source: John H. Mollenkopf, *New York City in the 1980s: A Social, Economic, and Political Atlas* (New York: Simon and Schuster, 1993), 93.

at a time when whites were fleeing the city in increasing numbers—two million whites left between 1970 and 1980—blacks became the largest component of a burgeoning nonwhite plurality.[2]

Historically, blacks played an extremely limited role in municipal politics. Before the Civil War state constitutions and statutes throughout the North as well as the South disfranchised blacks; the revision of New York City's municipal charter in 1821 did so as well. Even after the ratification of the Fifteenth Amendment, the small number of blacks living in cities kept urban politics primarily a white affair. In the days before the Great Migration of southern blacks to northern industrial cities, the leaders of local political organizations saw no need to field black candidates or cultivate black electoral support—especially when larger ethnic groups produced more votes and demanded to be rewarded for past loyalties. In short, blacks simply lacked the number of votes to compete effectively in the urban electoral arena. Individual black politicians often forged personal links with local political machines, receiving low-level appointive positions in government and honorary posts in civic and social agencies. This arrangement, which the political scientist Martin Kilson has called "clientage politics," flourished in a number of large cities around the turn of the nineteenth century. In New York City, Charles W. Anderson became the black intermediary with the local Republican organization and held a series of patronage jobs in federal agencies as a reward. Anderson and other black clients of predominantly white political organizations enjoyed heightened status in black communities but wielded scant influence citywide.[3]

By the twentieth century, more blacks lived in New York City than in any other community, but the black percentage of the city's overall population remained comparatively small. Because New York City's large, heterogeneous electoral districts spread black voters thinly, and because the vast majority of blacks voted Republican whereas the Democratic Party dominated city government, black candidates enjoyed little success in local contests. The election of the first black alderman came in 1919, the first black district leader ten years later. In the 1930s and 1940s the meteoric rise to prominence of the Reverend Adam Clayton Powell Jr. gave evidence of a newly aggressive style of black leadership in New York City. In 1944, after boundary adjustments created a new congressional district with a nonwhite majority, Powell became the city's first black member of Congress. Using his Harlem church (Abyssinian Baptist) as a base of support, he formed the Greater New York Coordinating Committee to politicize the emerging black middle class and the upwardly mobile skilled workforce. Powell criticized Harlem's black elites for their conservative politics and pioneered activist tactics like boycotts and picketing against racial discrimination. He gained national acclaim as a militant spokesman against old-style racial clientage politics and by the 1950s became, arguably, the best-known black political leader in the nation. His flamboyant personality and concentration of power in the Abyssinian Baptist Church made his appeal personal, however; his celebrity contributed little to the construction of a stronger black political organization in New York City.[4]

Sustained black population growth after the Second World War resulted in New York City blacks' gradually achieving more influence within the local Democratic Party. The primary practitioner of this expanding influence, J. Raymond Jones, held a series of increasingly important local posts during the time that Powell was engaged in national civil rights battles. A native of the Virgin Islands, Jones emigrated to Harlem during World War I and shortly thereafter launched a career in Democratic politics that lasted through the 1960s. Known as "the Fox" for his political acumen, Jones eschewed the role of racial spokesman and concentrated solely on the nitty-gritty of electoral politics. He succeeded well enough to become vice chairman of the New York County Executive Committee, Harlem's city council member, and New York County (Manhattan Borough) chairman. Despite these achievements, however, the local Democratic leadership never considered Jones a candidate for mayor. In 1969, when he resigned his last political post, blacks comprised only 19 percent of New York City's population and a smaller percentage of the electorate.[5]

The election of the liberal John Lindsay as mayor in 1965 and 1969, along with the growing number of minority candidates elected to municipal posts, suggested that a biracial, progressive coalition might have been viable by the 1970s. In fact, the essentially conservative mayoralties of Abraham Beame (1974–78) and Edward Koch (1978–90) rested upon a white ethnic political base and established policies that reversed the kind of redistributive spending initiated in the Lindsay years. In 1977 Manhattan Borough President Percy

Sutton became the first black New Yorker to mount a serious campaign for mayor but in a crowded field of candidates could do no better than fifth in the Democratic primary election. Dispirited by his lackluster showing, black leaders declined to field a candidate four years later against the incumbent Koch. In 1985 the black leadership of Manhattan declined to support a Puerto Rican or woman candidate against Koch and insisted upon the selection of an undistinguished black politician, Herman Farrell. He received only 40 percent of the black vote and 28 percent of Latino ballots and finished a distant third in the Democratic primary. The debacle soured black-Latino relations, heightened tensions between male and female black leaders, and exacerbated bad feelings between blacks from Manhattan and the surrounding boroughs.[6]

In the 1970s and 1980s New York City's disparate black political factions found uniting in common cause to be impossible. Black political leaders in Harlem, the traditional center of nonwhite political activity in the city, jealously resisted the growing power of the expanding minority communities in the outer boroughs—particularly in Brooklyn, where many young activists sounded themes of protest and black nationalism. Just as geography divided blacks politically, so did ethnicity. Although whites often saw black communities as homogeneous enclaves, native-born and immigrant blacks occupied quite different niches in New York City society. Black immigrants of first- and second-generation West Indian ancestry held subordinate economic and occupational positions and accordingly held unique political views. Considerations of class complicated racial politics as black newcomers frequently criticized what they perceived as the economic conservatism of native-born black voters.[7]

The second largest minority group in New York City, Latinos, seemed no more capable of forging a unified political front. Puerto Ricans had long been the dominant Caribbean group in the metropolis, but the arrival of growing numbers of Dominicans and other Latin American immigrants beginning in the 1960s altered the city's political demographics. Nor had the Puerto Ricans been a unified electoral force in the decades before their numbers declined relative to other Latin populations in the city. Puerto Ricans had failed repeatedly to unite behind one of their own candidates for citywide office. Although they were more inclined than the city's blacks to support the regular Democratic county organizations, the Puerto Rican leaders of the five boroughs seldom cooperated on matters of common interest. Moreover, the widespread belief among Puerto Ricans that their political leaders were selfish and ineffective kept voter registration low and political activity limited.[8]

The political fragmentation among the city's minority communities redounded to the benefit of Mayor Ed Koch, a shrewd politician whose ability to unite New York City's diverse white ethnic groups made him a formidable incumbent. A Democrat from the liberal stronghold of Greenwich Village, Koch became increasingly conservative during his years in city hall. Throughout his first two mayoral terms (1978–86), he remained relatively popular with nonwhite voters. His prickly personality and acerbic tongue seemed to offend everyone equally, and he cultivated a reputation for plain speaking that appealed to populist sympathies. If his diatribes against Great Society welfarism rankled liberals and poor blacks, his impassioned defense of the middle class cut across racial lines and won him favor among the expanding black and Latino bourgeoisie. During his third term, however, Koch's drift to the right politically seemed to quicken, and he became embroiled in a number of race-related controversies that undermined his popularity among minority voters. By the time of his third reelection campaign in 1989, he had become widely known as the champion of the city's white population.[9]

The apparent deterioration of race relations in New York City during the Koch years accelerated during his third term. Bernhard Goetz's vigilante shootings of four black youths who threatened him on the subway, and the sensational coverage of the event by the city's tabloids, highlighted the widespread fear of black violent crime. In December 1986 a gang of white youths beat three black men in the Queens neighborhood of Howard Beach; one victim died after he was struck by an automobile as he was fleeing his assailants. He died, according to Manhattan Borough President David Dinkins, at the hands of "a white gang [behaving] like a pack of dogs on a Sunday fox hunt." Accusations by a young black woman, Tawana Brawley, of abduction and rape by whites in Newburgh, New York, ignited another contretemps, and the disclosure that Brawley had fabricated the incident only contributed to a growing sense of mistrust between the races.[10]

Mayor Koch had been appropriately condemnatory of violence perpetrated against blacks, and had agreed to name an independent prosecutor in the Howard Beach case, but was nonetheless censured for doing little to dampen racial hostility in the city. His controversial role in the presidential primary campaign of Jesse Jackson in 1988 intensified the criticisms. Citing remarks that Jackson had made in defense of the Palestine Liberation Organization's Yasir Arafat and Jackson's acceptance of support from Black Muslim leader Louis Farrakhan, the mayor opined that Jews "would have to be crazy" to vote for Jackson.

The black press in New York City roundly denounced Koch's comments; the *Amsterdam News* published a series of front-page demands for the mayor's resignation. After weeks of bitter campaigning, Jackson won the New York

City Democratic primary along strict racial voting lines. Exit polls showed that Jackson received 88.2 percent of the black and 63.5 percent of the Latino votes cast, but only 17 percent of white votes and just 9 percent of Jewish ballots. What the local press portrayed as an electoral showdown between Koch and Jackson left the latter a clear-cut victor. Most important, with a mayoral election just a year away, Jackson's surprising victory and the numbers of new minority voters enrolled by his campaign led political pundits to speculate whether a black mayoral candidate might for the first time have a realistic chance at election.[11]

In 1989 David Dinkins emerged as Mayor Koch's principal opponent within the Democratic Party. Dinkins had grown up in Trenton, New Jersey, the son of a barbershop owner and a manicurist. He became one of the first blacks to serve in the U.S. Marine Corps and graduated from Howard University (where he and Atlanta mayor Andrew Young belonged to the same fraternity). After Brooklyn Law School, he practiced law in New York City for eighteen years. Through his wife, the daughter of a Harlem Democratic ward leader, he became involved in politics. An acolyte of the legendary Harlem Fox, J. Raymond Jones, Dinkins served one term in the state assembly and spent ten years as the city clerk before being elected Manhattan borough president (on the third try) in 1985. The veteran politico played a high-profile role in the 1988 primary, establishing good relations with Jackson's white liberal and Latino supporters. With a strong base in Harlem political clubs, the backing of the city's municipal unions, and the unified support of the city's black political leadership, Dinkins appeared well positioned to mount a formidable challenge to Koch.[12]

Despite the many strengths of his candidacy, however, Dinkins seemed in many respects an uninspiring choice. A quiet, nondescript clubhouse politician throughout his long and generally undistinguished career, he had managed even as Manhattan borough president to remain largely invisible to New York City voters. Known as a stolid and courtly gentleman but certainly not a dynamic or forceful leader, the sixty-two-year-old Dinkins surprised the experts with his decision to challenge the estimable Koch. Asked about Dinkins's candidacy, a minority political leader responded: "I think Dave's a wonderful guy, but let me tell you three things about him running for mayor: First, he'll make a lousy candidate. Second, in the unlikely event that he does win, he'll make a terrible mayor. Third, I will support him." The lack of enthusiasm for Dinkins notwithstanding, the political leader seemed to be saying that the time for a black mayor had arrived.[13]

The racial unease that animated Dinkins's candidacy persisted in the months preceding the August 1989 primary election. On April 20 the grisly rape and beating in Central Park of a white jogger, a young female investment banker, by black teenagers on a "wilding" excursion left the city in shock and constituted what *New York* magazine called a "psychic turning point for the city." In contrast to Mayor Koch's fulminations about law and order, Dinkins spoke about the need for racial rapprochement—a theme that became central to his campaign. On August 23, in the Brooklyn neighborhood of Bensonhurst, a gang of whites murdered sixteen-year-old Yusef Hawkins, a black man who had ventured into the Italian neighborhood to inspect a used car. Koch initially denied any racial motivation in the homicide and then lambasted blacks for protesting Hawkins's death in Bensonhurst; Koch's confrontational remarks seemed to intensify the crisis. Dinkins, who had earlier acted as an intermediary to calm tensions in the Howard Beach and Tawana Brawley episodes, earned praise once again for his conciliation efforts among blacks. Although Dinkins generally took the high road and spoke of racial reconciliation, he also hinted that Koch bore at least partial responsibility for the tragedy in Bensonhurst. "The tone and climate of this city is set at City Hall," Dinkins claimed. As racial animosities finally cooled in Brooklyn, New York governor Mario Cuomo implicitly endorsed Dinkins, suggesting that the next mayor should be the person saying to the city's factionalized populace: "I will bring you together."[14]

Excoriated for contributing to the city's racial volatility, Koch also found his candidacy damaged by a spate of scandals that emerged during his third term. A number of high-ranking city officials and dozens of lower-level functionaries left office in disgrace or went to jail, and one target of investigation, the Democratic borough president of Queens, committed suicide by plunging a knife into his heart. Koch lamely denied any knowledge of the widespread corruption that seemed to pervade his administration; he campaigned for reelection by reciting the achievements of his first two terms and questioning the extent of Dinkins's experience. Unable to campaign too aggressively for fear of conforming to the emerging picture of him as a racially insensitive politician, the mayor never attacked Dinkins as zealously as he might have. On September 12 a coalition of black, Latino, and white voters gave the challenger a decisive victory over the incumbent. With more than a million Democrats voting, Dinkins secured 50.8 percent of the votes to Koch's 42 percent. According to exit polls, the winner of the Democratic primary received 84.8 percent of black votes, 60.4 percent of Latino votes, and approximately 33 percent of white votes. To a substantial number of white as well as minority voters, David Dinkins seemed eminently better suited than Ed Koch to heal the city's gaping racial wounds.[15]

Registered Democrats outnumbered Republicans 5 to 1 in New York City, and Governor Cuomo and Mayor Koch endorsed their party's candidate, but a number of factors left Dinkins's election far from certain. Blacks, Latinos, and white liberals predominated in the Democratic primary but wielded less influence in the general election, in which whites, both Republicans and independents, voted in greater numbers. Although the mayor had dutifully pledged to support the Democratic nominee, it remained uncertain whether the more conservative elements of the Koch coalition—especially the Jews and Roman Catholics of the outer boroughs—would remain loyal to the party's candidate. In addition, the Republicans fielded a strong candidate in Rudolph Giuliani, a renowned federal prosecutor who had indicted a long list of Mafia dons and crooked politicians, as well as the infamous white-collar criminals Leona Helmsley, Ivan Boesky, and Michael Milken. In the Republican primary, Giuliani had easily dispatched Ronald Lauder, scion of the Estée Lauder cosmetics empire, and proved to be an eager, tough campaigner.[16]

At the outset of the eight-week mayoral campaign, Dinkins projected the image of a compassionate healer, an earnest if inarticulate man of good intentions. In early October he enjoyed a twenty-four-point cushion in the polls, but his comfortable lead gradually evaporated as the campaign grew nastier. Giuliani hired Roger Ailes, a notoriously aggressive media consultant who had spearheaded George Bush's ruthless campaign against Michael Dukakis in the 1988 presidential election. Under Ailes's ardent direction the New York Republicans attacked the front-running Dinkins with relish, especially by raising questions about questionable financial dealings in his past. Dinkins had failed to file income tax returns from 1969 to 1972, an embarrassing fact he had acknowledged in 1973. Referring to his nonpayment of taxes as a regrettable oversight, Dinkins promptly paid the taxes plus interest. His explanation, however, was as unsatisfactory as it was confusing: "I haven't committed a crime. What I did was fail to comply with the law." As another example of his opponent's cavalier attitude toward his personal finances, Giuliani cited the millionaire Dinkins's sale of stock valued at $1.2 million to his son, David Jr., for $67,800. Giuliani suggested that this was evidence of "moral laxity" and raised serious doubts about Dinkins's character. If he never quite said that the Democratic candidate lacked the intelligence to master the job of mayor, Giuliani repeatedly ridiculed the vague and confusing answers Dinkins gave to specific policy questions. Also, the Republican questioned whether an old-line liberal Democrat like Dinkins could assert his independence from the cloying interest groups (especially the municipal unions) to which he would be beholden because of their support.[17]

In response Dinkins pointed to his solid backing from state and local Democratic leaders as well as Giuliani's lack of managerial experience. Dinkins supporters also noted that, while acting as head of the U.S. Justice Depart-

ment's criminal division in the Reagan administration, Giuliani had personally oversaw the forced repatriation of Haitian exiles to the bloodthirsty de-
vices of the notorious Tontons Macoutes. To suggestions that his liberalism
bespoke a softness on crime, the Democratic candidate pledged to be "the
toughest mayor on crime this city has ever seen." Most of all, Dinkins emphasized his ability to bring the city together, to calm the roiling racial seas
that seemed to be lapping at the city from all sides. He spoke of creating a
rainbow coalition that would unite New York City's colorful racial and ethnic mosaic; the city's heterogeneity, he averred, could be made an asset rather than a liability.

On November 7, 1989, a slender majority endorsed Dinkins's optimistic
view and provided him with a 47,000-vote margin of victory out of 1.9 million votes cast in the closest mayoral election since 1905; he received 51 percent of the vote to Giuliani's 48 percent. Assured of heavy support from the
city's minority groups, Dinkins received the respectable showing among white
voters that he needed to win the election. Blacks and Latinos voted for him
in expectedly large majorities—89.0 percent and 73.6 percent, respectively—
and he received just enough white votes (about 25 percent of the total) to edge
Giuliani. In a city haunted by racial polarization, Dinkins's claim to be able
to defuse tensions apparently appealed to many voters of all colors. In that
respect the key to victory rested with his ability to be unthreatening enough
to attract uncertain white voters. As a white supporter of the mayor-elect
concluded: "David Dinkins is not really a black politician. He's a coalition
politician. For people who are white and for whom race is an important factor, Dinkins is not scary. They have nothing to fear."[18]

In the immediate aftermath of Dinkins's election blacks jubilantly celebrated the historic election of one of their own to the mayor's office, just as
many white voters expressed cautious optimism that the election of a minority politician would indeed be a good thing for New York City. Yet doubts
lingered about Dinkins's ability to govern the nation's largest city. In part,
the concerns stemmed from his putative timidity, indecisiveness, and mal-
leability. A halting, laborious orator whose campaign speeches offered little
but platitudes exalting brotherhood and cooperation, Dinkins did not appear to be the kind of dynamic leader the city required. Some observers questioned whether he would have the toughness Koch exhibited in managing
New York City's powerful bureaucracies. Indeed, could Dinkins be a reliable
steward of the city's resources by saying no to the special interests he had long
championed? Not even the black leadership that had rallied around the new
mayor's candidacy felt assured that their man was up to the task. Mindful of
Dinkins's reputation as a good soldier who loyally carried out policy rather

than challenged or made it, Calvin O. Butts III, pastor of Harlem's Abyssinian Baptist Church, warned: "Dinkins is as much a machine, clubhouse politician as he is African-American."[19]

Questions about Dinkins's mettle were magnified because of the staggering array of problems confronting the new mayor in 1990. New York City had for decades been precariously balanced over a precipice, and Koch left his successor no shortage of worrisome dilemmas. Dinkins inherited a $1 billion deficit and greater fiscal problems on the horizon. More than one fourth of the city's $26 billion budget went to pay its 360,000 municipal employees, and with contracts expiring in 1990–91, the new mayor faced contentious bargaining with union negotiators to hold down wages. City officials counted 75,000 homeless in New York City, only 35,000 of whom were able to find shelter nightly, and the city needed 250,000 more housing units. Schools, social agencies, and the health-care system lacked adequate resources. The closing of bridges, highways, and streets, and the frequent explosion of water mains gave the impression that New York City's aged infrastructure was collapsing. "In the seventies, we didn't have a crack problem, we didn't have an AIDS problem, and we didn't have a homeless problem," commented Felix Rohatyn, chairman of the Municipal Assistance Corporation, in reference to the many intractable social ills facing New York City in the 1990s. "These problems won't go away." Many pundits feared that the accumulation of problems would finally overwhelm the business community and the middle class, two groups already concerned about having a black mayor, and their exit from the city for greener suburban pastures would reduce an already declining tax base. Clearly, Dinkins would need all his famed poise and patience to impose order on crisis-ridden New York City.[20]

Throughout his administration Dinkins had to grapple with the intractable problem of how to balance the city's budget, satisfy the business community's demand for fiscal responsibility, and still find the resources to offer the costly social programs that much of his constituency and his own liberal beliefs demanded. As the new mayor quickly pointed out, the financial pressures on New York City had worsened during the preceding decade. Tax revenues had fallen abruptly after the stock market dive of October 19, 1987, exacerbating the effect of an economic recession that had struck the nation's cities especially hard. During the same years the federal government had withdrawn desperately needed financial assistance. By 1991 federal aid accounted for just 9.3 percent of New York City's budget, down significantly from 17.9 percent ten years earlier (an actual loss of $1.2 billion). During the 1980s, despite declining revenues, the Koch administration had restored the forty thousand jobs to the municipal workforce that had been eliminated

during New York City's 1975 budgetary crisis. Indeed, according to city comp-
troller Elizabeth Holtzman, the number of additional jobs with which the
incoming Dinkins administration was saddled by Koch approached fifty
thousand.[21]

The mayor's Herculean struggle with the city budget began immediately
and continued throughout his four years in office. Only two days after his
inauguration Dinkins announced the suspension of the upcoming police
academy class (1,848 cadets) as a cost-cutting measure—a politically risky
move in a city obsessed with rising crime rates. In June 1990 city contracts with
most of its unionized employees expired, and the neophyte mayor promptly
plunged into the thicket of collective bargaining. After protracted negotiations
Dinkins announced a 5.8 percent annual wage increase for the teachers' union
and comparable raises for other municipal workers—a curiously generous
augmentation just as his administration was detailing the depths of the city's
budgetary woes. To pay for these pay increases the mayor called for a series
of tax increases as well as a $1.6 billion reduction in such services as day-care
programs, public health clinics, and after-school and recreational programs.
The mayor's willingness to cut spending on health, education, and welfare
programs seemed to target the lower classes particularly and sparked immediate dissent from the city's poorer neighborhoods.[22]

Enhanced funding of social welfare programs remained difficult because
of the crushing weight of the municipal payroll. During the mayoral campaign Dinkins had promised to curtail the runaway growth of labor costs.
Dismissing the notion that he would be hamstrung by his political and economic ties to the municipal unions that had supported him so avidly, Dinkins told financier Rohatyn: "Don't worry, they'll take it from me." The city
paid its 360,000 employees (250,000 of whom belonged to trade unions)
annual wages totaling $7.7 billion. According to the U.S. Bureau of the Cen-
sus, New York City employed 575 workers per 10,000 residents, an extraordinarily high ratio that was second only to that of Washington, D.C., among
major U.S. cities. (By contrast, San Francisco employed only 344 and Chicago 146.) Custodians in the city's public schools earned average salaries of
$57,000, whereas the national average stood at $36,000. Such profligacy cried
out for reform, but Dinkins proved no more successful than his predecessors in significantly reducing the size of the bloated municipal workforce.[23]

New York City's recurring financial problems naturally interested Governor Cuomo, who had vigorously endorsed Dinkins in the primary and general elections in 1989. As governor of New York and as a potential presidential candidate, Cuomo had every reason to forestall a budgetary crisis that
would necessitate some sort of state or federal intervention to maintain New

York City's solvency. At the same time, however, the financial interests of the entire state did not always coincide with those of its largest city—just as the administrative and political priorities of the governor and the mayor were often at loggerheads. (One prominent Democrat put it more starkly: "David should understand a basic fact of life. Mario Cuomo is not his ally.") As a consequence, Cuomo lambasted Dinkins's refusal to curtail wage increases for city workers and deflected the mayor's repeated calls for financial aid from the state. Instead, the governor urged the city leadership to forsake patchwork remediation of recurring financial problems in favor of a long-range strategy that included tax increases and a permanent reduction in labor costs. When Dinkins balked, Cuomo threatened oversight of the city's finances by convening the Financial Control Board, as Gov. Hugh Carey had been forced to do during the 1975 budgetary crisis. (The Financial Control Board, which had not been assembled since 1981, consisted of the state and city comptrollers, three representatives of the business community, the mayor, and the governor.) The friction between New York City and Albany continued during Dinkins's administration, and the newspapers reported that the mayor threatened to "make this a black-white thing" if Cuomo activated the Financial Control Board.[24]

Like other black mayors who had been voted into office burdened by an imposing set of expectations, Dinkins had to be concerned about responding to the desires of the various elements of his victorious coalition—a collection of groups with numerous demands that had accumulated during the many years they had been excluded from power in city hall. Because he owed his election to a number of ethnic voting blocs, the first black mayor in the city's history could not afford to satisfy only black leaders. Nor could he use set-aside programs and "affirmative action hiring" strategies to reward black job seekers exclusively. Relations with Latinos, the second largest component of the political coalition, were sensitive from the beginning. Only slightly less numerous than blacks in the city, Latinos received about one third as many municipal jobs and many fewer patronage positions in the managerial and professional ranks. At a forum sponsored by the Institute for Puerto Rican Policy just months after the November 1989 election, a number of that community's leaders expressed their concern about the new mayor's early performance in office. The institute's president described the few decisions already made by Dinkins that affected Puerto Rican communities as lousy and put the mayor on notice that "we're going to be monitoring . . . the Dinkins administration to make sure our community gets its fair share." Latino discontent with the amount of patronage and other rewards received from city hall continued to nettle Dinkins throughout his tenure.[25]

Another violent racial episode erupted just seventeen days after Dinkins assumed office, dispelling the notion that a black mayor would somehow be immune to the simmering racial antipathies that continued to pervade the city. On January 18, 1990, an altercation ensued between a Haitian-American resident of the Flatbush section of Brooklyn and employees of the Family Red Apple Market, a neighborhood grocery store owned by Korean Americans. After a struggle that resulted in the shopper's treatment for superficial injuries at a nearby hospital, police arrested the grocery store owner, and blacks began pelting the Korean-American employees with bottles, fruit, and rocks. In the days that followed, blacks demonstrated in front of the Family Red Apple Market and across the street at the Church Fruits and Vegetable Store, another establishment owned by Korean Americans. A judge issued an injunction mandating that protesters stay at least fifty feet from the targeted stores, but the mayor refused to call for its enforcement and appealed the ruling to a higher court. The picketing and boycotts lasted for nearly a year as protesters used bullhorns to dissuade shoppers from patronizing the two businesses. Violence occasionally flared, most notably when demonstrators assaulted the wife of one store owner, causing her to undergo an emergency abortion. One reporter referred to the boycott as the "'ugliest crack' in the gorgeous mosaic of racial harmony in the city," a sardonic reference to the language used by Dinkins in his recent election as mayor.[26]

On April 21, as the boycott continued in Brooklyn, Dinkins appointed a committee to investigate the events of January 18 and to recommend action to restore peace to the neighborhood. On August 30 the committee issued a report that critics quickly labeled a whitewash. The report praised the New York City Police Department for its efforts to keep peace in the neighborhood, criticized media coverage as inflammatory and simplistic, and, calling the boycott "incident-based," denied that hostilities were racially motivated. The district attorney for King's County and the New York City Council's Committee on General Welfare subsequently issued statements condemning the report of the mayor's committee, especially for its refusal to acknowledge the role played by racism. On September 18, Asian Americans staged a civil rights demonstration in front of city hall that attracted a crowd of ten thousand onlookers and elicited considerable negative publicity for the mayor. Local newspapers urged the mayor to shop at one of the stores as a symbolic call for the end of the boycott, but Dinkins demurred. On September 21, accompanied by a horde of reporters and cameras, Dinkins finally bought some items at the two boycotted stores—a gesture some called long overdue. Meanwhile, violence between blacks and Asians persisted in the Flatbush area. In May 1990, for example, a gang of fifteen black teenagers attacked three Vietnamese-American men whom they mistook for Korean Americans; one victim suffered a fractured skull, and the others incurred similarly severe injuries.[27]

In 1992, in a comprehensive assessment of civil rights issues concerning Asian Americans, the U.S. Commission on Civil Rights again questioned Mayor Dinkins's handling of the grocery boycott. "The Flatbush incident illustrates what can happen when racial tensions are unchecked and racial incidents mishandled by local governments," concluded the commission's report. "An incident that might have been managed in such a way as to improve racial relations in New York City instead ended up worsening racial relations." Stung by the implication that he had been insensitive to the fate of the Korean Americans, Dinkins disputed the conclusions drawn by federal investigators and charged that the radicals who had organized the boycott had prolonged the episode to undermine his administration. In all, the contretemps proved particularly embarrassing to the new mayor, whose recent campaign had been so closely tied to the promise of lessened racial turmoil.[28]

The picture of a black mayor who cared little about violence perpetrated against other minority groups resurfaced the following year in another part of Brooklyn, Crown Heights. On August 19, 1991, a seven-year-old black boy was accidentally killed when struck by a car driven by a Hasidic Jew. In retaliation angry blacks fatally stabbed Yankel Rosenbaum, a twenty-nine-year-old Hasidic divinity student from Australia who happened to be walking in the area. A riot ensued in Crown Heights, a neighborhood of 211,000 residents, approximately 80 percent of whom were black and only about 2 percent of whom were Hasidic Jews. The black population, 80 percent of which hailed from the Caribbean, lived uncomfortably next to the diminishing Jewish population and complained that the white minority continued to receive favored treatment from city hall. An unruly crowd showered Dinkins with boos and catcalls when he attempted to address hundreds of blacks roaming the riot-torn streets of Crown Heights. At the same time, the mayor offended the Hasidic community by speaking at memorial services held for the dead black child but inexplicably failed to attend Rosenbaum's funeral. One outraged Crown Heights resident called Dinkins "the first mayor who made a pogrom against Jews in America," and the Jewish press first called for the mayor to resign and later for him to be recalled. Such unflattering newspaper headlines as "Dinkins' Mosaic Crumbles" appeared in the mainstream press as well.[29]

In December 1992 a jury acquitted the black man charged in the death of Yankel Rosenbaum, despite an apparent plethora of evidence (including the weapon and a legally obtained confession) linking the defendant to the crime.

After the verdict was announced, several members of the jury celebrated at a restaurant with the defendant's lawyers. Noting that the evidence seemed as incontrovertible as the videotape presented in the Rodney King case in Los Angeles, and that Dinkins had publicly deplored the King verdict, commentators wondered whether Dinkins's apparent sanguinity reflected the existence of a double standard. Dinkins appeared to compound his error by chastising the Hasidic community for questioning the verdict and by warning of a black backlash if Jews continued to complain about the city's role in the Crown Heights affair.[30]

The Crown Heights controversy resurfaced in 1993 with the publication of a state government report on the deaths and with the filing of a lawsuit against Dinkins and the city on behalf of the Hasidic residents of the beleaguered neighborhood. Investigators working for the state director of criminal justice had determined that police at times did nothing to protect Jews from attacks by black rioters and that, if he did not countenance police inaction, Dinkins was slow to respond to a situation that could have been handled more effectively with stronger mayoral leadership. Although most journalists simply suggested that Dinkins's dilatory response owed largely to inattention, a *New York* magazine writer speculated that Dinkins "felt that the expression of black rage was, up to a point, justified" or that he thought it politically imprudent to side with whites against blacks in a racial confrontation. An indignant Dinkins repudiated such notions, just as he defended his conduct in court when charged with permitting violence against Jews in Crown Heights. Testifying under oath for more than five hours in the mayor's residence at Gracie Mansion, Dinkins adamantly insisted that he had never ordered police to allow protesters to vent their anger against innocent bystanders and characterized the lawsuit as a transparent attempt by his enemies to sustain interest in the Crown Heights affair on the eve of the mayoral election of 1993. No doubt to Dinkins's dismay, discussion of Crown Heights continued.[31]

So did talk about the mayor's handling of yet another racial disturbance, a clash between police and rioting Dominicans in the upper Manhattan neighborhood of Washington Heights. On July 3, 1992, just days before thousands of delegates to the Democratic Party's national nominating convention began arriving in the city, a white police officer shot and killed a Dominican immigrant, Jose Garcia, under disputed circumstances. According to the arresting officers, Garcia brandished a handgun while resisting arrest; members of his family offered a completely different account of an unarmed victim killed by racist cops. Despite Dinkins's frequent attempts to cool the angry passions, five days of rioting followed in Washington Heights. The mayor promised that there would be no cover-ups in the city's investigation and offered extensive expressions of sympathy to Garcia's grieving family—so much so that police union officials accused him of making Garcia a martyr and thereby fueling the violence that resulted in one death and dozens of injuries. An autopsy revealed the presence of cocaine in Garcia's body, and police identified him as an active participant in the area's drug trade. Despite these disclosures, Dinkins arranged for the city to pay Garcia's funeral expenses and the cost of flying the corpse to the Dominican Republic for burial. The Policemen's Benevolent Association formally protested, a reflection of the mayor's plummeting standing with the city's law-enforcement personnel.[32]

By the time of his reelection campaign, events in Flatbush, Crown Heights, and Washington Heights—dramatic reminders of the continuing volatility in the city's race relations—had gradually eroded Dinkins's reputation as an effective architect of compromise. In each of these situations the mayor seemed susceptible to the charge of placating constituencies; worse, he seemingly had exerted no moral leadership. His ambitious rhetoric of four years earlier seemed full of bankrupt promises, and many questioned whether the mayor had become a hostage to the black community. The journalist Jim Sleeper accused Dinkins of "indulging the [black] militants" at the expense of other minority groups that sought a broad-based civic consensus. "It's a flawed mosaic," complained a disenchanted Dinkins supporter. "There aren't any Indians or Irish from the outer boroughs; it's as if Queens and Staten Island didn't exist." Dissatisfaction with the version of Dinkins's mosaic that had formed over the previous four years emanated not only from the Indians, Irish, and other ethnic groups in the outer boroughs who felt excluded but also from the Latinos, who complained of inadequate compensation for their crucial support in 1989.[33]

With his party eager to widen the fault lines visible in the Dinkins coalition, Giuliani easily secured the Republican nomination for mayor in 1993 and launched an aggressive campaign that hammered constantly at a single theme: In four years the mayor had repeatedly demonstrated his inability to manage the myriad affairs of a complex city. When the Campaign Finance Board fined Dinkins $320,000 for overspending in the Democratic primary that year, the Republicans cited the incident as yet another example of the mayor's incompetence. "It is patently clear that he can't manage a riot, he can't manage a boycott, he can't manage a budget, and he can't manage a campaign to keep it even vaguely in compliance with the law," proclaimed Giuliani. The challenger characterized the Dinkins administration as ineffective and wasteful, the mayor himself as inept and unresponsive. The result of such mismanagement, charged the former prosecutor, was evident in

the many ways that the quality of life had deteriorated in New York City—
and no more so than in the escalating crime rate that had become a major
focus of editorial comment in the press.[34]

Responding to the heightened public concern with lawlessness, Dinkins
had lobbied successfully in Albany for the "Safe Streets, Safe City" law that
allowed the city to levy a $500 million tax surcharge in order to hire twenty-
eight hundred new police officers. Yet public safety remained a concern as
the larger police force continued to make few arrests and seemed to countenance a disturbingly high level of street crime. "What's the difference if you've
got twenty-five thousand people sitting around doing nothing or thirty thousand?" asked a disgruntled cop in Harlem, who intimated that curbing street
crime required a stronger mandate from city hall than a simple increase in
the numbers of police. The rising fear of unsafe streets stemmed in part from
the highly visible and growing population of homeless people, a significant
portion of whom had been released from the city's overcrowded mental institutions. After initially dismissing the homeless as nothing more than the
products of a housing shortage, Dinkins refused to charge the police with
aggressive enforcement of the city's vagrancy laws. At best a daily irritant to
the middle class and at worst a real threat to public safety, the homeless served
as a persistent reminder of Dinkins's apparent indifference to the image of
New York City as a haven for panhandlers, muggers, and other predators. The
mayor's "softness on crime" presented Giuliani, a seasoned prosecutor and
nationwide symbol of tough law-enforcement policies, with a made-to-order
issue for the 1993 campaign.[35]

Dinkins's handling of the city's finances also came in for persistent criticism from his Republican opponent. Annual adjustments in the municipal
budget had resulted in substantial tax increases, the elimination of services
in bad times, and the partial restoration of those services when budget surpluses accumulated in subsequent years. Critics especially balked at the elimination or reduction of such social programs as day-care centers, public
health clinics, and parks and recreation programs. Despite the mayor's frequent announcements regarding the "rightsizing" of the municipal workforce, actual reductions totaled only about ten thousand workers (5 percent
of the total) during the four years. Rohatyn scored Dinkins for his slavish
devotion to the municipal unions, especially for lavishing these political supporters with generous pay raises at a time when other needs—particularly
education—went wanting. Robert Wagner Jr., Ed Koch's deputy mayor and
the son of former Democratic mayor Robert Wagner, similarly excoriated
Dinkins's spending priorities and piecemeal approach to budget making.
Instead of attempting to reduce the city's ravenous bureaucracy, Wagner

charged, Dinkins opted for quick fixes with less political cost. "He was not looking at productivity gains," Wagner concluded. "He was not looking at restructuring."[36]

Dinkins ardently defended the record he had compiled at city hall, conceding that he had made mistakes but arguing that overall he had done quite well during extremely trying times. The mayor noted he had constantly been frustrated by a lingering economic recession that cost the city 350,000 jobs and forestalled the kind of long-range financial planning he had very much hoped to initiate. He nonetheless had still balanced four municipal budgets and had done so without a hint of the kind of scandal that had besmirched his predecessor's reputation, Dinkins pointed out. He rejected the charges of incompetence leveled against his administration, defended his low-key management style, and ridiculed the bombast that had characterized the Koch era. If racial antipathies had risen nearly to the boiling point on several occasions, Dinkins asserted, his administration had kept the lid on; New York City had experienced no massive outbreak comparable to the riot in Los Angeles following the announcement of the Rodney King verdict.[37]

The issue of race, largely absent from the mayoral campaign in its opening weeks, surfaced dramatically in September because of comments made by President Bill Clinton. Appearing at a $1,000-a-plate fund-raiser for Dinkins at a New York City hotel, the president discarded his prepared remarks and launched into an extemporaneous plea for the reelection of the mayor on the basis of racial comity. In an atmosphere not unlike a religious revival the president emotionally suggested that the incumbent mayor faced an uphill battle for reelection because "too many of us are still too unwilling to vote for people who are different than we are." Careful to emphasize that he was not impugning the motives of New York City voters and explaining that "this is not as simple as overt racism," Clinton nevertheless implied that, in a city where Democrats outnumbered Republicans by such a huge margin, race could be the only explanation for the projected closeness of the vote. Dinkins commented that the president had drawn the obvious conclusions that he, as the candidate, could not.[38]

Once the president had freed the genie from the bottle, talk of race came to dominate the campaign. Not coincidentally, the tone of the political discourse worsened. Dinkins criticized Giuliani's opposition to affirmative action and suggested that minorities would have much to fear from a police department unleashed by a law-and-order Republican in the mayor's office. As Dinkins stood by his side, a black minister observed that "elements that can best be described as fascist seem to have grown up and flowered around Mr. Giuliani"; another of the mayor's supporters likened Giuliani to Ku Klux

Klan leader David Duke. Giuliani both attempted to link Dinkins with the anti-Semitic Louis Farrakhan and accused the mayor of injecting the campaign with racial divisiveness in order to win. Amid increasingly hysterical charges of old-fashioned racism and new-fashioned urban terrorism, with bizarre invocations of Benito Mussolini sprinkled in for good measure, the campaign stumbled to a welcome conclusion. By a narrow margin Dinkins lost the vote for reelection and became the first black mayor of a major U.S. city to relinquish the office after just one term. Giuliani, who had lost to Dinkins by 2 percent four years earlier, won in 1993 by almost exactly the same margin (50.7 percent to 48.3 percent). In an electorate strikingly polarized along racial lines, Dinkins secured more than 90 percent of the black vote and three fifths of the Latino vote but received fewer votes from whites than he had in 1989. A comparatively low black voter turnout, apparently caused by intraborough rivalries among black Democrats, also hurt Dinkins. Blacks in boroughs outside Manhattan, especially in Brooklyn, failed to campaign as hard for the mayor as they had for other black candidates in the city—a regrettable circumstance that Dinkins's supporters felt led to a reduction in the number of black votes cast for mayor. By contrast, Giuliani won because he swept the white ethnic neighborhoods of Queens, Brooklyn, and Staten Island and received an overwhelming majority of Republican votes. In a city in which whites constituted 60 percent of the electorate, a minority candidate faced an uphill battle in constructing a victorious coalition—a feat that Dinkins had accomplished in 1989 but could not duplicate after four contentious years in office.[39]

In his triumphant 1989 campaign David Dinkins had portrayed himself as being especially sensitive to the varied concerns of New York City's disparate populations and capable of brokering their many interests in a way that had not been done before. His failure to respond effectively to the racial incidents that scarred his mayoralty, along with the city's gradual economic contraction, seriously called into question the administration's ability to solve any crisis. New Yorkers still apparently liked Dinkins but felt that this decent, honorable man had neither managed the city's affairs well nor delivered on his promise to defuse racial tensions. The closeness of the vote in 1993 led to widespread speculation that, had it not been for Dinkins's detached leadership style and lackluster record, a black mayor could have been reelected. In polyglot New York City, with its diverse and constantly evolving population mix, the election of a black mayor depended upon the painstaking creation of multiracial coalitions. Rudolph Giuliani, capitalizing on Dinkins's frequent missteps, had parlayed a white electoral plurality into victory in 1993 and handily won reelection over another Democrat in 1997. A multiracial coali-

tion capable of trouncing a white-dominated electoral alliance could be constructed again, but the perils of incumbency—a lethal combination of bad
economic news and persistent racial strife—kept Dinkins from replicating
his 1989 triumph.[40]

Dinkins's mayoralty produced an ambiguous legacy. Because of New York
City's preeminence among the nation's urban places, his election constituted a landmark in U.S. politics. Unlike successful black candidates in other
large cities with black electoral majorities, Dinkins triumphed in 1989 in a
city where blacks comprised just 25 percent of the population. The *New York
Times* recognized Dinkins's achievement, calling his election a "political
coming of age" for African Americans. But in the same editorial the newspaper warned, "Now comes the hard part: governing." Dinkins's unsuccessful
reelection campaign in 1993 underscored the problems he encountered in
governing the city—problems that confronted black mayors in other cities
as well. His failure to solve the city's fiscal woes bespoke the difficulties facing a host of black mayors who arrived in city halls at a precarious time of
urban retrenchment, suburban expansion, and reduced financial aid from
the federal government. Dinkins's failure to convince voters of his ability to
deal fairly and evenhandedly with all ethnic groups and races in New York
City proved to be a lethal shortcoming because of the intense scrutiny inevitably applied to all black mayors when issues of race relations arose. Indeed,
the deficiencies of Dinkins's four years in city hall gave ample testimony to
the many pitfalls awaiting black mayors in the treacherous urban America
of the late twentieth century.[41]

Notes

1. On the history of black mayors see Roger Biles, "Black Mayors: A Historical Assessment," *Journal of Negro History* 77, no. 4 (Summer 1992): 109–25; H. Paul Friesema, "Black
Control of Central Cities: The Hollow Prize," *Journal of the American Institute of Plan-
ners* 35 (March 1969): 75–79; William E. Nelson Jr. and Winston Van Horne, "Black Elect-
ed Administrators: The Trials of Office," *Public Administration Review* 34 (November–
December 1974): 526–33; William E. Nelson Jr. and Philip J. Meranto, *Electing Black Mayors:
Political Action in the Black Community* (Columbus: Ohio State University Press, 1977);
and Michael Preston, "Limitations of Black Urban Power: The Case of Black Mayors," in
Louis H. Masotti and Robert L. Lineberry, eds., *The New Urban Politics* (Cambridge, Mass.:
Ballinger, 1976), 111–32.

2. Roger Waldinger, *Still the Promised Land? African Americans and New Immigrants in
Postindustrial New York* (Cambridge, Mass.: Harvard University Press, 1996), 47–51; Claire
J. Kim, "Cracks in the 'Gorgeous Mosaic': Black-Korean Conflict and Racial Mobilization
in New York City" (Ph.D. diss., Yale University, 1996), 89.

3. John Hope Franklin, *From Slavery to Freedom: A History of Negro Americans,* 5th ed.
(New York: Knopf, 1980), 162; Leonard P. Curry, *The Free Black in Urban America, 1800–*

1850: The Shadow of the Dream (Chicago: University of Chicago Press, 1981), 88, 216–24; Martin Kilson, "Political Change in the Negro Ghetto, 1900–1940s," in Nathan I. Huggins, Martin Kilson, and Daniel M. Fox, eds., *Key Issues in the Afro-American Experience,* vol. 2 (New York: Harcourt Brace Jovanovich, 1971), 171–74; Gilbert Osofsky, *Harlem: The Making of a Ghetto* (New York: Harper and Row, 1963), 161–67.

4. Edwin R. Lewinson, *Black Politics in New York City* (New York: Twayne, 1974), 16–17; Osofsky, *Harlem,* 168–76; Adam Clayton Powell Jr., *Marching Blacks: An Interpretive History of the Rise of the Black Common Man* (New York: Dial, 1945), 95–103; James Q. Wilson, *Negro Politics: The Search for Leadership* (New York: Free Press, 1960), 26–27, 35–36.

5. Lewinson, *Black Politics in New York City,* 144–60; Charles V. Hamilton, "Needed, More Foxes: The Black Experience," in Jewel Bellush and Dick Netzer, eds., *Urban Politics, New York Style* (Armonk, N.Y.: Sharpe, 1990), 370ff. On Jones's career see John C. Walter, *The Harlem Fox: J. Raymond Jones and Tammany, 1920–1970* (Albany: State University of New York Press, 1989). According to the 1970 census, blacks, Latinos, and Asians comprised 37 percent of New York City's population (John H. Mollenkopf, "New York: The Great Anomaly," in Rufus P. Browning, Dale Rogers Marshall, and David H. Tabb, eds., *Racial Politics in American Cities* [New York: Longman, 1997], 98).

6. John H. Mollenkopf, *A Phoenix in the Ashes: The Rise and Fall of the Koch Coalition in New York City Politics* (Princeton, N.J.: Princeton University Press, 1992), 103–13; Hamilton, "Needed, More Foxes," 379; John H. Mollenkopf, "Political Inequality," in John H. Mollenkopf and Manuel Castells, eds., *Dual City: Restructuring New York* (New York: Russell Sage Foundation, 1991), 347. In 1977 Herman Badillo, the Puerto Rican borough president of the Bronx, refused to renounce his mayoral candidacy to enhance Percy Sutton's chances at election. Consequently, blacks declined to support Badillo in 1985 and settled instead for the inferior candidate, Herman Farrell (Mollenkopf, "New York: The Great Anomaly," 82).

7. Mollenkopf, *Phoenix in the Ashes,* 90–91; Shirley Jenkins, "New Immigrants: Ethnic Factors in Governance and Politics," in Bellush and Netzer, *Urban Politics, New York Style,* 406.

8. Mollenkopf, *Phoenix in the Ashes,* 91; Angelo Falcon, "Black and Latino Politics in New York City: Race and Ethnicity in a Changing Urban Context," *New Community* 14 (Spring 1988): 370–84. Also see Nathan Glazer and Daniel Patrick Moynihan, *Beyond the Melting Pot: The Negroes, Puerto Ricans, Jews, Italians, and Irish of New York City* (Cambridge, Mass.: MIT Press, 1963).

9. On Mayor Koch's career see Mollenkopf, *Phoenix in the Ashes;* and Jack Newfield and Wayne Barrett, *City for Sale: Ed Koch and the Betrayal of New York* (New York: Harper and Row, 1989). Koch defends his mayoralty in the following first-person accounts: Edward I. Koch, *Mayor* (New York: Simon and Schuster, 1984); Koch, *Politics* (New York: Simon and Schuster, 1985); and Koch, *Citizen Koch: An Autobiography* (New York: St. Martin's, 1992).

10. Dinkins is quoted in *New York Times,* December 24, 1986. For an analysis of these events see Jim Sleeper, *The Closest of Strangers: Liberalism and the Politics of Race in New York* (New York: Norton, 1990), chap. 7.

11. *New York Times,* April 21, 1988; Mollenkopf, *Phoenix in the Ashes,* 172.

12. Mollenkopf, "New York: The Great Anomaly," 108.

13. Hilary MacKenzie, "A Breakthrough," *Maclean's Magazine,* November 20, 1989), p.

39; Joe Klein, "Can Dinkins Do It?" *New York,* July 31, 1989, pp. 34–35; "David Dinkins," *U.S. News and World Report,* November 20, 1989, p. 54. The political leader is quoted in Joe Klein, "Mr. Softy," *New York,* January 16, 1989, p. 20.

14. *New York Times,* April 21, 22, 1989; Michael Stone, "What Really Happened in Central Park: The Night of the Jogger—and the Crisis of New York," *New York,* August 14, 1989, pp. 30–43; "Gotham Rainbow," *Nation,* October 2, 1989, pp. 335–36; Fred Barnes, "The Mayor's Race," *New Republic,* October 9, 1989, p. 9. Dinkins is quoted in Joe Klein, "Brotherhood Week," *New York,* September 11, 1989, p. 36; Cuomo is quoted in Scott McConnell, "The Making of the Mayor, 1989," *Commentary* 89 (February 1990): 34.

15. *New York Times,* November 3, 1993; Joe Klein, "Now the Showdown," *New York,* September 25, 1989, p. 52; Mollenkopf, *Phoenix in the Ashes,* 178–80; John H. Mollenkopf, *New York City in the 1980s: A Social, Economic, and Political Atlas* (New York: Simon and Schuster, 1993), 82.

16. MacKenzie, "Breakthrough," 39; Mollenkopf, *Phoenix in the Ashes,* 180–81. In the Republican primary Giuliani received 67 percent of the vote to Lauder's 33 percent (*New York Times,* September 13, 1989).

17. Barnes, "Mayor's Race," 10; Eloise Salholz, "A Call for Racial Harmony," *Newsweek,* September 25, 1989, p. 22; Mollenkopf, "Political Inequality," 352. Dinkins is quoted in Klein, "Mr. Softy," 20. In 1992 the Internal Revenue Service ruled that Dinkins had not broken the law with the transfer of stock to his son (Eric Pooley, "Air Dinkins," *New York,* May 25, 1992, p. 33.

18. *New York Times,* November 8, 1989; "Gotham Rainbow," 335–36; Mollenkopf, *New York City in the 1980s,* 86; Mollenkopf, *Phoenix in the Ashes,* 181–82. Dinkins is quoted in Klein, "Now the Showdown," 52; his supporter is quoted in MacKenzie, "Breakthrough," 40.

19. Barnes, "Mayor's Race," 9; Butts is quoted in Kevin D. Thompson, "Can the Healer Mend New York?" *Black Enterprise,* January 1990, p. 49.

20. Thompson, "Can the Healer Mend New York?" 48–49; Joe Klein, "The New Mayor and the Crisis of New York," *New York,* November 20, 1989, pp. 38–39. Rohatyn is quoted in Peter Blauner, "The Big Squeeze," *New York,* April 2, 1990, p. 51.

21. Larry Black, "Running out of Money," *Maclean's Magazine,* June 3, 1991, p. 43; Bonnie Angelo, "Speak Softly and Carry a Big Hatchet," *Time,* May 27, 1991, p. 25.

22. Blauner, "Big Squeeze," 51; *New York Times,* October 24, 1993; Michael Mead, *Power Failure: New York City Politics and Policy Since 1960* (New York: Oxford University Press, 1993), 241; Joe Klein, "The Never-Ending Story," *New York,* July 15, 1991, p. 8.

23. Dinkins is quoted in Michael Tomasky, "Identity Politics in New York City," *Nation,* June 21, 1993, p. 860; see also Angelo, "Speak Softly," 25; Black, "Running out of Money," 42; Joe Klein, "New York to Dave: Get Real!" *New York,* May 27, 1991, pp. 12–13.

24. The Democrat is quoted in Klein, "New Mayor and the Crisis," 39, and Dinkins is quoted in Joe Klein, "The Real Deficit: Leadership," *New York,* July 22, 1991, p. 24.

25. Waldinger, *Still the Promised Land?* 249–50. The institute's president is quoted in Institute for Puerto Rican Policy, *The Dinkins Administration and the Puerto Rican Community* (New York: Institute for Puerto Rican Policy, 1990), 15.

26. U.S. Commission on Civil Rights, "Civil Rights Issues Facing Asian Americans in the 1990s," February 1992, 36. The fullest account of what happened in Flatbush appears in Kim, "Cracks in the 'Gorgeous Mosaic.'" She argues that the boycott should be seen

not as an example of racial scapegoating but rather as the purposeful action of a social movement; that is, the boycott against the Korean grocers was simply part and parcel of a larger black radicalism that inevitably clashed with the more moderate Dinkins administration.

27. U.S. Commission on Civil Rights, "Civil Rights Issues Facing Asian Americans," 36–39.

28. Ibid., 40; *New York Times*, February 29, 1992.

29. The resident is quoted in *New York Times*, August 22, 1991; the headline is cited in Andy Logan, "Syzygy," *New Yorker*, September 23, 1991, p. 108.

30. John Taylor, "The Politics of Grievance," *New York*, December 7, 1992, pp. 18–19.

31. The quotation appears in John Taylor, "The Pogrom Papers," *New York*, August 2, 1993, p. 25; see also *New York Times*, August 25, 1993; Taylor, "Politics of Grievance," 18–19.

32. *New York Times*, July 9, 14, 1992; Taylor, "Politics of Grievance," 18.

33. Tomasky, "Identity Politics in New York City," 862; Sleeper, *Closest of Strangers*, 301. The Dinkins supporter is quoted in Joe Klein, "Is He up to It?" *New York*, November 5, 1990, p. 39.

34. Giuliani is quoted in *New York Times*, October 24, ; see also *New York Times*, November 4, 1993. As in 1989, Giuliani ran as the fusion candidate of the Republican and Liberal parties.

35. Fred Siegel, *The Future Once Happened Here: New York, D.C., L.A., and the Fate of America's Big Cities* (New York: Free Press, 1997), 182–83, 190–91.

36. Pooley, "Air Dinkins," 34–35. Wagner is quoted in John Taylor, "What's at Stake," *New York*, November 1, 1993, p. 41.

37. *New York Times*, October 24, 1993. Dinkins easily won the Democratic primary in 1993, besting Roy Innis and Eric Ruano-Melendez (*New York Times*, November 4, 1993).

38. *New York Times*, September 27, 1993.

39. The minister is quoted in *New York Times*, November 4, 1993; see also the editions of November 3 and 7, 1993; Taylor, "What's at Stake," 38–39.

40. In 1997 Giuliani defeated Democrat Ruth Messinger, receiving 57 percent of the vote to her 41 percent. From 1993 to 1997 he increased his share of the black vote from 5 percent to 20 percent and the Latino vote from 37 percent to 43 percent (*New York Times*, November 6, 1997). Many white mayors elected in the 1990s followed the first generation of black mayors and won plaudits for their neoprogressive approach to governing cities. See, for example, Peter Beinart, "The Pride of the Cities," *New Republic* June 30, 1997, pp. 16–24.

41. *New York Times*, January 2, 1990.

6. Tom Bradley and the Politics of Race

HEATHER R. PARKER

I have disregarded what may be politically popular or unpopular. If I
felt it was right, if my heart told me it was right, if my gut told me this
is what you ought to do, then brothers and sisters, that's what was going to be done.
—Tom Bradley (1917–98)

IN 1973 LOS ANGELES elected Tom Bradley as its first African-American
mayor. His ascension to the mayoralty was remarkable in light of the heterogeneous nature of the city's population. Unlike other large cities that
had elected black mayors—among them, Cleveland, Newark, and Atlanta—
African Americans comprised only a small portion of Los Angeles's population—less than 18 percent.[1] To win the election Bradley needed support
from a large percentage of nonblack voters. His campaign strategy was to
appeal to the majority electorate without alienating his black support base.
His mild manner, moderate political views, and status as a member of the
city council and former police officer attracted white voters, but his five
consecutive terms as mayor witnessed a gradual deterioration in his relationship with the black community.

Anticipating that Bradley would serve as their spokesman in city hall, African Americans expected his election to usher in a bold new era of unprecedented social and economic advancement for black people. The mayor's
moderate, mainstream political style, however, bore little resemblance to the
brash, dynamic leadership many blacks had envisioned. Bradley's seemingly color-blind approach to politics and his efforts to distance himself from
the black community resulted in some African Americans' resenting him for
not using his position to pursue their concerns aggressively.

After his election Bradley granted an interview to a national African-American magazine. On the opening page of the article a photograph depicted the
tall, handsome Bradley standing before a large mural on which was painted

Abraham Lincoln to his right and John F. Kennedy to his left. In the center, directly above the new mayor's head, was pictured the Liberty Bell, and beneath Bradley's feet was a caption informing the reader that a Latino street gang had painted the mural.[2] Rather than pose before a mural created by a black artist depicting African-American activists and political leaders, Bradley had chosen to stand before an image of white American political icons venerated by the majority culture for their support of racial justice. Bradley's decision to be photographed with this mural behind him symbolized his identification with the political system. He believed that the tenets of democracy and equality applied to all people—a concept to which many African Americans, oppressed by racism and discriminatory practices, could not relate.

A high school classmate recalled, "He never once considered the handicap he might have because of his race. He seemed to be . . . a true believer in the American Dream."[3] Bradley believed that hard work and honesty within the avowedly egalitarian system could lead to material prosperity. While conceding that blacks were victims of discrimination, he scoffed at those who maintained that African Americans could not achieve the American Dream without upsetting the established rhythm of the system. He used his own experience as an example and cited how he had, in all stages of his life, refused to allow racial barriers to impede his progress. Bradley labeled himself an "eternal optimist" and acknowledged that he had "been accused of being Pollyanna-ish" in his dreams for the future.[4] No matter what the obstacles, Bradley believed that black people could succeed if they were determined. Reiterating many similar pronouncements, he asserted, "Young people of every race, creed, and color—I want them to know if they work hard, they can achieve. They can look at . . . [me] and say, 'If he can do it, so can I.'"[5]

As the son of a poor Texas sharecropper and a maid, Bradley in fact exemplified the American Dream. He was born in Calvert, Texas, in 1917 and moved with his family to Los Angeles in 1924 where his mother, who had divorced his father, earned a meager living as a domestic. Despite these hardships, Bradley excelled in his scholastic and athletic endeavors and was rewarded with a full athletic scholarship to the University of California, Los Angeles. During his junior year at UCLA Bradley was recruited by the Los Angeles Police Department and served for the next twenty years. Although he endured much discrimination as a law-enforcement officer, he eventually achieved the rank of lieutenant, one of only a few African Americans ever to hold such a prominent position in the LAPD. During his tenure with the department, Bradley attended law school at night and, after retiring from the police force, practiced law for a brief period until his election to the Los Angeles City Council in 1963. Despite the obstacles of poverty and racial discrimination, Bradley had worked hard and enjoyed remarkable success. Confident that the American Dream was possible for all to attain, Mayor Bradley operated as though this concept was a reality. He believed that Los Angeles's electorate would learn to ignore his skin color and judge him solely according to his merits. In return, he promised the city that he would be fair and impartial and that he would not allow issues of race to influence his decisions as mayor.

This essay examines the mayor's turbulent relationship with Los Angeles's African-American community and argues that while many blacks supported Bradley, others resented him because he refused to allow their particular concerns to dominate his actions as mayor.

*   *   *

Following his election Bradley became a symbol of black progress, and his presence in the mayor's office was a source of considerable pride for African Americans. As the first African American in the Los Angeles Police Department to attain the rank of lieutenant, the first black elected to the city council, and the first black mayor, Bradley was considered a true African-American hero. "If you had grown up a Black kid in my generation," stated a Los Angeles–based newspaper columnist, "Tom Bradley would have been almost a sacred icon to you; he was everything your parents wanted you to be. Somebody to be looked up to, admired, used as a role model as what Black people . . . could accomplish."[6] Bradley's heroic status gradually dissipated, however, as many blacks began to resent the manner in which he executed his duties as mayor.

Bradley rarely addressed black issues boldly and publicly. Rather, he instituted many programs that benefited blacks but were not specifically designated as "black programs." Such initiatives allowed Bradley to improve African-American access to housing, employment, and other benefits without jeopardizing his support from within the white community. Bradley's decision to maintain a calculated distance from issues uniquely affecting the black community, however, was not simply a response to pressures related to his political situation. As an elected official, he earnestly believed that his duty was to represent the needs of the entire city. "A black leader's duty to his own people," stated Bradley, "is identical to his duty to the larger community."[7] Bradley believed that the well-being of the black community was inextricably connected to the strength of the entire city. "If you don't supply the kind of support that a community needs to survive," asserted Bradley, "it's not going to be a very livable area and that has an effect on the entire . . . [population] eventually."[8] In instituting programs to address pervasive problems, such as unemployment, that ailed Los Angeles, Bradley was convinced that blacks, along with the entire population, would reap the benefits of general improvements. For example, he justified his support of an ordinance aiding small business and minority contractors by citing the benefits of such programs for the entire city. "An increase in the number of small contractors," said the mayor, "can only mean more profit for them and better economic health for the city."[9]

Confident that blacks were aware of his efforts to help them, Bradley saw no need to explain publicly how his programs would explicitly benefit African Americans. "I would say," he asserted, "that the Black community does not anticipate overnight miracles—they know that my reputation is that I have worked hard [and] that I am fair."[10] However, because they believed that he was ignoring them, blacks often did not recognize Bradley's subtle efforts on their behalf, such as his support of programs that provided quality low-income housing in Los Angeles's black neighborhoods. Further fueling African-American resentment was Bradley's expectation that blacks would respect his commitment to serving the needs of the entire electorate without focusing primarily on the African-American community. Most blacks understood the political necessity of rhetoric that centered on moderate issues and would not alienate his white supporters. The tension between the more militant members of the black community and Bradley increased, however, when they realized that this color-blind rhetoric was a genuine expression of the mayor's political ethos.

Tom Bradley was a mild-mannered black man who occupied a position of political power that he could retain only with continued white support. In public speeches and interviews he emphasized his commitment to the entire city and distanced himself from the black community. When within the confines of the black community, however, many African Americans expected Bradley to tell them that the moderate views he publicly espoused and his reluctance to be identified with black issues were political necessities. Blacks wanted Bradley to assure them that he truly wished to be a vocal advocate for African-American issues but could not do so if he hoped to remain in office. African Americans received no such message.

In a 1974 interview with *Black Enterprise* magazine, for example, Bradley avoided African-American issues until his frustrated interviewer asked him to discuss the implications of Los Angeles's decision to elect a black mayor. In reply Bradley asserted, "I don't anticipate any problems related to my color. I think we've overcome that major hurdle."[11] The interviewer then asked whether blacks could expect any increased attention to their problems now that the city had elected a black mayor. To this Bradley replied, "I will do everything that I can to help the black community *as I would the rest of the community*."[12] Even when he was responding to questions posed by a black interviewer for a publication written for African Americans, Bradley said nothing different from what he said to white audiences. He not only said what whites wanted to hear, he fully accepted this rhetoric. As a consequence, many blacks began to view Bradley as an Uncle Tom; that his name was "Tom" only facilitated the comparisons. For example, when in 1983 Bradley endorsed Walter Mondale rather than Jesse Jackson for president, a militant member of the black press maintained that this was "par for Mayor Tom," a reference to the traitorous Uncle Tom.[13] Many blacks believed that in refusing to unconditionally align himself with causes of concern to the African-American community, Bradley repeatedly betrayed them throughout his five terms as mayor.

Blacks who had followed Bradley's career as a member of the city council should not have been surprised by his failure to give special attention to the African-American community. In his ten years on the council, Bradley demonstrated that he would not solely serve the interests of the black community and that he was committed to representing the entire city of Los Angeles. Bradley's council tenure was noteworthy because of the wide range of issues about which he was passionate. Of special interest to him was bringing money and jobs into Los Angeles and finding ways to address the city's many social problems without raising taxes. For example, he protested an initiative that would require Los Angeles city residents to subsidize the cost of hiring additional sheriff's deputies for suburban areas, rejected efforts to tax municipal bonds, and supported tax relief for homeowners. He also continuously endeavored to attract federal funding for Los Angeles programs and on two occasions expressed concern about the decision of Columbia Records, a major employer, to leave the Los Angeles area.[14] Similarly, Bradley endeavored to save the city money by identifying services duplicated by the city and county.[15] He also addressed himself to noneconomic issues, initiating discussion regarding the opera, the symphony, consumer protection, the environment, the formation of citizen grievance committees, various health and safety regulations, highway and rapid transit construction programs, and a host of other issues unrelated to the particular concerns of the African-American community.[16]

As a member of the city council, Bradley spoke explicitly on behalf of black people on only two occasions, both of which involved police misconduct. He once criticized the LAPD's excessive use of force during the 1965 Watts rebellion and, on another occasion, called into question the department's procedures when, unprovoked, a police officer shot a young black man.[17]

These uncharacteristic instances of identification with the black community would haunt Bradley during his unsuccessful 1969 bid for the mayoralty. In that race Bradley, whose main support base was comprised of black

ministers and liberal African-American and Jewish Democrats, received the
most votes in the primary election and faced the incumbent in a runoff. His
opponent, Sam Yorty, had not expected such strong support for an African-
American candidate and resorted to racist tactics to discourage the electorate from voting for Bradley. Citing Bradley's criticisms of the police department's response in Watts and the shooting, Yorty endeavored to portray him
as a militant with ties to radical elements within the African-American community. On one occasion Yorty asserted that, if Bradley were elected mayor,
"the militants would come down and intimidate the city council . . . and then
what could the police do? How are they going to handle the [black militant]
friends of the mayor who are there to back [him]?"[18]

To detract attention from Yorty's racist appeals, Bradley distanced himself from issues related to race and portrayed himself as a candidate for the
entire city. While this might have been problematic for an African-American candidate unaccustomed to representing the interests of the nonblack
community, it was a challenge for which Bradley was particularly well suited. He compared himself to John F. Kennedy, remarking that just as Kennedy
was a president who happened to be Catholic, he intended to be a mayor who
just happened to be black.[19] He pledged to preside over an "honest, clean
government, open to all, responsive to all, serving all."[20] The phrasing of
Bradley's speeches and statements was designed to allow liberals, moderates,
and conservatives of all races to identify with his message. "I have no sympathy for lawlessness, but even less for injustice, poverty, unemployment and
slum housing. I would seek to involve private enterprise in massive training
and employment programs," he told the *Los Angeles Times* during that first
campaign.[21] In this carefully constructed statement Bradley assuaged liberals by making a commitment to the eradication of injustice and poverty while
appealing to moderates and conservatives by decrying crime and proposing
the use of private capital rather than public funds to address unemployment.

The campaign issues Bradley embraced also reflected his desire to appeal
to a large cross-section of the electorate. He called for an "end to graft and
corruption in city hall" and vowed to "fight lawlessness and violence wher-
ever it occurs," to "represent this city better in Washington, D.C., and Sacramento" and to "fight for a master plan for downtown Los Angeles and the
entire city."[22] Despite these attempts to draw attention away from the race
issue, Yorty's racist tactics were effective. For example, after the Yorty campaign deluged her neighborhood with mailers warning of black militant rule
should Bradley be elected, a resident of an affluent white area remembered,
"Liberal Democrats in my home neighborhood started saying they couldn't
vote for a black because the neighborhood would no longer be safe."[23] Sim-

ilarly, a Bradley campaign worker recalled that "voters . . . had been frightened out of their minds [by Yorty's racist tactics] in 1969."[24] And, commenting on the effects of Yorty's racist campaign, Bradley said, "People who had been inclined to support me, finally in the last few weeks of the campaign, got so scared that they backed away."[25] With an 80 percent voter turnout, Yorty narrowly defeated Bradley in 1969, 53 percent to 47 percent.[26]

When he once again faced Yorty in the 1973 race for the mayoralty, Bradley was backed by a loose coalition comprised largely of black and Jewish liberals. According to Bradley, he made no deliberate effort to form a coalition. Rather, the people who supported him were simply friends he had made during his many years of public service as a police officer and as an active member of the Democratic Party. "Old friends, loyal and supportive, responding to the friendship which we had established over the years, became the essence of that multiethnic community that became my campaign supporters," he said.[27] Maury Weiner, one of Bradley's most trusted aides, described Bradley's core support as being "formed by people from the . . . African-American community and from the . . . Chicano community . . . and some Asians and an enormous number of . . . [white] men and women, most of whom were Jewish and most of whom came from the liberal . . . California Democratic Council club movement."[28] While black ministers and their congregations and Jewish activists provided much of the grassroots support, the large amounts of money needed for advertising and other campaign expenses came from several wealthy investors, many of whom were liberal Jews.[29]

Backed by this coalition of liberals, Bradley continued to emphasize his broad approach to the issues and tried to appeal to all segments of Los Angeles's electorate. Carl Stokes, the African-American mayor of Cleveland, remarked that Bradley understood the importance of not allowing race to become a major issue in the 1973 campaign. "In 1973, Bradley conducted a low-key campaign in which he did not use any black leaders from outside Los Angeles as I had counseled him in 1969. When [Black Panther] Bobby Seale, fresh from his defeat for the mayoralty of Oakland, gratuitously endorsed Bradley's candidacy, Bradley quickly moved to publicly reject Seale's endorsement. He didn't want to do it. But he had to if he wanted to keep those white voters whose fears he had so carefully allayed over the four years."[30]

During the campaign Bradley also avoided references to racial topics even when addressing such issues as appointments to various city boards and law enforcement. For example, when asked how he would best use his power as mayor, Bradley replied that he would appoint board members who "shared his views on [city] planning and other issues."[31] He did not mention appointing people who shared his views concerning racism, discrimination, the inner city, unemployment, poverty, or any other issue immediately affecting many members of the African-American community. Rubin Hightower, a resident of voter precinct 2008, which was predominantly black, astutely observed, "Bradley doesn't come around here much. Maybe he feels he got the blacks' votes."[32] Similarly, Charles Williams, a resident of the same precinct, commented, "Bradley doesn't speak out on issues that concern this area . . . but I'm voting for him because he's black."[33]

Indeed, despite his reluctance to associate himself with the black community, Bradley captured huge majorities in both the 1969 and 1973 elections. Voter precincts 2052, 2054, 2055, and 2530 were all located within the eighth and ninth city council districts, majority-black areas of South Central Los Angeles. The returns from these districts reveal that in the 1969 primary election Bradley received 1,082 votes to Yorty's 31, and in the runoff election Bradley polled 1,253 votes to Yorty's 48. Similarly, in the 1973 primary election Bradley received 769 votes, while Yorty polled only 32, and in the runoff election of the same year these precincts gave 1,160 votes to Bradley and a mere 33 votes to Yorty.[34] In 1973 the eighth councilmanic district was 87 percent black, and its residents voted for Bradley over Yorty 44,693 to 3,629. This majority-black district had the highest voter turnout in the city at 74.42 percent, compared to a 63.89 percent turnout citywide.[35] The city council district with the second-largest voter turnout was the ninth district, also largely African American. Thus Bradley enjoyed near-unanimous support from the black community. Not insignificantly, if every ballot cast by voters from the eighth and ninth council districts were disqualified, Bradley still would have been elected by more than 16,000 votes.[36] In 1973, therefore, Bradley's victory was not dependent on the African-American vote. However, African Americans believed their vote was pivotal and expected the new mayor to be attentive to their needs.

From the outset Bradley instituted programs intended to benefit the entire city, and although he rarely specifically addressed problems unique to the African-American community, many of his programs greatly assisted poor and working-class blacks. For example, he increased police patrols, instituted after-school programs, and combated housing shortages and unemployment, all of which benefited Los Angeles's large population of low-income black residents.[37] Despite the contentions of some, he did not ignore issues of importance to African Americans. Rather, he did not publicly or aggressively emphasize the many ways in which his programs addressed the needs of Los Angeles's less fortunate blacks. Bradley adviser Art Gastelum commented on the mayor's inherent "modest quality" stating, "It's so frustrating . . . because we know what he does on a day-to-day basis that affects so many aspects of people's lives, but he has never let us package him with the press releases or pictures that he deserves."[38] As a consequence, struggling African Americans were not always aware of the ways in which the mayor's programs, though not instituted exclusively for blacks, were enhancing their quality of life. Many middle-class African Americans, however, were quite aware of the mayor's efforts on their behalf. This relatively small segment of the black community immediately benefited from Bradley's affirmative action policies and his commitment to placing in influential positions prominent members of minority groups that had previously been excluded from city government.[39]

Bradley's most important task as the new mayor in 1973 was to appoint city commissioners who would reflect his political ethos and spread his influence throughout the city's many boards. He had 140 appointments to make; of these, Bradley retained only seventeen Yorty appointees, none of whom occupied seats on the most important boards. By appointing twenty-one African Americans, thirteen Latinos, and ten Asians, Bradley significantly changed the composition of the commissions, underscoring his commitment to affirmative action.[40]

For instance, the Civil Service Commission was the body most responsible for determining hiring policy for city jobs. In appointing African Americans to policy-making positions on this board, Bradley ensured that his affirmative action hiring policies would immediately benefit the African-American community. Throughout his twenty years as mayor Bradley continued to appoint large numbers of African Americans to commissions. In 1981, 31 of 170 commissioners were black; in 1992, 51 of the 222 commission seats were occupied by African Americans—23 percent of all commissioners—whereas blacks accounted for 13.9 percent percent of the city's population.[41] Additionally, Bradley was the first to appoint an African American to the prestigious position of harbor commissioner in 1984.

More important, Bradley explicitly made public his commitment to affirmative action when, immediately after his swearing-in, he issued Executive Directive No. 1. This order stipulated that "the recruitment, employment, promotion, compensation, benefits, training and layoff of all employees . . . be conducted without regard to their race, religion, national origin, sex or age."[42] To ensure the success of this program, Bradley initiated the "Equal Opportunities Policy Resolution for the City of Los Angeles," which explicitly outlined the method by which the affirmative action program would be executed.[43] He then placed African Americans committed to affirmative action in positions where they could directly influence policy related to this program. He appointed to the powerful Civil Service Commission Arnett Hartsfield, an African-American activist dedicated to affirmative action, and he created a position, special assistant to the mayor on affirmative action, and gave the job to African-American Bill Elkins, a tireless advocate of equal opportunity.[44] In a 1974 memorandum Elkins blasted Bradley for not recognizing the inadequacy of an affirmative action ordinance regarding minority contractors. He told the mayor, "Affirmative Action and contract compliance both for construction and nonconstruction as well as personnel in my judgment is a *major, major, major* issue."[45] Bradley responded to Elkins's memorandum by issuing Executive Directive 1-C, which read, "All departments which issue calls for bids or requests for proposals for work . . . are hereby directed to consult with the Mayor's Office of Small Business Assistance to determine the level of minority and women business participation which will be required of the contractors in the performance of such contracts."[46]

In another instance the Advisory Affirmative Action Committee, a panel comprised of representatives from the city's African-American, Latino, Asian-American, and Native American populations, commissioned a report on the effectiveness of Executive Directive No. 5. Within the bounds of a merit system, this directive was intended to facilitate the appointment of ethnic minorities and females to positions but did not clearly state the importance of recruiting qualified candidates from underrepresented groups. The report found major problems with the directive and suggested that it be revised.[47] In response Bradley issued "Executive Directive No. 5—New Series," which reflected his intention to personally enforce compliance with affirmative action policy.[48] Throughout the course of his terms as mayor, Bradley demanded that his staff cooperate with the city's affirmative action programs and insisted that they be well trained in this area. In 1975 he convened the first of many training sessions for his executive staff, emphasizing his personal commitment to the program and stating that his employees must "have a clear understanding of and commitment to the goals and objectives promulgated by this Affirmative Action Plan for Los Angeles."[49]

True to form, while Bill Elkins and others closely associated with the affirmative action programs often specifically mentioned African Americans, Bradley rarely mentioned blacks in particular. However, they were the ethnic group that most benefited from his affirmative action programs. Table 6.1 illustrates the marked increase in the number of African Americans holding high-paying positions, where they had been severely underrepresented, and a slight decrease in their numbers in low-paying jobs, where they had been overrepresented.

According to the "Mayor's Affirmative Action Audit Report" in 1975, minorities and women were "considered to be underrepresented when the Office's

Table 6.1. Demographics of Los Angeles City Employees, 1973 and 1992

	White-Collar, Higher-Paying Positions					
	Protective Service[a]		Officials/ Professionals[b]		Administrators[c]	
	1973	1992	1973	1992	1973	1992
Blacks	9.5%	23.9%	5.0%	12.0%	1.3%	10.6%
Latinos	7.8	25.5	4.6	11.4	2.6	8.1
Asians	0.5	3.2	8.0	16.2	1.3	8.1
Whites	81.5	45.9	81.4	53.8	94.7	70.2
	Skilled and Unskilled, Lower-Paying Positions					
	Skilled Craft[d]		Service/ Technicians[e]		Maintenance[f]	
	1973	1992	1973	1992	1973	1992
Blacks	24.2%	17.0%	7.8%	9.5%	57.6%	41.5%
Latinos	9.5	18.9	6.4	14.4	14.4	30.6
Asians	2.5	5.4	5.8	8.7	1.7	2.0
Whites	63.2	55.8	79.4	62.7	25.7	24.5

Source: City of Los Angeles Affirmative Action Statistics, Box 3847, Bradley Papers, Special Collections, Los Angeles Research Library, University of California.

a. For example, police officers.
b. For example, accountants.
c. For example, project directors.
d. For example, carpenters.
e. For example, electrical linemen.
f. For example, janitors.

representation in an occupational category [was] lower than the City population parity of 17.9% Blacks, 18.4% Spanish-Surnamed, 4.8% Asian, .3% American Indian, and 51.8% women."[50] Between 1973 and 1991 the percentage of African Americans in Los Angeles decreased from 17 to 13 percent because of the growth of the Latino population, from 18 percent in 1970 to 28 percent in 1980.[51] Throughout Bradley's administration, however, the hiring of African Americans, especially for desirable jobs, remained constant even as their proportion of the population declined within Los Angeles. African Americans comprised 21.9 percent of Los Angeles's overall workforce in 1973 and 22.1 percent of the total workforce in 1992.[52] The Latino population, which was experiencing phenomenal growth, represented 9.3 percent of the total workforce in 1973 and 20.1 percent of the overall workforce in 1992.[53] However, unlike blacks, who were overrepresented in high-paying municipal positions, Latinos were greatly underrepresented in local positions that were considered desirable.

In addition to affirmative action programs, Bradley tried to institute programs that would improve the quality of life for underprivileged Los Angeles residents. In 1975 he created a summer recreation program for disadvantaged youth. Of the 48,276 children selected to participate in these activities, 25 percent were African American.[54] Two years later Bradley embarked on a project called "Urban Rx," which rehabilitated abandoned houses and sold them to Los Angeles residents for the amount of the repairs. The cost of the houses ranged from $10,000 to $15,000, and the loans were financed at 3 percent interest or less. The first phase of this program focused on fifty properties in South Central Los Angeles and made homeownership a possibility for many low-income African-American residents.[55] In another overture to residents of this area, Bradley created the South Central Los Angeles Task Force to make recommendations regarding housing and business development and employment opportunities within the black community.[56]

The year 1985 witnessed what may have been Bradley's most publicized show of solidarity with the black community. In September, Louis Farrakhan came to Los Angeles, and local Jewish leaders implored the mayor to censure the Black Muslim for anti-Semitic statements he had made. At the request of both conservative and more militant black leaders, however, Bradley refused to censure Farrakhan before the minister's scheduled speech, maintaining that it would not be ethical to do so when he had no indication that the Muslim leader planned to include anti-Semitic remarks in his address. While blacks respected Bradley's decision, Jewish leaders asserted that "Farrakhan's record as a bigot [was] clear" and that they were "outraged that Bradley [had] not spoken out."[57] In taking this stand Bradley ran the risk of losing one of his most important sources of support—liberal Jews. James H. Cleaver, executive editor of the Los Angeles Sentinel, the area's largest black newspaper, wrote, "He has made a decision that was not popular with some of his former supporters and they will, in all probability, seek vengeance. Hopefully they will recognize the wisdom of Tom Bradley's decision."[58]

Despite these and many other attempts to address issues that concerned the black community, Bradley failed to convince many African-American Los Angeles residents that he had their best interests at heart. Some resented Bradley for not doing more to bring attention and solutions to the police-related problems plaguing the African-American community. In a 1979 editorial the Sentinel castigated the mayor for "not [making] noise where the public could hear him" when dealing with issues of concern to blacks. "Because he is a black man . . . and should be . . . empathetic to the problems of black people, many members of this community are disappointed by his inaction. It is time for Mayor Bradley to consider the needs of the black community and understand its frustrations and concerns."[59] This editorial was accompanied by a cartoon that depicted Bradley casually strolling through the black community, oblivious to police harassment and police-related kill-ings. Another article gave the mayor credit for having "taken steps to end certain practices on the part of the police department which might have gone unnoticed by his predecessor." However, the article continued, "because the mayor is a part of [the black] community, there is [a] . . . feeling by some that much more could have and should have been accomplished by now. No matter that much of the progress we now recognize has come about under the leadership of Tom Bradley. To these people it has been a matter of too little too late."[60]

In 1985 sixty South Central Los Angeles residents met with the mayor to voice their frustration with his lack of attention to their request for more police to patrol their gang-infested neighborhoods. Responding to this need, Brad-ley vetoed a popular measure that would have provided only one hundred new police officers in favor of a less popular proposition (referendum question) that would add more than seven hundred new officers.[61] Nevertheless, resi-dents maintained that officers did not respond to emergency calls in a timely manner and that police-related problems in their neighborhoods required the mayor's personal attention, not just the efforts of his aides.[62] They complained that Bradley's suggestions that blacks "take more responsibility in educating their children to become good citizens" and that they set up more effective "Neighborhood Watch" programs did nothing to protect them from being terrorized by gangs.[63] Virginia Taylor Hughes, then president of the Merchants 4 Community Improvement, said she organized the meeting because "peo-ple in the community feel neglected by the mayor."[64]

Bradley's failure to connect personally and politically to the African-Amer-ican community negatively affected his relationship with younger blacks. One young black minister stated that he would vote for Bradley only if Bradley promised to "spend more time in the Black and Brown communities . . . talk-ing to and listening to the rank and file people on the street."[65] The matter that especially galvanized Los Angeles's young people against Bradley was his re-sponse to the March 16, 1991, shooting death of a fifteen-year-old black girl named Latasha Harlins. Harlins was attempting to steal a bottle of orange juice from a Korean-owned market when Soon Ja Du, the market's proprietor, con-fronted her. A scuffle ensued during which Harlins physically assaulted Du, who then shot Harlins in the back of the head as she ran from the store. The lenient sentence imposed upon Du aroused anger within the black commu-nity. Shortly thereafter a different Korean-owned store was firebombed, and the mayor, having never acknowledged the Harlins family's grief, came to the site to express sympathy for the Korean community. This enraged Harlins's family, and her brother criticized Bradley for his insensitivity, stating, "We felt that if he could come out to the site of the firebombing of a Korean-owned store and express support that he could publicly show some compassion for the death of a Black child."[66]

Another issue that illustrated Bradley's apparent distance from the black community was his 1984 endorsement of Walter Mondale during Jesse Jackson's bid for the presidency of the United States. Boasting an unblemished record and nationwide visibility as the mayor of Los Angeles, Bradley was on the short list of Mondale's choices for a running mate. To the consternation of conservative, moderate, and militant blacks, Bradley was disinclined to support Jackson. Los Angeles's African-American community responded by publicly chastising him. Conservative black Republican Uriah Fields called for Bradley to withdraw his endorsement of Mondale, and Ralph Bailey Jr., a *Sentinel* columnist, wrote, "Bradley has offended his Black base by stressing the importance of his strong White political base—which might . . . [not support him] . . . if Bradley was behind Jackson."[67] In response to Bradley's decision to endorse Mondale rather than Jackson, the more militant *Sentinel* columnist Booker Griffin wrote, "Tom has a history of going against Black people and turning his back on the sufferings of the masses of Blacks. He is 'their' kind and not 'our kind.' He left our race, in practice, a long time ago."[68]

Indeed, many blacks believed that Bradley was more committed to the interests of other groups than he was to problems African Americans were experiencing. Earl Ofari wrote that blacks resented Bradley's allegiance to the many ethnic groups that had supported him. "Some Blacks," he stated, "feel that he could take stronger stands on specific problems that concern the Black community."[69] In a letter to the *Sentinel*'s editor, one reader wrote, "We have become numb with shock over [Bradley's] blind devotion to other ethnic interests while seemingly taking our community for granted. His seeming indifference toward his own people and the issues that most affect them has caused me grave concern."[70]

Much of the tension between Bradley and segments of the black community was related to his relationship with Los Angeles's Jewish community, which had supported him since his 1963 campaign for election to the city council. Although Bradley knew he could be assured of votes from certain liberal segments of the Jewish community, he made considerable efforts to maintain this support and to attract more conservative Jewish voters. During the 1973 campaign, for example, he marched with Los Angeles's Jewish community to protest the treatment of Jews in Soviet Russia, and he attended a block party commemorating the twenty-fifth anniversary of the founding of Israel.[71] These and other overtures to the Jewish community did not go unnoticed and served to increase Bradley's standing among members of this group. Herb Brin, editor of the *Heritage Southwest Jewish Press*, continuously praised Bradley, urging Los Angeles Jews to support him. Brin also lauded Bradley's "tremendous knowledge of city government . . . [and] enormous intellect and resourcefulness."[72]

Despite Bradley's relationship with the Jewish community, he defeated Yorty by only narrow margins in key Jewish precincts in the 1969 and 1973 mayoral elections. Precincts 2227, 2224, 2272, and 2235 were heavily Jewish neighborhoods in the late sixties and early seventies. Table 6.2 shows how Angelenos within these precincts voted in the 1969 and 1973 primary and runoff mayoral elections.

The figures demonstrate that Yorty gained an impressive number of votes in the period between the 1969 primary election and the runoff election of the same year. Bradley was the clear favorite in the 1969 primary, but after Yorty stepped up his racial attacks, he pulled ahead of Bradley in the runoff, picking up 406 votes to Bradley's paltry 125. In 1973 Bradley responded to Yorty's campaign by lavishing time and attention on the Jewish community. Despite his extensive efforts, however, he gained only 10 votes more than Yorty between the primary and runoff elections. These numbers reveal that while the Jewish community was more loyal in its support of Bradley than any group other than African Americans, Jews were still not immune to Yorty's fear tactics. A Jewish Bradley campaign worker commented that she was "alarmed at the large amount of racial propaganda pouring forth from the Yorty camp" to areas of the city heavily populated by Jews. Though many Jewish residents were in favor of Bradley, she continued, some "indicated Yorty support because of racial prejudice or anti-Semitic fears."[73] In order to strengthen his Jewish support, Bradley paid special attention to Jewish interests throughout his tenure as mayor.

This commitment to Jewish concerns was a constant source of tension between Bradley and many of the black community's more militant members. In a letter to the mayor one disgruntled African American wrote, "I was disappointed to see your name supporting Zionist racism. [Some blacks have] not been emancipated from [their] old Negro mentality. But what is the prob-

Table 6.2. Vote Totals in Key Jewish Precincts

Candidate	1969		1973	
	Primary	Runoff	Primary	Runoff
Tom Bradley	566	691	282	610
Sam Yorty	193	599	181	499

Source: City of Los Angeles Official Election Returns, Office of the City Clerk, Records Management Division.

lem with you, Brother?"[74] Booker Griffin, a militant *Sentinel* columnist, accused Bradley of being a stooge for supporters of the Zionist movement. Claiming that Bradley was "trapped by his loyalty to his manipulators," Griffin stated, "if he does not wish to help black liberation, he should not allow himself to be used cheaply against it."[75] He also complained that Bradley had failed to denounce the atrocities committed by white minorities against black Africans but had "ranted and raved with the most militant rhetoric in support of Soviet Jewry."[76]

The busing issue exacerbated the discord between Bradley and blacks regarding his relationship with Jews. Although many African-American parents were in favor of plans to have Los Angeles students bused to schools in areas outside their neighborhoods, Jewish parents strongly opposed such measures. Recognizing the volatile nature of this debate and unwilling to disaffect blacks or Jews, Bradley remained silent. His failure to lend vocal support to blacks in favor of busing infuriated many African Americans. One woman exclaimed, "Mayor Bradley could have given the 'busing to achieve school integration' program a decided emotional and moral uplift if he had come out strongly in favor of the program. I wonder if . . . he wasn't playing the role of political expediency too heavily . . . [and] took the easiest way out?"[77]

Speaking to Bradley's relationship with Jews, one columnist wrote, "[Bradley's] entire political career has been based on strong black and Jewish support [and he] is caught in a high-pressured tug of war between the two groups."[78] Additionally, Earl Ofari asserted that Bradley's obligations to the largely Jewish coalition that enabled his election had "consigned blacks to political second-class citizenship."[79] This coalition, he continued, made it necessary for Bradley to "stress that he is not a black mayor, but rather a mayor who is an impartial representative of all interests. This angers blacks who feel that he could take stronger stands on specific issues that concern the black community."[80] Many African Americans believed that Bradley owed them, not Jews, his allegiance. "No group," wrote a black Los Angeles resident, "has been more supportive of Bradley at the polling place than the Black people who gave him his start."[81] Similarly, a *Sentinel* editorial read, "It is time for him to realize that while the bulk of his support comes from other communities, the black community was the first to stand behind him and . . . he does in fact owe [us] more than just a passing nod."[82]

Throughout Bradley's tenure at city hall Los Angeles's moderate and conservative middle-class black leaders continually commented upon the various manifestations of the tension that existed between the mayor and segments of Los Angeles's black community. Aware of Bradley's long-established method of dealing with African-American issues, these leaders attempted to demonstrate that Bradley's style, though cautious, was the most effective way to create opportunities for blacks in a city with only a small percentage of African-American voters. "Which does . . . [the black community] prefer," asserted the Reverend Thomas Kilgore, "outcry or action? If it has observed over the years the man's way of taking care of business, then it should know that, as mayor, Tom Bradley's actions often speak louder than words."[83] Such leaders acknowledged the mayor's shortcomings but also enumerated his many efforts on behalf of blacks and entreated discontented African Americans to continue to support Bradley despite their frustration with him. The primary concern of the black middle class was to convince African Americans that a vote for Bradley was a step toward a victory that all blacks could claim. "Whatever happens to one Black person," wrote Jim Cleaver, "happens to all Black people."[84] To middle-class leaders like the *Sentinel*'s editor, Bradley embodied the American Dream, and his value as a symbol far outweighed whatever grievances African Americans voiced concerning his methods.

Even their arguments in Bradley's favor, however, are laden with references to the ambivalence Bradley demonstrated toward the black community. It was as though Bradley had become so inextricably linked with his quiet and cautious method of addressing black issues that not even his most ardent supporters could praise him without including a disclaimer. For example, before proclaiming Bradley a "fair, unbiased mayor" who had "attempted to deal with all the city's problems on a fair and equitable basis," a *Sentinel* editorial acknowledged, "some blacks have accused Tom Bradley of not working hard enough to support his black constituency."[85] Another editorial read, "The . . . [mayor] has not moved as swiftly as many would have liked, but he has moved and he has moved decisively."[86] Similarly, Jim Cleaver wrote that blacks should support Bradley "despite the fact that he may not have done all we think he should have done for his own people."[87] "To be sure," wrote Cleaver on another occasion, "there were times when we were angered by one or another of the things he did or did not do . . . when we were angry at him for what we perceived to be his failure to react."[88] Following this disclaimer, Cleaver went on to assert that Bradley would be remembered by history as a great mayor and therefore warranted black support. "Even if there had been nothing more than symbolism to be gained from his winning," wrote the respected columnist A. S. "Doc" Young, "that would have made support of him worthwhile."[89]

Other, more militant blacks, however, maintained that regardless of what Bradley was able to accomplish for blacks behind the scenes, symbolism without public decisive action in support of the African-American community was worthless. Booker Griffin asserted in his column, "Tom Bradley will never give Blacks anything but psychological satisfaction. He offers image and ambition for the people but little of substance or significance."[90] Griffin and others believed that in placing importance on symbolism, influential black community leaders had encouraged blacks not to engage in the responsible activity of critically analyzing Bradley's tenure as mayor. In trying to lead blacks to believe that voting for Bradley was an exercise in self-affirmation, Bradley supporters inferred that criticizing him was tantamount to reproving themselves as black people. Stanley G. Robertson, a *Sentinel* columnist, stated, "Many feel that it is almost 'sacrilegious' to criticize Bradley openly."[91] As a result of this pressure, one columnist commented, "Even Blacks who disagreed with [Bradley] would not speak out or criticize him for fear of doing something which would 'harm the race.' I think this is very unfortunate because it has given people the impression that we were all satisfied with the job the Mayor was doing."[92]

When in the spring of 1992 a Simi Valley jury acquitted four Los Angeles police officers of charges in the brutal beating of Rodney King, the city erupted in violent protest. The First African Methodist Episcopal Church opened its doors to all who wished to discuss the ramifications of this verdict, and black Los Angeles's religious, community, and political leaders addressed the tense and massive African-American crowd gathered there. One leader after another approached the pulpit to thunderous applause, but when Mayor Tom Bradley rose to speak, the church reverberated with deafening boos and jeers. Because he had refused to embrace them in the manner they expected, many blacks rejected this mayor whom they no longer recognized as their own.

* * *

When Bradley became the first black mayor of Los Angeles, he promised to be impartial, that he would not allow issues of race to dominate his administration. Convinced that no other way to properly administer the city existed, Bradley was committed to fulfilling his pledge to run an unbiased administration. To Bradley this meant giving equal attention to all segments of Los Angeles's population, not focusing primarily on the African-American community's needs. However, blacks had been subjected to prejudice and discrimination more than any other group in Los Angeles, and they anticipated that Bradley would aggressively address the problems, born of racism, that plagued their communities. Struggling poor and working-class African Americans, therefore, began to resent the mayor when it became clear that he did not intend to be their decisive, steadfast, and vocal advocate. They expected Bradley to boldly respond to their need for entry-level jobs, affordable housing, better schools, and protection from crime by immediately allocating funds for inner-city programs. Bradley, a fiscal conservative, avoided increasing taxes whenever possible. Rather, he sought to raise money for social programs by applying for federal grants, a process that provided money for specific projects within underprivileged communities.[93] Although some of these programs were effective, the complicated process of applying for federal grants meant that projects could not be implemented immediately, and seldom were funds sufficient to adequately administer services to all that sought assistance. Dissatisfied with Bradley's efforts on their behalf, few poor and working-class blacks believed that he was working hard enough to improve conditions in their communities.

Upwardly mobile African Americans had a separate set of concerns. These college-educated blacks sought high-paying professional and administrative positions, and they wanted a voice in city government. In the past racial discrimination had posed a nearly impenetrable barrier to such advancement. However, Bradley instituted affirmative action hiring policies that substantially increased the numbers of minority, female, and disabled professionals employed by the city. He also appointed to city boards commissioners who reflected the diverse nature of the city's population and endorsed for elective office many minority candidates.[94] Middle class, rather than poor and working-class members of the African-American community, were the beneficiaries of these Bradley efforts.

These middle-class, moderate blacks comprised a vocal support network for the mayor.[95] While they acknowledged poor and working-class blacks' frustration with Bradley's approach to their concerns, they encouraged all African Americans to recognize advances, such as affirmative action, that the mayor had initiated. They asserted that his presence in city hall as a symbol of African-American success was far more important than any controversy regarding his methods. Supporting the mayor, they maintained, was an exercise in self-affirmation—a way to demonstrate pride in black accomplishments, not merely an expression of approval for Tom Bradley.

Indeed, Los Angeles's socially and economically diverse black population was remarkably united in its electoral support of Bradley. Yet, while they continued to vote for him, many poor and working-class blacks were often critical of what they perceived to be Bradley's inattention to their particular concerns. An influential group of middle-class African-American ministers, journalists, professionals, and community leaders encouraged dissatisfied blacks to continue to support the mayor and tried to convince them that Bradley was to be commended for what he had accomplished as mayor of a large, diverse city. As mayor, they asserted, Bradley's foremost responsibility was to protect the interests of the entire city, and he had never pledged to use the power of his office primarily to advance the black cause. Rather, they continued, Bradley was committed to creating an equitable society in which all people, including blacks, could reap the benefits of the city's strength and prosperity. In this effort, they maintained, Bradley had been remarkably successful and for this reason blacks should be proud of him and continue to vote for him. Other, more militant middle-class blacks, together with many poor and working-class African Americans, disputed the wisdom of continuing to support an African-American mayor whose commitment to the black community had been questioned repeatedly.

Convinced that the mayor refused to identify with them because he lacked the courage to defy his white supporters, many African Americans considered Bradley weak and an Uncle Tom. What they failed to recognize was that Bradley's leadership reflected his political values and his belief that his approach was the most effective way to bring black Angelenos into the political and economic mainstream. In his own worldview he could not be an outspoken advocate for African Americans and, at the same time, impartially serve the multivariate interests of Los Angeles's diverse electorate. Bradley's strength was his courage to remain true to his ideals even when, in doing so, he alienated many of his own people who had so strongly supported him and provided the political foundation for his election.

Notes

1. The 1970 census shows that blacks comprised 17.7 percent of the Los Angeles population, while whites accounted for 59 percent and Latinos 18.3 percent. Carl Stokes was elected mayor of Cleveland in 1968, which two years later had a population that was 37 percent black, according to the U.S. Census Bureau. Newark, New Jersey, with a population that was 47 percent black, elected Kenneth Gibson in 1970. In 1973 Coleman Young became the mayor of Detroit and Atlanta elected Maynard Jackson. According to the 1970 census, Detroit was 50 percent black, and Atlanta was 54 percent black.

2. "The Example of Los Angeles Will Encourage Others: An Interview with Mayor Tom Bradley," *Black Enterprise*, January 1974, pp. 34–37.

3. J. Gregory Payne and Scott C. Ratzan, *Tom Bradley: The Impossible Dream* (Malibu, Calif.: Roundtable, 1986), 46.

4. Tom Bradley, "Vision and Responsibility: The Role of States in Planning for Full Employment," *Urban League Review* 10, no. 1 (Summer 1986): 60.

5. Payne and Ratzan, *Tom Bradley,* 249.

6. Stanley G. Robertson, "A Time for Direction, Leadership," *Los Angeles Sentinel,* April 6, 1989.

7. *Heritage Southwest Jewish Press,* March 13, 1969.

8. "Bradley Identifies Self as Best Candidate," *Los Angeles Sentinel,* July 7, 1982.

9. "Ordinance Aids Small Business," *Los Angeles Sentinel,* May 1, 1980.

10. "The Example of Los Angeles," *Black Enterprise,* January 1974.

11. "The Example of Los Angeles."

12. Ibid., emphasis added.

13. Booker Griffin, "Endorsing Mondale Was Par for Mayor Tom," *Los Angeles Sentinel,* October 27, 1983.

14. Opposition to sheriff's deputies' subsidy, September 8, 1967, File 135972; opposition to taxing municipal bonds, March 7, 1969, File 143200; support of homeowners' tax relief, February 7, 1968, File 137971, and January 3, 1972, File 71-71; federal funding, April 19, 1973, File 72-808; and Columbia Records, July 25, 1963, File 114526, and March 3, 1964, File 114526, all in Los Angeles City Council files, Office of the City Clerk, Records Management Division.

15. Duplicate services investigation, July 19, 1963, File 114425, and January 31, 1969, File 142656; processing fee for gun sales, May 16, 1968, File 139379, all in Los Angeles City Council files.

16. Opera, January 26, 1966, File 127777; symphony, October 15, 1964, File 121090; consumer protection, July 30, 1971, File 71-3035, and April 3, 1972, File 1282; environment, October 5, 1967, File 13633, February 25, 1970, File 148075, and February 15, 1973, File 73-300; citizen grievance committees, July 11, 1968, File 140088, and January 21, 1969, File 142506; and health and safety regulations, March 20, 1967, File 133615, February 8, 1968, File 138032, and December 5, 1972, File 72-4592, all in Los Angeles City Council files.

17. On February 18, 1968, a Los Angeles police officer shot Gregory Clarke, an eighteen-year-old African American whom the medical examiner later determined was facedown on the pavement when the fatal wound was inflicted. Witnesses testified that the young man had not resisted arrest, but a coroner's jury rendered a 4-3 decision of justifiable homicide. On March 12, 1968, Tom Bradley, then a member of the city council, made a motion that the city "conduct an inquiry into the incident and report its findings to the city council" (March 12, 1968, File 138454, Los Angeles City Council files).

18. *Los Angeles Election Gazette,* May 20, 1969.

19. *Heritage Southwest Jewish Press,* March 13, 1969.

20. *Los Angeles Times,* May 26, 1969, pt. 1, p. 4.

21. *Los Angeles Times Magazine,* January 1969.

22. *Los Angeles Times,* May 26, 1969, pt. 1, p. 4.

23. Irene Winston, a resident of Woodland Hills, is quoted in Payne and Ratzan, *Tom Bradley,* 102.

24. Student activist Rick Fehrenbacher is quoted in Payne and Ratzan, *Tom Bradley,* 122.

25. Tom Bradley, interview by author, May 22, 1995, Los Angeles. See Heather Rose Parker, "The Elusive Coalition: African-American and Chicano Interaction in Los Angeles, 1960–1973" (Ph.D. diss., History Department, University of California, Los Angeles, 1996), p. 215.

26. "Result of Vote Cast for Mayor," 1969, Box C-129, City of Los Angeles, City Records Center and Archives.

27. Bradley interview.

28. Maury Weiner, interview by author, July 24, 1995, Tarzana, Calif. See Parker, "The Elusive Coalition," 309–10.

29. Bishop H. H. Brookins, interview by author, August 10, 1995, Bel Air, Calif. During the 1960s and 1970s Brookins pastored the First A.M.E. Church, one of the largest and most

influential black congregations in Los Angeles. He orchestrated Bradley's 1963 election to the Los Angeles City Council and was instrumental in Bradley's first campaigns for the mayoralty. See Parker, "The Elusive Coalition," 333, 335. Also see Payne and Ratzan, *Tom Bradley,* 116–17.

30. Carl B. Stokes, *Promises of Power: A Political Autobiography* (New York: Simon and Schuster, 1973), 271–72.

31. *Los Angeles Times,* May 27, 1973, sec. 1, 26.

32. *Los Angeles Times,,* May 2, 1973, pt. 1, p. 3.

33. Ibid.

34. "Result of Vote Cast for Mayor," 1969 and 1973, Boxes CC-03-25 and CC-03-26, City of Los Angeles, City Records Center and Archives.

35. "Result of Vote Cast for Mayor" (by council district), 1973, City of Los Angeles, City Records Center and Archives. Also see *Los Angeles Times,* June 10, 1973.

36. *Los Angeles Times,* June 10, 1973.

37. The majority of Los Angeles's black population was affected by problems associated with low income levels. According to the 1970 census, the median income for blacks in Los Angeles was nearly $4,000 less than for whites, and the high school dropout rate for blacks was 27 to 54 percent, whereas the white dropout rate was 1 to 34 percent. Additionally, 96 percent of Los Angeles's black children attended segregated schools, a reflection of the city's segregated neighborhoods. According to a study by Howard J. Nelson and William A.V. Clark, *Los Angeles, The Metropolitan Experience* (Cambridge, Mass: Ballinger, 1976), Los Angeles's black neighborhoods were considered the worst areas of the city when judged according to such criteria as per capita and household income, soundness of housing, percentage of white-collar employment, percentage of owner-occupied housing, and crime, welfare, unemployment, and high school dropout rates.

38. Gastelum is quoted in Payne and Ratzan, *Tom Bradley,* 169.

39. The black middle class was a small segment of the black population and lived in three small neighborhoods (Baldwin Hills, Ladera Heights, and View Park) far to the west of the black section of Los Angeles. For a detailed analysis of how the black middle class benefited from Bradley's administration, see Byran O. Jackson and Michael B. Preston, *Racial and Ethnic Politics in California* (Berkeley, Calif.: Institute of Governmental Studies, 1991).

40. "1974 Commissions Roster," Box 0899, Bradley Papers, Special Collections, Los Angeles Research Library, University of California. For a detailed account of Bradley's commission appointments, see Raphael Sonenshein, *Politics in Black and White* (Princeton, N.J.: Princeton University Press, 1993).

41. "1981 Commission Roster," Boxes 4715 and 2150, and "1992 Los Angeles City Commissioners Ethnicity Report," Box 1163, Bradley Papers.

42. Executive Directive No. 1, October 29, 1973, Box 3813, Bradley Papers.

43. "Equal Opportunities Policy Resolution for the City of Los Angeles," 1975, Box 0781, Bradley Papers.

44. "Implementation of the Affirmative Action Program for the Mayor's Office," 1975, Box 0781, and Bill Elkins, "Affirmative Action Record of the Tom Bradley Administration," Box 3813, 1982, both in Bradley Papers

45. Bill Elkins, memo to Mayor Bradley, "Affirmative Action Ordinance for Non-Construction Contractors (vendors, suppliers, etc.)," March 22, 1974, Box 3115, Bradley Papers.

46. Executive Directive No. 1-C, March 30, 1987, Bradley Papers (Box 3858).

47. Samuel M. Sperling, "The Impact of Directive #5 on the Appointment of Minorities and Women: A Report to the Advisory Affirmative Action Committee," February 13, 1975, Box 779, Bradley Papers.

48. Executive Directive No. 5—New Series, 1975, Box 779, Bradley Papers.

49. Bradley to Mrs. Wanda Moore, executive assistant to the Mayor, regarding "Affirmative Action Training for Executive Staff of the Mayor's Office," November 10, 1975, Bradley Papers.

50. Office of the Mayor, "Affirmative Action Audit Report for October," December 5, 1975, Bradley Papers.

51. See the U.S. Census for 1970, 1980, and 1990: Bureau of the Census, *Census of Population: General Population Characteristics of Urban Areas* (Washington, D.C.: U.S. Government Printing Office).

52. Affirmative action pie charts, 1992, Box 3847, Bradley Papers.

53. Ibid.

54. City of Los Angeles Recreation Support Program, Project Narrative (Participant Characteristics Plan), 1975, Box 3107, Bradley Papers.

55. "Urban Recovery Program Slated," *Los Angeles Sentinel,* May 19, 1977.

56. "Mayor's South-Central L.A. Revitalization Plans Defended," *Los Angeles Sentinel,* March 1, 1990.

57. "Bradley Promised Silence on Farrakhan," *Los Angeles Sentinel,* September 13, 1985.

58. James H. Cleaver, "What Happens to Tom Bradley Now?" *Los Angeles Sentinel,* September 19, 1985.

59. "The Time Is Now," editorial, *Los Angeles Sentinel,* March 1, 1979.

60. "You Can't Be Everything to Everybody," *Los Angeles Sentinel,* March 22, 1979.

61. "Supporting the Mayor," *Los Angeles Sentinel,* May 30, 1985.

62. "Mayor Queried on Lack of Police Service," *Los Angeles Sentinel,* October 31, 1985.

63. Ibid.

64. Ibid.

65. Robertson, "A Time for Direction, Leadership."

66. "Supporters: Mayor Insensitive to Harlins Family," *Los Angeles Sentinel,* September 12, 1991.

67. Ralph Bailey Jr., "Jesse Jackson Wreaking Havoc with Local Politicians," *Los Angeles Sentinel,* March 31, 1988.

68. Griffin, "Endorsing Mondale Was Par."

69. Earl Ofari, "Is Bradley's Coalition Politics the Answer?" *Los Angeles Sentinel,* October 7, 1982.

70. Legrand H. Clegg II, letter to editor, *Los Angeles Sentinel,* December 2, 1982.

71. *Heritage Southwest Jewish Press,* March 23, 1973, and *Los Angeles Times,* May 7, 1973, pt. 1, p. 2.

72. *Heritage Southwest Jewish Press,* February 13, 1969.

73. Shirley Wolf is quoted in *Heritage Southwest Jewish Press,* June 12, 1969. Also see

"Rabbis Warn Against 'a Negro Confrontation' Should Bradley Become Mayor," *Heritage Southwest Jewish Press,* May 29, 1969; "Jewish Resident Expresses Hope That Jews Would Not This Time Be 'Taken in by the Blatant Racist Appeals of the Yorty Campaign," *Heritage Southwest Jewish Press,* March 30, 1973; and "Yorty's Racist Campaign Proved Very Effective in Jewish Areas That Bordered Black Neighborhoods," *Los Angeles Times,* June 10, 1973.

74. Dr. M. T. Mehdi, Mailgram to the mayor, November 24, 1975, Bradley Papers.

75. Booker Griffin, "Bradley 'Mum on Human Rights in Southern Africa,'" *Los Angeles Sentinel,* August 25, 1977.

76. Ibid.

77. *Los Angeles Sentinel,* April 9, 1981.

78. *Los Angeles Times,* September 13, 1985.

79. Earl Ofari, *Los Angeles Sentinel,* October 7, 1982.

80. Ibid.

81. Clegg letter to editor.

82. "The Time Is Now."

83. "Rev. Tom Kilgore Censures the Sentinel," *Los Angeles Sentinel,* March 22, 1979.

84. James H. Cleaver, "Blacks Must Keep a Voice in City Hall," *Los Angeles Sentinel,* January 24, 1985.

85. "We Need Him Now," editorial, *Los Angeles Sentinel,* March 24, 1977.

86. "Cause Behind the Cause," editorial, *Los Angeles Sentinel,* December 4, 1980.

87. Cleaver, "Blacks Must Keep a Voice."

88. James H. Cleaver, "Kleaver's Klippins," *Los Angeles Sentinel,* July 8, 1993.

89. A. S. Young, "Class Taught by Crabs," *Los Angeles Sentinel,* February 10, 1983.

90. Griffin, "Endorsing Mondale Was Par."

91. Stanley G. Robertson, "L.A. Confidential," *Los Angeles Sentinel,* April 13, 1989.

92. Robertson, "A Time for Direction, Leadership."

93. "Correspondence Regarding Grant for Youth," 1974, Box 3107; "U.S. Department of Health . . . Youth Gang Drug Prevention Program," 1990, Box 4857; "Poverty Programs," 1974–1983, Box 3630; and "City of Los Angeles Recreation Support Program 1975," Office of Economic Opportunity—Application for Community Action Program, 1975, Box 3107, all in Bradley Papers.

94. In 1973 Bradley appointed Manual Aragon as his second deputy mayor, the first Latino to occupy this position. Bradley appointed African-American Warren Hollier to the presidency of the Board of Public Works and William Elkins, also African American, as executive assistant to the mayor. When confronted with a choice between endorsing for his vacant Tenth District city council seat David Cunningham, an African American, or Ronald Takei, an Asian American, Bradley endorsed his close friend Cunningham but appointed Takei to the Board of the Southern California Rapid Transit District. Some other black candidates who received Bradley endorsements were Robert Farrell (Eighth [city council] District), Kenneth S. Washington (Twenty-ninth District state senate seat), and Maxine Waters (Forty-eighth District assembly seat).

95. This influential and vocal group included such people as the Reverend Thomas Kilgore, pastor of one of Los Angeles's oldest and most respected African-American churches; the respected newspaper columnist A. S. "Doc" Young; James H. Cleaver, exec-

utive editor of the *Los Angeles Sentinel;* Bishop H. H. Brookins of the African Methodist Episcopal Church; Ron Smothers, president of the Crenshaw Chamber of Commerce; Los Angeles City Council members Robert Farrel, David Cunningham, and Gilbert Lindsay; California Assemblywoman Teresa Hughes; the Reverend P. J. Ellis, president of the Baptist Ministers' Conference of Los Angeles and Vicinity; and California lieutenant governor Mervyn Dymally. In addition, one hundred clergy representing nine Christian denominations pledged support for Bradley in 1981, as did the Democratic Minority Conference, a group of black lawyers that sought to increase the representation of minorities in elective office.

7. African-American Mayors and Governance in Atlanta

RONALD H. BAYOR

ATLANTA ALWAYS HAS been a business-oriented city. The white business elite long dominated the decision-making process and effectively determined the city's priorities. Problems relating to race and class often were largely neglected unless they immediately affected Atlanta's economic vitality and racially progressive reputation. From the 1940s through the 1960s especially, white business leaders ran city hall and controlled the changes that occurred when racial issues dominated the headlines. This power structure included a relatively small group of men consisting of the leaders of such companies as Coca-Cola and Rich's Department Store, top officials from Atlanta's banking, utility, and insurance firms, and from the most important law, real estate, and construction businesses.

The development of an assertive, politically powerful black community, which eventually elected African-American mayors and wanted standing equal to that of the white power structure, set the stage for a confrontation between the goals of business leaders and the priorities of the black community. In seeking to address the long-neglected concerns of Atlanta's blacks, African-American mayors initially found themselves challenging a white business community that expected to set the city's agenda along traditional lines favorable to its interests. This clash and its outcome largely determined the effectiveness of black mayors in reorienting city policies.

For many years black Atlantans were convinced that simply securing a powerful political voice would solve *all* the community's problems. "Eventually, and ultimately, most of our problems will be solved and settled at the ballot box."[1] So spoke John Wesley Dobbs, a civil rights pioneer and political activist, in expressing in 1856 the hoped-for value and power of voting.

For decades black Atlantans had their eyes on the prize of voting and making that vote a significant one in the city. Registration campaigns in the 1930s and 1940s, and particularly in 1946 when the federal courts ended Georgia's white primary, exhorted blacks to register in order to help get more and better schools, streets and lights, and police protection. These efforts reflected the symbolic and real importance attached to the vote. The salience of that vote was evidenced over the years in numerous ways and underscored the significance of the election of Atlanta's first black mayor in 1973.[2]

In the late 1940s William Hartsfield was the first mayor to recognize the racial changes in Atlanta. His views were best captured when black leaders earlier asked that the city hire black police officers and make basic infrastructure improvements in the black community. Hartsfield responded, "Come back to see me when you have ten thousand votes."[3] In 1947 the mayor understood that black voters were now substantial and important and agreed to the hiring of the first African-American police.

Hartsfield's victories came to depend on the black vote in coalition with upper-income whites. At this point in the city's history, blacks were able to secure limited neighborhood improvements and prevent openly racist whites from gaining office. Hartsfield had used the black community to maintain his political strength, but black leaders had also used him. While change was evident in Atlanta, the city was far from embracing equal representation for the races.

The 1961 election of Ivan Allen and the defeat of segregationist Lester Maddox, in the midst of civil rights efforts to desegregate the city, represented the ascension to city hall of a pragmatic moderate politician who was principally concerned with Atlanta's economic growth and reputation. Fully aware that change was needed, Allen hired the first black fire fighters and provided more services and amenities to black neighborhoods. Racial issues received greater attention from Allen than they had from any previous white mayor.

But while Allen represented an improvement over Hartsfield on issues of concern to Atlanta's blacks, limitations in a white mayor's approach still were evident. City schools remained largely segregated, black neighborhoods received less attention than white ones, hospitals were segregated, and blacks remained invisible in municipal policy-making positions. Allen also failed to appoint a single African-American department head. Moreover, the city had yet to provide equality of services, rights, and benefits for black residents. The problem, as Allen noted, was that the "white community tends to define [racial harmony] as absence of disturbance, [the] Negro Community as establishment of their full rights as American citizens."[4] Basic change for the city, or so it seemed increasingly to many black voters, would come only with the election of a black mayor.

The election of the last white mayor, Sam Massell, in 1969 once again made clear to black residents the limitations of white leadership. Massell certainly fulfilled some of the black community's goals. He secured the appointment of the first black department head, set up (but did not fill) the position of affirmative action officer in the personnel department, and pushed for a higher percentage of minority employees in city jobs. Yet could a white mayor, even Massell, really be trusted? When Massell saw that the black vote was increasing, he realized that he probably would face a black opponent in his reelection bid in 1973. At that point he began to appeal for white support. Several of his actions reflected this shift: his 1971 aldermanic committee changes, which left some committees without black members; an annexation scheme that would have increased the white population in the city; and his criticism of his black opponent in a way that was widely interpreted as racist. Massell's use of "Atlanta, Too Young to Die" as a campaign slogan in 1973 suggested to voters that a black mayor would mean the end of the city.

Mayors Hartsfield, Allen, and Massell did effect a number of positive changes for the black community. They were, in fact, the first white mayors to address seriously the problems of black neighborhoods. Yet they would go only so far. Working within a paternalistic relationship, they viewed blacks as junior partners in the city's political coalition of upper-income whites and black voters. More and more, and especially after Massell's actions at the end of his first term, Atlanta's blacks saw the election of a black mayor as the only solution to their problems.

What difference did the election of a black mayor make for Atlanta and its black community? What changes occurred? And how has the city been transformed, if at all, after more than twenty-five years of a black-run city hall?

Maynard Jackson's 1973 victory against Massell was surely a turning point and a symbolic event for a city that was now majority black (51.3 percent in 1970). By capturing 95 percent of the black vote (and 17.5 percent of the white vote), Jackson demonstrated the ability of blacks to elect one of their own to the city's highest office. Jackson was well grounded in Atlanta politics from his position as vice mayor and through his grandfather John Wesley Dobbs, who had been co-leader of the Atlanta Negro Voters League, long active in registering African Americans to vote, and was widely respected for his political activism. Jackson's election brought into office an articulate individual who could stand up to whites. It also sparked tangible changes, as Jackson set out to correct years of neglect of the city's black population. Nonetheless, the new mayor recognized that fulfilling black aspirations would be difficult. Soon after the election he noted that "the level of expectation of black people when a black mayor is elected is so intensely emotional until it is almost exaggerated. It may be impossible for any human being to satisfy the level of expectations." Working within an atmosphere of "exaggerated black expectations" alongside "exaggerated white anxiety," Jackson sought to calm white fears yet secure greater opportunities for all African Americans.[5]

At first, this was impossible to do. Efforts to shift traditional business priorities, increase minority hiring and promotion, expand affirmative action and minority business set-asides, and upgrade neglected black neighborhoods met with disfavor from the white business leaders. Each program brought a test of wills. In Jackson's first year as mayor, African Americans made up 80 percent of new city hires and 59 percent of the top two job classifications. Jackson appointed twelve whites and fifteen blacks to head city departments and agencies.[6] Opening up many leadership positions that had largely been withheld from blacks represented an important first step for biracial power sharing in city government. In the private sector the mayor pressured white-run banks to appoint blacks and women as executives and used deposits of city money to push the banks into compliance. As Jackson observed subsequently, he wanted to secure a policy of equal opportunity. This goal was the basis for "moving a half-million-dollar account out of a bank that would not comply with the city policy to a bank that had come in on the twenty-ninth day of a thirty-day last ultimatum." Jackson took this action after eighteen months of discussion on the issues of affirmative action and equal opportunity.[7]

The new mayor expanded Massell's affirmative action efforts and the minority set-aside program of the Metropolitan Atlanta Rapid Transit Authority (MARTA). Furthermore, his administration made special efforts to recruit African Americans for city positions and to increase the number of of blacks appointed to serve as department heads. Jackson also appointed an affirmative action director. The results were impressive. In 1970, before Jackson took office, 38.1 percent of the total Atlanta municipal workforce was black, along with 7.1 percent of the administrators and 15.2 percent of the city's professionals. By 1978, into the mayor's second term, the percentages were 55.6, 32.6, and 42.2, respectively.[8] Jackson also established a city Minority Business Enterprise (MBE) program to ensure that a significant level of city contracts would be awarded to black-owned firms. Under MBE stipulations the city had to award about 25 percent (later 35 percent) of city contracts to minority-owned firms outright (through contracts or subcontracts) or through joint ventures in which a white and minority firm would join for the contract.

The MBE program proved especially important in developing the new airport terminal, and it was in relation to MBE and airport construction that the white business leaders became incensed. Jackson, however, would not back down on this issue and proclaimed he would see grass grow on the runways before he would relent. In fact, he held the project up for a year until he received compliance with his demands. As a result of the MBE efforts, 19 percent of city contracts went to minority businesses by the end of Jackson's first term and 34 percent by the end of his second term in 1981. These figures compared to 1 percent in 1973.[9] The MBE program enabled black-owned firms and numerous black workers to share in the city's economic success. Minority workers made up 71 percent of MBE firms' employees. The mayor saw his efforts as "economic integration."[10] Changes in federal laws helped Jackson during these early years. The clause in the 1964 Civil Rights Act dealing with private-sector employment discrimination was enhanced by the 1972 Equal Employment Opportunities Act to include local government positions. And the Equal Employment Opportunity Commission required cities to note in annual reports the race of their workers, thereby making public the results of affirmative action programs.

African-American neighborhoods also initially benefited significantly from Jackson's efforts. He shifted city hall priorities to the protection of residential areas instead of the downtown business district and supported the development of additional housing, particularly for low-income residents. After he secured federal funds from Community Development Block Grants, he said that the city would use the money mainly for the "revitalization of deteriorating neighborhoods." Money went toward housing rehabilitation, housing code enforcement, sewers, streetlights, recreation centers, and social services—and he made black neighborhoods targets for these improvements.[11]

The deterioration of public housing was a special concern to black residents. White mayors had long neglected this housing. In 1974 Jackson spent one weekend at Bankhead Courts, a low-income housing project, and was so appalled by the conditions that he immediately ordered improvements. He assigned city workers to clean up the grounds and to provide better sanitation services. The city also improved police protection, opened a day-care center, renovated a recreation center, and organized a youth program. The mayor also appointed a female tenant to the Atlanta Housing Authority board and began meeting with Citywide Tenants, an organization consisting of tenant groups from Atlanta's public housing projects. These meetings represented the first and only time low-income residents were part of the policy-making process.[12]

Jackson's leadership was also important in reforming the police department, which had a long history of brutality and racist hiring and promotion policies. He waged a long battle to oust the police chief, John Inman, who had been appointed to an eight-year term in 1972 by the previous mayor. Inman opposed affirmative action and did little to deal with numerous charges of police officers' excessive use of force against blacks. Although he failed to remove Inman, Jackson removed his powers in 1974 and placed them in the hands of Reginald Eaves, an African American who held the newly created post of public safety commissioner. Cases of police brutality declined sharply under his command. Eaves, however, was a controversial commissioner. As head of both the police and fire departments, he wanted to improve minority representation in both departments by hiring more blacks. Charges of reverse discrimination, and Eaves's involvement in a cheating scandal regarding police promotion exams, eventually embroiled the department in years of suits and countersuits regarding hiring and promotions. Eaves was eventually forced to resign in 1978 because of the cheating allegations and the unremitting pressure on Jackson from the white business community. Nonetheless, Eaves, following Jackson's lead, had increased the number of blacks on the force. By 1976, 74 percent of those hired as police in the previous two years were African Americans. Blacks also received more promotions than they had under Inman.[13]

Jackson's initial years demonstrated that a black mayor could make long overdue changes, present a policy focus different from his white predecessors', and begin to transform a city. Most of all, the black community and its neglected problems became the focus of city hall concern. Jackson said one way in which he was different from the white mayors was that he placed the black community on the daily agenda of his thinking. The issue, he noted, is whether the mayor wakes up each morning asking what can he do for the people of Atlanta, including the black community, which was most in need. Unless a special effort was made to include the black community, it often was ignored.[14] Andrew Young, Atlanta's second black mayor, also thought Jackson filled a special role for the black community. As Young noted years later, Jackson was important for implementing and expanding affirmative action and understanding what this meant for the black community and for improving long-neglected black neighborhoods.[15]

As effective as he was in his early years, Jackson encountered economic and political pressures that subsequently forced him into the traditional way of leading Atlanta. His two administrations illustrate both the possibilities and realities of governing a large, complex city. Jackson confronted two major obstacles—the white business community, which resisted change, and the

Atlanta economy, which limited long-term improvements for low-income blacks.

Maynard Jackson's election and his subsequent support for affirmative action, MBE, and neighborhood revitalization issues received substantial criticism from the white business community, which, as Jackson said, felt "that I was forcing them to change." According to Dan Sweat, executive director of the powerful downtown business group Central Atlanta Progress (CAP), the business leaders looked at Jackson, and his new social agenda, with "a great sense of apprehension, fear, and in some cases bordering on panic." The business community began to realize that Atlanta was going to see some dramatic changes and that it would no longer be able to call the mayor and tell him what to do. Black political power and a black mayor meant that the business community would need a new way of communicating with city hall.[16] These feelings were reflected in a September 1974 letter to Jackson from Harold Brockey, who was president of CAP and chairman of Rich's Department Store. This letter was based on a CAP survey of the business community, which believed the mayor was ruining downtown, mismanaging the city, doing little to prevent whites and businesses from leaving Atlanta, and being antiwhite. Brockey's letter brimmed with fear, a sense of displacement, a longing for the old business-government relationship, and an unwillingness to accept the racial shift. Jackson held firm against these charges, stating that his goal was to include others in the leadership of the city and that charges of being antibusiness or antiwhite were false.[17]

In an attempt to reconcile the business group with Jackson, former mayor Ivan Allen gave public voice to the intensity of the negative feelings toward the new mayor. Allen noted at a reconciliation meeting that "some of us have gotten too concerned with wanting the city government to fail because it's black." He added that Atlanta would be destroyed unless the white business leaders and the black political leaders worked together. Jackson later contended that Allen's words revealed what most black leaders believed—that "there was a Vietnam type burn-and-reclaim strategy. Let the city go to hell, blame it on the blacks and they [whites] will come back and rebuild, come back to reclaim it."[18] After the intensity of the dispute caught the attention of the national press, the business leaders, fearing harm to Atlanta's economy, pulled back. Jackson too tried to ward off any harm to investments. In 1974 he went to Chicago and New York, along with the Chamber of Commerce president, to convince potential investors of the excellent business situation in Atlanta and to deny any reports of business–city hall tensions. Jackson claimed that such reports resulted from "preconceived notions as to the disposition of a black administration toward the predominately white business community."[19] But the tensions were real, and they continued.

The leading newspapers in the city picked up the battle flag. The *Atlanta Constitution* warned that the city was moving away from its earlier racial harmony and was "in severe danger of dividing along racial lines." In 1975 the paper ran a series on Atlanta as a "city in crisis" that was critical of Atlanta's leadership, its racial divisiveness, and the lack of cooperation between business and government. The *Atlanta Journal* suggested that the mayor was guilty of demagogic actions on behalf of low-income Atlantans. The newspapers blamed problems in the city on its black leadership. During Jackson's first term, black leaders called two press conferences specifically to express discontent with what they felt was unfair newspaper treatment of the Jackson administration.[20]

The constant battering began to have an effect on the mayor. Jackson defended his actions by noting that "black people do not want to take over Atlanta. Black people want to participate and to have our influence felt in fair proportions." He accused white leaders of failing to foster harmony between the races and urged them to resist racial fears. White resistance to a black mayor continued through Jackson's second term, but the mayor had realized early, as he said in 1974, that "Atlanta can't prosper without city hall and business 'in bed' together." What this meant in terms of policy changes was that Jackson at first pushed for his more inclusive agenda but eventually toned down certain aspects of it and redirected some initial priorities. As one student of Atlanta politics concluded, "Black control of political power is dependent on corporate control of vast economic resources, and the mere threat of corporate disinvestment is sufficient to curtail serious consideration of redistributive public policy."[21]

The neighborhood revitalization program illustrated this change in priorities. Dan Sweat of CAP reflected the attitude of white business leaders in 1975 when he criticized the use of the Community Development Block Grants for residential rather than downtown commercial use. Claiming that the money would be better spent in the central business district for parking lots and the Underground, a tourist and entertainment center, Sweat questioned how the city could make any decisions about how to spend the grant money without the participation of the business community, which had always shaped development. In reaction to this criticism and pressure, Jackson announced the creation of a Mayor's Office of Economic Development in 1977 (the year of his reelection campaign) to maintain a commercially strong business district. He subsequently used almost 50 percent of the block grant money for "public works improvements in the downtown area." The shift from a focus on black neighborhoods to commercial development was abrupt. The mayor's rhetoric also changed as he spoke about the "revitalization of the central business district as an 'utmost priority.'" However, even with continued good intentions toward residential areas, Jackson and his successors would have found maintaining improvements difficult. Park space represents a good case in point. Under white mayors, Atlanta's black neighborhoods had less park development than white neighborhoods, and Jackson initially tried to correct that historic neglect. As much as the Jackson administration tried to equalize park space, doing so proved impossible. By 1970, 50 percent of the city money allocated for parks had to be put toward the amortization of bonds issued for the building of Atlanta–Fulton County Stadium.[22] The fiscal obligations incurred by earlier mayors had tied Jackson's hands.

The mayor's opposition to a sanitation workers' strike in 1977 offered further proof of shifting priorities. In 1970 Jackson, then the vice mayor, had strongly supported the workers' demand for higher pay and a strike. Now the union incurred his opposition. Although he had been critical of the previous mayor for not meeting the workers' demands, Jackson proceeded to take the same position. The white business community opposed the union's demands, but so did the Reverend Martin Luther King Sr. and the Atlanta Urban League.[23] Part of King's and the AUL's opposition stemmed from their support of Jackson as the city's first black mayor, but it also reflected a class preference. An established, as well as a rising, black middle class could only benefit from a city in which the racial priorities but not the class priorities had changed. As one analyst of Atlanta's history concluded, "The interests of a growing professional-managerial stratum within the black community dovetailed with those of pro-growth white elites."[24] Policies of redistribution had little support. The sanitation strike revealed this clearly. As another student of Atlanta's politics noted, in regard to the strike, "The incorporation of the Black business and political elites forced their members to choose in such situations between their racial and their class allegiances. Further progress depended more on cooperating with the white business elite than in solidarity with the Black working class." Essentially, the "White leaders deflected and absorbed the Black challenge to their authority by co-opting the Black economic and political elites."[25] It was revealing that King and other black leaders were in the Atlanta Chamber of Commerce offices when they issued their statements against the striking workers. Jackson also had some very real budget concerns regarding a pay increase for the sanitation workers. Nonetheless, the firing of nearly one thousand poorly paid black workers reflected the mayor's new perspective.

Affirmative action and joint venture, so strongly touted in the administration's early years, also had a lower priority. Joint venture tended to favor the black middle class, those who were ready to make use of new opportunities. The number of minority-owned businesses increased significantly by the 1980s, and the city contract compliance office did well in overseeing the process. However, employment opportunities were not a major concern. Aiding low-income blacks by increasing job opportunities became of secondary interest. The city failed to continue to push Jackson's early efforts at economic integration and asked only that businesses make a good faith effort. Even with joint venture some questioned Jackson's changing priorities. Emma Darnell, Jackson's commissioner of administrative services, was removed from office in 1976 and her department abolished, according to her statement, because white business leaders had viewed her as overly aggressive regarding the airport's joint venture program. She claimed that the mayor fired her because of complaints from the white business community.[26] Jackson also fired other department heads, one of whom was a black commissioner not in the good graces of the white business leaders. They had attacked this department head, who led community and human services, for opposing the use of Community Development Block Grants mainly in the downtown business area.[27] And, as noted earlier, Eaves was forced to resign in 1978.

By the end of his first term Jackson had accomplished a great deal. He had secured a fairer share of the city's economic growth for middle-class blacks and had done much to deal with police mistreatment of black Atlantans. Both were notable accomplishments, but his priorities gradually shifted to embrace the goals of the business leaders. As one study of Atlanta concluded, "Black business and professional leaders were simply asking that doors closed on a racial basis be opened. They were seeking to use, not challenge, the strategically important place that the white business elite held." The business of the city was still business, not class uplift. Black and white leaders spoke the same language of Atlanta's economic growth. Atlanta's mercantile milieu was best expressed by one observant individual, who said that "a room full of black and white leaders in Atlanta 'is nothing but a room full of people trying to cut a deal.'"[28]

As a result of his need and willingness to acknowledge the priorities of the business leaders and his strong support in the black community, Jackson faced little opposition in his reelection bid in 1977. Emma Darnell, his former commissioner, was the main opposition, and she failed to secure many votes, which demonstrated that no significant black political opposition to Jackson arose even as he shifted priorities. Prominent black politicians were few, and not many individuals in the African-American community wished to split the black vote at this time. Also, the city's white leaders did not field a white candidate because they realized Jackson would win. Nonetheless, the racial split in the city was evident. Jackson received 93.2 percent of the black vote and only 19.5 percent of the white vote (up from 17.5 percent in 1973).[29]

Opposition to black political empowerment and black acceptance of white business priorities were only part of the explanation for why Atlanta did not see greater change, particularly for lower-income blacks. Jackson, like the mayors who followed him, believed that the benefits of economic growth would trickle down to the poor. Jackson did speak about unemployment. In fact, his rhetoric suggested that his second term would focus on the problems of poverty and unemployment. However, he supported economic development as the business community envisaged it. Specifically, the business community claimed that improving the business environment for Atlanta's private sector would benefit low-income blacks.[30] The shift in block grant money to the downtown area reflected this approach.

At the same time, the city's economy was changing, and the changes did not benefit low-income residents. The city lost industrial jobs to the suburbs and overseas—jobs that would have helped many unskilled and semiskilled blue-collar workers among Atlanta's poorer population. Meanwhile, the city's new jobs called for office, managerial, and technological skills. The mismatch between the skills of the inner-city population and the available jobs increased. Black mayors could not control the employment boom in the suburbs, the movement of middle-class whites and then blacks out of the city, the expansion of suburbia, or the inability of inner-city blacks to reach those suburban jobs. Michael Lomax, a leading black politician, said in 1981 at the end of Jackson's second term that low-income blacks had assumed a black mayor would "change significantly how they lived." In fact, Lomax stated, "You can't change the American economy and social system from a local unit." The result by 1980 was an unemployment rate of 10.5 percent (up from 7.3 percent in 1969) for Atlanta's blacks, whereas it was 4.1 percent for whites, and black workers remained overwhelmingly concentrated in blue-collar jobs. Jackson and his successors were fighting a national economic trend, one that Atlanta illustrates well: the city saw a net loss of more than eight thousand manufacturing jobs between 1970 and 1978.[31]

Jackson had tried to shift the city's priorities, but when he met with both criticism and marginal success, he became more accommodating to the city's business elite. In embracing the priorities of the business community, he set the tone for his successors. None of them, including Jackson in his third term (1990–94), tried to resist the will of the business leaders.

Although challenging Jackson at the ballot box had been an exercise in futility, Andrew Young, the prominent civil rights leader, former U.S. ambassador to the United Nations, and member of Congress, drew opposition when he ran for mayor in 1981. Sydney Marcus, a state legislator, was the business community's "great white hope," but he ran an unsuccessful campaign in a city that had a black majority. On election day no one secured a clear majority. Young received 41 percent of the vote to Marcus's 39 percent, with the rest going to another black candidate, Reginald Eaves, the public safety commissioner Jackson had forced to resign. In the Young-Marcus runoff, voting fell strongly along racial lines, and Young won 55 percent of the vote to secure the mayoralty. Young had gained the endorsement of just one significant white business leader, Charles Loudermilk, but he did get the backing of the *Atlanta Constitution*. After the runoff Young quickly moved to bring the business elite into his coalition.[32] Right after the election Loudermilk set up a luncheon to bring the mayor-elect and the white business leaders together. Young told the group: "I didn't get elected with your help, but I can't govern without you."[33] Jackson too had understood that simple fact and eventually moved or was pushed toward a business agenda. Young, aware of Jackson's experience, focused quickly on business concerns.

As Jackson had done before him, Young sought economic growth for Atlanta in which "economic prosperity would trickle down." According to Young, the rich could get richer, so long as the economic boom trickled down to the poor. This goal could be achieved only through a business-government partnership. As the mayor said, "Politics doesn't control the world. Money does. And we ought not to be upset about that. We ought to begin to understand how money works and why money works." Young believed his role involved guarantees that "whites get some of the [political] power and blacks get some of the money." Young was certainly concerned about Atlanta's poverty and social problems, but his vision was little different from the white business group's. The mayor stated, "If you want to bring about what we preachers preach about— feeding the hungry, clothing the naked, healing the sick—it's going to be done in the free market system. You need capital. You need technology. You need marketing."[34]

Young was elected in 1981, the first year of Ronald Reagan's presidency, and understood the new political realities. His approach was pragmatic. The mayor's thinking reflected that of a nation on the make, with increasing numbers of rich citizens and a federal government less interested in urban problems. For Atlanta this new but old thinking resulted in a business-oriented approach that the previous white mayors would have felt comfortable supporting.

Although Young's policies in some respects enhanced Jackson's pioneering efforts in MBE and affirmative action, they reflected the new outlook. In regard to African-American political empowerment and access to decision-making positions, Young increased the number of blacks in the city bureaucracy to 59 percent by the end of his first term.[35] MBE guidelines for the proportion of city contracts that should go to minority firms increased to 35 percent. As with Jackson, Young's MBE efforts benefited many blacks by aiding black businesses and the workers they would hire. All these accomplishments were important, but they amounted to still more economic opportunities for black middle-class Atlanta. Young did little to shift resources to black neighborhoods or to target the black poor for help.

Instead, the mayor, as one article in the *Atlanta Constitution* noted, "after six years in office had become the darling of the business community. He has traveled the world selling the city." Young was effective at marketing Atlanta to the world, but as Tyrone Brooks, a black state representative, commented, "I think the downside has been that under his administration the city has realized a larger poverty population. The poor people in this community, particularly the homeless, are really disillusioned with his administration."[36]

A telling example of Young's thinking was his handling of the redevelopment of Underground, the recreational-commercial downtown mall that the business community had sought to help revitalize the downtown. The mayor diverted to the Underground's development $6 million in federal funds that had been designated for the poor (the money was granted under the Housing and Community Development Act). Although the law stated that the money had to benefit the poor, city officials claimed that this diversion was legitimate because Underground would provide jobs for low-income residents. Others were not convinced. Brooks stated that the decision "was a slap in the face of poor people who need housing." Rob Pitts, a member of the city council, commented that "it's difficult to explain to the usual [low-income] recipients how taking that money and putting it into Underground is going to benefit them. They see it as a glamorous upscale project that will benefit tourists and the power structure. I have not tried to explain it, because I can't."[37]

The focus on economic development and downtown revitalization was filled with promises of better times for poor Atlantans, but rarely were these promises fulfilled. In 1982 city officials pledged that the building of an industrial park would result in two thousand new jobs, 80 percent of which would be filled by the low- and moderate-income people living in the slum areas along Bankhead Highway. The park was built but created only five hundred jobs—and just 8 percent went "to the poor in whose name $4 million was spent." The neighborhood poor did not get first chance at the jobs. Most positions went to individuals already associated with the companies relocating there. One problem was that the city enticed these companies with tax breaks but neglected to secure written assurances that the companies would hire from the neighborhood. The firms initially said they would but reneged on their verbal guarantees.[38]

None of the projects fulfilled the grandiose promises that using federal community block grants to fund economic development would produce jobs for the low income. As one *Atlanta Constitution* article noted, "Sometimes, the city has had to stretch to find any low-income benefits in its spending." For example, from 1977 to 1986, a period that spanned the Jackson and Young years, the city spent $1.1 million in grant money to revitalize the downtown business area of Fairlie-Poplar. When federal officials questioned how the refurbishing of this area would benefit low-income Atlantans, all a city administrator mentioned was how the aesthetic improvements might benefit bus riders who waited for transportation in the area. Nothing was said about providing better housing or jobs for the low income, which was the intention of the federal grants.[39]

Although the grants were reduced in the Reagan years, the Young administration still put a higher percentage of this money into economic development than was done nationally and less into housing than the national percentage. If the focus on economic development had created jobs, the money would have been well spent. But the end result was that jobs did not materialize, and housing deteriorated further. According to the *Atlanta Journal-Constitution,* "Young administration officials acknowledge that the shift toward economic development has meant that some much needed housing rehabilitation in the city had been sacrificed."[40]

Young's business orientation resulted in other actions that hurt poor Atlantans. He supported a 1 percent local option sales tax for MARTA and an accompanying 1 percent property tax decrease—a swap that benefited property owners and was supported by the business community.[41] In 1987 the mayor also backed the building of the Georgia Dome stadium for the city's football team, a structure that destroyed housing in the low-income and black Vine City neighborhood. The dome, like other sports facilities in the city, did nothing to improve these areas. Replacing housing with sports facilities and their attendant parking lots benefited only tourism and the commercial interests.

This situation was a particularly interesting one because the neighborhood had long been promised improved housing. Vine City was not supposed to become another Summerhill, the neighborhood where the Atlanta–Fulton

County baseball stadium had been built despite the opposition of residents. Building the stadium and displacing residents in Summerhill had ruined the area. Politicians in the Vine City neighborhood initially tried to provide a better outcome for their area. However, by 1997, despite the leadership of the city by black mayors, the construction of the dome had led to the further deterioration of the community. Churches were torn down, a promised $10 million trust fund—to rebuild the neighborhood and provide new housing—was never forthcoming, and residents were still waiting "for city officials to fulfill their promises to fix streets, deal with crime and otherwise improve the neighborhood."[42] Vine City residents simply did not matter within a business-oriented mind-set, but football teams and tourists did.

Young, following Jackson's lead, recognized the power of the business community and seemed to assume that no matter what he did he would receive support, as Jackson had, from the majority of black Atlantans. Most black leaders, including ministers and others who spoke for the poor, had little desire to undermine a black mayor and thereby undermine black political power.[43] Although Jackson and Young surely faced some criticism for their willingness to support business interests, this criticism never materialized into serious political opposition. And the black middle class, on the make, agreed with the business-oriented approach.

By the time Maynard Jackson was elected for a third term in 1989 with white business support, and Bill Campbell, a Jackson protégé, was elected for two terms in 1993 and 1997, Atlanta's policies and priorities were fully established in a probusiness, middle-class agenda that certainly benefited some black Atlantans but left many more mired in poverty. Examples from the 1990s, including the planning and development of the Atlanta Olympics, are plentiful. During the late 1980s Bill Campbell, a city council member who represented part of Vine City, fought for housing in the area. He opposed the construction of a state labor department building in the neighborhood on land originally designated for housing. After he became mayor, Campbell was still interested in Atlanta's housing but primarily for the middle class, which he sought to attract to Atlanta. Low-income housing was no longer a priority. Campbell worked closely with an Atlanta Renaissance group made up of the city's business executives and civic and academic leaders. This group's plans called for creating new jobs by expanding the Georgia World Congress Center (the city's main convention facility), promoting the city as a tourist destination, boosting the city's technology industries, and setting up new job development programs. The emphasis was still on a business-oriented approach. Revitalization of poorer neighborhoods languished, a job-training program was accused of mismanagement, and empowerment zone activities were failing.[44]

The site selection for and development of the 1996 Olympics are prime examples of city priorities under more recent black mayors. Promises to poor neighborhoods about revitalization and the benefits that would result from this world event were made from the beginning of the planning stage. But the results revealed the usual Atlanta pattern. Improvements were made on streets near Olympic sites or those used by tourists walking to those sites but not elsewhere. As the *Constitution* reported, Peoplestown, "the most distant of these neighborhoods affected by construction of the Olympic Stadium, didn't have much to show off for the Olympics except for a few affordable Habitat for Humanity homes." Only Summerhill, where the new stadium was built, and the Techwood–Clark Howell Homes area (the public housing projects), across from the Olympic Village on Georgia Tech's campus, saw some redevelopment. Summerhill, which had opposed the building of the first stadium in the 1960s, now found itself the site of a second one. Protest from neighborhood residents failed to change the result—further destruction of the housing stock. The original stadium was eventually torn down (and the space used for parking), and some housing was rebuilt (but sold at prices only the middle class could afford). The situation of low-income residents was actually worse than before.[45]

The group responsible for neighborhood revitalization during the Olympics period was CODA (Cooperation for Olympic Development in Atlanta), a nonprofit cooperative venture of city government and the business community. Their initial plans were extensive, but funding was limited. The business community, which was to provide the money for neighborhood development, lost interest in this aspect of planning and became captivated by the development of Centennial Olympic Park, a large project that would eliminate a run-down commercial area in downtown Atlanta. With the Chamber of Commerce actively raising money for the park, neighborhoods suffered. As one study of this process stated, "Financing the park largely with corporate contributions severely reduced CODA's already limited ability to obtain financing from the private sector for neighborhood redevelopment."[46]

The Olympics provided Atlanta with a major new park, better sports facilities, an economic spur, and a way for more tourists and conventioneers to see the city. Low-income areas and low-income Atlantans, however, benefited little. Essentially, even a mayor who had fought for the downtrodden would have found changing these results difficult. This event was the business community's show—it sought the Games, planned for them, and raised the money for the outcome it wanted. City money did not play a large role, and in this respect city officials were not major players. Jackson, who was mayor when plans for Centennial Olympic Park were announced, found out about it by reading his morning newspaper.[47]

Whatever interest existed in the redevelopment of low-income areas during the planning of the Olympics largely evaporated afterward. As Joe Brown, senior vice president of NationsBank's community development corporation, stated in 1998, "In 1996, the city was more focused in its direction because of the Olympics. Now you don't have that kind of focus to solve the city's housing woes."[48]

The redevelopment of Techwood–Clark Howell Homes as a mixed-income housing project renamed Centennial Place also served as a notable example of the city's approach to housing. Techwood–Clark Howell was located across from Georgia Tech, close to the Coca-Cola Co. headquarters, and occupied an important section near the main business district. It had long been viewed as an impediment to the downtown's economic vitality. The Olympics provided the opportunity to remove this eyesore. Although Jackson had promised to plan the area with residents' concerns in mind, and occupants of Techwood Homes had initially been informed that, as long as they "left in good standing," they would be able to move back into the new development, they found that requirements had tightened once Centennial Place opened. Most (92 percent) of the former residents are no longer living at that site; instead, many received Section 8 vouchers (rent subsidies) for other housing. A substantial number of units at Centennial Place are reserved for fair-market renters. Renee Glover, the Atlanta Housing Authority director and a rising African-American star in the city's administration, reflected the general business viewpoint by noting that "providing housing for the jobless and homeless is better handled by organizations that cater to residents with 'special needs.'" The housing units set aside for low-income residents were to be reserved for a higher level of poor. The very poor were not going to be allowed back in. Similar rebuilding for mixed-income populations is evident in other housing projects in the city today.[49]

After more than twenty-five years of black mayoral control, Atlanta today has problems strikingly similar to what was evident decades earlier under white mayors. Like many other cities, Atlanta has lost factory jobs—thirteen thousand during the 1980s alone—and this reduction has deeply affected the working-class areas. With both the black and white middle classes leaving the city, Atlanta has become home to the very rich and the very poor. Atlanta was the ninth-poorest city in the United States in 1993. Most city neighborhoods were poorer in 1990 than in 1980. In 1997 Atlanta had "12 percent of the region's population but 65 percent of the area's public housing and 78 percent of its impoverished households." It is not surprising that the problems have been difficult to solve. Even former president Jimmy Carter's The Atlanta Project, begun in the early 1990s as a war on Atlanta's poverty and supported by the city's major corporations, failed to change much. The program saw some modest successes and created some entry-level jobs, but because the problems developed over many years and were rooted in long-term racial and class issues, this effort had lost much of its steam by 1996.[50]

Black mayors consistently failed to appreciably improve the housing stock for low-income residents. Atlanta officials remained interested in attracting the middle class to the city and did not address long-term laxity in enforcing housing codes or in targeting poor neighborhoods for improvements. As the *Constitution* reported in 1998, "By the end of 1996, one in four of the city's then 6,000 pending housing code cases had been on the books for five years or longer." Low-income housing, after Jackson's early years, was not a city priority, whatever the political rhetoric. Although Mayor Young spoke about building or repairing approximately eighty thousand low-income housing units, in 1987 the Atlanta Housing Authority was forced to give back to the federal government a $3.5 million housing grant because the city had failed to secure a place to build the new housing. At that time, city council member Rob Pitts complained, "I don't think housing is a real priority of the city. Not compared with the sexy projects—a new City Hall, a new zoo, Underground Atlanta, a new stadium." Housing plans for the homeless also languished. At the beginning of his third term in 1990, Jackson promised to construct thirty-five hundred single-room occupancy units for the homeless by the time he left office in 1994. Instead, the city built only 625 and an additional 330 were under construction. By 1998, with housing still a serious problem, Mayor Campbell had directed his attention to saving Underground, which was once again in financial straits.[51]

Given the continuing problems and the mayoral priorities, how have black mayors changed the city and what has been their importance and place in Atlanta's history? One view comes from the civil rights activist and city council member Hosea Williams, who said in 1987, "All these Black politicians—they're Black until they're elected."[52] It was a harsh statement that reflected disappointment with policies that were inextricably linked to traditional white business interests. In several ways, however, the black community clearly benefited from having African-American leadership at city hall. Paternalism and a second-class citizenship were gone. Govern-

ment-sponsored racism was a thing of the past. Blacks were also well positioned in city government jobs. However, as racism faded, class divisions
in the black community became more prominent. Jackson's efforts in his
first term to reach out to all black Atlantans and to shift priorities away from
the interests of the business community lasted a relatively short time. The
needs of business leaders (increasingly a biracial group) once again became
the focus of city hall. Upper- and middle-income blacks certainly benefited from MBE and political empowerment. But the black poor, although
they secured benefits from affirmative action and the end of official racism, saw their neighborhoods neglected again, with services declining and
stadiums being built instead of housing. Their hopes for better schools,
housing, jobs, and police protection went unfulfilled.

The vote and political success had its limitations because of the many
political pressures on the mayor and the national and regional economic
changes. Also, politics necessitates compromises. A mayor has limited power, which is perhaps not fully understood until the job is secured. Jackson was
bound to disappoint some in the black community because expectations were
so high. And to govern and unite the city, he *had* to disappoint some. Insurgency, which was the style of many early black mayors, could not last as a
policy because it alienated the economic powers in the city, a group that many
blacks were becoming a part of or were aspiring to join.[53] Thus the reality of
governing, the necessity of accommodating the business leaders, forces beyond a mayor's control, and the salience of class, once official racism was
eliminated, all limited the ability of black mayors to change the city's historic priorities.

Notes

1. John Wesley Dobbs, speech before Georgia Voters League, March 10, 1956, Box 3,
Dobbs Papers, Amistad Research Center, Tulane University, New Orleans.

2. A fuller discussion of this political background appears in Ronald H. Bayor, *Race and
the Shaping of Twentieth-Century Atlanta* (Chapel Hill: University of North Carolina Press,
1996), 15–48.

3. Warren Cochrane, executive director of the Butler Street YMCA in the 1940s and 1950s
and executive director of the Atlanta Negro Voters League, interview by author, October
10, 1985; Clarence Bacote, chairman of the All Citizens Registration Committee, undated
interview in Living Atlanta Collection, Atlanta Historical Society.

4. Council on Human Relations of Greater Atlanta, tentative draft report, March 27,
1964, Southern Regional Council Papers, Atlanta University Center, Robert W. Woodruff
Library, Atlanta.

5. Jacob E. Butler Jr., "Racial Conflict and Polarization as a Constraint on Black Mayoral Leadership in Urban Policy: An Analysis of Public Finance and Urban Develop-

ment in Atlanta During the Mayoral Tenure of Maynard H. Jackson, 1973–1977" (Ph.D. diss., Atlanta University, 1989), 90–91; Maynard Jackson, interview by author, November 23, 1987.

6. Richard A. Keiser, *Subordination or Empowerment? African-American Leadership and the Struggle for Urban Political Power* (New York: Oxford University Press, 1997), 148–49.

7. Jackson interview, November 23, 1987.

8. Peter K. Eisinger, "Black Employment in Municipal Jobs: The Impact of Black Political Power," *American Political Science Review* 76 (June 1982): 385. See also *Atlanta Journal-Constitution,* February 18, 1979.

9. Bayor, *Race and the Shaping,* 123; Dan Sweat, executive director of Central Atlanta Progress, interview by author, January 21, 1988; Clarence N. Stone, *Regime Politics: Governing Atlanta, 1946–1988* (Lawrence: University Press of Kansas, 1989), 88; Keiser, *Subordination or Empowerment?* 149.

10. Keiser, *Subordination or Empowerment?* 149; Maynard Jackson, interview by author, January 4, 1988.

11. Butler, "Racial Conflict and Polarization," 179–82.

12. Georgia A. Persons, "Atlanta: Black Mayoral Leadership and the Dynamics of Political Changes" (Ph.D. diss., MIT, 1978), 211–19; *Atlanta Journal,* November 1, 1974.

13. Bayor, *Race and the Shaping,* 183–86; Stone, *Regime Politics,* 88; Mack H. Jones, "Black Political Empowerment in Atlanta: Myth and Reality," *Annals of the American Academy of Political and Social Science* 439 (September 1978): 111, 114; *Atlanta Constitution,* March 12 and July 21, 1978.

14. Jackson interview, November 23, 1987.

15. Andrew Young, interview by author, February 13, 1986.

16. Jackson interview, November 23, 1987; Sweat interview.

17. *Atlanta Constitution,* September 21 and 25, 1974. See also Bayor, *Race and the Shaping,* 50.

18. *Atlanta Constitution,* September 26, 1974; Jackson interview, January 4, 1988.

19. Stone, *Regime Politics,* 90; Butler, "Racial Conflict and Polarization," 137–38.

20. *Atlanta Constitution,* September 24, 1974, and March 23 and 28, 1975; *Atlanta Journal,* December 27, 1974; Jones, "Black Political Empowerment," 113.

21. *Atlanta Constitution,* October 10, 1974; Bayor, *Race and the Shaping,* 51; Claude W. Barnes, "Political Power and Economic Dependence: An Analysis of Atlanta's Black Urban Regime" (Ph.D. diss., Clark Atlanta University, 1991), 88.

22. Butler, "Racial Conflict and Polarization," 183–84, 298–99, 302–3; Bayor, *Race and the Shaping,* 153.

23. *Atlanta Constitution,* April 5, 1977.

24. Adolph Reed Jr., "Black Urban Administrations," *Telos* 65 (Fall 1985): 51–52.

25. Stephen Burman, *The Black Progress Question: Explaining the African-American Predicament* (Thousand Oaks, Calif.: Sage, 1995): 170, 192–93.

26. Bayor, *Race and the Shaping,* 123; Stone, *Regime Politics,* 166; Butler, "Racial Conflict and Polarization," 310–11.

27. Jones, "Black Political Empowerment," 114.

28. Clarence Stone and Carol Pierannunzi, "Atlanta and the Limited Reach of Elector-

al Control," in Rufus P. Browning, Dale Rogers Marshall, and David H. Tabb, eds., *Racial Politics in American Cities*, 2d ed. (New York: Longman, 1997), 166, 175.

29. Butler, "Racial Conflict and Polarization," 314; *Atlanta Daily World*, October 9, 1977.

30. Adolph Reed Jr., "A Critique of Neoprogressivism in Theorizing About Local Development Policy: A Case from Atlanta," paper presented to the meeting of the American Political Science Association, Washington, D.C., August 28–31, 1986, pp. 12, 13.

31. Bayor, *Race and the Shaping*, 124–25; Gary Orfield and Carol Ashkinaze, *The Closing Door: Conservative Policy and Black Opportunity* (Chicago: University of Chicago Press, 1991), 23, 24. Lomax is quoted on p. 55.

32. Stone, *Regime Politics*, 109–10.

33. *Atlanta Constitution*, August 11, 1987.

34. *Atlanta Constitution*, September 22, 1985, and August 14, 1987; Stone, *Regime Politics*, 136.

35. Keiser, *Subordination or Empowerment?* 150.

36. *Atlanta Constitution*, August 14, 1987.

37. Ibid. (for Brooks quote); Pitts is quoted in *Atlanta Journal-Constitution*, March 2, 1986. Also see the *Journal-Constitution* for August 16, 1987; and Bayor, *Race and the Shaping*, 147.

38. *Atlanta Journal-Constitution*, March 2, 1986.

39. Ibid.

40. Ibid.

41. *Atlanta Business Chronicle*, 1997.

42. *Atlanta Constitution*, March 20, 1986; *Atlanta Journal-Constitution*, November 1, 1987, and July 31, 1988. For the material quoted, see the *Atlanta Constitution*, February 19, 1997.

43. Stone, *Regime Politics*, 167.

44. *Atlanta Journal-Constitution*, November 1, 1987; *Atlanta Constitution*, October 21, 1996, December 10, 1997, and April 3, 1998; *Atlanta Business Chronicle*, November 14–20, 1997.

45. *Atlanta Constitution*, February 23, 1996; Steven P. French and Mike E. Disher, "Atlanta and the Olympics: A One-Year Retrospective," *Journal of the American Planning Association* 63 (Summer 1997): 388–89; *Fences and Neighborhoods* (video on Atlanta Olympics and low-income neighborhoods), University of California Extension, Center for Media and Independent Learning, 1997.

46. French and Disher, "Atlanta and the Olympics," 384, 388. See p. 390 for the material quoted.

47. Ibid., 390–91; *Fences and Neighborhoods*.

48. *Atlanta Business Chronicle*, July 24–30, 1998. Since the merger of the two banking behemoths, NationsBank is known as Bank of America.

49. Barnes, "Political Power and Economic Dependence," 36; *Atlanta Constitution*, September 15, 1997, March 5, 1998, and December 17, 1998. Glover is quoted in the *Atlanta Journal-Constitution*, February 15, 1998.

50. *Atlanta Constitution*, October 14, 1993, September 15, 1996, and May 26, 1997; Bob Holmes, ed., *The Status of Black Atlanta, 1993* (Atlanta: Southern Center for Studies in Public Policy, Clark Atlanta University, 1993), 2.

51. *Atlanta Journal-Constitution,* March 22, 1998; Orfield and Ashkinaze quote Pitts in *Closing Door,* 89; *Atlanta Constitution,* December 26, 1993, and February 20, 1998.

52. Gerald H. Foeman II, "An Interracial Comparative Analysis of the Impact of Central-City Mayors During the Urban Transition of the 1980s: Social, Political, and Economic Indicators of Effect" (Ph.D. diss., Temple University, 1992), 86.

53. A discussion of insurgency as a style of early black mayors appears in Georgia Persons, ed., *Dilemmas of Black Politics: Issues of Leadership and Strategy* (New York: HarperCollins, 1993), 45.

8. Protest and Power in Washington, D.C.: The Troubled Legacy of Marion Barry

HOWARD GILLETTE JR.

MORE THAN TEN thousand people stood and cheered his entry to Washington, D.C.'s new sports arena. For nearly four hours young and old, famous and obscure, black, white, and those of colors in between, praised his accomplishments. While the five-part video that flashed across the giant screens trumpeted his triumphs, it did not ignore the pain of his disgrace. When the hour passed eleven in the evening, his spiritual adviser and his pastor stemmed the stream of departures by rousing the crowd to the power of redemption. When trouble came, he did not pretend it did not exist, the Reverend Willie Wilson bellowed. He did not descend into the storm, he ascended it. As Marion Barry rose in the front row to acknowledge Wilson's declaration, the crowd issued yet another roar. Counted out after his arrest and conviction for smoking crack cocaine while mayor of Washington, D.C., in 1990, Barry defied all predictions by coming back to win another term in office. Now that he was finally retiring, his admirers offered him one last emotional tribute.

Once one of the most charismatic and compelling black politicians on the national scene, Marion Barry, despite the adulation he received that October night in 1998, was but a shadow of his former self. For the greater part of the last of his four terms in office, Congress had limited his powers by imposing a financial oversight board. For more than a year it had restricted his control of a $5 billion budget to several departments that represented less than $100 million. Although many people he had recruited had moved up to powerful administrative and judicial appointments, Barry remained without a certain future himself. An early supporter, the white civic activist Sam Smith, put it most starkly, comparing the situation to witnessing "an old rusting-out hulk of a car and trying to imagine what it was like when it was brand new. What people are seeing now is that corroded shell of what Barry was, and if you don't remember that, it's very hard to see."[1]

Diminished as he was as he left office, Barry had dominated local politics for virtually a generation. Although Washington's unique political status under Congress's ultimate financial as well as political control makes that story unusual, it nonetheless remains deeply revealing, not just the account of a single flawed individual but also the story of the shifting tide of racial politics in the last quarter of the twentieth century.

The carefully orchestrated tribute to "forty years of service" represented Barry's own effort to cast the most positive light on his legacy in terms that clearly continued to resonate with his core constituency. A statement issued from his office when he decided to step down remained defiant, describing Barry as standing tall "against all fashions of criticism and disrespect from Congressional leaders" and "the humiliation regularly heaped on the District of Columbia." Barry, it asserted, had governed the city on his own terms: "He has weathered any number of assaults from a hostile media, Congress, the Financial Authority and other elected officials but he has stood firm. Though he has sometimes been bloodied he remains unrepentant and unbowed. Whatever history determines Barry's legacy to be, his re-election to an unprecedented fourth term as Mayor in 1994 solidified his image as one of the purest examples of redemption, rebirth and resurrection."[2]

The weight of critical opinion, in Congress and in the press, was harsher. Not just the *Washington Post,* with which Barry had maintained a running battle for years, but also the *New York Times* used the occasion to describe him in unflattering terms. The black journalist Jonetta Rose Barras charged in a recent book on his tenure that Barry looked bad compared to the new breed of pragmatic black mayors, whom she praised for "avoiding confrontation, racially divisive rhetoric, empty symbolism, and bravado" to "reconstruct governments and communities from durable cloth." In a direct reference to Barry she asserted that "for many African-Americans who waited through aborted political promise, prostituted goodwill and squandered potential, the final change from symbolism to substance will have come none too soon."[3]

As in any complex story, none of these representations fully captured the central dilemma of the last quarter of the twentieth century: could oppositional tactics forged in the heat of the civil rights movement translate effectively to ensure political empowerment for African Americans? Could this happen on the national stage provided by the capital city, where Congress, while acceding to the District of Columbia basic elements of home rule, retained ultimate political and financial authority?

In many ways Marion Barry was destined to seize that challenge. Born in 1936 in the Deep South and raised by his hard-working mother after his father left the family, Barry threw himself into the civil rights movement as a young man. After sitting in at segregated lunch counters in Memphis, Tennessee, and joining voter registration efforts in Mississippi, he was selected to be the first chairman of the Student Non-Violent Coordinating Committee. Determined to take the struggle north, Barry moved to Washington, D.C., to set up a SNCC office in June 1965. Undoubtedly, Barry chose to work in Washington not just because it was the national capital but also because in 1957 it had become the first major U.S. city with a majority-black population. Here, in a southern city that had only recently seen its schools officially desegregated, the tight rein of southern congressional committee chairmen had thwarted every effort to attain the home rule that had been denied for nearly a century.[4] Barry brought new energy to the drive for self-governance by organizing the "Free D.C." movement. By threatening to boycott Washington businesses that refused to display emblems of support for home rule, Barry took civil rights tactics well beyond those used in a limited don't-buy-where-you-can't-work campaign in the 1930s.[5] Although the Free D.C. movement was thwarted when opponents threatened to take the issue to court, Barry continued to raise his profile. He helped organize a successful campaign against a hike in bus fares that the city's working poor greatly appreciated, and he joined in challenging a massive highway program that would have displaced many black residents in the pursuit of the city's ambitious urban renewal program.

Barry was a central figure among younger civil rights activists, and his political style initially conformed with the approach prescribed by fellow SNCC activist Stokley Carmichael, whom he helped mentor while Carmichael was still a student at Howard University. In his 1967 book on black power Carmichael stressed the importance of using collective action to enhance the material well-being of the entire black community and proposed a race-based approach to politics that diverged from contemporary integrationist norms. Barry adapted the basic principles of that approach to his later electoral strategy, maintaining throughout his political career, as the political scientists David Sears and John McConahay have described it, an ability to project symbolically a powerful ideology built on the power of black group identity as well as to promise the tangible benefits that flow from government power.[6] But to secure that power Barry assumed quite early a pragmatic streak that permitted alliances with whites when necessary. When Carmichael took SNCC in the direction of black power after his election as president in 1966, he criticized Barry for reformist tactics that included working with liberal white clergy. A year later Barry formally resigned his SNCC position in Washington, retorting, "The civil rights direction of protest is dead. Now we must concentrate on control—economic and political power."[7]

Indeed, Barry's distinctive ability, forged in his early years in Washington, was that of the activist able to navigate the shifting tide of militancy to maintain his support in the black community even as he extracted concessions from the white establishment. In resigning from SNCC, he demonstrated that strength by securing from Secretary of Labor Willard Wirtz money to train hard-core unemployed youth in Washington. Improvised during a weekend in response to Wirtz's invitation to apply for funding, Barry's proposal to form Pride Inc. appeared to ensure the Johnson administration's immediate goal would be met: that Washington be spared civil disorders. Pride quickly established itself as an emblem of self-help in the inner city as it recruited some of the area's toughest unemployed youth and attempted to give them structure as well as job training. The organization generated considerable controversy for sloppy bookkeeping and questionable contracts, but it retained Wirtz's support for its ability to build community participation.[8] Barry, the black *Washington Star* columnist William Raspberry reported, was "fast becoming the leading catalyst for change in Washington."[9]

Barry's ascent to elective power was equally pragmatic. In running for the school board in 1971, he recruited David Abramson, a white communications specialist, to handle his media relations, although Barry was aware that Abramson had helped squelch the Free D.C. movement. When Abramson asked why he had been hired anyway, Barry replied that his earlier transgression did not matter because Abramson's role in electing the first nonvoting District delegate to Congress earlier in the year had made him indispensable to the Barry campaign.[10] When opposition to home rule finally collapsed after John McMillan, chair of the House District Committee, lost his reelection bid in the South Carolina Democratic primary in 1972 and Congress authorized an elected city government, Barry was elected to the first elected city council in 1974. There, as chair of the council's finance committee, he overcame business hostility to him that dated to the Free D.C. campaign by fashioning tax policies to business's liking.

Four years later Barry entered the Democratic primary for mayor, challenging the incumbent, Walter Washington, and Sterling Tucker, who chaired the city council and who was a leader in the Washington Urban League. By habit, as well as the necessity of facing two African Americans widely respected in the black middle class, Barry forged alliances with liberal and gay whites as well as low-income African Americans who were energized by his activist agenda. His narrow 1978 victory was thus accepted as a triumph of civil rights activism. Supreme Court Justice Thurgood Marshall swore him in as mayor. Sen. Teddy Kennedy offered a rousing speech, proclaiming that Washington, D.C., as "a model for the nation and the world," would attract the attention of millions "to see how you meet the challenge you face—the challenge to demonstrate that home rule works."[11]

Barry took that charge seriously. After years of contesting the power of Congress, he was now determined to demonstrate his ability to govern effectively, both to showcase African-American managerial talent and to keep Congress, which had retained final budgetary powers and the right to disapprove local legislation, from meddling too much in the city's affairs.

Promising at his inauguration "an open, compassionate and responsive administration," as mayor he asserted his determination to empower those who had been excluded from power, not the least women, whom he appointed to a number of prominent positions. To critics who questioned his dedication to the civil rights movement as an elected official, he responded that his goals remained consistent, only the forum had changed. "People see myself as a symbol of success because of where I've come from economically and socially," he declared in allying himself with his most dispossessed supporters.[12] In the 1970s, following years of civil rights agitation, few questioned the appropriateness of making this racial appeal. Only later would Barry come to be criticized by some of his former admirers for inappropriately playing "the race card."

Indeed, having secured less than 30 percent of the black vote in the Democratic primary, Barry's first task lay in shoring up his African-American power base. He did so, following the formula of black power, both by being a constant presence at black community events and by actively pursuing tangible benefits to meet the city's most pressing social needs. He launched an expansive summer jobs program for youth, established a goal of assuring that 35 percent of government contracting would go to minority-owned firms, and actively pursued housing rehabilitation, returning ten thousand units to active use in his first term.

Barry's appeals to racial solidarity would prompt dissent, as in February 1980, when the *Washington Star* chastised him for "flailing away" at rampant discrimination against blacks in federal employment. "The adversary stance is comfortably familiar for a Marion Barry, and racism has always been an effective stick for beating the establishment," the *Star* editorialized. "The only trouble is they don't make quite as much sense for the person who's supposed to be running things."[13] But Barry's scrupulous attention to administrative details tended to mute such criticism. He had inherited both an unwieldy bureaucracy and a significant debt, which Walter Washington had passed down from the pre–home rule period. Barry threw himself into administrative reforms. Working closely with his city administrator, Elijah Rogers, the former city manager of Berkeley, California, Barry fashioned a program of job cuts and administrative savings to pull the city government out of debt. From the start Barry immersed himself in budgetary matters, becoming so well acquainted with details that he could ask his budget director to add money when he spotted a program area where he knew it was needed. According to an associate, he loved the political game and played it brilliantly, orchestrating, for example, a complicated maneuver to stave off fines from the Environmental Protection Agency by inducing the suburban counties surrounding the city to join a cooperative arrangement to meet the challenge.[14]

Politics and administration could clash, however, as it became obvious in his first term that Barry could not satisfy each constituency he courted. Even as the media started to question race-based politics, others, looking at Barry's budgetary cuts, questioned the sincerity of his appeals to African Americans when they suffered the most from the cuts. "Barry pleads his color and asks that he be spared criticism because he is black," lawyer Hunter C. Clark, an African American, charged in May 1980. "In short, he is attempting to stir racial resentments in order to divert attention from the failures of his administration."[15]

Despite his accomplishments, then, Barry drew considerable opposition in the 1982 Democratic primary. The main challenge came from Patricia Roberts Harris, secretary of Housing and Urban Development under President Jimmy Carter and a Washington native. Questioned about his commitment to delivering needed services to African Americans, Barry acknowledged he had tailored his political style to work with business and congressional leaders. In announcing his candidacy for reelection, however, he stressed his record of dealing with the social welfare concerns of crime, poor housing, and the creation of jobs. Then, finding himself trailing in the early polls, Barry shifted his emphasis from tangible benefits to a racial and emotional appeal that he was the "blacker" of the two candidates. He contrasted his own humble background to Harris's patrician roots and her association with Walter Washington, which prompted the *Washington Post*'s Juan Williams to write, "In a town where a majority white Congress has dominated local black political life for decades, many blacks still blame Capitol Hill for the problems of the District Government. Barry wants to attract all the racial sympathies that a black mayor can get to wipe away the memory of the problems that plagued his administration."[16]

Barry's strategy worked. In a sharp reversal of the voting pattern that had given him his 1978 primary victory, Barry carried the predominantly black and especially poorer sections of the city, even as his support dropped by more than a third among whites (see table 8.1).[17]

Race-specific appeals were not new to Barry, but in the context both of evolving national attitudes toward race as well as his own political role, they assumed a sharper and more divisive edge. Ronald Reagan's election as president in 1980 had ushered in a more conservative era, and even though Congress remained in Democratic control, both funding for inner cities and national sympathy for social causes were waning. Such trends offered black big-city mayors convenient targets against whom to rally urban constituencies, but Marion Barry's behavior undermined the authority of his position.

Shortly after Barry's reelection, Ivanhoe Donaldson, his closest political associate and a fellow civil rights activist, was indicted on charges of illegally obtaining nearly $190,000 in government funds. While Barry distanced himself from the scandal, other close allies also left the Barry administration, most notably Deputy Mayor Alphonse Hill, who was forced to resign in March 1986 after acknowledging he had received $3,000 in illegal payments from city contractors. Further scandals dogged Barry's second term as no less than eleven of his appointees were forced to resign, prompting sustained criticism, most notably from the *Washington Post*'s Juan Williams. Williams, author of the

Table 8.1. Selected Election Results, Washington, D.C., 1978–98

Election and Year	Candidate	Ward 3 Votes	Ward 8 Votes	Citywide Percentage
Democratic primary (mayor, 1978)	Marion Barry	5,918 (46.8%)	1,842 (29.7%)	34.6
Democratic primary (mayor, 1982)	Marion Barry	3,734 (34.3%)	4,495 (65.6%)	58.0
General election (mayor, 1986)	Marion Barry	3,550 (15.2%)	7,165 (86.0%)	61.2
General election (council at large, 1990)	Marion Barry	703 (14.0%)	6,065 (42.8%)	19.8
Democratic primary (mayor, 1994)	Marion Barry	620 (3.4%)	10,875 (82.0%)	47.0
General election (mayor, 1994)	Marion Barry	1,920 (6.8%)	14,243 (93.0%)	55.0

Source: Figures compiled from official reports, Washington, D.C., Board of Elections and Ethics.

Note: As the most affluent of the city's eight wards and the only one that is predominantly white, Ward 3 stands in starkest contrast with Ward 8, the city's most concentrated area of poverty among its predominantly African-American population. According to 1990 census statistics reported in the *New York Times* of July 26, 1996, Ward 3 was 88 percent white; Ward 8, 91 percent black. Ward 3 reported that 70 percent of its population was older than twenty-five with four or more years of college; Ward 8, 8 percent. Ward 3 recorded 97 percent of its homes valued at $200,000 or more; Ward 8, fewer than 1 percent. Births out of wedlock were 6 percent in Ward 3 and 84 percent in Ward 8. The two wards thus serve as effective proxies for race and class differences.

book *Eyes on the Prize,* which accompanied the highly acclaimed public television series on the civic rights movement, charged:

> Barry did more for his people when he was working in the civil rights move-
> ment to gain power than he did after he had that power. The constant bouts
> with petty corruption have diverted attention from Barry's policy failures and
> from the larger agenda of reforms that black voters might demand of practi-
> cally white development firms, real estate companies, banks and utilities. Con-
> sequently the promise of black political power in Washington and the change
> it could bring for the city's black residents, particularly the poorest, has gone
> down the drain.[18]

Beyond such overt difficulties, Barry's ego grew over time in office and
clouded his judgment. As early as his first reelection campaign, he determined to retaliate when Oliver Carr, a prominent Washington developer,
sided with Patricia Harris in the 1982 primary. Although aides warned him
not to, Barry canceled Carr's exclusive rights to develop a prime location
near the downtown subway exchange known as Metro Center. As Barry's
advisers had warned, that decision prompted the Hecht department store
chain to announce it would be leaving the city rather than building a new
anchor store in Washington; the Hecht store was considered the key to downtown revitalization. Barry had to quickly rescind his directive against Carr.
At that point he was still surrounded by long-time allies to whom he would
listen. But as his original allies began to leave government, whether under
legal pressure or for new employment opportunities, fewer voices served to
check what Jonetta Barras ultimately labeled Barry's imperial tendencies as
mayor. Without such checks Barry's personal indulgences grew and thus
became subject to more intense public scrutiny.

No one who knew Barry in his early years as mayor disputed his incredi-
ble energy. When he was focused on city matters, he could be an effective
manager. But as his second term advanced, his personal indulgences got him
increasingly in trouble, and the city suffered. A known womanizer from his
civil rights days, Barry included among his intimate associates outside marriage a woman named Karen Johnson, whom authorities charged had used
drugs with the mayor. Johnson accepted a jail term in 1984 rather than answer a grand jury's questions about Barry, and the mayor escaped legal action. During the next several years, however, Barry became the target of sustained federal surveillance. A robust economy, Barry's courtship of downtown
developers, and weak primary opposition allowed his third election as may-
or in 1986. Although he continued to lose support among whites, he picked
up voters in the city's poorer areas (see table 8.1). His charmed life was not

to continue, however. During his third term, vicissitudes in both the economy and his personal life combined to break his hold on office.

In March 1989 the FBI arrested Barry's close associate, Charles Lewis, for drug use in the Virgin Islands, and prosecutors arrested Lewis again in December after a raid on his hotel room in Washington only moments after Barry had left the premises. Once again Barry had appeared to escape disaster, but increasingly it seemed that he had given up even the pretense of governing. According to his city administrator at the time, Carol Thompson, he was coming to the office late, sleeping there until early afternoon, and ignoring requests for decisions from his staff. City government, she asserted, stopped functioning.[19] The social welfare goals established in the first term, such as housing rehabilitation, lagged even as drug-related violence soared. Barry repeatedly denied charges he used drugs himself, making a brave show of personally leading police teams into drug-infested areas. But on January 18, 1990, FBI agents arrested the mayor after he was seen smoking crack cocaine in a hotel room where he had been lured by a former girlfriend, Hazel Diane "Rasheeda" Moore. Caught on videotape, not only was the mayor in a most compromising position but his words—"Bitch set me up"—were also subsequently immortalized throughout a host of late-night talk shows and on commemorative t-shirts.

Viewers of the infamous tape could see for themselves that Barry was more interested in sex than drugs. Moore clearly used her considerable sex appeal to entice the mayor to smoke cocaine, lending credence to Barry's claim that he had been entrapped although not to his charge that the experience had been a political lynching.[20] Citing his decision to "stand up and fight" what he called an abusive federal government, the mayor described his controversial case as "not an embarrassment but an inspiration" and a source of hope to citizens who, he said, had also suffered from abuse by the federal government. His most fervent supporters, including Louis Farrakhan, discerned a nationwide pattern of indictments designed to bring down strong black mayors.[21] Meanwhile, as Barry's energies were taken up preparing for trial, his administration encountered the second of its major fiscal crises.

The real estate boom of the 1980s masked Washington's structural weakness in the regional economy. A strong federal presence and a boom in downtown office building helped sustain the city's economic importance, but economic growth was concentrated largely in the suburbs. Among those jobs created in the city, only a small portion went to city residents. When the construction boom came to a halt with the recession of the late 1980s, both local jobs and revenues dried up. By 1990 the city faced a severe budget deficit. A commission chaired by the economist Alice Rivlin and charged by Barry to develop a five-year plan for balancing city budgets, insisted on the elimination of six thousand city jobs and other cost-cutting measures, without which, it predicted, the city's deficit could reach $700 million by 1996.

Facing a fiscal as well as a political collapse, Barry chose not to seek reelection in 1990 but became instead a candidate for an at-large seat on city council. He did better before the jury than he did at the polls. He was convicted on just one count of drug possession, leading his supporters to claim vindication. For the first and only time in his life, however, he lost an election. While he retained support in the city's poorest sections, in predominantly white Ward 3 his vote fell from a high of 5,918 in 1978 to a paltry 703 (see table 8.1). Barry's subsequent incarceration for six months and a highly publicized incident involving oral sex in a public waiting room solidified his negative image. Barry confounded his critics, however, by clawing his way back to elective office.

Shortly after he returned from prison in a caravan of buses organized by Cora Masters, the woman he would soon make his new wife, Barry moved to the city's impoverished Ward 8 and launched his political revival. He subsequently crushed the incumbent there to gain election to the city council in 1992. Now deprived of any significant political support from whites, he embraced black nationalist themes in rhetoric as well as in his attire. Two years later he took his message aggressively into the black community in yet another run for mayor. Mercilessly criticized in the media, especially the *Washington Post,* which had endorsed him for office twice before, Barry nonetheless defeated the incumbent mayor, Sharon Pratt Kelly, and a fellow council member in the 1994 Democratic primary. Wrapping himself in the cloak of the recovered alcohol and drug user, playing to strong class as well as race biases, and building a formidable registration and get-out-the vote drive in the city's poorer wards, Barry managed to overcome the adamant opposition of whites, who gave him less than 5 percent of their primary votes (table 8.1). While the white establishment was predictably appalled at the election results, the cover story in *Emerge,* a journal describing itself as "black America's newsmagazine," proclaimed Barry's comeback as sweet. Pointing to African Americans' resentment at being subordinated to congressional control, the publisher, George Curry, explained that Barry's candidacy allowed "people considered powerless to exercise power in a major way. This was a chance to thumb their noses at the 'system,' to say, in effect, that regardless of whom the White power structure desired, the people would go in the opposite direction."[22]

In such economic times, however, victory could be hollow. With a significant deficit already apparent, Barry's transition team members met with representatives of the previous administration and learned the city's finances had been in free fall.[23] Even before Barry took the oath of office, he announced the deficit would reach more than $700 million if spending continued at current levels. Added to this crisis was the coincidental capture of congressional majorities by Republicans. Now, in place of the sympathetic and hands-off approach of Democrats chairing committees overseeing the District of Columbia would be Republicans intent not just on rolling back the programs associated with Lyndon Johnson's Great Society but on using Washington to test their own pet ideas, such as school vouchers and a flat tax. In Barry, as one Republican put it, Congress perceived the symbol of "a corrupt city, a decaying city."[24]

Barry thus assumed office again with a formidable burden to overcome, not only his past indiscretions but also the political opposition of his ideological enemies. Such challenges required him to draw deeply on his considerable political abilities. Promising at his inauguration to "delve into the very root of our city's problems and rebuild from the ground up," Barry had every incentive to prove himself in office again. His friends reported the same sense of mission that drove him in 1979 was back in the forefront, but the situation did not allow any room for error.

During his 1994 campaign for mayor Barry had courted yet another endorsement from the *Washington Post,* as unlikely as that might have been. When he did not receive the paper's support, he pointed to its backing of his Republican opponent in the general election as an issue in order to rouse suspicion and hostility among his black constituents. The *Post* was hardly forgiving. An ardent supporter of Barry's 1990 successor, Sharon Pratt Kelly, the paper pressed her in her last year in office to address the looming deficit. It was especially critical of her proposal early in 1994 to defer $230 million in District pension payments in order to conserve cash to meet immediate expenses.[25] Kelly's weakened position was fully revealed when she failed to carry a single precinct in the 1994 primary. Yet with Barry's election, the *Post* consistently refused to blame Kelly for the city's financial problems. The editorial board downplayed its own admission of complicity in the city's problems because it had backed Kelly initiatives that had exacerbated the deficit.[26] Its editorials ignored information it had reported in its news sections: that the city suffered a severe structural financial imbalance because of federal restrictions on the city's taxing power as well as the unfunded pension liability.[27] When Robert Pohlman, Barry's former deputy mayor for finance, testified to the debilitating effects of Kelly's decision to build fifteen months of receipts into one budget cycle, thereby starving future budgets, the *Post* acidly retorted that such self-serving testimony could not hide Barry's having "bequeathed to his successor a government that was broke and that the tax base no longer could support." Rather, the *Post* insisted, the deficit could be traced to Barry's own padding of the city payroll during his previous terms in office. This theme also was adopted by the *New York Times,* which, in reporting the crisis even as Barry assumed office, remarked, "A bloated, sometimes surly and indolent bureaucracy, packed onto the payroll by Mr. Barry in flusher times, is draining the treasury while providing perhaps the worst municipal service in the country. . . . The flamboyant Mr. Barry, brought down by his craving for women and cocaine, is seen by some as the very personification of the problem."[28] When the city's credit skidded to "junk bond" ratings in February, the *Post* ran a Herblock cartoon captioned "Some places have floods, fires and mudslides—we have the mayor."[29] In so personalizing the fiscal crisis by focusing negative attention on the incoming mayor, the media provided additional reasons for an already hostile Congress to rebuke him.

Barry thus would have had to make an extraordinary effort to forge a positive relationship with congressional representatives in whose hands rested the District's fate. Once Wall Street lowered the city's bond rating to junk status in February, it became clear that Washington would have to revert to borrowing from the U.S. Treasury as a measure of last resort. Under the circumstances some kind of financial review board was inevitable. But Barry was not compliant. Rather, he responded boldly, blaming the fiscal crisis not on mismanagement alone but on a structural imbalance between the city and the federal government. He agreed to cut the city workforce by another four thousand employees. But in declaring the city could no longer survive "half-slave and half-free," he demanded that the federal government assume those functions shouldered under the home rule act by the District of Columbia but that traditionally had been borne by the states. These included, most notably, the administrative costs of prisons and courts. In addition, he asked Congress for $267 million in one-time aid to cover escalating Medicaid costs as well as money to meet a federally mandated but unfunded pension liability that had grown to nearly $5 billion. Barry's assessment would ultimately gain acceptance, but the immediate reaction was harsh. The *Post* not only stressed in its news story that Barry "would dismantle major parts of the local bureaucracy he helped build in the 1980s," but its editorial condemned the proposal as a beg-and-borrow approach that "won't wash any more. . . . The worn-out woe-is-us, bail-us-out abdication of local responsibility won't do."[30]

Barry had a second chance to make his case when he appeared before the first meeting of newly reorganized congressional committees on the District of Columbia on February 22. But he was already in a bad position, having incurred hostility by appearing to say that as mayor he would be willing to make only a modest step toward resolving the deficit if Congress would take a much bigger step. The challenge became even more formidable when, on the eve of the hearings, a General Accounting Office audit of city finances questioned the reliability of Barry's budget figures. According to Barry's city administrator, Michael Rogers, the new committee chairs, Tom Davis of nearby Fairfax County, Virginia, and James Walsh of New York, were deeply affected by the GAO report, and it showed in their hostility to Barry's position in the hearings. Barry's attitude, Walsh charged, was emblematic of the cycle of denial and inaction that had characterized the responses of city officials to the financial crisis. Referring to Barry's claim that the District had received an unfair deal in the home rule charter, he retorted, "You made your bed; now you have to lie in it." Even the more sympathetic Democrat Julian Dixon of California complained of inadequate figures on the budget, noting Barry failed to help himself by presenting rambling testimony in place of the tightly structured paper he submitted to the record.[31]

His credibility on Capitol Hill already shattered, Barry acquiesced in the formation of a financial control board, the details of which he left to be worked out by the city's nonvoting delegate in the House of Representatives, Eleanor Holmes Norton.[32] Once Congress formed the oversight authority in April 1995, Barry appeared at first to be willing to work with it, describing himself in his State of the District address as a "captain in a changing sea." There is, he said, "a steady hand on the wheel, and we'll take charge of today and tomorrow."[33] In fact, from its earliest days Barry's last term was largely reduced to the distasteful job of trying to keep the city operating while still attempting to maintain a semblance of political support by rallying constituents to the local government's side in its dispute with Congress.

Once Congress denied the city the emergency funding it needed to bridge the budget gap in the first months of 1995, the only choice was to cut expenses dramatically. In Barry's first nine months back in office, the city cut $189 million from the budget, including rolling back city wages and reducing services to the poor, moves that adversely affected his core constituency. The city asked the new financial oversight board for an additional $300 million to satisfy the remaining deficit. On August 1, with only a month to go in the fiscal year, the board replied that it could approve only $149 million for deficit reduction. In light of the response, city administrator Rogers had to publicly announce that in order to meet bedrock obligations—the city's debt payment, its payroll, and its third-party payments—it would have to delay paying other vendors. What followed was a public relations disaster: fire trucks in hock, police cars without gas, trash not picked up, bodies piling up in the morgue.[34] As Barry approached the end of his first year in office, his old nemesis at the *Washington Post,* Juan Williams, described the control board as the only defense from Barry's incompetence:

> Barry, who once carried the banner for District home rule, has now decided that cause is less important than his own self-preservation. Having earlier assumed the role of hapless victim of a prejudiced judicial system and then, later, prodigal son seeking redemption, Barry now appears in the guise of genial passerby who happens upon a terrible fire. The fact is that this mayor is neither victim, nor passerby. Much of the blame for the raging fire that is the city's current financial crisis can be placed squarely on the four-time mayor and the excesses he oversaw during his first 12 years in office. Barry—having sold out the city's political independence and self-respect, having divided the races and chased off the middle class, having raised taxes and frightened off commercial enterprise, having trapped the poor in shameful schools and having left the city with inadequate and inefficient services—is now left to protect the only two things he truly cares about: his pension and his political future.[35]

Compromised in his ability to deliver services, Barry responded to such negative attacks by further personalizing the city's crisis in presenting himself as the city's last best hope against an unsympathetic Congress. By the time of the Million Man March on Washington in the fall of 1995, he no longer pictured himself as the confident captain. Instead, he evoked the image of the federal government as slave master: "Six hundred thousand of us live here in political and economic bondage. . . . Remove this political and economic yoke from our neck. Let my people go!"[36] Ordered by the control board to dismiss the head of the Department of Human Services, an old friend who had helped organize the bus caravan that brought him back from prison, Barry likened the action to those of Nazi Germany. He described his own cuts in the workforce as necessary because "enemies of the people" were poised to suspend self-government altogether if local officials did not take dramatic action quickly.[37] Barry's worst predictions were realized when Republican senator Lauch Faircloth of North Carolina slipped a rider into the 1997 District appropriation that stripped the mayor of control of all but several small elements in government. Barry screamed that the city had been raped.[38]

Such confrontational politics conformed to at least one element of Barry's and the city's history. As James Gibson, Barry's first planning director, put it, "If you have a conquered people, what is your psychology about assimilation, about joining the enemy? There is a deep maintenance of boundaries. To fully collaborate or assimilate to some extent has connotations of capitulation to the conqueror. In a sense, because race is such a factor, as are issues of equity and concepts of fairness, you see Marion trying to find a stance that retains integrity for him and the people he represents."[39] Indulging in such rhetoric, however, assured Barry's continued harsh treatment in Congress and in the press, even as he actually made hard decisions to bring the budget under control.

Although a 1996 audit showed the city had reduced the deficit from $335 million in 1994 to $54 million, Republican control board member Steven Harlan denounced Barry's statement at the time that he had made as many cuts in government as he was able and willing to do. Calling the mayor irrelevant, Harlan proposed to cut all his staff and overhead items, commenting, "He ought not be supported or paid if he is not contributing to the welfare of the city."[40]

Barry attempted one alliance of convenience in an effort to shore up his position in Congress. In Republican House Speaker Newt Gingrich he appeared briefly to have found an unlikely ally who was willing to protect the city's home rule from some of the more offensive experiments his fellow Republicans wanted to implement in the District. As a writer for the New York Times put it, "Barry, a pragmatist and, above all, a self-preservationist, is ideologically elastic enough to agree with Gingrich, the man who must pay the city's bills, on most everything he says. Barry is the ultimate insider-as-outsider. In the 70's, rich white liberals voted him in as Mayor, in the 80's, rich white developers paid for his re-election campaigns. Now, he needs the rich white Republican Congress to fund his government."[41] The core of their relationship became a plan to "transform" city government as part of a broader response to the fiscal crisis. At Gingrich's suggestion Barry hired the Atlanta-based consultant and former alcohol and drug abuse counselor Daryl Conner to produce a plan to "reinvent" District government. Drawing from the "human potential" movement of the 1960s and 1970s, Conner's approach dovetailed precisely with Barry's sustained attempt to identify his own recovery process with that of the city. A number of people who participated in the process initially thought the effort might actually provide a blueprint for management reform. Spelling out this plan before the city council in February 1996, Barry asserted, "I am serious about this. This is not a joke. This is not pie in the sky. . . . We have to change because there are forces out there that would change for us, and not do as good a job."[42] In fact, a number of elements in the 147-page plan were finally implemented, including new procurement procedures for government contracting and the privatization of some government functions. Barry also achieved the essential budgetary goals the plan laid out. But despite Barry's enthusiasm for what he called the joy of commitment to radical change, he never pursed the recommendations with the level of intensity that was necessary to shift the culture of the city bureaucracy. As a consequence, he failed to convince either Gingrich or his media critics that he had done what was necessary to reform city management.[43]

It was more than ironic, then, that when the control board offered its own strategic plan for the city in December 1996, it claimed that the city's financial stability depended on the federal government's taking over about $1 billion worth of city programs, including Medicaid and prisons. "In making a pitch to Congress today for services that typically are the responsibility of state government," the *Post* reported, "the control board is mirroring the position staked out by D.C. Mayor Marion Barry early last year when he declared that the home rule government established two decades ago is broken and that Congress should take over the state functions."[44] Within months President Clinton proposed and Congress adopted as part of its 1997 budget a plan that looked very much like what Barry first, and then the control board, proposed. Barry's credibility had sunk so low in Congress, however, that the entire plan was quietly developed without his participation. To bring the point home, as part of the same budget Congress required that the greater portion of District government be placed under the control of an externally hired manager appointed by the control board.

As he approached the end of his term, Barry began to appear as the game but badly battered prizefighter who had stayed in the ring too long. This was the image projected in a 1997 *City Paper* lead story, under the title, "Is Barry Down for the Count?" While acknowledging Barry's accomplishments in reducing the deficit, Jonetta Rose Barras nonetheless stressed that Barry, once on the ropes, "will come flying back with the race card." The city, she asserted, "will never get the respect and resources it deserves until it shakes its addiction to the man who once proclaimed that he *is* the District of Columbia."[45] In stark contrast to his first term, Barry's staff included few veterans of District government who could hold their own with him in a policy argument. Instead, he turned most assiduously to his wife, Cora Masters Barry, for advice and counsel, not exactly a perfect check on his judgment. Thus compromised in his ability to set broad policy, Barry acquiesced as federal authorities assumed responsibility for much of city government, including public housing and child welfare. Stripped of any power he might have sought in Congress, Barry decided to retire rather than continue fighting.

Once the mayor made his decision, the *Post* rushed an overwhelmingly negative assessment of his tenure into print. In addition to quoting the locally detested Senator Faircloth as saying "he has been a terrible mayor," along with a host of other critics, staff writer Vernon Loeb summed up the man-

tra the paper had been repeating for four years: "The mayor's personal indiscretions mirrored an equally sharp decline in his public performance. By
the end of his third term, his bloated government had been rocked by one
scandal after another while residents complained bitterly about inadequate
city services. After five years of robust growth and healthy surpluses, the
District's finances were suddenly running seriously in the red, and the city's
per-capita murder rate became the highest in the nation."[46]

Revealingly, the same issue of the *Post* carried a column strikingly sympathetic to the mayor. Written by Courtland Milloy, it reported Barry's personal views about his stewardship. As the two men played tennis on the courts
that Barry's wife had helped secure in an underserved part of the city, Barry
told Milloy:

> The only way you can survive in this world, buy food, put a roof over your head,
> is to make money or take money. One of the things that makes me the most
> happy is knowing that I helped provide the opportunities for so many people
> to make it legitimately. You listen to some of these Republicans over the last
> three years, and what they say goes beyond personal disrespect towards me. It
> is a collective disrespect of all citizens, a disregard for humanism, just when you
> think we had gotten past much of that history, and I think a lot of it is racial.
> When I was growing up in the South, it wasn't just the Jim Crow signs, which
> I saw all the time, or having to move to the back of the bus, which I had to do,
> or sitting in the colored-only balcony at the movies, where I had to go. When
> they talked to you, there was an unmistakably disrespectful tone that was used—
> and with [Senator Lauch] Faircloth, [Representative Tom] Davis, and [Repre-
> sentative Charles] Taylor, all white men from the South—I have heard it, over
> and over again, and I recognize it for what it is.[47]

In a single day Washington's most important media outlet ran two starkly contrasting visions of Marion Barry. Not surprisingly, the second vision,
highlighting race pride, was featured at the October tribute to the retiring
mayor. Time and again, speakers praised Barry's decision to set aside contracts for minorities, to promote minorities and women in office, to give kids
summer jobs. One of the most moving moments came when Ella McCall-
Haggan, describing herself as a young woman made homeless when drugs
and alcohol destroyed her life, credited Barry with rescuing her through a job
at Pride, Inc. Now a licensed social worker, she spoke from the heart about
Barry's ability to offer the hand up, not out. No less a civil rights icon than
Coretta Scott King praised Barry's unswerving dedication to human liberties. And Marc Morial, a second-generation mayor of New Orleans whose
father, Ernest, was first elected in 1977, stressed the continuity of the struggle for civil rights. Milloy had certainly identified Barry's sustaining passion

to secure civil liberties as a strength. That passion also constituted a limitation, according to his recent critics.

Building on criticism made most consistently over time by Juan Williams, Jonetta Rose Barras concluded her recent assessment of Barry by charging that his chief failure was that he "could not shed his formative years' legacy of poverty and racism":

> It remained a complex, multifaceted presence in his adult life with an unfortunate propensity for rearing its head at the most inopportune of moments. A psychological burden too heavy to remove, Barry's childhood in the deep South was also like a clouded crystal ball through which he tended to prognosticate about African-Americans' future. Predictably, it also generated a sometimes overpowering fear of whites, making it nearly impossible for him to ever fully trust them—even those whom he grew to like. In consequence, Barry was never able to fully liberate either himself or his people.[48]

In less sympathetic hands such imprisonment by race appears more menacing. In 1991 the *Newsday* editorial writer Jim Sleeper, whose book *The Closest of Strangers* had offered a neoconservative take on racial politics, used a review of Jonathan Agronsky's *Marion Barry: The Politics of Race* to raise new questions about Barry. Citing a decision by the U.S. Attorney's Office not to prosecute Pride officials in connection with a fencing operation run from one of Pride's facilities, Sleeper challenged Washington's African-American community to unlearn the destructive lessons Barry and his counterparts had taught. One lesson, "born of real hurts and injustices," he said, was that "since white society cannot be redeemed, it might as well be ripped off."[49] The Manhattan Institute's Fred Siegel pursued Sleeper's lead by making Barry a centerpiece of the thesis that once stalwarts of the civil rights movement moved into positions of power, they effected an elaborate scheme to extort public funds through threats of civil unrest. Siegel built on Agronsky's provocative account of Pride, "Mau-Mauing the U.S. Labor Department," and tore into the 1960s liberal alliance of the federal government and inner-city neighborhood organizations. Siegel described Barry as the carrier of a broad political consensus "out of a mix of Great Society liberalism and the movements for home rule and black separatism—all of which were leveraged by the threat of renewed rioting." Asserting Barry's capacity "for investing blackmail and intimidation with the higher moral purposes of the civil rights movement," Siegel linked Barry's brand of race politics with the most controversial of contemporary activists, including New York firebrand Al Sharpton. "In an ironic re-creation of the very segregationists they once fought," he concluded, "Marion Barry and his allies and admirers have created in the District a 'volkish' democracy, a Dixie-like political culture based on the organized cultivation of racial resentments. If in the segregationist South 'white made right,' in the Crow Jimism of the District 'white must be wrong.'"[50]

As exaggerated as it was, Siegel's caricature of the mayor reflected the times. In a period of widespread hostility to affirmative action and other race-based programs, Barry's reassertion of black nationalist and race-specific appeals could hardly have found a sympathetic mainstream audience. But Siegel missed the terrible irony of Barry's position. Barry had implemented the draconian cuts and many of the alterations in government practice that Congress had demanded. While he hardly received credit, Barry left office with a $400 million surplus, a $1.1 billion turnaround from the time he entered his last term. Still pilloried by the white mainstream despite his accomplishments, Barry nonetheless retained a high standing among District residents. A poll taken just before he announced his decision not to seek another term in office showed him with a 2-to-1 lead over his nearest probable challenger.

Throughout his Washington career Marion Barry dealt with dualisms: city and capital, black and white, words and deeds. At his best Barry managed to bridge each of these divides, forging consensus, transcending racial hostility and suspicion, integrating the symbolic trappings of power with the execution of programs targeted at his most needy constituents. That capacity, so effectively demonstrated in his first term as mayor, disintegrated over time. Ultimately, Barry became much like a very different politician, Richard Nixon, whose rhetorical and policy strategies diverged so dramatically that his chief political adviser, Attorney General John Mitchell, asserted, "Watch what we do, not what we say." In bending the axioms of black power to his immediate political needs, Barry mastered the proper symbols without securing the means to deliver its tangible rewards. Because national values became more conservative and because Congress maintained considerable control of District affairs through its power of exclusive jurisdiction, Barry's job was even more difficult than that of other black mayors of major cities also beset with the flight of human and monetary capital. A thorough assessment of Barry's tenure reveals that his weaknesses have been better recognized than his strengths. He nonetheless left even his most fervent supporters a troubled legacy, for he managed most effectively to fuel their discontent without in the end being able to assuage its root causes.

Notes

I wish to thank David Abramson, James Gibson, Michael Rodgers, Eric Schneider, Janet Golden, and my wife, Margaret Marsh, for comments and suggestions made on an earlier version of this chapter.

1. *Washington Post,* May 22, 1998.

2. Barrington Salmon, "The Barry Years," Office of Communications, District of Columbia, August 1998, p. 16.

3. Jonetta Rose Barras, *The Last of the Black Emperors: The Hollow Comeback of Marion Barry in the Age of New Black Leaders* (Baltimore, Md.: Bancroft, 1998), 295.

4. Bound by the clause in the Constitution granting Congress "exclusive jurisdiction" over the seat of national government, the District of Columbia underwent a number of political changes in the nineteenth century. The city of Washington's first charter, adopted in 1802, allowed for an elected local government without representation in Congress, but Congress revoked that system in 1874, placing the District under the direction of three presidentially appointed members of a board of commissioners. This system remained without modification until 1967, when Lyndon Johnson, failing to secure Congress's approval for an elected local government, used his executive authority to name a larger and more representative city council headed by a mayor-commissioner.

5. Michele F. Pacifico, "Don't Buy Where You Can't Work: The New Negro Alliance of Washington," *Washington History* 6 (Spring–Summer 1995): 66–88. Barry defended his tactics by saying that because the Washington Board of Trade, the city's most powerful business and civic organization, had taken out ads opposing pending legislation to authorize home rule, this was a chance for merchants who held other views to make them count. See column by William Raspberry, *Washington Star,* March 10, 1966.

6. Stokley Carmichael and Charles Hamilton, *Black Power: The Politics of Liberation in America* (New York: Vintage, 1967); David O. Sears and John McConahay, *The Politics of Violence: The New Urban Blacks and the Watts Riot* (Boston: Houghton Mifflin, 1973). The connection between Carmichael's book, which was dedicated to fellow SNCC activist Ivanhoe Donaldson, and Barry's career was hardly incidental. Donaldson became Barry's closest political adviser during his early years as mayor.

7. *Washington Star,* May 17, 1966, January 16, 1967. Barry is quoted in Harry S. Jaffe and Tom Sherwood, *Dream City: Race, Power, and The Decline of Washington, D.C.* (New York: Simon and Schuster, 1994), 55.

8. *Washington Star,* December 18, 1970.

9. Jonathan I.Z. Agronsky, *Marion Barry: The Politics of Race* (Latham, N.Y: British American Publishing, 1991), 126.

10. Mark Desautels, "The White Shadow," *Regardies,* May 1985, p. 58; Jaffe and Sherwood, *Dream City,* 98. Abramson confirmed this story when I interviewed him on September 29, 1998.

11. *Washington Star,* January 3, 1979.

12. Ibid.

13. "Which Marion Barry Is Mayor?" editorial, *Washington Star,* February 28, 1980. The *Star*'s criticism was consistent with its editorial support for Barry of November 4, 1978, which praised Barry precisely for having made "the transition from the street conflicts of a decade ago" to dealing with "intractable problems of taxation, housing, jobs and schools."

14. James Gibson, interview by author, October 14, 1998.

15. *Washington Star,* May 25, 1980.

16. *Washington Post,* June 22, 1982. More details of this campaign, as well as Barry's first

three terms as mayor, appear in Howard Gillette Jr., "The Limits of Social Protest Politics," in *Between Justice and Beauty: Race, Planning, and the Failure of Urban Policy* (Baltimore, Md.: Johns Hopkins University Press, 1995), chap. 10, 190–207.

17. While Barry's support among nonblacks fell from an estimated 52 to 34.3 percent, it rose from 27.3 to 68.2 percent among African Americans (Jeffrey R. Henig, "Race and Voting: Continuity and Change in the District of Columbia," *Urban Affairs Quarterly* 28 [June 1993]: 554).

18. Juan Williams, "A Dream Deferred: A Black Mayor Betrays the Faith," *Washington Monthly,* July–August 1986, p. 39.

19. Jaffe and Sherwood, *Dream City,* 244, 252–53, 283.

20. *Washington Post,* February 16, 1990. Barry had used the lynching metaphor before in response to reports that he would be implicated by Karen Johnson's testimony. See Jaffe and Sherwood, *Dream City,* 172.

21. Gillette, *Between Justice and Beauty,* 201–3.

22. *Emerge,* December–January 1995. Hardly a proponent of Barry, the columnist William Raspberry acknowledged Barry's appeal to the growing number of voters personally familiar with the criminal justice system: "They are not shamed by Barry; they are redeemed by Barry, and by their redemption of him" (*Washington Post,* September 16, 1994).

23. *Washington Post,* September 27, 1994; Barras, *Last of the Black Emperors,* 165.

24. Jeffrey Goldberg, "Marion Barry Confronts a Hostile Takeover," *New York Times Magazine,* October 29, 1995, p. 51. Barry had been generating damning imagery well before his arrest in 1990. The Washington business journal *Regardies* was especially critical in the late 1980s, capping its attack with a May 1989 cover showing Barry's enlarged head popping out of Congress under the title "Jerk in the Box." The subtitle read, "Marion Barry's Made a Farce of Home Rule. Should Congress Take D.C. Back?"

25. *Washington Post,* March 21, 25, 1994.

26. In a March 25, 1994, editorial, "How D.C. Reached the Cliff," the *Post* noted, "May we say as enthusiastic endorsers of Mayor Barry and Mayor Kelly but also as enthusiasts for some of the spending initiatives based precariously on evaporating credit—that we don't think we can exactly take our distance from those who participated in the boom before the bust."

27. *Washington Post,* March 25, September 28, 1990; "Assessing the District of Columbia's Financial Future: A Report to the Federal City Council," report from McKinsey and Co. and the Urban Institute, October 1994. James Gibson, who during Barry's last term was director of D.C. Agenda, the civic organization built in part to respond to this report, directed the staff that assembled this report. Gibson also played a role in getting the Brookings Institution to underwrite the most thorough assessment of Washington's structural financial difficulties, Carol O'Cleireacain, *The Orphaned Capital: Adopting the Right Revenues for the District of Columbia* (Washington, D.C.: Brookings Institution Press, 1997). Under the heading "Findings," O'Cleireacain states firmly, on page 6, "The District's long-term fiscal problems stem largely from its very nature as the nation's capital."

28. *New York Times,* February 12, 1995. The same story also reported the structural issues plaguing the city. Quoting Peat Marwick consultant Larry Herman, who had served as staff director of the Rivlin Commission, the *Times* reported, "The problem is not Marion Barry. He didn't make it. The problems go back to home rule. The Feds gave them a

lousy deal. And, as best as I can tell, Mrs. Kelly chose not to take quick action. There were studies up to here telling Mayor Kelly this is a big-time problem."

29. *New York Times,* January 12, 1995; *Washington Post,* February 17, 1995. An editorial that accompanied the Herblock cartoon, "The Message Is in the Junk," blamed Barry personally for the bond rating.

30. *Washington Post,* February 3, 1995. Although Barry's critics condemned his request, in particular for Medicaid funding, only the District was responsible for 100 percent of the nonfederal share of all Medicaid expenditures.

31. Michael Rogers, interview by author, January 15, 1999; *Washington Post,* February 22, 23, 1995. See especially the editorial, "D.C. Finances: Today's Hill Test," *Washington Post,* February 22, 1995, which warned that the paper wanted "no more excuses, promises or floppy numbers from a city that is flat on its financial back."

32. For Norton's ability to keep Congress from vesting some powers in the authority, as it had wanted to do, see David A. Vise and Howard Schneider, "Who's in Charge?" *Washington Post Magazine,* December 17, 1995, esp. pp. 29–30.

33. *Washington Post,* April 28, 1995.

34. Michael Rogers, interview by author, October 13, 1998.

35. Juan Williams, "Why Brimmer Won't Blink," *Washington Post,* December 3, 1995, Outlook sec. For a summary of Washington's fiscal problems, see the two-part series "Budget Blues," *Washington Post,* March 16–17, 1996. The *New York Times* soon followed with its own extended litany of urban woes in the capital in a series entitled, "Monument to Decay," July 25–27, 1996.

36. Vise and Schneider, "Who's in Charge?" 27.

37. "Loose Lips," *Washington City Paper,* July 7, 1996; *Washington Post,* February 21, 1996.

38. *Washington Post,* August 7, 1997. As always, such rhetoric from the mayor did not go without negative response. The *City Paper*'s Ken Cummins, who became one of Barry's severest critics, dismissed Barry's claim caustically, writing in the August 22, 1997, issue, "While his behavior seems almost pathological, Barry makes no apologies. . . . Barry believes that such brattish conduct resonates with a disenfranchised electorate that can still be wooed by hackneyed civil rights rhetoric."

39. Barras, *Last of the Black Emperors,* 191.

40. *Washington Post,* February 2, 1996. The same issue of the paper reported that Cora Masters Barry, very much a presence during the last Barry term, lashed out at the paper's editors after an extended interview with her husband, saying they had no idea of the pain that cuts in service had caused the mayor.

41. Goldberg, "Marion Barry Confronts a Hostile Takeover," 44. For Republican goals see also *Washington Post,* May 12, August 2, 1995; Vise and Schneider, "Who's in Charge?"; and David Plotz, "The Laboratory of Dr. Gingrich," *Washington City Paper,* June 2–8, 1995.

42. *Washington Post,* November 6, 1995, April 30, 1996.

43. The *Post* provided the most extensive review of Barry's managerial shortcomings in a series that began July 20, 1997.

44. *Washington Post,* December 12, 1996.

45. *Washington City Paper,* January 24–30, 1997.

46. *Washington Post,* May 22, 1998. In typically derivative fashion, the *New York Times* chimed in with a similarly critical editorial May 25 under the title, "Marion Barry's Sour

Legacy," which charged, "through his last years and in his final speech as Mayor, Mr. Barry turned into an apologist for his own weaknesses. He railed in his farewell against 'the mean-spirited Republican Congress.' But no one in that body ever did as much damage to the capital as did Mr. Barry's cronyism, incompetence and hubris." Faircloth's controversial views on the District are reported in the *Washington Post,* March 3, 1997, and November 5, 1998, at the time he lost his bid for reelection.

47. *Washington Post,* May 22, 1998.

48. Barras, *Last of the Black Emperors,* 114.

49. Jim Sleeper, review of Jonathan Agronsky, *Marion Barry: The Politics of Race, Washington Post Book World,* June 9, 1991, p. 5.

50. Fred Siegel, *The Future Once Happened Here: New York, D.C., L.A. and the Fate of America's Big Cities* (New York: Free Press, 1997), 66, 73, 110.

9. Rethinking the Collapse of Postwar Liberalism: The Rise of Mayor Coleman Young and the Politics of Race in Detroit

HEATHER ANN THOMPSON

COLEMAN ALEXANDER YOUNG, accused Communist Party sympathizer, United Auto Workers activist, state senator, and leader of the Michigan Democratic Party, became the first African-American mayor of Detroit in 1974. Although Young won the mayoral seat by a hairsbreadth, his narrow victory was followed by a remarkable twenty-year career as leader of the nation's fifth-largest city. And yet, as interesting as is Young's leadership of Detroit, his mayoralty is even more significant for what it tells us about American politics during the 1970s. Young's rise to power not only reflects an important moment in the history of the Motor City but also illuminates a dramatic transformation taking place in urban politics across the United States after the Second World War.

By the mid-1970s, in urban centers all over the United States, civic power had shifted into the hands of African Americans, signaling the most dramatic political ascendancy of the twentieth century. In 1973 forty-eight U.S. cities had black mayors and by 1990 there were 316.[1] A vast political science literature has analyzed this phenomenon in detail, focusing largely on the differences between how black and white mayors ruled their cities as well as on the various obstacles that the black leaders in particular faced. Political scientists, however, have not adequately placed the rise of black mayors into the broader context of postwar political and social history. Thus some of the most fascinating aspects of this African-American ascendancy have been overlooked.

Historians, on the other hand, increasingly have addressed the evolution of twentieth-century politics, largely in terms of the rise and fall of American liberalism. Because historians have sought primarily to explain the rise of white working-class conservatism during the postwar period, a consensus has emerged in their scholarship that widespread white disillusionment with the tumultuous 1960s is what marked the beginning of the end for liberalism as a potent force in U.S. politics. The historians Gary Gerstle and Steven Fraser's influential collection of essays, *The Rise and Fall of the New Deal Order,* makes this argument, as do numerous other scholars writing from a quite different perspective, such as Fred Siegel.[2] Because the liberal strategies for social equality and racial integration promoted by Lyndon Johnson in his agenda for the Great Society were repudiated by many whites during the 1970s and because Reagan Republicanism swept across the country soon thereafter, historians are persuaded that liberalism itself had collapsed by 1980.

In sounding the death knell of liberalism, however, and specifically by arguing for the withering of any support for the social welfare and civil rights programs promoted during the Great Society, this historical scholarship has overlooked the key fact that urban Americans were electing black mayors from the 1970s onward precisely because of their commitment to these programs. Black mayors had campaigned successfully to continue the initiatives of the Great Society, particularly the social welfare components of the War on Poverty and key civil rights measures such as affirmative action. However moribund in much of the white working-class's political ideology, sixties-style liberalism was alive and well in the municipal politics of cities like Detroit well past 1980. Clearly, the task remains for scholars to account for the rise of black liberal power within the larger context of a growing white conservatism.

This essay examines the historical context within which one such black liberal mayor took office in one major urban industrial center. After first chronicling the dramatic events that set the stage for the election of black Democrat Coleman Young in Detroit, the essay will analyze the broader political significance of his leadership. One important factor is that the political moment that made Young's election possible was born out of a series of bitter and protracted battles waged during the late 1960s by increasingly conservative urban whites and increasingly radical urban blacks over how the liberal coalition forged during the New Deal, and then led by proponents of the Great Society, should deal with the racial problems and divisions that plagued the Motor City. Ultimately, however, neither conservative whites, who argued that liberals had come to cater to black over white interests during the 1960s, nor radical blacks, who maintained that this same sixties-style liberalism was far too timid in its approach to combating entrenched racism, were able to secure power in the city. Indeed, it was the vision of the city's politically moderate poor, working-, and middle-class black community, and that of the city's racially progressive whites who long had championed biracial cooperation and coexistence within a liberal framework, that triumphed in Detroit. Neither group could accept the premises of white conservatives, nor were these groups ultimately willing to embrace the more revolutionary agenda for the city promoted by civic radicals. Coleman Young successfully mobilized these voters, and his mayoral victory is clear evidence that a significant reaffirmation of sixties-style liberalism was occurring in urban centers such as Detroit just as it was atrophying elsewhere in the country. As African-American leaders like Young took power in cities across the United States during the 1970s, they reiterated their support for liberal programs to effect social and economic equality even while these same programs were being rejected by those who moved in growing numbers to the nation's suburbs and into the Republican Party fold.

From the moment that Young took office in Detroit, he not only championed fundamental principles of, and programs for, Great Society liberalism without equivocation but he also made it very clear that the goals of the civil rights movement would be a vital part of his political agenda. Thus, when Detroit's politically moderate black and racially progressive white communities elected Coleman Young in 1973, they had real reason to hope that the city would make major inroads against poverty and discrimination. But while the Young administration certainly met many of the civil rights goals its supporters had long sought, producing far greater racial equality and civic integration than had ever before existed in that city, this administration failed to effect the economic equity envisioned by the architects of the War on Poverty. To a significant degree Young's inability to improve living standards in this city stemmed from the deep hostility with which racially conservative white Detroiters had responded to his victory and their decision, soon after he took office, to abandon Detroit, taking their taxes and businesses with them. By 1980 the Motor City had become a predominantly black but increasingly impoverished urban center surrounded by overwhelmingly white, extremely hostile, and disproportionately wealthy, suburbs. In the face of white suburban opposition, the African-American and racially progressive white urban supporters of social welfare and civil rights liberalism would be left to carry out their agenda with few resources.

In analyzing Young's rise to power in Detroit, we can see clearly that the support base of sixties-style liberalism did not fully collapse after that turbulent decade, as so many would have it, but rather that it had noticeably changed color and had become overwhelmingly urban. And with that metamorphosis the programmatic initiatives of both the Great Society and the civil rights movement became barricaded within inner cities. Although conservatism was gaining in popularity among a significant number of white voters during the 1970s and 1980s, the Reagan revolution was never complete, and pockets of liberalism still existed throughout the United States. America's urban centers would remain important islands of liberal vision, perhaps dampened but not washed away by the vast sea of suburban conservatism surrounding them.

1945–67

During and after World War Two Detroit experienced a massive demographic transformation as many thousands of African Americans arrived from southern states seeking racial equality as well as economic opportunity during what historians call the Second Great Migration. By the mid-1960s Detroit's African-American population comprised more than 40 percent of the city's population; these Motor City residents had come primarily from the states of Arkansas, Alabama, North Carolina, South Carolina, Georgia, Mississippi, and Louisiana.[3] Because racial discrimination existed in Detroit, often as glaringly as it did in the South, African-American migrants quickly realized that the Motor City was not the promised land of which they had dreamed. Almost immediately, an African-American civil rights leadership, embodied in organizations such as the NAACP, the Urban League, and the Trade Union Leadership Council, led important battles for racial equality in Detroit. After 1961, when a coalition of black and racially progressive white city residents elected a liberal mayor, Jerome Cavanagh, civil rights leaders worked closely with his predominantly white administration in city hall for progressive change. Indeed, Mayor Cavanagh owed a great deal to these black leaders, without whose support he could not have been elected.

Throughout the 1960s Detroit's African-American leaders continually encouraged the larger black community to maintain faith in the various new civil rights initiatives of liberal whites as well as in their own multifaceted efforts to eradicate discrimination. Yet despite black leaders' commitment to work for progressive change, both alone and in cooperation with liberal whites, racial exclusion continued to thrive in Detroit. As the historian Thomas Sugrue has shown, city blacks had long been battling the rigidly segregated housing market of Detroit.[4] Particularly galling to them, however, was that despite the efforts of both progressive white city leaders and the black middle class to achieve integrated living, exclusionary practices still flourished. By the mid-1960s the inability of civic liberals to reverse housing segregation was clear; in fact, it was actually becoming more entrenched. As the scholars Albert Mayer and Thomas Hoult have pointed out, "In 1930, 51% of all Negro residents lived in white or predominantly white areas [yet] by 1960, only 15% of the Negro residents lived in so-called white areas."[5]

Detroit's growing black population still was barred not only from adequate housing as the 1960s wore on but continued to be shut out of decent jobs as well. Like segregated housing, employment discrimination had long been a problem for black Detroiters. According to scholars such as Joseph Darden, in "June 1948 close to 65 percent of all job openings in Detroit contained written discriminatory specifications, and those that did not discriminate in written form did so at the gate."[6] Despite the NAACP's successful agitation to have fair employment legislation enacted in Michigan, and even though a civil rights–oriented liberal was mayor, Detroit's black citizens by the late 1960s remained concentrated in the least skilled, lowest paying, and most dangerous occupations in the city.

Not surprisingly the continuation of housing segregation and workplace discrimination slowly eroded the black community's faith in liberal leaders' prescriptions for change. The deteriorating state of police-community relations in the city would breech that faith completely. The Detroit Police Department remained less than 5 percent African American throughout the 1960s, for example, which had enormous implications for city blacks. The department was notorious not only as the one institution in the city most opposed to racial integration but also for fielding officers well known to act upon their racial prejudices, both physically and verbally.[7]

Well aware of the scandalous treatment meted out to black residents of Detroit by police officers, the NAACP stepped up its efforts to bring the reality of police brutality to the attention of the mayor's office. As the NAACP described it in a 1964 report, the police "operate under the bigoted misapprehension that most Negroes are criminals" and noted further that "the NAACP has personally investigated numerous episodes of police brutality to Negro citizens which, even when verified by the courts or the Civil Rights Commission, has never resulted in any effective action against the guilty police officers."[8] The leaders of a prestigious black social organization, the Cotillion Club, put the problem of continuing police brutality even more pointedly when they wrote directly to Cavanagh in 1965. As they noted, "Records available to you and the police commissioner show that between May of 1961 and February, 1964, more than 1,000 citizens sustained physical injuries at the hands of Detroit policemen. Over 600 of these were Negro."[9]

Given the state of housing, employment, and police-community relations by the late 1960s, poor and working-class blacks, who had enthusiastically supported liberals in the mayoral elections of 1961 and 1964, had become skeptical indeed of leadership promises that racial equality and economic

opportunity soon would be realized. Intense white resistance to desegregation, and the inability of liberal city leaders to end discrimination while simultaneously appeasing racially conservative whites in Detroit only fueled
black frustration. By 1967, with poor and working-class blacks growing disenchanted with liberals' strategies for effecting racial equality, with conservative whites increasingly convinced that liberals were catering to black needs
over white, and with white and black liberal leaders still fully committed to
both the pace and parameters of their agenda for change, the Motor City was
veering toward a severe political crisis.

1967–73

That Detroit was in trouble became fully evident when a riot erupted there
during late July 1967. This grassroots rebellion, sparked by yet another confrontation between the all-white police department and poor blacks, was
followed in 1968 by a series of bitter black-led wildcat strikes in the city's
auto plants. Such dramatic events reflected the degree to which ordinary African-
American citizens had become fed up with conservative white resistance to
sharing the city and its workplaces. As significant, however, was that these
events demonstrated that many city blacks had lost faith in traditional means
of redress, in the formal political process, and in the efficacy of strategies for
achieving racial equality espoused by their liberal leaders from city hall to
the union hall to the pulpit.

Despite the social and political tensions erupting in the Motor City, May-
or Cavanagh remained undaunted and tried to mend his riot-fractured liberal coalition in order to save the city from further polarization. In response
to the urban upheaval of July 1967, Cavanagh established several committees
and commissions to address citizen grievances. Through organizations such
as the Mayor's Development Team and the New Detroit Committee, city
liberals—both black and white—worked feverishly to heal the wounded city
and to repair fissures in the local Democratic Party.[10]

When neither the Mayor's Development Team nor New Detroit was able
to quell the criticism that still raged in the black community, city leaders set
their sights on the mayoral election of 1969. They hoped that a political new-
comer, Richard Austin, a black liberal, could bridge the growing gap between
leadership liberals and the black community at large and thus defeat a conservative white law-enforcement candidate by the name of Roman Gribbs,
who played continually upon white fears of black "criminality" and "dependency." Austin was a migrant from Alabama who had become a successful
certified public accountant and was a well-respected member of the black

middle class. Austin identified himself as a moderate liberal, and in his campaign he insisted that "all citizens must be given equal treatment under the law" and that Detroit needed "better communication between the black community and the police."[11]

Austin's willingness to tackle the dicey issue of police-community relations, and ultimately his advocacy of "civilian control of police and all other city departments," made him quite popular with white progressives and the black community alike. Yet his views drew the ire of conservative white Detroiters, who now were completely suspicious of liberalism and of black liberals in particular. As one such self-described white Detroiter made clear in a particularly virulent letter to Austin before the election, "Your BLACKNESS is the only reason all those BLACK APES voted in the primaries! . . . All you BLACKS know how to do is have illegitimate children, drink, tear up schools, rob, rape, and constantly expect to get handouts from tax-paying whites! If by any fluke you become mayor of Detroit, you will be mayor of a dung heap because any WHITE who is able to do so will move out."[12]

Detroit was temporarily saved from this threatened exodus when, on November 4, 1969, Gribbs became mayor of Detroit with 257,312 votes to Austin's 250,000 in what the political scientist Joseph Darden and colleagues have deemed the "closest race in the history of Detroit."[13] This election, to an even greater degree than the 1967 riot, showed just how divided Detroit had become since World War II. As the *Detroit Free Press* put it, "quietly, and with little fanfare, the majority of Detroit's white voters went to the polls on Tuesday and cast their ballots for Roman Gribbs. . . . Gribbs received about 85 percent of the white vote and about 4 percent of the vote in the black community."[14]

But if racially conservative white Detroiters had hoped that the ousting of a liberal mayor with civil rights sympathies would restore the racial status quo or discourage greater black activism, events in the city between 1969 and 1973 left them sorely disappointed and even more disaffected with the state of city politics. Indeed, Gribbs's victory did not spell the end of social welfare and civil rights–sympathetic liberalism in Detroit, particularly because liberal voters, both black and white, had managed to retain all six liberal incumbent city council members and add three new liberals (including a third African American) to the council.[15] Gribbs's victory also did not defuse criticism in the black community. The combination of Gribbs's pro–law enforcement platform and Austin's defeat not only led poor and working-class blacks to become even more politically active but made many far more radical than Austin had ever been.

Indeed, it was after the upheaval of 1967, but more specifically after the election of 1969, that Detroit witnessed the birth of a new grassroots black challenge to the racial inequities in the city. After 1969 a key minority of African Americans throughout the city and in the auto plants formed militant black revolutionary organizations that advocated far more radical avenues for effecting change than the city's Great Society liberals were willing to embrace.[16] As *Detroit Scope Magazine* noted, even before the 1969 election took place, the ever-optimistic members of New Detroit were beginning to recognize that "if anything, the conflict is in a more advanced state than it was in late July, 1967" because "New Detroit's greatest grass-roots failure has been its inability to win support from the black militants."[17] According to the Coleman Young biographer Wilbur Rich, by the late sixties "individuals such as Edward Vaughn (Pan African Congress), Kenneth Cockrel (League of Revolutionary Black Workers), Milton Henry (Republic of New Africa), and Reverend Albert Cleage (Black Christian Nationalists), all emerged as challengers to the more established black leadership."[18] Indeed, between 1969 and 1973 battles over black representation and civic equality raged throughout the city's neighborhoods, schools, workplaces, churches, and courtrooms.

Despite the rise of black radicalism in Detroit, however, political battle lines in the Motor City during this period were not drawn simply between a group of conservative whites and a group of black militants. In fact, the battles that raged to shape Detroit's future were far more complex than this model suggests. Between 1969 and 1973 the political landscape of Detroit was divided into *three* ideological camps, all of which crossed class lines and two of which crossed the color line as well. In one camp white conservatives from across the class spectrum were beginning to mobilize so that their vision of white dominance could triumph. And in another camp black radicals (both working and middle class, with a number of white allies) certainly were beginning to articulate a far more militant approach for bettering the city than either Detroit's liberals or its white conservatives were willing to consider. Significantly, however, in a third camp black and white liberals (both working and middle class) still were fighting desperately to improve the city within the framework of the Great Society.

The actions of the Detroit Police Department brought an increased sense of urgency to the battles being waged within the Motor City after 1969. To city blacks it increasingly appeared that despite the civil rights gains of the past decades, and despite the various liberal programs to get the department to reform itself after the 1967 riot, the Detroit police were never going to change their ways. By July 1969 the department was still only 9 percent black, and of the 225 complaints registered with the Citizen's Complaint Bureau in 1968 regarding police treatment of black citizens, 167 were for physical abuse.[19] An additional problem brought to light by Detroit's Commission on Community Relations was that police routinely dismissed citizen complaints despite substantial evidence that they were justified; the commission also noted that "staff members [of the commission were] usually not permitted to see police reports that are important to development of sound conclusions."[20]

In the opinion of many community blacks, the police had become even more of a problem after Gribbs had taken office. In January 1971, for example, the Gribbs administration encouraged the department to form a special undercover decoy unit called STRESS, which stood for Stop the Robberies, Enjoy Safe Streets. STRESS was just what Gribbs had promised his constituency of white racial conservatives—a tougher division within the department that would target crime in the city's poor black neighborhoods. Not surprisingly, after the birth of STRESS the already severely strained relationship between the police and the black community deteriorated further as STRESS officers killed an alarming number of city blacks taken into their custody. By the police commissioner's own admission, by October 1971 ten suspects had died at the hands of STRESS officers and thirty-eight had been injured.[21]

Although few Detroiters thought the situation in the city could become more tense than it had been during July 1967, the formation of STRESS dramatically heightened civic conflict. Through their growing number of radical grassroots organizations, segments of the African-American community stepped up the drive to root out racism in the police department and to gain greater representation in the city as a whole. In response the city's conservative white community dug in its heels and continued, with renewed energy, to do everything in its power to strengthen police presence and to assert its control in Detroit. Predictably, as the black community mobilized to disband STRESS, many conservative white Detroiters made it clear in letters to local newspapers that their support of this police unit was unequivocal.[22]

Because liberal politicians in Detroit, influenced by the LBJ-commissioned Kerner Report, also believed that the local police had to be monitored, conservative whites became even more certain that these liberals no longer represented their interests and became more vocally opposed to the Democratic Party, both locally and nationally. A series of controversial legal battles that unfolded between 1969 and 1973—involving cases in which city blacks were charged with killing whites (such as a number of police officers and plant foremen)—served to cement conservative white Detroiters' opposition to Great Society liberalism.[23]

To the surprise of almost everyone, during the course of these trials the

African-American community's struggle for equality spilled over into Detroit's courtrooms. Various militant black organizations began mobilizing the
black community around these cases, and the radical black lawyers who represented the poor African Americans accused of murder readily used the jury
trial as a venue in which to air long-held grievances about racial discrimination in the city. In each of these contentious trials black defendants were
acquitted, often because radical defense attorneys had managed to shift the
jurors' focus away from the alleged wrongdoings of the accused to the racially discriminatory actions of the victims. Conservative white Detroiters
took these outcomes as confirmation that the Great Society liberals had abandoned them in favor of black criminals. In the minds of such white Detroiters, by 1973 the liberals in their city no longer merely facilitated dependency
through the myriad community programs in the ghetto; now they were actually catering to black criminals in the legal arena. As A. J. Kalber asked
in his letter to the editor of the *Detroit News,* after a controversial acquittal
in one of the post-1969 trials, "was it by good luck or arrangement of council that black groups . . . had their case assigned, through the so-called blind
draw assignment system, to the only black judge in Wayne County Circuit
courts?"[24]

Detroit's black and white liberal leaders who came of age in the optimistic
years of the early sixties (politicians, administrators, hearing referees, or
judges) viewed the outcomes of these trials very differently. To them, Detroiters' resolving their differences in courtrooms instead of on city streets testified
directly to the strength and successes of liberalism and its efforts to achieve
greater racial and economic parity. To them the trials of 1969–73 were not
about criminals winning out over cops; rather, these legal proceedings reflected the practical application of the long-held civil rights–sympathetic principle that white legal atonement for racial sins was a component of making
progress toward racial equality.[25] In ways that even they did not predict, however, the pragmatic application of such lofty sixties-style liberal principles
would have dramatic consequences for the political future of the Motor City.
Indeed, when the struggle for racial equality changed venue, from the streets
to the courtrooms, when blacks emerged victorious from this struggle, and
when liberals set out to take credit for their triumph, the fate of liberalism in
Detroit was in many ways decided—albeit in a surprising fashion.

To the utter dismay of civic militants, civic liberals were able to capitalize
on the radical courtroom victories of 1969–73. Liberals made it clear that they
had been instrumental in overseeing these landmark trials in which racial
discrimination had been condemned so dramatically, and this important fact
did not escape the notice of those in Detroit's black community who had long

been suspicious of both the legal system and the liberals who ran it. Almost overnight, their faith in liberalism was fully restored. Ironically, the civic radicals who had so successfully pushed the legal system to its most progressive limits during these trials had effectively lost their support base by 1973. But of course the legacy of both radical and liberal activism in the legal arena was that conservative whites, believing that liberals had catered to criminal blacks in the trials of 1969–73, had become more determined than ever to wrest political control of the city from liberals and to make sure that blacks got no more power than they already had managed to secure. Thus by 1973, with black radicals no longer contenders for Detroit's destiny, the political spectrum became divided in a new way altogether. By that year white liberals were still seeking to lead Detroit through a coalition with blacks. The largely liberal black community, however, now trusted only a black leader. Moreover, conservative whites wanted a law-and-order leader for the city. Each group began mobilizing in unprecedented ways during this election year, and each had a candidate ready and waiting to reshape Detroit in its image.

1973–94

By 1973 the black middle class had come to believe that Detroit would be best served by a mayor who was not only liberal but black, and it chose its candidate carefully. Sensing the desire in the larger black community for an African American more outspoken and daring than Austin had been, black leaders in Detroit decided that Coleman Alexander Young would be perfect. Young had been born in Tuscaloosa, Alabama, on May 28, 1918, and, like so many southern African Americans, moved to Detroit with his family in 1923. Throughout the 1950s and 1960s he was in the public eye, engaged in numerous political and labor activities. Unlike Austin, Young was not a political or social moderate. He had activist roots in the labor movement, and he had a reputation for being highly combative and uncompromising in local and state politics. Although he had stated publicly on numerous occasions that "I am not now and never have been a member of any organization that was subversive or whose design was to overthrow the United States in any way," in his early years many considered Young sympathetic to the far left. In 1954, for example, the head of the Detroit office of the FBI wrote to J. Edgar Hoover, noting that "this man is a dangerous individual and should be one of the first to be picked up in an emergency and one of the first to be considered for future prosecution."[26]

Young attracted FBI attention in part because he had been the first black organizing secretary of the Wayne County Congress of Industrial Organizations until the Reuther caucus of the United Auto Workers (UAW) ousted him.[27] In addition, Young was the executive director of the National Negro Labor Council, a radical black labor organization that came under fire from the House of Un-American Activities in the 1950s.[28] Young managed to survive McCarthyism, however, and in 1960 Michigan voters elected him to serve as a delegate to the state constitutional convention. Four years later he won a seat in the Michigan State Senate representing the East Side district of Detroit, and in 1968 he became one of the first black members of the Democratic National Committee. Young also played a prominent role in the NAACP, the Trade Union Leadership Conference, and the American Civil Liberties Union throughout these years while working aggressively to secure a state open housing law as well as to create the Michigan Civil Rights Commission.

Because Young and Cavanagh shared a deep commitment to civil rights, Young stood firmly behind this white liberal when Detroiters elected him mayor in 1961. But by 1968 Young's support of Cavanagh had become qualified. As Young put it, "I've been for Jerry [Cavanagh] until recently. . . . But the one thing I've got against him is he has been capitulating to the police."[29] As the Cavanagh administration gave way to the Gribbs administration, and as police brutality escalated, state senator Young became even more vocal about the need to rein in the police department.

By the early 1970s Young was not only speaking out against police power but he was arguing publicly that blacks needed a stronger voice within liberal coalition politics. As he saw it, the Democratic Party of Detroit was dependent upon the votes of white and black city residents alike, yet blacks still were second-class citizens within the party. Young shared the frustration of Detroit's black community, specifically that racial discrimination continued to flourish under the aegis of the liberal coalition politics in the Democratic Party. When black civil rights leaders in Detroit began looking for a candidate whom they trusted to keep the struggle for racial equality at the fore, who was firmly within the liberal Democratic fold, and who was committed to reforming the police department, Coleman Young was an obvious choice. Young had assured them that he was "a Negro first and a Democrat second."[30]

While middle-class black liberals were mobilizing the poor and working-class African-American community to support Young, Detroit's white conservatives were initiating their own effort to keep a law-enforcement advocate in the mayor's office. Soon they approached the police commissioner, John F. Nichols, to run for office. White conservatives appreciated Nichols's aggressive stance against crime as well as his staunch defense of the police department's independence. After the 1967 riot state senator Young spoke in favor of establishing a civilian review board for the police department, while then-superintendent Nichols argued that not only could the department oversee its own affairs but that it must have the right to do so.[31] His vocal protection of the police in the face of mounting community criticism made him a natural to become the city police commissioner in 1969. And Nichols's no-nonsense approach to the maintenance of law and order led him to create the highly controversial STRESS unit in January 1971.

Although Nichols did not fashion himself as a political figure, he found himself increasingly in the public eye as the controversy over STRESS escalated. When he was named a defendant in a major anti-STRESS suit filed by black radicals in 1972, Nichols was given a public forum to voice his long-held and passionate belief that the city needed a strong police force to prevent it from falling prey to social and political degeneration.[32] By early 1973 Nichols recognized that the events of recent years had given him a ready-made political constituency, a group of Detroiters who, like him, saw a future in Detroit primarily through its toughest city organization, the police department. Nichols announced his candidacy for mayor that year. Even though Nichols had never run for political office, the *Detroit News* opined on October 8, 1973, that "if white voters follow their usual pattern of higher turnout than black voters . . . Nichols will be the next tenant in the Manoogian Mansion."[33]

In fact, the Detroit media overestimated how clear-cut the 1973 election would be. Nineteen candidates had entered this race, and, within the group of the five most popular, Mel Ravitz, the white liberal city council president, was a serious contender indeed. As the *Detroit News* itself reported, Nichols and Ravitz were neck and neck as the primary approached, which meant that Detroit's white vote was most unpredictable.[34] Ravitz was very popular, particularly with white liberals from the Cavanagh days, because his election strategy was to "put together a coalition of white and black votes" rather than appeal to one or the other.[35] According to Ravitz, "if this election brings us a mayor who is supportive of only a segment of the community—any segment—then heaven help Detroit . . . because the next four years will be spent in further polarization."[36] This message resonated loudly within a number of powerful liberal institutions in the city, such as the UAW, which endorsed Ravitz in the primary.

But Ravitz surprised many by finishing third, behind Nichols and Young, in the September primary.[37] In rejecting Ravitz, despite the UAW endorsement, the city's black electorate had made it clear that it would not settle for just any liberal mayor. Black Detroiters had lost faith in the ability of white liberals to represent them, and they now were determined that a black liberal would be at the helm in Detroit. Of course, conservative white Detroiters had made it equally clear that they vigorously opposed a liberal mayor of any color running their city. The results of a *Detroit News* poll taken before the primary showed clearly the complex ways in which race and politics intersected in the Motor City by 1973. Young received 77 percent of the black vote and 15 percent of the white vote, while Nichols received 13 percent of the black vote and 75 percent of the white. In yet another *Detroit News* poll Young received 80 percent of the black vote and 21 percent of the white, while Nichols received 9 percent of the black vote and 69 percent of the white.[38] In the primary itself Nichols received 96,655 votes and Young 68,075. But when the *Detroit News* concluded after the primary that "each of the [city's] two major racial blocks nominated a candidate of their own," with whites promoting Nichols and blacks supporting Young, it had missed the significance of Ravitz's showing. He too had done quite well in the primary, receiving 52,527 votes.[39] By turning out in large numbers for Ravitz, white liberals showed that they still were committed to running the city in the Cavanagh tradition. Indeed, it would prove pivotal for the future of Detroit that these voters felt compelled to swing into the Young camp after Ravitz was defeated because their only alternative at that point was the conservative Nichols.

As the Young and Nichols campaigns unfolded after the September primary, it was Young who most defined the election issues. Although he campaigned for housing reform, educational reform, and other issues that had long been central to blacks and white progressives alike, Young's primary pledge to Detroiters was to create a "people's police department."[40] And before long, police-community relations in Detroit became the central issue for both candidates. By making law enforcement a focus of his campaign, Young ran the risk that Nichols would use the bogey man of "escalating black crime," as well as the pervasive argument that only a strong police force can combat crime, to win the votes he needed. But in a surprising move Young went on the offensive, insisting in his campaign literature that "safe streets are a necessity," and promising that "no criminal or thug, black or white, can expect special favors from me."[41] This left Nichols in the curious position of having to argue that Detroit really was not that dangerous. Young challenged Nichols to explain why the level of crime in Detroit was so high, which forced Nichols to defend his own track record as police commissioner. To do this Nichols routinely cited statistics showing that in fact "Detroit had been controlling crime and that it had dropped over the last years."[42] Ironically, the law-enforcement candidate himself, Nichols, was forced into claiming that any voter preoccupation with urban crime was unfounded.

When Young pointed to Detroit's high crime figures to argue that the existing law-enforcement system was ineffective, and when he argued that only by "joining people and police in cooperation, [will we] wipe out crime," he stole Nichols's thunder.[43] Ironically, Young had capitalized on crime statistics that had been inflated by the police department itself during a vigorous bid years earlier for more federal funding.[44] Nevertheless, Young was able to use these figures to persuade many undecided voters that, although STRESS had contributed immeasurably to the racial tension in the city, it had not solved its crime problem.[45]

As election day approached, however, the outcome remained difficult to predict. Both Young's and Nichols's chances depended on how many blacks turned out to vote, on how many liberal whites would in fact vote for Young, and on how many black votes Nichols could win from Young. It is notable that in the September primary Young had won fewer white votes than Austin had in the 1969 race, which did not bode well for Young's chances. But neither could Nichols solely rely on there being more white registered voters in the city than black. In fact, by election day the city had 79,624 more registered voters than in 1969 when the law-enforcement candidate, Gribbs, was elected, and the bulk of these new registrants were African American.[46]

On November 6, 1973, tensions ran high as voters went to the polls. Detroiters waited anxiously for the votes to be tabulated because they knew intuitively that the outcome of this election could change the city forever. When the final ballots were tallied, Coleman Young had become Detroit's first black mayor with 233,674 votes to John Nichols's 216,933.[47] However, Young had won by a very slim margin—3.7 percent of all votes cast—which meant that he would face many critics from the moment that he took office.

Although Young was ultimately victorious because he had put together a coalition of blacks, unions, and white liberals, the fact remained that the city's conservative whites had backed Nichols and were vehemently against the city's having a liberal, let alone a black liberal, mayor.[48] As important was that many of those who had mobilized for Young soon found his victory bittersweet. According to Gene Cunningham, a Detroit activist, while Young had needed the full support of radicals to win office, thereafter he told them, "Thanks for your help in getting us here, but we don't need you now."[49] And even some of the white liberals who had supported Young's candidacy also felt slighted after he took office. Overnight, white liberals lost the bulk of civic power to the black leaders within the liberal coalition of Detroit. The political agenda of these black leaders, while similar to that of the white leaders, placed far more emphasis on combating racial, as opposed to simply economic, inequality in the city. Just as the black militants had been undone by their successes in pushing the legal system to its limits, some of the city's white liberals soon felt undone by their success in electing Young.

But of all Young's critics, white conservatives would prove to be the most troublesome. As Young prepared to take office on January 6, 1973, he issued "a warning to all dope pushers, rip-off artists and muggers [that] it's time to leave Detroit. Hit the road! . . . I don't give a damn if they're black or white, if they wear Superfly suits or blue suits with silver badges."[50] The city's criminal element, of course, did not take Young's victory as its cue to abandon the city, but the city's white conservatives did—at least those with the economic means to flee. And among those financially unable to participate in the post-1973 exodus, "there remain[ed] a virulent racial bias that many believe [to be Young's] biggest challenge."[51] As one of Nichols's campaign workers told reporters after Nichols read his concession speech on the night of November 7, "The city will go to hell now."[52] The local media, clearly seeking to connect with its growing suburban readership, tended to minimize the political legitimacy of Young's victory. As the *Detroit News* opined, "In a real sense it might be said that Young socialized his way into the Manoogian Mansion, the official residence of the mayor."[53]

The hostility of white conservatives, however, did not cause Young to alter his plans for running the Motor City. Indeed, he immediately embraced much of the programmatic agenda of the Great Society and infused it with more deliberate measures to promote racial equality in Detroit. Of course, Young had long supported liberal initiatives such as welfare and integration. Well before he became mayor, Young had unapologetically voiced the opinion that "all welfare assistance should be extended and received AS A MATTER OF SOCIAL RIGHT. I am opposed to any and all efforts to degrade the recipients of public assistance and to their use as forced labor."[54] And Young had made his support of broad liberal integration initiatives equally clear early in his career when he supported a fair housing ordinance because, as he put it, the "segregation in the schools can never be eliminated while segregated housing is allowed to exist."[55]

It is notable that Young did not waiver from these sixties-style liberal views even when the national political context in which he was trying to promote them grew increasingly inhospitable. Immediately upon taking office, for example, Young decided to tackle the issue most important to his constituents—deteriorating police-community relations—with the weapon of integration even when affirmative action was coming under severe attack elsewhere in the country. Young began the process of integrating the police force with his Executive Order #2.[56] In 1972 the 5,558-member force was still only 15 percent nonwhite, and the Young administration believed that "when the police department is fully integrated, all segments of the community will have a chance to feel more directly involved in the department because their sons and friends will be a part of the force."[57] Though Young retained the white police chief, Phillip Tannian, he replaced the four-member police commission. Three of his four appointees were African American, and eventually Detroit boasted a black police chief as well. Gradually, Young achieved a far more integrated police department than any mayor had before him. By 1981, 1,126 of the 5,013 police officers, or 22 percent, were African American, and ten of the twenty police commanders were black as well. The number of women on the force also increased after Young became mayor. Whereas women comprised only 2 percent of the department in 1967, by 1987 they made up 20 percent of the police force. The department also had three female commanders and one female deputy chief that year.[58]

In addition to desegregating the Motor City's police department, Young paved the way for countless African Americans to become heads of key city agencies as well as to staff these units in unprecedented numbers. He eventually would also "set a national record for awarding contracts to minority firms."[59] That Young largely succeeded in his attempts to integrate Detroit and to bolster several Great Society initiatives for the city's poor only affirmed the conviction of his supporters that liberalism was a sound political philosophy. Indeed, even though the federal government was busily dismantling Great Society programs like Model Cities throughout the 1970s and 1980s, Detroiters' decision to give Young four terms in office, always by comfortable and sometimes by spectacular margins, shows that they still were optimistic that liberalism would prove the salvation of urban America.[60]

Several new projects designed to revitalize the city's economy and improve its image fueled their optimism. Young built many new parks and erected recreation centers, low-income housing units, and even a downtown civic center. In 1976 he also proudly unveiled a huge hotel, office, and shopping complex on the city's riverfront. This massive project, architecturally similar to the Peachtree Center in Atlanta, was appropriately named the Renaissance Center. Young intended it to draw both tourists and new businesses into Detroit.

Unfortunately for the Young administration, and for the city of Detroit itself, the mayor's ambitious urban renewal projects did not offset the hostility to his rule of racially conservative whites. As the political scientist Wilbur Rich has noted, many such whites "believed that Young would treat them like second-class citizens. This misconception among whites came from the belief that a black mayor cannot be even-handed in his approach to racial issues."[61] Clearly, Young did not remove all whites from positions of power. Nevertheless, as Young's tenure as mayor unfolded, the hostility of white conservatives only grew, and their exodus from the city continued. According to data collected by the city, 891,000 whites had lived in Detroit in 1969, but by 1976, when Young was proudly unveiling his Renaissance Center, only 543,000 remained.[62] Reflecting the sentiments behind such flight, metro-area resident Theodore J. Popwitz argued in a letter to the *Detroit Free Press* that "Mayor Young has polarized the city to a greater degree of racism than was displayed in the two race riots the city has experienced."[63] As a result of the massive out-migration of urban whites, between 1970 and 1990 the percentage of blacks in Detroit rose from 44.5 to 78.4 percent, giving the Motor City one of the largest African-American populations in the urban North.[64]

Although increasingly fewer racially conservative whites remained in the city proper, they nevertheless took every opportunity to blame Young for every Detroit problem and to accuse him of everything from reverse discrimination to corruption to downright poor manners and slovenly behavior. Young soon tired of such criticism that was, in his mind, so clearly born of racist stereotyping. One popular charge was that Young was uncivilized and could not even keep the mayor's mansion presentable. This rumor particularly rankled Young, and he decided to defend himself publicly. In an interview with the *Detroit Free Press* Young referred directly to the comments about the Manoogian Mansion and said, "I do resent, though, the implications that I didn't keep that place up. We spent over one million on it in the last couple of years."[65] When the local media implied, at a later time, that Young was corrupt, he pointed out that the FBI had continued to keep close tabs on him, and, if he was doing anything illegal, the agency would more than happily have exposed that fact. The most prevalent criticism that Young faced, however, was that he was a reverse racist. To this Young always responded that his attempts to improve opportunities for urban blacks clearly had not altered the fact that whites still held the most of the economic power in Detroit. Thus, he maintained, the charge of reverse racism was nothing short of absurd. Young's retorts, however, peppered as they usually were with four-letter words and direct jabs at the suburbs, did not help his cause.

In fact, nothing Young ever said stemmed the tide of white flight, and the effect of this exodus was to bring severe economic distress to the city. When Detroit lost much of its white population, it also lost a significant portion of its economic base. As the social geographers Bryan Thompson and Robert Sinclair have pointed out, when white Detroiters left the inner city, they took "the majority of the important service, professional, and leadership activities of the Detroit Metropolitan system" with them.[66] Soon it was no longer inner-city Detroit but the surrounding suburbs that housed the core of the region's auto industry. And, in time, industry foremen, supervisors, inspectors, and many white workers no longer called Detroit their home, either. Increasingly, they moved to suburbs such as Royal Oak Township, Troy, East Detroit, the Grosse Pointes, Dearborn, Hazel Park, Ferndale, Madison Heights, Sterling Heights, Southfield, Redford Township, Westland, Farmington, Allen Park, Melvindale, and Lincoln Park.[67] Increasingly, they moved to nearby suburbs that had few, if any, blacks within their borders.[68]

As Detroit became more impoverished after 1973, its neighboring suburbs grew ever wealthier.[69] By 1980 the median income in Detroit was $17,033, whereas in the bordering suburb of Grosse Pointe Woods it was $35,673.[70] That same year in Detroit 27 percent of blacks and 6.8 percent of whites were receiving some type of public assistance and 25 percent of blacks and 7 percent of whites lived below the poverty level.[71] By 1983 "the $11,685 gap in average household income between the overall region of Metropolitan Detroit ($33,241) and Detroit City ($21,556) . . . was the widest of the 33 largest metropolitan areas in the United States."[72]

To be sure, the urban renaissance that Mayor Young and his supporters had dreamed of was not thwarted simply by white flight. When Young took office, the nation as a whole was heading into a major oil crisis–induced economic recession. As a result of this national downturn, Detroit experienced "its worst fiscal crisis since the Great Depression" in 1975.[73] That year the city had to lay off more than four thousand employees, and in time Chrysler's Jefferson Avenue plant (one of the city's largest factories) closed its doors. By 1977 the city had lost 56,400 jobs, and Detroiters clearly were suffering.[74] As Young put it, "No city in America has been harder hit by the national economic recession. Detroit's unemployment rate is three times the national average."[75] Indeed, black unemployment had reached a full 25 percent in 1977 as Young began campaigning for his third term.[76]

Even though the national recession clearly hindered the Young administration's ambitious goals, hard times alone cannot explain the economic evisceration of Detroit.[77] Every major industrial city in the urban North suffered the recession of the 1970s—but few suffered to the extent that Detroit did. When Detroit lost most of its white population, tax base, and political support, its future was severely compromised.[78] As Rich notes, Detroit was irreparably harmed by "the impact of changing demographics, especially the loss of revenue occasioned by white flight."[79] Not coincidentally, while Detroit had lost 56,400 jobs by 1977, the suburbs had gained 36,500 jobs.[80] As the city grew poorer, its social deterioration escalated, setting in motion a vicious cycle of greater suburban antipathy toward the inner city and, in turn, greater social malaise. As Arthur Johnson, the long-time Detroit NAACP leader and public schools administrator, opined bitterly in 1990, "Whites don't know a god damned thing about what's gone wrong here. . . . It's Apartheid. They rape the city and then they come and say, 'look what these niggers did to the city' as if they were guiltless."[81]

Despite the social and economic deterioration of the Motor City, Detroit's black community and many of its white liberals remained fiercely loyal to Coleman Young, believing that, with him, their long-held goals of integration and greater racial equality were finally being tackled head-on. Although Detroit was clearly losing ground in its War on Poverty, city residents could nevertheless point to real gains in racial equality there. In the end, Detroiters gauged the success of their new liberal leadership primarily in racial, rather than economic, terms. Although Young's supporters could point to limited victories in the areas of economic development downtown and the successful management of two fiscal crises, the mayor's real appeal was best summed up by the Detroit Chapter of the National Negro Labor Council (NNLC) when it placed him firmly in the context of a broader struggle for African-American equality. According to the NNLC, Young "'damned the odds,' he took up the cudgels, the causes, and the confrontations of those martyred souls of the past. . . . The torch that they carried to guide us through the dark tunnels of slavery and injustice has been taken from their fallen hands by Coleman A. Young to guide us to freedom and equality."[82]

Although Detroiters had won the battle for greater black representation and civic equality under Young's leadership, it seems clear that they ultimately lost their war on poverty. The exodus of anti-Young whites after 1973 had played a critical role in draining the lifeblood of the city that blacks and white progressives had fought to share since the 1950s.[83] Despite Young's ambitious revitalization plans, such as those that wooed a General Motors and a Chrysler plant to the city with major tax incentives in the 1980s, Young was never able to compensate for the economic losses occasioned by white flight. In fact, Detroit atrophied further each year that Young remained in office.

To suburban whites, and to much of the United States for that matter, the disintegration of cities like Detroit seemed to be as irrefutable evidence that the politics of liberalism, and the programs of the Great Society in particular, had been a terrible social and economic mistake. Detroit-area suburbanites in particular made it clear that they wanted nothing whatever to do with the inner city or with the particular brand of politics still promoted therein. If there could be any doubt about the degree of suburban white hostility to Young's Detroit, and to the liberal political solutions to inequality still proffered within its borders, the visceral reaction to an areawide school desegregation decision in the early 1970s is instructive. Whites who had abandoned Detroit were shocked and appalled when a U.S. District judge ordered that fifty-three suburban school districts would have to participate with the school system of Detroit in a cross-district busing plan designed to balance the educational opportunities of city children with those in the suburbs.[84] Almost overnight, antibusing groups sprang up everywhere, some numbering more than forty-eight thousand people, which used legal and extralegal tactics to defeat the plan. To them, Detroit, embodied in the figure of Young, had become black, decayed, crime-ridden, and the epitome of all that had gone wrong with the politics of liberalism after LBJ.

* * *

While a noticeable white disengagement from the Democratic Party, and from America's urban centers, is indeed a remarkable chapter in postwar political and social history, historians have been too quick to pronounce the death of sixties-style liberalism as a potent force in U.S. politics. Scholarly overemphasis on disaffected and hostile whites has obscured the ways in which black and white progressives were an equal part of the political equation, and the degree to which their actions also would determine the viability of social welfare and civil rights liberalism in the United States. Indeed, when whites chose to abandon Detroit in the 1970s and to vote for Ronald Reagan in 1980, they did so as *losers,* not as victors of the political battle to lead urban America into the future. As important as it was for the contours of the United States that many whites chose to abandon inner-city living and liberalism after the politically tumultuous and racially rancorous 1960s, it was equally important that, because of this same tumult and rancor, urban centers across the United States in the 1970s witnessed the most dramatic ascendancy of black liberal political power ever seen in American history.

Undoubtedly, scholars have overlooked the political significance of the black liberal rise to power in the 1970s at least in part because they have underestimated the political and racial complexity of the postwar period as a whole. It is crucial to recognize, for example, that urban black militants were key political players not simply because they alienated white conservatives but also because they inadvertently paved the way for white progressives and the black community at large to keep a liberal as mayor at the very height of the Reagan revolution and beyond. Indeed, only by paying greater attention to the political and racial complexity of the postwar period can one see most clearly that liberalism oriented to social welfare and civil rights did not die at all.[85] To be sure, much white support for such a politics did disappear by 1980, but clearly the faith of the nation's African-American and white progressive urbanites in liberal prescriptions for effecting economic and racial equality thrived well past that year.

Not only did citizen support for the tenets of sixties-style liberalism not disappear by 1980 but the often disparaged and marginalized centers of black liberal power that sprang up across the United States after 1970 also wielded significant political influence well beyond their borders. In fact such inner cities have been, and continue to be, crucial to the evolving contours of both politics and social policy in the United States. Any electoral hope that the Democratic Party had in 1992, for example, lay with these black-led liberal enclaves still supported by many a white progressive. Evidence from Detroit clearly shows that the black and white liberal vote has mattered and matters today. Specifically, by looking carefully at the complex social and political roots of Mayor Coleman Young's rise to power in the Motor City, we can better see just how tenacious support for both Great Society liberalism and the U.S. civil rights movement has been.

Notes

1. Frank McCoy, "Black Power in City Hall," *Black Enterprise,* August 1990, 148–51.

2. Gary Gerstle and Steve Fraser, *The Rise and Fall of the New Deal Order: 1930–1980* (Princeton, N.J.: Princeton University Press, 1989); Fred Siegel, *The Future Once Happened Here: New York, D.C., L.A., and the Fate of America's Big Cities* (New York: Free Press, 1997).

3. For a great deal of interesting information on the African-American migration from south to north, as well as many U.S. census statistics on the migration, see Marcus E. Jones, *Black Migration in the United States with Emphasis on Selected Central Cities* (Saratoga, Calif.: Century Twenty-one, 1980); Fred R. Harris and Tom Wicker, eds., *The Kerner Report: The 1968 Report of the National Advisory Commission on Civil Disorders* (New York: Pantheon, 1988), 12. Also see Joseph Darden, Richard Child Hill, June Thomas, and Richard Thomas, *Detroit: Race and Uneven Development* (Philadelphia: Temple University Press, 1987), 69.

4. Thomas Sugrue, *The Origins of Urban Crisis: Race and Inequality in Postwar Detroit.* (Princeton, N.J.: Princeton University Press, 1996).

5. Albert J. Mayer and Thomas F. Hoult, "Race and Residence in Detroit," in Leonard Gordon, ed. *A City in Racial Crisis: The Case of Detroit Pre– and Post–the 1967 Riot* (New York: Brown, 1971), 5.

6. Darden et al., *Detroit,* 68.

7. Former police commissioner George Edwards actually estimated "that 90 percent of the 4,767-man Detroit Police Department are bigoted, and that dislike for Negroes is reflected constantly in their language and often in physical abuse" (William Serrin, "God Help Our City," *Atlantic Monthly,* March 1969, p. 115).

8. Statement of the NAACP, "NAACP Proposals for Effective Law Enforcement and Crime Prevention," by the Reverend James Wadsworth, president; Robert Tindal, Executive secretary; Bruce Miller, Chairman Legal Redress Committee, 1964, Pt. 2, Box 24-3, NAACP Collection, Walter Reuther Library of Labor and Urban Affairs, Detroit.

9. Cotillion Club to Mayor Jerome P. Cavanagh, January 22, 1965, Pt. 2, Box 24-3, NAACP Collection.

10. Almost immediately after the riot, the Mayor's Development Team published a 750-

page report on the city's problems and how they might be addressed. New Detroit was a thirty-nine-member group of business and civic leaders, including nine blacks, who both wrote reports and generated money in its attempt to revitalize and repair the city. On the problems of the Democratic Party, see Donald Lief, "Community Consensus as a Goal Seeking Constructive Change," and "Power Struggle Among Black Militants," *Detroit Scope Magazine,* both in Gordon, *City in Racial Crisis.*

11. "Richard Austin Plans a Better Detroit," pamphlet, Box 30-4, Richard Austin Papers, Reuther Library.

12. "*WHITE* Tax-Paying Honky" to Richard Austin, September 30, 1969, Box 30-12, Austin Papers.

13. *Detroit Free Press,* November 5, 1969; Darden et al., *Detroit,* 209.

14. *Detroit Free Press,* November 5, 1969

15. *Detroit News,* November 4, 1969.

16. By 1969 black radical activism had taken off in Detroit in grassroots organizations such as Parents and Students for Community Control, the Inner City Voice, Black Student United Front, and National Committee to Combat Fascism (the local Panthers), to mention but a few. In the auto plants of Detroit, also by 1969, numerous black nationalist in-plant organizations sprang up, including several chapters of the Revolutionary Union Movement and the citywide League of Revolutionary Black Workers. By the close of the 1960s ordinary black Detroiters had also begun to criticize local churches, and the traditional theology that they espoused, for their role in maintaining the racial status quo through black nationalist religious organizations.

17. "Power Struggle Among Black Militants," 115.

18. Wilbur C. Rich, *Coleman Young and Detroit Politics: From Social Activist to Power Broker* (Detroit: Wayne State University Press, 1989), 82.

19. See "Memo to: Subcommittee on Police Community relations, From: Detroit Commission on Community Relations Staff. August 1, 1969," Pt. 3, Box 68-4, and "Memo to: Commission on Community Relations from: Staff r.e. Analysis of 1968 Citizens Complaint Bureau Report, December 12, 1969," Pt. 3, Box 68-19, Detroit Commission on Community Relations Papers (hereafter DCCR Papers), Reuther Library.

20. "Memo to: Denise Lewis and Commission on Community Relations, From: Field Division Staff, r.e. the Detroit CCS Procedure: Problems and Potential for Contributing to Community Stability," April 26, 1973, Pt. 3, Box 68-19, DCCR Papers.

21. "Statement by Commissioner John F. Nichols to Common Council. October 4, 1971," Pt. 3, Box 66, DCCR Papers.

22. As one Detroit woman, a Mrs. Orb, wrote in the *Detroit News* on April 20, 1972, "STRESS has . . . created an atmosphere of hope and confidence among honest, law-abiding citizens of Detroit." In the same paper a Mrs. Wsp registered her support of STRESS even more forcefully: "I beg Detroiters not to be carried away by sympathy for criminals! We need STRESS! The choice is between STRESS and Crime!" See letters to editor, *Detroit News,* April 20, 1972, Pt. 3, Box 67-13, DCCR Papers.

23. Space constraints prevent me from detailing these cases—New Bethel One and Two, the murder trial and subsequent workers' compensation trial of black auto worker James Johnson Jr., and then three trials involving a man accused of attempting to murder or assault several STRESS officers—but in each of them, city whites knew, as did blacks, that

liberal judges, hearing referees, and juries had afforded the defendants unprecedented leeway.

24. A. J. Kalber to editor, *Detroit News,* April 20, 1972.

25. As Mayor Jerome P. Cavanagh had put it to the Kerner Commission several years earlier: "We must frankly face up to the need to consider and accept a new principle . . . the principle of reparation for long standing injustice dating back to the generations preceding ours. . . . The price that they [blacks] have paid has been incalculable. Now the nation must, I believe, begin to make reparation—for the deeds of past generations, and of our own." See "Mayor's Recommendations Before Governor Kerner's Committee in Washington on August 15, 1967," Pt. 3, Box 2-19, DCCR Papers.

26. See interview with Young in the *Detroit News,* August 15, 1973, and FBI memo printed in the *Detroit News,* January 27, 1985, Young Biographical File, Reuther Library.

27. Darden et al., *Detroit,* 213.

28. Ibid.

29. *Detroit News,* November 8, 1968.

30. *Detroit Free Press,* September 22, 1968.

31. Radio and TV Reports, Inc., April 14, 1972, WWJ-TV, News 4, Box 3, Charter Revision Commission Papers, Burton Historical Collection, Detroit Public Library, Detroit.

32. A copy of the suit may be found in Box 11, Kenneth Cockrel–Sheila Murphy Papers, Reuther Library.

33. *Detroit News,* October 8, 1973.

34. *Detroit News,* August 19, 1973.

35. *Detroit Free Press,* September 9, 1973.

36. "Ravitz for Detroit," campaign newsletter, June 20, 1973, Vertical Files, Sociology and Economics Department, Detroit Public Library.

37. Rich, *Coleman Young and Detroit Politics,* 102. Also see the *Detroit Free Press,* September 13, 1973.

38. *Detroit News,* October 14, 1973.

39. *Detroit Free Press,* September 12 and 13, 1973.

40. *Detroit News,* July 11, 1973.

41. Ibid.

42. *Detroit News,* October 20, 1973.

43. Ibid.

44. For more information on how the police department altered crime statistics, see Gebhard Long, William Deane Smith, David O. Porter, Delores Weber, and L. L. Loukopoulus, "The Detroit Police Department—A Research Report on Previous Studies; Criminal Statistics; and Police Technology, Productivity, and Competence," May 1970. This exhaustive report includes seventy-four pages of text, sixty pages of graphs and tables, and a forty-three-page appendix; a copy may be found in Box 37, Cockrel-Murphy Papers. Also see L. L. Loukopoulus, "The Detroit Police Department," and "The Detroit Police Department—Statistical Section," May 1970, an independent study conducted by a fact-finding team at Wayne State University and its Urban Studies Department, Charter Revision Commission Collection, Detroit Public Library, and at the Harlan Hatcher Graduate Library, University of Michigan, Ann Arbor.

45. *Detroit News,* October 24, 1973.

46. Desmond Brandy, elections specialist, City of Detroit, to author, November 14, 1990.

47. Detroit Election Commission, "Official Canvas of Votes, 1953–1978," Vertical Files, Sociology and Economics Department, Detroit Public Library.

48. *New York Times,* January 6, 1974.

49. Cunningham is quoted in Robert H. Mast, ed., *Detroit Lives* (Philadelphia: Temple University Press, 1994), 315.

50. Ibid.

51. Ibid.

52. *Detroit News,* November 7, 1973.

53. *Detroit News,* December 20, 1973.

54. "I Take My Stand," campaign brochure, Coleman A. Young for Common Council, Young Biographical File, Reuther Library.

55. Ibid.

56. Mayor's Office Press release, February 13, 1974, Box 11, Cockrel-Murphy Papers.

57. See Detroit Police Department and Michigan Office of Criminal Justice Programs, "A Turn Around in the Seventies," 1973 booklet, Pt. 3, Box 68-19, DCCR Papers. Also see WJR radio editorial by Denise Lewis of the Detroit Commission on Community Relations, March 27, 1974, Pt. 3, Box 68-19, DCCR Papers.

58. B. J. Widick, *Detroit: City of Race and Class Violence* (Chicago: Quadrangle, 1972), 24.

59. *Detroit Free Press,* December 5, 1997.

60. No matter how many hard times befell Detroit, residents still stood by Young and his liberal agenda in election after election. Note the voter returns from the mayoral elections of 1977, 1981, 1985 and 1989.

	Young	Opponent
1977	164,626	63,626 (Browne)
1981	176,710	91,245 (Koslowski)
1985	141,551	90,907 (Barrow)
1989	138,312	107,073 (Barrow)

Figures courtesy of the Department of Sociology and Economics, Detroit Public Library.

61. Rich, *Coleman Young and Detroit Politics,* 266.

62. See City of Detroit Department of Health Data Book, 1969, 1973, 1976, Detroit Municipal Library.

63. *Detroit Free Press,* January 22, 1985, Young Biographical File, Reuther Library.

64. U.S. Bureau of the Census, *Summary Characteristics for Government Units and Standard Metropolitan Statistical Areas—Michigan* (Washington, D.C.: U.S. Government Printing Office, 1970, 1990).

65. *Detroit Free Press,* April 28, 1994.

66. Bryan Thompson and Robert Sinclair, *Metropolitan Detroit: An Anatomy of Social Change* (Cambridge, Mass.: Ballinger, 1977), 14.

67. Darden et al., *Detroit,* 109.

68. Ibid., 96, 138.

69. Thompson and Sinclair, *Metropolitan Detroit,* 54.

70. Darden et al., *Detroit,* 101.

71. Ibid., 70.

72. Ibid., 100.

73. Rich, *Coleman Young and Detroit Politics,* 112.

74. Sheldon Friedman and Leon Potok, "Detroit and the Auto Industry: An Historical Overview," UAW Research Department, UAW International, December 1981.

75. Coleman Young, "Mayor's Press Release," April 10, 1975, Box 38, Cockrel-Murphy Papers.

76. Darden et al., *Detroit,* 217.

77. *New York Times,* January 22, 1975.

78. For an examination of how conservative white hostility to black mayors compromised the viability of inner cities other than Detroit, see Jack White, "The Limits of Black Power," *Time,* May 11, 1992.

79. Rich, *Coleman Young and Detroit Politics,* 241.

80. Friedman and Potok, "Detroit and the Auto Industry."

81. Z'ev Chafets, "The Tragedy of Detroit," *New York Times Magazine,* July 29, 1990, p. 51.

82. In 1981 Young saved the city from a $113 billion budget deficit. See *Jet,* July, 12, 1993; "An Evening with . . . Coleman A. Young," pamphlet, Detroit Chapter of the National Negro Labor Coalition, August 13, 1994, Young Vertical File, Reuther Library.

83. As Andrew Brimmer points out in his article, "Political Power and Urban Decline," *Black Enterprise,* September 1992, the phenomenon of black mayors witnessing the wholesale flight of both white residents and a viable business base was common to many cities other than Detroit (p. 45).

84. For further information on how this famous desegregation case unfolded, see *Bradley v. Milliken,* 433 F.2d 897 (6th Cir. 1970); *Bradley v. Milliken,* 338 F. Supp. 582 (E.D. Mich. 1971); *Bradley v. Milliken,* 345 F. Supp. 914 (E.D. Mich. 1972); *Bradley v. Milliken,* 484 F.2d 215 (6th Cir. 1973); *Milliken v. Bradley,* 418 U.S. 717 (1974).

85. Although several scholars have recognized not only that black politics are key but also that there was a real "threat of radical black politics—or at least politics to the left of black moderates in the liberal coalition—[which] posed problems for the established black politicians," they have concluded that "the threat never materialized into any substantial challenge" (Darden et al., *Detroit,* 206). They too have missed a full understanding of the ways in which pushes from the left helped civic liberals, and black liberals in particular, to secure power in the face of the growing opposition of urban white conservatives.

Contributors

JEFFREY S. ADLER, an associate professor of history and criminology at the University of Florida, is the author of *Yankee Merchants and the Making of the Urban West* (1991), as well as articles on urbanization and violence that have appeared in the *Journal of Social History*, the *Journal of Urban History*, *Social Science History*, and other journals. He is completing a book on murder in Chicago from 1875 to 1920.

RONALD H. BAYOR, a professor of history at Georgia Tech, is the founding and current editor of the *Journal of American Ethnic History*. His most recent books are *Race and the Shaping of Twentieth-Century Atlanta* (1996), which received an outstanding book award from the Gustavus Myers Center for the Study of Human Rights in North America, and the coedited volume *The New York Irish* (1996), winner of the James S. Donnelly Sr. Prize of the American Conference for Irish Studies for the best book in history and the social sciences.

ROGER BILES, a professor of history at East Carolina University, is the author of "Black Mayors: A Historical Assessment," which appeared in a special issue on black mayors that he edited for the *Journal of Negro History*. He is also the author of five books, including *Big City Boss in Depression* and *War: Mayor Edward J. Kelly of Chicago* (1984), and *Richard J. Daley: Politics, Race, and the Governing of Chicago* (1995).

DAVID R. COLBURN, a professor of history and director of the Reubin O'D. Askew Institute on Politics and Society at the University of Florida, is author or editor of ten books, including *Government in the Sunshine State* (1999; coauthored with Lance deHaven-Smith), *The African-American Heritage of Florida* (1995; coedited with Jane Landers), and *Racial Change and Community Crisis: St. Augustine, Florida, 1877–1980* (1989). He writes regularly on state and national politics for the *Orlando Sentinel.*

HOWARD GILLETTE JR., a professor of history at Rutgers University's Camden campus, is the author of *Between Justice and Beauty: Race, Planning, and the Failure of Urban Policy in Washington, D.C.* (1995), among other books, as well as a number of articles on American urban history that have appeared in a range of scholarly journals in the United States and abroad. A founder and the first director of the Center for Washington Area Studies at George Washington University, he is also a former editor of *Washington History,* the journal of the Historical Society of Washington, D.C. He is writing a history of the impact of disinvestment on the city of Camden, New Jersey.

ARNOLD R. HIRSCH, a member of the Department of History at the University of New Orleans since 1979 and now the Herman and Ethel Midlo Professor of History and New Orleans Studies at that institution, was a senior fellow of the American Council of Learned Societies in 1993–94. His publications include *Making the Second Ghetto: Race and Housing in Chicago, 1940–60* (1983; reissued in 1998) and the coedited volumes *Creole New Orleans: Race and Americanization* (1992) and *Urban Policy in Twentieth-Century America* (1993), as well as numerous book chapters, articles, and reviews in the *Journal of American History,* the *Journal of Urban History, American Historical Review,* and *Reviews in American History,* among others.

JAMES B. LANE is a professor of history at Indiana University Northwest, codirector of the Calumet Regional Archives, and editor of *Steel Shavings* magazine. He is the author of *"City of the Century": A History of Gary, Indiana* (1978) and coauthor (with Edward J. Escobar) of *Forging a Community: The Latino Experience in Northwest Indiana, 1919–75* (1987).

LEONARD N. MOORE is an assistant professor of history at Louisiana State University, where he teaches courses in African-American and urban history. He is writing a book entitled *The Ballot and the Bullet: Carl B. Stokes and the Rise of Black Political Power in America.*

HEATHER R. PARKER is an assistant professor of history at Hofstra University and a past recipient of an National Endowment for the Humanities Summer Institute Fellowship (1998). She is revising her doctoral dissertation, "The Elusive Coalition: African-American and Chicano Political Organization and Interaction in Los Angeles, 1960–73," for publication.

HEATHER ANN THOMPSON is an assistant professor of history at the University of North Carolina at Charlotte. Her first book, forthcoming from Cornell University Press, seeks to challenge how scholars think about race and the postwar evolution of inner cities, urban politics, and the urban labor movement in the United States. She has received a grant from the National Endowment for the Humanities to work on her next book project on the politics of school desegregation and busing in the urban North and South after *Brown v. Board of Education.*

Index

Abbott, Carl, 8
Abramson, David, 203, 219n.10
Abyssinian Baptist Church, 132
Activism, African-American, 28, 36, 90;
Bradley and, 156; in Brooklyn, 133; in Chicago, 122, 129n.26; in Detroit, 50n.17, 230, 231–33, 245n.16, 248n.85; in Evans incident, 90; Hatcher on, 57, 75n.2; in New Orleans, 122; during Reagan era, 243; role in African-American politics, 48n.4; Stokes and, 98. *See also* Civil rights movement; Political power, African-American
Affirmative action: African-American mayors and, 224; Bradley's policies on, 161–64, 171; Coleman Young's initiatives in, 238; Hatcher's initiatives in, 71; Maynard Jackson's policies on, 181, 184, 187, 190, 196
African Americans: access to city government, 15; Caribbean immigrants, 130–31, 133, 143; change-oriented values of, 51n.32; civic power of, 223; economic empowerment of, 71; effect of New Federalism on, 8; entrepreneurship of, 58, 72, 74; Great Society programs for, 32; homicide rates for, 9; investors, 75n.3; migration to cities, 23, 244n.3; in New York municipal politics, 131; political participation by, 4; poverty rates of, 7, 21n.33; unemployment rates for, 7, 33, 107; upwardly mobile, 171; urban flight of, 20n.19. *See also* Middle class, African-American; Voters: African-American

Afro-Set (organization), 98
Agronsky, Jonathan, 217
Ailes, Roger, 137–38
Aim-Jobs program (Cleveland), 88
Ali, Muhammad, 64
Alkalimat, Abdul, 56n.94
Allen, Dozier T., 66, 67
Allen, Ivan, 179, 180, 184
Anderson, Charles W., 131
Anti-Catholicism, 3
Anti-Semitism, 3
Anzelmo, Sal, 117
Arafat, Yasir, 134
Aragon, Manual, 176n.94
Arrington, Richard, 15
Asian Americans: civil rights demonstrations by, 142
Atlanta, Ga.: African-American administrators in, 14, 190; African-American community of, 178–79, 196; African-American neighborhoods of, 180, 181, 182; African-American politics in, 53n.55; African-American population of, 37, 172n.1; African-American voters of, 6, 189; Bankhead Courts area, 182; business community of, 18, 178, 184–85, 188, 196; Centennial Olympic Park, 193, 194; Citywide Tenants (organization), 182; Community Development Block Grants for, 182, 185–86, 187, 188, 191; downtown revitalization in, 190; economic growth in, 17–18, 187, 189, 190, 191; empowerment zones of, 193; Fairlie-

Typeset in 10.5/13 Minion
with Minion display
Designed by Paula Newcomb
Composed by Celia Shapland
for the University of Illinois Press
Manufactured by Maple-Vail Book Manufacturing Group

University of Illinois Press
1325 South Oak Street
Champaign, IL 61820-6903
www.press.uillinois.edu